W9-ABI-380

Managing Literacy, Mothering America

Pittsburgh Series in Composition, Literacy, and Culture

David Bartholomae and Jean Ferguson Carr, Editors

Sarah Robbins

Managing Literacy, Mothering America

Women's Narratives on Reading and
Writing in the Nineteenth Century

University of Pittsburgh Press

Title page illustration from *The Child's Book,* by Lydia Sigourney (1844).
Courtesy, American Antiquarian Society

Published by the University of Pittsburgh Press, Pittsburgh, Pa., 15260
Copyright © 2004, University of Pittsburgh Press
Manufactured in the United States of America
Printed on acid-free paper
10 9 8 7 6 5 4 3 2 1

LIBRARY OF CONGRESS CATALOGING-IN-PUBLICATION DATA
Robbins, Sarah.
    Managing literacy, mothering America : women's narratives
on reading and writing in the nineteenth century / Sarah Robbins.
        p. cm — (Pittsburgh series in composition, literacy, and
culture)
    Includes bibliographical references and index.
    ISBN 0-8229-4235-6 (cloth : acid-free paper)
    1. American prose literature—Women authors—History and
criticism.   2. Women—Books and reading—United States—History—
19th century.   3. Women and literature—United States—History—
19th century.   4. American prose literature—19th century—History
and criticism.   5. Literacy—United States—History—19th century.
6. Domestic fiction, American—History and criticism.   7. Women—
United States—Intellectual life.   8. Books and reading in literature.
9. Motherhood in literature.   10. Authorship in literature.
11. Narration (Rhetoric)   12. Women in literature.   I. Title.
II. Series.
    PS374.B67R63 2004
    818'.308099287—dc22
                                            2004010929

34.96

Contents

Acknowledgments

When I began the research that eventually led to this book, my daughters, Margaret and Patty, were in middle and elementary school. As the project finally goes to press, Margaret is in her first year of teaching high school English, and Patty is a junior in college, majoring in political science and psychology. They have, literally, grown up with the book. In the final stages of manuscript preparation, my daughters have become true colleagues in the writing process, with Margaret sharing exciting stories about "managing literacy" in her first classroom, Patty carefully checking endnotes and bibliography entries, and both of them giving powerful pep talks when my energy flagged. I doubt my daughters can remember a time when this book was not in our lives. We are happy, finally, to be sharing it with a larger audience.

I hope that my teachers will see their influence here. Major thanks go to Anne Ruggles Gere, Julie Ellison, June Howard, Marlon Ross, and Karen Wixson at the University of Michigan; all of them pushed me to write a book by letting archives gradually shape my arguments. David Scobey and Jay Robinson taught me to think critically about education's place in public culture. At the University of North Carolina, Chapel Hill, scholars like Donald Kennedy and Aldo Scaglione taught me to love research but also to admire the best teaching.

I worked on this book while teaching at Kennesaw State University. Serving as director of the National Writing Project's (NWP's) local site there slowed down my own writing progress but also enriched my thinking about the place of literature and education in American life. By collaborating with schoolteachers on a number of grant-funded programs, I had the chance to think deeply about social interactions between home and school, school and university, learning and public culture. I thank all my colleagues at the Kennesaw Mountain Writing Project (KMWP) for their contagious energy and their dedication to teaching; both have shaped this book considerably. Special thanks to the KMWP advisory council chairs and grant project codirectors, whose leadership enabled me to make some time for scholarship while also directing an NWP site.

Having the opportunity to develop several grant-funded curriculum programs has provided substantial intellectual support for my research. While codirecting several projects funded by the National Endowment for the Humanities (NEH)—"Domesticating the Canon," "Making American Literatures," and "Keeping and Creating American Communities"—I met some of the nation's best scholars in women's studies, American literature, American studies, literacy studies, and more. Colleagues involved in these programs patiently answered my questions about "managing literacy," national culture, literature making, and nineteenth-century American women's lives while driving from airports to workshops for teachers, planning syllabi for summer institutes, or writing project evaluations. Thanks, in particular, to these mentors: Randall Bass; Frances Smith Foster; Joyce A. Joyce; Paul Lauter; Cristine Levenduski; Sandra Zagarell; and, at the NEH, Janet Edwards and Bob Sayers.

Another crucial network supporting this book's development was the Nineteenth-Century American Women Writers' Study Group. Topics we explored at our study sessions often worked their way into my research, and advice the group's leaders gave me about scholarly publishing has been invaluable. Thanks to all, especially Ellen Garvey, Karen Kilcup, Jean Pfaelzer, Susan Harris, Carla Peterson, Karen Sanchez-Eppler, Ellen Garvey and Jean Yellin for much encouragement.

At Kennesaw, I have benefited from having many energetic colleagues in the English department and across campus. I am most grateful to Ann Pullen and LeeAnn Lands for pushing me to "think historically" about women's studies and American literature. And thanks to my students for their enthusiasm about my research. I am particularly grateful to the Faculty Incentive Grant program and to the Kennesaw State University Foundation for providing funds that supported my research.

Locally, the interlibrary loan managers at Kennesaw State and many librarians at nearby Emory University (especially in the Pitts Theological Library and the Special Collections Department of the Robert W. Woodruff Library) provided ongoing aid. Librarians affiliated with the following institutions also gave invaluable time and expertise: American Antiquarian Society, Bancroft Library of the University of California at Berkeley, Boston Public Library, Cincinnati Historical Society, Free Library of Philadelphia, Gutman Library at Harvard University, The Huntington Library, Jane Addams Memorial Collection at the University of Illinois in Chicago, Library

Company of Philadelphia, Massachusetts Historical Society, Schlesinger Library at Radcliffe Institute, Schomburg Library of Nineteenth-Century Black Women Writers, University of Michigan, and Wake Forest University.

Portions of chapter 2 appear here by permission of the Children's Literature Association, publisher of the *Children's Literature Association Quarterly;* other portions of the same chapter are published by permission of the *Lion and the Unicorn,* from Johns Hopkins University Press. Other sections of chapter 2 and some sections of chapter 1 appeared originally in the December 2002 issue of the *New England Quarterly.* Anonymous reviewers for all of these publications provided very helpful feedback, as did readers for *American Literature, American Quarterly,* and the forthcoming *Women in Print* anthology. Special thanks to Lucy Maddox, Linda Rhoads, Jeanne Gunner, James Danky, and Wayne Wiegand for expert editorial guidance.

Several libraries provided permission for the use of archival material essential to the book. The 1851 letter from Harriet Beecher Stowe to Sarah Hale (which appears in chapter 4) is reproduced by permission of The Huntington Library, San Marino, California. Letters from Harriet Beecher Stowe to Calvin Stowe, which are excerpted in chapter 4, appear with permission of the Schlesinger Library, Radcliffe Institute, from the Beecher-Stowe Family Papers. Several items from the Fannie E. S. Heck Papers appear in chapter 4 with permission of Wake Forest University Archives and Special Collections, Z. Smith Reynolds Library, Wake Forest University.

The editorial staff at the University of Pittsburgh Press has been unfailingly attentive. I am particularly grateful for detailed, supportive responses from the press's anonymous reviewers and for the expert, collegial editing of Carol Sickman-Garner and Deborah Meade.

My generous friends Sandra Zagarell and Carolyn Karcher read and critiqued the entire manuscript; the book has profited substantially from their insightful attention. Special thanks to Anne Ruggles Gere and June Howard for thoughtful advice at many stages of my work, as well as to my mother, my mother-in-law, and my sister, Pat, for believing I would finish.

I wrote this book on domestic literacy management in a home shared with another busy writer. Friends have sometimes kidded me for sending e-mails to my husband, John, when he was just downstairs, typing away on his own multimedia and video script projects. But we have worked hard at appreciating the need for protected time, as well as enjoying occasional shared lunch breaks, when we could talk about our very different writing tasks. Thank you, John, for your patience with this project and for the inspiring example of your own writing.

Introduction

Domestic Literacy and Social Power

He diligently read to her his lessons.

Lydia Sigourney, *The Faded Hope*

In the introductory pages for her 1865 *Looking Toward Sunset* anthology, Lydia Maria Child reflected back on her long, prolific writing career. Child used her preface to position her book within a far-reaching circuit of exchanges with readers, while characterizing herself as a congenial manager of others' domestic literacy. "I occasionally meet people," she confided, "who say to me, 'I had many a pleasant hour, in my childhood, reading your *Juvenile Miscellany;* and now I am enjoying it over again, with my own little folks.'" As a motherly teacher of these domesticated readers, Child suggested in her self-characterization, she had established their personal literature-reading habits in ways that were later replicated when they became parents themselves, with their "own little folks." The power of this cultural reproduction process was relatively easy—and perhaps strategically important—for Child to downplay: "Such remarks remind me," she declared, "that I have been a long time in the world; but if a few acknowledge me as the household friend of two generations, it is a pleasant assurance that I have not lived altogether in vain."[1]

Despite Child's modesty about her print texts' guidance of others' family literacy, such stories about domestic teaching merit more careful scrutiny than has been given to them so far.[2] As a cultural history, then, *Managing Literacy, Mothering America* explores what it meant to the nation, to visions of American motherhood, to middle-class women readers, and to writers such as Child herself for numerous nineteenth-century women authors to construct themselves as "household friend[s]" teaching multiple generations. Drawing upon an archive of narratives by authors whose writing was more influential in its own day than appreciated in our own, this study examines social composing processes, recurring internal traits, shared reading practices, and educational values associated with a body of narrative literature *about* domesticated literacy. These texts, using plots focused on guided literacy acquisition, provided middle-class women with indirect yet influential avenues into a political culture from which they were legally excluded, from the beginning of Constitutional government in 1789 until they were finally given the vote in 1920.

This flexible genre circulated in a variety of publishing venues in the United States during the long nineteenth century. Through interactions with children and adult readers, these narratives contributed to the formation of an idealized "American" moral identity to be guided by feminized, home-based literacy practices. The core premise of *Managing Literacy, Mothering America* is that sustained management of a particular brand of literacy (in particular, for studying literature) was promoted by a long line of authors depicting middle-class maternal teaching through print text as essential to leading the nation. Exploring how this adaptable narrative form addressed socially significant teaching goals, this study emphasizes connections linking middle-class home reading practices; shifting literature production and consumption models; gender-, race-, and class-based educational agendas; and sociopolitical issues facing the United States at different times in the genre's developmental history.

At the heart of this analysis are stories that appear to be quite transparent: narratives showing maternal figures teaching young Americans to read, write, and learn about the world through oral and written language, thereby giving them an idealized moral character to benefit their national community. The very simplicity of this recurring plot is surely one cause of its functional influence—as well as its literary significance—having been underexamined for so long. This study counteracts that neglect by situating literary analysis more directly within the interpretive framework of literacy studies and by viewing home education through an American studies/cultural studies lens. This interdisciplinary move is particularly necessary since the genre in question—the domestic literacy narrative—itself portrayed American literature as living at the center of nineteenth-century home-based learning. That is, in its then-familiar scenes of mothers and children discussing stories together, this genre valued literature not only as an aesthetic product but also as a source of social knowledge and improvement—for the characters successfully learning within the narratives and, by extension, for the circle of readers outside that fictive world yet presumably reenacting its values.

A review of Emma Willard's 1830s *Journal and Letters* in the *Ladies' Magazine,* an early and enthusiastic promoter of the form, demonstrates how overtly such writing could be bound to motherly teaching. The reviewer praises Willard for taking on "the improvement of her own sex" and observes that addressing this goal had "enabled her to do so much in the work of education." To define Willard's character, the *Ladies' Magazine* describes her as going ever "'onward, and upward,' in the career of morals and literature." Conflating the book with the author's own identity, the reviewer links both print text and writer to "the relation of *mother,*" with its "high aim, of training . . . children for a life of goodness and usefulness," then imagines an extension of Willard's example to other American women, until "we should have no doubt respecting the destiny of our Republic."[3]

Whether an "aim" attributed to authors like Willard, or a role being enacted by the imaginary maternal characters in these narratives, managing literacy involved guiding learners' interpretation of social messages embedded within print texts. In either case, the "literacy management" being achieved was closely aligned with gender- and class-related strategies for acquiring community-wide influence. As a gendered activity, the literacy management depicted in these narratives assumes that the maternal teacher's political power was mainly indirect, achieved through her guidance of others' (her children's, and primarily her son's) literacies. By directing their reading, writing, and oral language acquisition, she also shaped their public behavior and thus, eventually, their influence on the nation. At the same time, this purposeful "management" enterprise was closely associated with middle-class status. Cast as a parallel to the evolving model of male middle-class management in the workplace, the middle-class mother figure in these stories directs learning by managing the use of print text. Like the male middle-class manager, this motherly administrator depends upon the physical labor of other classes (such as the domestic workers who free her up for fireside teaching). Assuming the nationwide generalizability of her daily activities and their associated value system, she promotes self-validating patterns for social interaction while reinforcing the very class divisions her work requires yet pretends not to see. The ideology of maternal domestic literacy management, therefore, caused social power to accrue to middle-class (primarily white) women at the expense of others, while claiming to serve the national welfare.

On both an internal and an extratextual level, domestic literacy narratives advocated the type of literacy they portrayed—one defining middle-class reading/writing practices as ideally home based or at least home inflected and affirming the special responsibilities (and powers) of maternal teachers. At the same time, this vision of guided domestic literacy contributed to contests over the nature and social position of American literature in a nation bent on defining itself and preparing moral citizens, at least in part, through communal literate activity. Accordingly, this literary genre's managers of literacy were, on one level, the mother figures *in* stories about domesticated literacy development. But they were also an extratextual group of readers, since the stories' maternal characters served as accessible role models inviting women (or some women, at least) to see themselves as part of a community, undertaking a shared educative enterprise.[4] Along the way, by associating good citizenship with mother-managed literacy, the narratives gained advantages for both the print-constituted middle class (being nationalized through its own norm-setting literacy practices) and the genre's authors (who self-identified as active members of this same class).

Perhaps no better example of the domestic literacy narrative's social positioning of the mother-teacher and her instructional program exists than Lydia Sigourney's *The Faded Hope* (1853). A memoir of her son's literacy development, the book blends her biographical narration with edited entries from his voluminous journals.[5] Sigourney published this text in the 1850s, when white middle-class women writers' domestic literacy narratives were already well established as a literary genre. Serving both as sentimental eulogy and as didactic model for other mother-teachers, *The Faded Hope* synthesizes three important identities for Sigourney—writer, mother, and teacher—in ways that are sometimes difficult for twenty-first-century readers to appreciate. Throughout the biography, Sigourney uses Andrew's own writing and her sentimental anecdotes about him to emphasize that their shared literacy molded his character, one she presents as an ideal for other American youth to emulate. In the process, as is typical of the genre, Sigourney celebrates her own maternal management of reading and writing while seeming to concentrate on praising the well-educated son. In its treatment of mother-led literacy within a complex social context, *The Faded Hope* embodies both the empowering vision and the troubling limits typical of domestic literacy narratives.

For instance, Sigourney devotes one section of the memoir to a close reading of Andrew's early attempts to write, himself, for a juvenile audience, as he was observing his mother doing on a regular basis. Although she admits his "childish simplicity" in these efforts, Sigourney stresses the care that he gave to entries for "his little volume" and his "pen and ink pictorial illustrations"—products that he hoped would make "a useful contribution to juvenile literature" (111). Even as she is lauding the energy devoted to these "simple pages," however, Sigourney evidently cannot resist underscoring her own influence on the enterprise. She records his tendency to write "I will wait, and ask my mother" in places where he was not certain of his wording or idea (112). Similarly, rhetorical strategies evident in his early efforts at authorship are clearly modeled on her work. For example, Sigourney fondly quotes his closing address to readers in a February 1839 piece for children whom he imagined as being in need of his nine-year-old wisdom:

> And now, dear children, I am about to end this
>   little book, and to bid you farewell.
> May you have gotten some good from it.
> Farewell! Farewell, little reader!
> May this short book do you much good. (110)

Here Andrew's text clearly echoes his mother's educative voice by imitating scenes like those in "The Little Girl That Could Not Read," one of Sigourney's own domestic literacy narratives from an anthology (*Songs for the Little Ones at Home* [1852]) published by the American Tract Society. (See figure 1.) Andrew casts himself as a feminized teacher, a motherlike manager of literacy even beyond his home, just as his mother was through her own publications.

At the same time, of course, his literacy use reaffirms her social belief system. Thus, for example, a key argument of Andrew's "short book" is to show that life after death will be a "happy land," with "no pain, nor sorrow, nor sighing"—a place of "perfect joy" with God. Innocuous as such flowery verbiage may seem today, we should note connections between its content and the values of the white New England middle class, whose close ties to Protestant religious life were reflected in and supported by the kind of communal literacy Andrew mimicked from his mother's writing. In this passage, like other sons in narratives throughout the century, Andrew endorses the efficacy of his mother's domestic teaching, thereby also exalting the cultural power of her gendered and class-linked values.

Similarly, Sigourney's description of Andrew's increasing involvement in her authorial career as he grew older and became a better writer himself casts their shared literacy as reciprocally beneficial.[6] In this case, Sigourney relates how Andrew's tendency to "industry" in "writing and reading" became supportive of her authorship as he asked to "take charge of any arrangement with publishers that she might feel disposed to depute to him, and rendered her essential aid as an amanuensis" (198). Besides handling business dealings, Sigourney's well-trained son provided material for direct interpolation into her texts. For instance, because he had great "power of retaining dates and numerical statements," she would often "appeal to him on these points as to unerring authority" (199). Andrew also assisted her writing with details from his vast knowledge of "history and chronology," wherein "his precision and readiness were remarkable" (199).

Even if we assume that Sigourney was simply reporting straightforwardly, we need to realize how appealing these scenes would have been for other white, middle-class women readers. Balancing anecdotes about the contributions he made to her books with parallel details portraying her encouragement of *his* literacy development, Sigourney reconciles her initial advantage as an adult mother controlling a child's access to literacy-oriented activities with her son's eventual ability to call on knowledge from educational experiences that were not as directly available to her. For example, on an occasion when she was "wishing a few nautical terms" for a piece of her writing, "he poured them forth in such profusion" that she wrote out pages of terms "with explanations, which were afterwards arranged in the form of a lexicon" (199). Relating such collaborative writing back to her earlier home teaching, Sigourney admits: "It was sweet to her, that the hand she had guided in infancy, to form the letters of the alphabet, should bring forth its pen so willingly and skilfully [sic] when she needed its aid. Large portions of the manuscript of two or three volumes were copied by him, in an incredibly short time. . . . Indeed, it was difficult to keep him supplied with work, so rapidly did he bring sheet after sheet, not only without error, but if either omission or obscurity existed in the original, they were sure to be rectified and rendered lucid" (199). This anecdote confirms authority for both participants in the domestic literacy management relationship. Although at first Andrew merely copies her words, in the end he can rewrite— to correct "either omission or obscurity [that] existed in the original," so that it is "rectified" and "lucid."

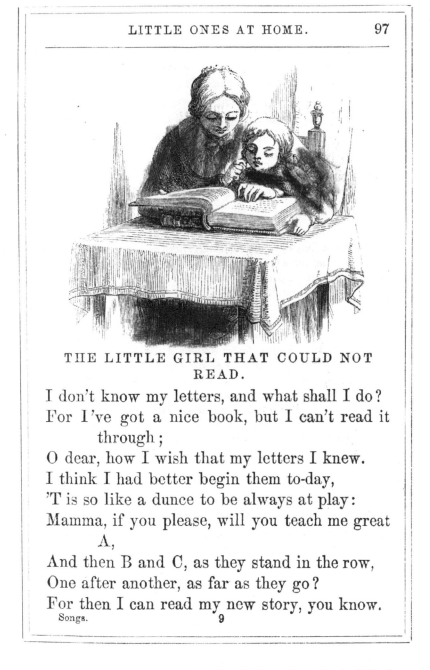

THE LITTLE GIRL THAT COULD NOT READ.

I don't know my letters, and what shall I do?
For I've got a nice book, but I can't read it
    through;
O dear, how I wish that my letters I knew.
I think I had better begin them to-day,
'T is so like a dunce to be always at play:
Mamma, if you please, will you teach me great
    A,
And then B and C, as they stand in the row,
One after another, as far as they go?
For then I can read my new story, you know.

Songs.   **9**

Fig. 1. "The Little Girl That Could Not Read," from *Songs for the Little Ones at Home* (1852). Yale Collection of American Literature, Beinecke Rare Book and Manuscript Library

But what does this rewriting entail, in terms of shared cultural power and influence over others? And how does the maternal literacy manager react if/when her youthful charge asserts a rewriting that is not in accord with her own values? Sigourney's *Faded Hope* depicts a specific case of this complex issue, one revealing the limited social vision often, unfortunately, evident in these maternal teaching narratives. She recounts the episode in a maternal voice unconcerned about how her depiction of a domestic worker's situation might reflect upon her own moral sense. For the doting mother, in fact, the character at the center of the story is still her son, and she writes primarily to praise his generous teaching impulses, presumably learned via the home education she has provided:

> He found a delight in knowledge which he was desirous of imparting, not only by written, but by oral teaching. There was a colored servant in the family, somewhat advanced in years, whom he endeavored to allure to become his pupil. He diligently read to her his lessons, —and was grieved when he found her employments of such a nature, as to preclude her bestowing on him undivided attention. He sometimes expressed a childish indignation that she should have so many labors to perform, and be so much fatigued as to fall asleep when he wished her to study; and proposed that we should have fewer dishes at table, that her cookery need not interfere with her intellectual prosperity. As she retired early, he would take a seat near the entrance of her bed-room, and read in a clear, distinct voice his lessons, or repeat and simplify portions of them for her especial behoof. If his labors, as not unfrequently [sic] happened, were repaid by echoes of that heavy breathing which denotes undoubted sleep, it only aroused him to more earnest efforts at the next period of instruction. "I am determined," he would say, "to improve Ann's mind." (117–18)

The story opens with a sentence reconfirming connections between middle-class children's mother-directed literacy acquisition and their desire to constitute themselves as teachers of others. Andrew, in particular, has a "delight in knowledge" that he longs to share through both "written" and "oral teaching." To this point, and even through the next few sentences identifying his favored pupil as "a colored servant in the family," we would probably find relatively little with which to charge Sigourney (or, more precisely, the maternal narrative voice behind the story). However, once she classifies as "childish" Andrew's frustration that Ann's duties get in the way of the servant's potential learning, we see an uncomfortable distance emerging between the speaker's view of the deserving recipients of domesticated literacy and Andrew's. While the maternal teacher (Sigourney) depicts as humorous his wish for "fewer dishes at table" so that his would-be pupil could have more time "to study," and while she similarly portrays as laughable his determined oral reading outside the door of the sleeping "colored ser-vant," we are left with a cluster of unanswered questions. Why does this mother-teacher assume that the "undivided attention" of her servant would be inappropriately devoted to study? Why is no attempt made to determine the servant's wishes in regard to her own literacy? Why does Andrew's mother make no effort to remedy the conflict between his wish "to improve Ann's mind" and the faithful servant's exhausted sleeping? What are the "lessons" that, from the mother's perspective, are rightfully "his"—that is, necessary for the white, middle-class boy (and his mother) but not the for the "colored" domestic worker? How does that same servant's ongoing la-bor, which continually leaves her "fatigued," make possible the privileged mother's teaching of her son in the first place?

These questions must stand at the heart of any effort to recover the do-mestic literacy narrative for American literary and cultural history. That is, even as we assemble a story of the genre's positive constructions of (white) middle-class American motherhood, we must take equal note of its ten-dency to constrain others' uses of literacy. Along with analysis of ways in which the genre exalted motherly teaching, therefore, *Managing Literacy, Mothering America* will highlight its moves to exclude some Americans from full participation in national civic life.

Taken together, the book moves from the dawn of the narrative form's development in Americanized versions of Anna Laetitia Barbauld's prim-ers, to its apex of political influence in Harriet Beecher Stowe's *Uncle Tom's Cabin,* to the near-twilight of its activity on the American literary scene. The opening of *Managing Literacy* explicates the early history of the genre, emphasizing its close connections to the ideology of republican motherhood, debates about women's education, white women's social ac-tivism, and the emerging print marketplace for women's writing. After this limning of the genre's history in broad, interdisciplinary strokes, I juxta-pose extended readings of two important midcentury literary texts (*Uncle Tom's Cabin* and Frances E. W. Harper's *Minnie's Sacrifice*) that have, up to now, been underinterpreted as educational initiatives tied to domestic lit-eracy management. Then I examine the genre's usefulness for more imperi-alistic (if still purportedly "benevolent") teaching designs in white women's turn-of-the-century missionary literature. Finally, I show how echoes of the genre through the twentieth century and into the twenty-first bear traces of a challenging question: is it possible for writers and readers to use this flexible narrative form to claim social influence without constraining oth-ers?

Whatever the specific era of composition and use, *Managing Literacy, Mothering America* sees the domestic literacy narrative as shaped by individual women writers' rhetorically astute efforts to make literature serve their personal teaching goals. At the same time, however, this study positions these authors' composing processes within a dynamic cultural context and thus also interprets authorship, audiences, and texts as socially constructed. Overall, while connecting the development of this resilient narrative form with shifting conceptions of literary value and purpose, I present a view of this genre as grounded in social literacies; I rewrite American literary history to include enhanced emphasis on its gendered education goals; and I revise understandings of middle-class American motherhood to highlight its nation-building agenda.

Literacy and Literature in Nineteenth-Century America

The happiest and holiest use to which women can devote their talents and education is, to help *those of the other sex with whom they are connected, their fathers, husbands, brothers, sons. And this kind of literary companionship is more needed in our country than any where in the world.*

(Review of Lydia Maria Child's biography of

Madame Roland, *Ladies' Magazine*)

Genre, Gender, and Political Society

In recuperating the domestic literacy narrative, we uncover a form whose muted traces in American literature, education practices, and gendered social roles still have significant implications for our national culture today. The task is complex, however, and requires using several analytical tools in concert. Partly because the genre often participated simultaneously in several related literary modes (including sentimentalism, advice literature, and protest writing such as abolitionist texts), its distinctive rhetorical characteristics have been submerged. To recover a sense of the genre in action, we also need to examine connections linking its aesthetic, political, and educational work. Consideration of this body of texts as a "genre," therefore, includes identifying historicizable, shared reading and writing practices that gradually built a community whose members would have responded positively to elements within these texts not always easily accessible to us today. So, in this study, specific examples from the domestic literacy narrative genre are certainly interpreted as sharing internal textual traits. But rather than focusing primarily on the relative "merits" of particular texts from a formalist perspective, this analysis of individual narratives and the genre as a whole emphasizes *interactions* among those texts and a national identity-building process, as engaged in by groups of readers, along with the writers imagining their responses.[1] In this sense, my readings of specific narratives interpret genre in a Bakhtinian sense—as constructed (and always developing) out of dialogic exchanges involving writers, texts, and readers, with each of those three elements responsive to the other two.[2] Thus, I socially situate "genre" as a literary category for cultural analysis, including literacy practices associated with production and use of these narratives. Domestic literacy narratives were shaped by social forces such as changing curricula in women's education and new venues for publishing that welcomed women's writing.[3] For this study, then, the analytical tool of "genre" is broadly conceived, situated in particular material-culture conditions and viewed as part of an array of sociolinguistic exchanges involved in culture making. To emphasize the genre's interplay between textual portrayals and community-building actions, I examine ways that depicting domesticated literacy as socially beneficial would encourage readers to appreciate internal textual features as literary elements but also to imitate the literacy-oriented actions seen there.

The outlines of this genre's history can be traced in episodes from an evolving ideology favoring women's literary teaching of the nation. Initially, in the late eighteenth and early nineteenth centuries, these narratives advocated American middle-class women's public influence through maternal management of children's reading and writing at home. As the nineteenth century progressed, the genre increasingly advocated domesticated instruction in the common schools and benevolent activities (e.g., urban infant schools, training for servants). By its twilight phase, the genre was delineating the social benefits of feminized literacy management in hybrid educational sites ranging from women's clubs to the mission movement.

Individual texts built upon a core premise—that motherly literacy management could create enlightened members of the national community. Authors intervened in the political sphere to address an array of national concerns by portraying idealized cultural actors at work, guided by literacy-centered, domesticated instruction. So, for example, these types of portraits emerged: Catharine Maria Sedgwick's empathetic consideration of Lucy Lee as a well-taught domestic employee in *Live and Let Live* (1837); Harriet Beecher Stowe's portrayal of young George Shelby as a maternally molded leader in *Uncle Tom's Cabin* (1852); and Jane Addams's depiction of settlement house–trained immigrants' successful assimilation efforts in *Twenty Years at Hull-House* (1910). These celebratory stories about domestic literacy experiences ranged from extended narratives, such as Lydia Sigourney's *Lucy Howard's Journal* (1858); to short tales published in inexpensive form for children and their mothers, such as Lydia Maria Child's *Flowers for Children* collection (1854) and her sixty-three-page *Emily Parker* tale (1827); to narrative poems like Frances Harper's "Chloe" series on post–Civil War literacy acquisition by former slaves. Shorter forms of the narrative appeared as anecdotes about maternal literacy management woven into advice pieces for manuals such as Sigourney's *Letters to Mothers* (1839).

The genre was highly gendered. With that in mind, the overarching goal of this study is to write a feminist cultural history of a nineteenth-century genre closely associated with feminized constructions of literacy, literature, education, and nation building.[4] Donna Landry describes a "feminist literary history" as necessarily involving archival recovery—as in this study of "historical figures who were women, and sometimes men, but also figures of femininity and masculinity as they structure textual systems."[5] The development of the literary genre under review here, in fact, was often implicated in questions about the proper place of women (and men) in society. For instance, Harriet Beecher Stowe did not come under criticism for her 1830s–40s parlor literature—even when she began to write in support of the temperance movement. But in the 1850s, the most vehement attacks against her extension of the domestic literacy narrative into the highly charged political arena of slavery framed their condemnations as questions about her sexuality, suggesting she was absurdly trying to act the part of a man. Although the authors and women readers of domestic literacy narratives certainly cannot be classified as feminists, they were fully engaged in consideration of woman's place in society.[6]

Tracing the genre's history requires taking an extended view of the nineteenth century and situating the narrative form in a political context. We can locate its beginnings in the years just after the Revolution, when civic rhetoric's vital position in the new nation raised questions about the specific goals of women's reading and writing.[7] In 1789, when adoption of the new Constitution signaled the continued exclusion of women from suffrage, alternative routes to political influence gained heightened importance and so became the focus of many middle-class women's texts. The genre faded as an explicit form around 1920, when American women's increasing access to higher education and the professions was broadening their opportunities to exercise management-oriented roles beyond the home. Also, finally gaining the vote made the effort to guide others' politics through literacy management seem less essential than before. Overall, such a time frame foregrounds the political context of the genre's development to affiliate this study with Fredric Jameson's conception of "narrative as a socially symbolic act" and Larzer Ziff's view that literary and political culture are always interacting.[8]

One risk of constructing this roughly chronological narrative of the genre's history is giving the impression that its development was teleological. In fact, its growth and decline were both uneven and recursive. Another limitation to this chronological presentation is that, given my focus on the genre's stages, individual authors' simultaneous activity in other related literary modes cannot be elaborated, so productive interactions like those between the domestic literacy narrative and Lydia Sigourney's poetry or Frances Harper's abolitionist speeches may be obscured. Nonetheless, by stretching the boundaries for women's nineteenth-century literature in both directions, we can avoid a compartmentalized sense of this period. On the one hand, early nineteenth-century writers developing the domestic literacy narrative drew from sources situated in the eighteenth century, yet forward-looking in their views on gendered literacy. On the other hand, women writing in the early twentieth century could still deploy elements from the genre to great rhetorical advantage, even if they were resisting some of the constraints associated with its earlier versions.

Taken as a whole, the period focused on here loosely matches one (1780–1920) set by historian Paula Barker, and the stages she describes for women's political activism parallel phases in the history of domestic literacy narratives.[9] Thus, where Barker describes a first phase in American women's political involvement as represented by the republican motherhood ideal, I see nascent equivalents in literary texts such as Hannah Foster's *The Boarding School* (1798) and Judith Sargent Murray's *The Story of Margaretta* (1798), as well as in full-fledged domestic literacy narratives by Lydia Sigourney, Catharine Maria Sedgwick, and Lydia Maria Child. Barker characterizes a second phase, around the middle of the nineteenth century and through the Civil War, when women's domestication of politics extended the republican mother model into the community by way of benevolent activities. In that vein, Harriet Beecher Stowe's *Uncle Tom's Cabin* is a second-stage domestic literacy narrative. Finally, where Barker outlines a third historical stage when women moved to more direct action in politics, I interpret narratives reconfiguring the domestic literacy narrative to represent mission and settlement teaching as professionalized yet still domesticated literacy management.

Literacy in the Domestic Setting

While taking a *literary* tradition as my primary subject, I foreground *literacy* to stress how, for authors and audiences involved in the development of this genre, the role that social reading and writing played in molding public culture was considered crucial and therefore necessary to control. In particular, how and why Americans interacted with literature were questions of great political importance. The word "domestic" in "domestic literacy narrative" both locates the social acquisition of literacy in a feminized, home-oriented context and constructs that process as reaching outward beyond the home by suggesting that American literacy itself was being domesticated. So, in cultural terms, domesticating literacy represents both the subject the authors using this genre wrote about (feminized management of reading and writing, especially reading and writing of literature) and the related sociopolitical process they were trying to carry out discursively (taking control of the public's reading and writing by "domesticating" these activities). The characteristics of this national teaching enterprise, meanwhile, were shaped by nineteenth-century assumptions about literacy itself.

Significantly, recent research in literacy studies has indicated how the conception of literacy that guided the production and reception of these texts was very different from familiar ideas about literacy at today's turn into the twenty-first century. Our own everyday assumptions about literacy are closely tied to a twentieth-century phenomenon: the mass public-education system shaped by industrialization's factory model of goods-making and of schooling (itself geared to "producing" effective goods-makers).[10] But in the nineteenth-century United States, educational theorists—as well as leading political thinkers and women writers working in the domestic literacy genre—conceived of literacy in more creative, interactive, and moral terms. Furthermore, literacy-based civic nurturance was seen as a key responsibility of middle-class mothers in the home. As Catharine Maria Sedgwick observed in *Means and Ends* (1839), for example, "reading families" "cultivated" not only a "taste for reading" in their children but also a knowledge of "how to read"; and the agent specifically assigned this important teaching task was undoubtedly "the intelligent mother who understood the history and condition of her country" because of the "attention" she gave to her own well-managed reading program.[11] Texts like Sedgwick's help show that the view that current public-education policies such as standardized testing promote today—that literacy is a neutral set of skills related more to the ability to perform tasks in the job market than to a set of ideologically charged social practices—did not yet dominate in the nineteenth century.[12] Instead, social links between literacy learning and proactive citizenship were more explicitly valued then than now. Though writers producing domestic literacy narratives did not employ a phrase exactly like Theodore Sizer's "public literacy," they often theorized as self-consciously as today's progressive educators about the cultural aspects of language development and about the national political implications of communal literacy practices.[13] Specifically, many nineteenth-century writers advocated a national literacy nurtured by maternally managed literature study that generated a moral sense in readers and therefore encouraged appropriate social actions for the polis.

Sedgwick's 1848 preface to *The Boy of Mount Rhigi* provides an apt example of this conception. Situating her text as "the first of a series to be published by Mr. Charles H. Peirce for the young people of our country," Sedgwick explains that the narrative had been written "to awaken, in those of our young people who have been carefully nurtured, a sense of their duty." Declaring that "the safety of the republic depends" on "the young" acquiring "goodness" and spreading it to others, Sedgwick hopes that "after reading the following story" her audience can enact a generous form of civic responsibility.[14] As Sedgwick's preface suggests, nineteenth-century women who developed the domestic literacy narrative were fostering a view of literacy similar to Charles Schuster's recent definition, constructed partly to refute narrow, skills-related conceptions of literacy. Schuster posits a broadly proactive brand of literacy. He declares that being literate is having the "ability to make oneself heard and felt, to signify," so that literacy can be "the way in which we make ourselves meaningful not only to others but through others to ourselves." Such a vision, Schuster says, conceives of literacy as "socially constituted meaning-making" rather than simply as decoding print text, with a literate person being able to use language "to organize experience" through "speech genres," as described by Bakhtin.[15]

Schuster's invocation of the inclusive Bakhtinian "speech genre" is, in fact, particularly relevant to this study. Setting Bakhtin's formulation of the "speech genre" (as any purposeful utterance aimed at an anticipated audience) within Schuster's even larger framework of literacy as the ability to make socially significant meaning, we can position both of these ideas next to Sedgwick's description of the reading process she desires to elicit from her audience. Sedgwick's hope for enlightened behavior as a result of reading, then, becomes more complex than acknowledged by the dismissive view of didactic texts' goals that has been dominant in literary studies. We can see how, for writers and readers of such teaching narratives, the traits linking genre conventions within print texts to literacy practices and shared beliefs were often more purposeful than we might think today. Further, we can draw on social literacy theories like those of Brian V. Street to demonstrate how these narratives affirmed a view of literacy as ideologically charged yet still allowing for individual agency—by both writers and readers.[16]

One approach for recovering a clear picture of how the genre represented a social view of literacy is to note how particular texts portray occasions of shared, home-based reading and writing as recurring practices with results that could be anticipated by readers. For instance, the narratives often use a scene of a maternal figure asking her naive charges (whether children in a Sigourney story or immigrants in an Addams essay) questions about a reading designed to lead them toward appropriate behaviors. A nineteenth-century reader would have recognized this oral literacy exchange as a frequent activity in properly guided American homes. She also would have recognized particular linguistic techniques depicted in the scene—for example, using figurative language or Biblical allusions for explanations—as teaching models she could replicate in her own management of domestic reading. One reason this response to such a scene would have been possible is that the genre reinforced views of what Shirley Brice Heath would call "literacy events" (or particular occasions of literacy being used) as potentially becoming what Street would call "literacy practices" (regular patterns of literacy use linked to shared beliefs about social action).[17]

A brief narrative essay from the 1831 *Ladies' Magazine*, "Social Lyceum," provides an apt window into the kind of social literacy practices that the genre both reflected and promoted. This submission narrates the history of a parlor reading-and-writing club. This group's shared applications of literacy were clearly more in line with Heath's, Street's, and Schuster's conceptions than with the constant, casual references to the term today in political speeches decrying students' and workers' limited literacy (generally cast as inability to read in a narrow skills context). Throughout the essay, in fact, we see interactive views of social and familial literacy, used for "mutual improvement" that joins "pleasure with profit" (in a behavioral rather than a monetary sense). For example, the author, "Noel," stresses that, although the "number of the Literary Association was gradually swelled from the circle of our friends" to a size of about thirty members, the group still saw itself as "our family." Similarly, the meetings of the club are characterized as having a "communion together"—an experience simultaneously "public" yet of a *family nature*," leading to "sociality," so that "the intellect was cultivated, the moral affections called forth, and manners improved." Discussing and writing about "choice selections from English and American classics," as well as newer pieces of "literature and science," this Social Lyceum encouraged a free exchange of ideas among men and women members in a domestic setting. The results included personal and group growth, as members became "brothers" and "sisters" to each other: "It is a family who meet in the quiet light of their own hearth, to hold communion together on subjects which quicken the heart to virtue and stimulate its best affections, as well as course the intellect to action, and summon up the powers of mind."[18] Here is a picture, in other words, of literacy as proactive and unabashedly ideological—not simply decoding print text. And a crucial element in this productive brand of literacy, as signaled in the essay's repeated invocation of "family" and fireside, is the domestic setting being used for social improvement.

While twentieth- and twenty-first-century shifts in understandings of literacy have made it difficult to recognize domestic literacy narratives' proactive place in the nineteenth-century United States, an equally significant factor obscuring this history has been the tendency to reify domesticity. As long as "home" was seen as separate from the "outside" culture, it was difficult for critics to see how nineteenth-century women's management of literacy there shaped public arenas. (Contrasting the critical model of the separation of spheres with the "Social Lyceum" essayist's comments on the overlap between "public" and family is, of course, noteworthy in this regard.) Fortunately, recent scholarship has begun to undo the private/public dichotomy and to reemphasize that women's actions within the home constantly interacted with and influenced public culture.[19]

Amy Kaplan's incisive essay "Manifest Domesticity" provides a case in point.[20] Kaplan demonstrates the efficacy of nineteenth-century separate spheres rhetoric for practitioners like Sarah Josepha Hale even while emphasizing ways in which it masked imperial designs behind a cloak of moral domesticity. The sphere of domesticity was hardly separate from the field of imperial conquest; instead, the two were mutually reinforcing. Like Kaplan, I want to emphasize the flexibility of domestic discourse and the ways in which it exercised a feminized political power. Building upon her view of domesticity as an outward-reaching social force but focusing especially on literacy management within domesticated spaces as a key source of that power, I see this cultural work as actively constructing a citizenry regulated by (the best and the worst of) "white" feminized morality. Literacy and domesticity, when acting together through a literary genre portraying the very process it was promoting, molded the larger political society. Domesticating literacy, this genre repeatedly indicated, could also domesticate the nation.

The "Social Lyceum" essay offers an apt illustration of this interplay between literacy and domesticity, as well as the positive effects the interaction could have on public culture. After brushing aside readers' possible questioning of the propriety of having men and women together for extended literacy exchanges, the writer describes the lady participants' positive influence. Significantly, the essayist explains, these gatherings could be counted on to remain genteel precisely because they were held in the "domestic circle." In the "family" setting of the Social Lyceum, no lady needed to fear exposure to raw, unregulated behavior. Her very presence assured the opposite. Thus, the sketch's author praises both the group's social literacy and its cause-effect link to the feminized domestic setting. Although they did not need to "rise into the attitude of public orators," and while "still sitting as in the domestic circle," female participants in the Social Lyceum exercised the "gentle influence" needed to "govern" the "hearts" of its male members, thereby promoting a feminized literacy. As editor Sarah Josepha Hale observes in her succeeding "Remarks," the "beneficial" effects of the lyceum were derived from "intellectual sociality." In fact, the feminized literacy practices of the group were at the core of their "mental improvement": "reading judicious selections"; "offering their own observations on given questions"; and collaboratively producing "written reflections" combined "to stimulate the intellect, increase the knowledge, and cultivate the benevolent and truly Christian feelings of the community." Like the maternal figures who populated so many fictive domestic literacy narratives throughout the nineteenth century and into the twentieth, Hale here *manages* interpretation of a printed representation of the same social literacy practice (domesticated reading, writing, and discussion) that she is advocating in her argument. The "intellectual drama," as Hale describes it, occurs on two levels—inside the printed text of the magazine but also between the printed text and readers. So, although she does not explicitly designate herself as another "gentle influence" who is "govern[ing]" her audience, Hale is clearly casting herself as a maternal literacy manager.[21]

It is easy to fault Hale today for failing to acknowledge her own specific social position here. Standpoint theory helps us see how her affirmation of the domestic lyceum's work—especially its sanctioned role for female club members—supported her own program of educational advancement for women without admitting to the class- and race-linked limitations of this role. Who cleaned the parlor where the Social Lyceum gatherings were held? Not the "ladies" whose "gentle influence" "Noel" extols, ladies like those in Hale's own reading audience. However, when we critique the reluctance of Hale and other writers to use domestic literacy narratives to interrogate their own standpoints, we should also take note of the complicated authority issues facing them. For the occasion and, to some extent, the right to speak in her "Remarks," Hale was dependent upon authorization provided by male figures like the "Social Lyceum" author—just as the women participating in that club were dependent upon the good will of their male literacy sponsors. In this sense, white women's domestic literacy narratives often anticipate Sandra Harding's standpoint theory question about "what happens when marginalized peoples begin to gain public voice."[22] Both the lady participants in the lyceum and the lady writer (Hale) affirming its influence were still "marginalized peoples," just "begin[ning] to gain public voice" in the postcolonial United States of the 1830s. But they were also claiming that voice from a position of relative privilege. This position would lead many domestic literacy narratives, in Harding's words, to illustrate how "the failure by dominant groups critically and systematically to interrogate their advantaged social situation" actually placed them in a "scientifically and epistemologically disadvantaged [position] for generating knowledge" that could "end up legitimating exploitative 'practical politics' even when those who produce[d] them [had] good intentions" (54).

Motherhood's Teaching Duties

At the center of the social process domesticating literacy—whether set literally in the middle-class home or (later in the century) in domesticated institutions such as women's seminaries, mission schools, or female-run settlement houses—was an idealized, overgeneralized vision of the American mother. This ideal was refined over the course of the nineteenth century with the shifting ideology of the "sphere" where her cultural work was purportedly situated.[23] In this view, the prime agent who could cultivate the nation was the American mother, and one of her major tools was the literary genre celebrating her own management of literacy in the home.

Marilyn Jacoby Boxer argues in *When Women Ask the Questions* that "motherhood" has not yet "commanded sufficient attention in women's studies and feminist theory." Citing Jean Bethke Elshtain's approach for studying motherhood, Boxer suggests that scholarship on this "vital aspect of women's lives" should aim "to 'trace historically, or better, genealogically paradigms'" of motherhood "that have served as catalysts for action and sources of female authority" but also as agents of constraint.[24] In line with Elshtain's call, this study examines how a paradigm casting mothers as literacy guides simultaneously enabled and restricted white middle-class women and others.

Social histories of literacy indicate that American middle-class women were the directors of home reading and writing. Accordingly, the version of motherhood associated with the domestic literacy narrative was doubly empowering for the authors of these texts. As Nina Baym points out in broader terms, literary publication offered a relatively open avenue of influence to nineteenth-century women, and often "their allotted occupation of domestic ground became precisely women's justification for professional authorship."[25] In fact, many useful studies have shown connections between domesticity and the professionalization of women's writing, as well as its popularity during the nineteenth century.[26] Yet connections linking the home-based social consumption of literature and the didactic features of many literary texts have been underanalyzed, as has the unique entrée that writing *about* maternally guided reading practices would have provided for women writers. Nonetheless, a clear sign of nineteenth-century women writers' own awareness of literacy regulation as a route to social power appears in their frequent use of rhetorical techniques presenting themselves as mother-teachers.

In that vein, critics have often commented on the motherly voice of Harriet Beecher Stowe in *Uncle Tom's Cabin* but have tended to react to this rhetorical self-positioning as a distracting or sentimental intervention, rather than an apt device consistent with the author's understanding of her relationship with her readers and the text's didactic purposes. In contrast, when we reread *Uncle Tom's Cabin* alongside the mother-child dialogues of Anna Barbauld's *Lessons,* arguably the first domestic literacy management narrative, both Stowe's maternal voice and its directing of our reading process take on a different tenor. Lydia Sigourney's seemingly self-effacing preface to *The Boy's Book* (1845) is another case in point:

> The writer hopes [this book] may sometimes be a companion of the child, who, loving truth for its own sake, voluntarily devotes a part of his leisure, to what is useful, and sits in the long winter evenings, reading aloud to his mother by the quiet fireside. Sons of my people, —this book has been constructed for you, carefully, and with pleasure. May it bear on its pages, a blessing to you, who now, under the discipline of education, will so soon emerge from its tutelage, to take the places of the fathers. Then, may you stand forth, amid the green vales, and broad prairies of our native land . . . like the blessed tree, "whose leaves are for the healing of nations."[27]

Despite this passage's use of passive voice to reference the female author's writing process, and its purported focus on the upcoming influence of "the fathers," a nineteenth-century reader schooled in the domestic literacy narrative genre would have recognized the motherly guidance of literacy behind *The Boy's Book*. For such a reader, "the discipline of education" from which the boy reader would soon "emerge" (the "tutelage" preparing him "to take the places of the fathers") was undeniably a maternal enterprise grounded in guided study of texts like this one. And the author's own written teaching would have been seen as maternal work for public good. Imagining her text being read in the domestic setting (at "the quiet fireside") by a son under the direction of his mother, Sigourney's preface presents her book and herself as motherly teachers, guiding home-based literacy.

And yet, the genre's argument that domestic literacy management was the most important aspect of women's work was potentially very limiting— and not only because it reinforced "separate spheres" ideas. For one thing, starting with a conception of the maternal role as home-based literacy management by biological mothers prevented unmarried women from claiming a politically significant position in the nation. Writing by Catharine Beecher and Catharine Maria Sedgwick, among others, would try to overcome this limitation by arguing that sisters and aunts could help manage domestic literacy or carry it into the schoolroom. Even then, single would-be practitioners of this literacy-oriented version of motherhood were sometimes supported, sometimes constrained, by their era or region. Augusta Evans's orphaned title character in 1859's *Beulah*, for example, could hardly achieve the kind of proactive social agency through her guidance of schoolchildren's literacy in the patriarchal antebellum South as the well-to-do Jane Addams would in urbanized Chicago fifty years later.

Similarly, the genre's representations of motherhood tended to portray this literacy guidance role as universally accessible to any mother-reader, yet the unspoken assumption was that such readers were white and middle-class. Significantly, efforts by white authors to extend the model of maternal literacy manager to nonwhite or working-class women and moves by nonwhite authors to appropriate it both showed that the national class of educated/educating mother portrayed in these texts could be quite difficult for some women to attain. So, for instance, the Native American author Zitkala-Ša's 1900 transposition of the mother-child dialogue, which had been the touchstone of early domestic literacy narratives, into the radically different "domestic" setting of her girlhood on the plains signaled parallels between her Indian mother's oral, experience-based literacy management and white maternal direction of children's learning. But it also underscored ways in which the motherhood model of the dominant white culture was tied to objects and practices (such as reading printed books) that could be inaccessible for many nonwhite American families.[28]

Finally, to classify the domestic literacy narrative as "women's" literary pedagogy oversimplifies its interactive relationship with "men's" writing and reading. Notable male authors were shaped by and shaped the genre. Some forcefully adapted it to their needs, as Charles Chesnutt did in *The House Behind the Cedars* (1900). Others actively resisted its influence to assert a masculine alternative (as Herman Melville and various midcentury high-culture editors sometimes did).[29] Additionally, the genre was constantly being read by males, including young sons studying with their mothers but also adult men selecting periodicals like the *National Era,* which aimed at a mixed-gender audience. Just so, in an enthusiastic report on Lydia Maria Child's book on ideal wives, the May 1833 *Ladies' Magazine* imagined a socially efficacious blending of male and female reading audiences. A review signed "U. U." closes with this comment: "we recommend to *gentlemen* the following anecdote, as worthy of their imitation: A young friend of ours, after reading 'Good Wives,' exclaimed, that if he ever got married, he would present the lady before her wedding-day with a volume of 'Good Wives.'"[30]

Earlier on, the 1828 inaugural number of Sarah Josepha Hale's magazine (which would be home to many domestic literacy narratives) had sketched a broad, instrumental view of the mixed-gender readership Hale anticipated for the new periodical. Writing what could itself be termed a domestic literacy story in action, Hale describes the place she hoped the *Ladies' Magazine* would hold in American life, while staking claim to maternal guidance of home literacy through cooperation between men and women. Hale delineates the various stances from which male readers might approach her publication, including "the husband," "father," "brother," and "lover." In each case, Hale outlines reasons why the male should, at the very least, welcome the magazine into the home (specifically, by paying for a subscription) and, at best, become a supportive reader himself. Each of her examples is framed as male sponsorship of female literacy, with social implications beyond the home. The husband, Hale says, could "rejoice" that the *Ladies' Magazine* provided a socially productive way for his wife to spend her spare time while he was away at work, with her reading actually enhancing her ability to provide support when he returned home. Father could count on the magazine to "be a source of improvement" to daughters, since it would discipline them through "reading and reflection." Brothers about to enter the public arena not open to their "dear and tender relatives" could use the magazine to reinforce "ties of kindred affection" overcoming the separation. Similarly, the male "lover" could make the magazine his ally, preparing his beloved for proper domestic duties through her reading, which he could regulate by buying a subscription.[31] With its backhanded acknowledgment of nineteenth-century male anxieties about female literacy, Hale's description of the wished-for support of male readers simultaneously expanded the gendered readership expectations for genres like the domestic literacy narrative, promised benefits to males who supported female reading of her product, and mounted an argument for reading and the direction of others' reading as important work women could do for society.

For example, although Father needed to purchase the subscription, he would not be at home throughout the day to direct the hoped-for reading, but Mother would. Similarly, by controlling the "gaze" of his beloved—sending her to "pure pages" that would improve her mind—the lover prepared her for her paramount duties as educator of his sons. Hale's introduction clearly situates this vital, gendered work in a domestic setting that was also a national one, due to the print-linked learning going on there.

Hale's overview of her new publication's position in national society is closely related to her gendering of two groups of imagined readers around their distinctive social roles. Significantly, although a good deal of Hale's language stresses separation (e.g., women will not "usurp" the rightful labor of males "or encroach on the prerogative of the man"), careful reading also reveals major overlaps between the two gendered identities outlined here. For instance, whereas Hale pictures the "sons of the republic" as crucially supportive "polished pillars in the temple of our national glory" and the "daughters" as (mere) decorative elements ("bright gems to adorn it"), both genders are a part of the same edifice. More important, although adult American women need to be "agreeable friend[s]" for their spouses, Hale insists they should also become "rational" ones who can do serious "instructive" work. Furthermore, even as she declares that the American woman exercises influence most directly "within her sphere," consistent with her natural "delicacy" and "retirement" from the outside world, Hale also underscores both "the importance of the privileges now accorded" women and the implications of the "training" they provide for the larger culture. When we ask ourselves how this maternal figure is to perform these "domestic duties" that have national influence, we can see that her interactions with print texts—like the very narrative that is constituting her identity on the magazine's pages—simultaneously position her work within the home (literally, as she reads) and beyond it (giving her access to the larger sociopolitical milieu). So, Hale suggests, these interactions with "literature" will ensure the "character and happiness of our society" since "mothers" are continually "instructing their children" (2). Overall, Hale uses this early domestic literacy narrative to situate a reading program for middle-class women within an ideology of distinctive yet complementary gender roles; to relate this cultural work to nation formation; and, not coincidentally, to sell magazines. Constituting "maternal" identity in a culture dependent on print, she also contributes to a genre-definition process binding shared literacy practices to the formation of social values, especially through the use of "American" literature.

Americanizing Motherhood's Social Role

In American studies today, scholars carefully avoid conflating "America" and the United States, as "American" has rightfully become a more hemispheric term. However, in the post-Revolutionary United States, through the nineteenth century and on into the twentieth, the term "American" was self-consciously employed to designate the new postcolonial nation, intent on establishing its own identity and, later, on exporting that identity around the globe. In that regard, the *Ladies' Magazine*'s frequent invocations of "American" society are typical rather than unusual, as is Hale's observation in her inaugural introduction that her periodical would "be national—be American" (3). So closely connected were the agendas of domestic literacy management, the dissemination of mass-circulation print texts to women readers, and the coalescing sense of a national identity that, when Hale found out "there was a British periodical called the 'Ladies' Magazine,'" she "altered the title of our work" to *The American Ladies' Magazine,*" even though she insisted that any "examination of its contents, to be sure," would have revealed "its character" as quite distinctive from the English publication.[32]

Benedict Anderson's influential *Imagined Communities* argues that the nineteenth-century formation of national identities was such an intense enterprise that virtually every cultural activity became involved in the process. Certainly, literacy practices—especially those related to the marketplace of print—were central to nation building, as Hale well understood then and as they still are today. Anderson underscores such a linkage: "What, in a positive sense, made the new communities imaginable was a half-fortuitous, but explosive, interaction between a system of production and productive relations (capitalism), a technology of communications (print), and the fatality of human linguistic diversity."[33] Anderson's emphasis here is on connections among varying languages and a major means for sustaining them—purchasable print text—that vastly expanded during the nineteenth century, thereby enabling the organization of diverse nationalities around those different languages. Nineteenth-century U.S. domestic literacy narratives were built on a related premise about the role interactions with print text could play in nation building. An ideology supporting maternal regulation of language development (and thus beliefs and behaviors) was created in part through the genre celebrating women's domesticated literacy management. With their control of literacy, middle-class mother figures could, in Anderson's terms, facilitate an "imagined community"—one whose defining traits would embody a properly domesticated citizen.

A major element in this defining process, especially in the decades after the Revolution but to some extent throughout the nineteenth century, was an effort to distance the "American" identity from its European forebears, particularly England. Yet the dominant culture of the new country was clearly indebted to England, so that a major task for American cultural arbiters was to find ways of delineating difference while still affirming connections with Britain. Domestic literacy narratives became one important site for this process of affiliating and distinguishing.[34]

Enthusiastic American packagings of didactic writers such as Anna Barbauld, Maria Edgeworth, and Hannah More demonstrate the ongoing influence of English models for the domestic literacy narrative. Lydia Sigourney's 1832 edition of More's *Works,* for instance, proselytizes for the domestic literacy genre within a biographical sketch that portrays the British author as teaching American readers. Having celebrated "the diffusion of the works of Mrs. More" around the world, Sigourney describes the domestication of the American wilderness through the distribution of More's texts by enlightened mothers of the new nation: "In this far country of England's planting [More's texts] have been incorporated with the elements of a young nation's literature, and blended with the sources of its happiness and glory. Companions of the Bible, they have travelled with the family of the emigrant to our uncultivated wilds, and forest frontiers. There . . . the isolated matron . . . introduces by the evening fireside the 'Shepherd of Salisbury Plain' to her delighted household."[35]

Sarah Hale was one of many women writer-editors who extolled English models, while simultaneously insisting that the domestic literacy narrative and its associated social literacy practices should be Americanized. Besides her enormous *Woman's Record* set of biographies, bringing together hundreds of European and American women's life histories as educational tools, Hale also published sketches underscoring ties between British and American domestic authorship. Harriet Martineau was one favorite subject, as exemplified in an enthusiastic April 1834 *American Ladies' Magazine* biographical piece.[36]

Even as they capitalized on their class-related access to a European heritage and to print texts sustaining that tradition, however, writers like Hale insisted upon the unique vitality of the new national identity they were helping to generate. For instance, in her introduction to *Women and Work* (1859), a British pamphlet being published in America, Catharine Sedgwick explains: "Religious works and moral essays written for the English public, require some modification to meet the wants of the American people. We are at a different stage in civilization—in a different position. We have different modes of education, different modes of life, and far different prospects."[37] This effort to import, and then reframe, European norms formed a major goal for American women writers of domestic literacy narratives.[38]

One of the strategies nineteenth-century Americanists used to exalt their new nation over England was bound up with calls for enhanced education for women in the United States. The argument was, actually, a circular one. American women had unique civic duties and therefore needed more advanced education.[39] In the first days of republican motherhood, proponents argued for reforming American female education so as to make women better teachers of their children for the good of the nation. Dr. Benjamin Rush, one of the leading male articulators of the republican motherhood theory, posited a kind of indirect citizenship for women with a level of education in accordance with that role: "Let the ladies of a country be educated properly and they will not only make and administer its laws, but form its manners and character."[40]

Using just such language, Sarah Josepha Hale, by the 1820s, was already carrying out a *Ladies' Magazine* campaign for improved female schooling. Yet she carefully couched her calls within the conservative ethos of domesticity.[41] Advocating a deemphasis on the "accomplishments" in the curriculum of girls' schools, Hale based her case on the idea that educated women made better mothers. Hale often printed male-voiced pieces in support of this position, as in an 1831 essay by John A. Bolles. Bolles followed the lead of Rush, Susanna Rowson, and other advocates of women's education by offering a celebratory yet conservative view of female agency. He summarized his theme as the "mighty influence exerted on society by woman, and of the education which, in view of this influence, she ought to receive."[42] Building on writing like Bolles's, throughout the nineteenth century, domestic literacy narratives sought support for American female learning based on women's need to serve as teachers for the nation. Even at the turn into the twentieth century, variations on this theme were still being invoked to support expanded educational programs for women, turning seminaries into colleges and allowing women into universities with men.

Management as a Middle-Class Prerogative

"Middle-class" is an important qualifier for discussion of the domestic literacy narrative because its nineteenth-century writers and readers saw themselves as belonging to this group, whose identity was becoming cohesive through shared social values; related, self-conscious work at nation building; and the use of print text to achieve their goals. Along those lines, the term "middle-class" is not used here in the classic Marxist formulation emphasizing various individuals' and groups' relationships "to the structure of ownership and paid labor."[43] Rather, in this study, social class membership resides mainly in such "symbolic capital" elements as "the control over knowledge and skills"—following Bourdieu to employ cultural as well as materialist correlates of class.[44] Antebellum New England writers developed class-inflected strategies for mothers to dispense "knowledge and skills" needed for success in school, work situations, and politics. Language itself as symbolic capital served as the vehicle for women's indirect control over the sociopolitical system: middle-class mothers could manage children's social progress by guiding home-based interactions with written texts, thereby also facilitating young readers' internalization of class-sustaining values.

A historical as well as a theoretical view of class is essential for interpreting the cultural work of domestic literacy narratives. In the nineteenth century, authors and readers of this genre identified with a subset of the growing American middle class—an influence-seeking group whose own members knew who they were and recognized their vital social responsibilities.[45] Often constructing their group identity as who they were *not*—the manual laborers, the newly rich but boorish, the suffering poor—this wing of the middle class allied itself with interrelated institutions of culture making and preservation, such as publishing, education, artistry, and the law. This subgroup, which Louise L. Stevenson describes as the *Victorian intellectuals* and Stow Persons as the *gentry*, self-consciously assumed the responsibility for creating and guarding the right kind of national identity.[46] Stevenson accordingly describes them as "energetic, public-spirited citizens" whose male members "were usually doctors, lawyers, college professors, journalists, and in lesser numbers, businessmen" (62). Though generally successful in their own careers, Stevenson argues, these middle-class intellectuals tended to look down upon the "mere capitalists" who concentrated only on material gain (62). Nonetheless, although "profoundly committed to the idea of republicanism, and scornful of those who disdained the American people," this social group still "distrusted . . . universal suffrage and majority rule" because they feared the masses' insufficient preparation for citizenship (43). (Andrew Jackson was one of their favorite satirical targets.) Stevenson suggests that their main endeavor was to educate society—including those entering the ranks of the middle class through new wealth that made them potentially dangerous to conservative values.[47]

The tools for this ongoing education movement included everything from lectures and lyceums to publication of texts representing the class's value system. Stevenson classifies *Uncle Tom's Cabin* as just such a work, aiming "to educate the public morally and intellectually" (180). Jane Addams's autobiographical accounts of the Hull-House program, along with other books like *A New Conscience and an Ancient Evil* (1914), also illustrate that agenda.[48] (One common trait in all such writing, Steven Mintz indicates, is its linkage of gentility, social commitment, and belief in the power of language to effect community reform.)[49] In that vein, Persons describes a gentry-class cluster of female writers (including Sedgwick, Stowe, and Hale) who shared a firm sense of their social responsibility, which they addressed in didactic texts. All in all, such nineteenth-century writers' adoption of the domestic literacy narrative was an apt strategy for constructing a highly influential class-based identity still consistent with con-

servative expectations about American middle-class womanhood. In guiding
home literacy for the public good, nineteenth-century middle-class women
were carrying out a variation on the kind of male middle-class social leadership Dana D. Nelson describes as closely related to American national values.[50] The domestic literacy narrative allowed for a gendered version of a
class-based role that would accommodate women's writing as well as their
reading of such texts.

Female Authorship and Didactic Literature

Numerous studies have chronicled the increasingly impressive sales
nineteenth-century women writers claimed in the literary marketplace, doc-
umented their influence on multiple literary forms, and explicated their intense connections with their readership.[51] Despite these successes, women
writers continued to elicit male discomfort—and occasional overt resistance—on into the twentieth century. For example, in *Doing Literary Business,* Susan Margaret Coultrap-McQuin revisits the infamous 1877 *Atlantic
Monthly* dinner party to which the magazine's many "lady" contributors
were not invited. Her explanation for their exclusion emphasizes the "am-
biguous response of nineteenth-century American society to the woman
writer." Coultrap-McQuin sees editor Henry O. Houghton's "mistake" of
"not inviting 'lady contributors'" as an example of the way male publishers,
reviewers, and writers supported and devalued nineteenth-century women's
authorship at the same time.[52] From Mary Kelley's perspective, the com-
modification of female texts—the money exchange involved—made female
authorship problematic.[53] A woman's writing for money meant her rightful
position as object of male protection had been disrupted. A male writer's
bank account shrinking from female competition was similarly troubling. In
both situations, the economic underpinning of the ideology of domesticity
was undone, with the purportedly helpless woman providing for herself, in
the first case, and the supposedly self-sufficient male unable to provide adequately for his family in the second.

Yet it was not the market exchange alone that made women writers potentially dangerous to society. In some cases, threats to social mores embedded in their texts generated negative responses. Perhaps unsurprisingly,
content that might in any way be construed as immoral could bring especially forceful censure on a female writer (hence Harriet Jacobs's concern
about how to present her relationship with Mr. Sands in *Incidents in the
Life of a Slave Girl* [1861]). In contrast, content that upheld morality or,
better yet, taught a healthy moral lesson was usually considered worth-

while.[54] In other words, the same ideology at the heart of republican motherhood's home pedagogy and its various extensions (into the schoolroom and social reform movements) was also invoked to justify women's entrance into the literary domain—and their management of literature consumption by others. Similar to the circular quality of arguments about female education, the advocacy for female authorship often spun back onto itself. Women's special abilities to nurture and refine meant they could have a beneficent influence on literature, both as readers and as writers; and once literature itself had been feminized, it could have a nurturing influence on social behaviors. Social interactions around consumption of literature, in turn, would shape individuals into ideal community members, ready to refine others, possibly by creating and circulating more morals-guiding American literature.

This view of literature is, of course, quite at odds with New Critical conceptions of literary value, as feminist critics such as Jane Tompkins and Cathy N. Davidson have repeatedly pointed out.[55] This nineteenth-century idea about literature's moral influence—and the concomitant goals of authors—was closely related to gendered, middle-class-oriented nation building. For one thing, assigning an educative duty to literature helped ensure that making and circulating it could be cast as proper feminine activities. For another, it helped position literature consumption ideologically in a domesticated setting, where middle-class women (as guardians of social literacy) could guide that use.

Privileged middle-class women continually used their own publishing venues to reassert interrelated arguments about their needs for learning, their nation-building duties in teaching, and the special role that a feminized American literature—emphasizing the didactic over the aesthetic qualities of texts—would play in these connected enterprises. John Bolles's "The Influence of Women in Society" in the June 1831 *Ladies' Magazine,* for instance, offered a view of literature as rightfully becoming a women-led pedagogy for the national good. Bolles went so far as to posit an American literature with *"a more* SOCIAL CHARACTER *than literature has ever possessed"* based on women's influence. Juxtaposing masculine and feminine imagery to imagine a shift in literature's character, he also predicted that, under the enlightened guidance of women, literature would "lose its air of stiffness and chilling dignity, and . . . come home to all hearts with cheering influences." Making his gendered contrast even more explicit, he added, "It will . . . , under female management, like rustic manners, be polished and softened, and domesticated." Unlike some male writers who expressed fear about what such an impact on the national character might be (e.g., a loss of manly strength), Bolles asserted the positive social power of literature, if nurtured by women's improved education and their successful ventures into publication: "The whole body of our literature will undergo a mighty transformation, assuming in the change a social charm, a moral loveliness, a power over the heart, as yet unknown. The beautiful results that have already followed from woman's efforts to divide with man the field of literary triumph—from the labors of female poets, and novelists, and editors—more than warrant our expectations" (265–66). Linking all these related enterprises to "an elevation of national character, and an increase of national spirit" (266), Bolles justified his predictions in part by citing personal experience. The "little Lyceum" to which he belonged, after all, had been dramatically reformed by adding women members. "Let us compare our present literary efforts with those which date earlier than the commencement of our association with our sister members," Bolles opined, "and we shall discover increased delicacy of taste and expression, superior gentleness and friendliness of thought, and a more polished style and manner—the fruits of mental communion with the fairer and gentler sex" (265).[56]

For all his enthusiasm over the crucial part women could play in American literature making, it is noteworthy that Bolles's definitive example emphasizes feminine influence over men's text making more than women's work on their own literary products. Whereas American women's responsibility to guide (and support) others' reading and writing was clear, writing for print publication placed them in a potentially more tenuous social position, as was suggested by the tentative considerations of female authorship in an 1832 *Ladies' Magazine* review of Child's Madame Roland biography. Hesitant to extol Madame Roland's own literary endeavors, the reviewer hints at her abilities as a writer but stresses even more the importance of her support to her husband:

> He found in her zeal and skill that assistance in his literary pursuits and political writings which it is not probable any man on earth could have rendered him. We think the happiest and holiest use to which women can devote their talents and education is, to *help* those of the other sex with whom they are connected, their fathers, husbands, brothers, sons. And this kind of literary companionship is more needed in our country than any where in the world. . . . Our men are so engaged in active business they have but little time for writing, but our ladies are comparatively at perfect leisure; and might they not employ such hours, under the direction and for the aid of those they are bound to assist as well as honor with advantage to both? If they had the zeal and industry of Madame

Roland, they might lighten their husband's labors by copying if no more.[57]

In both its enthusiasm over American women's potential in "literary pursuits" and its contention that such enterprises still needed to be framed primarily as "help" for "those of the other sex," this passage's use of Madame Roland pulls back from an overt challenge to gender roles. Clearly capable, American women like Madame Roland had adequate "leisure" for literature making, but their work in this arena might still need to be structured, at least in part, as "copying" that could "lighten their husband's labors." By implication, then, if/when she did write on her own, an American woman's literature would focus mainly on nurturing others.[58]

Furthermore, even as this ideological construction of feminized literature—always sensitively reinforcing true American social values—was being advanced, an alternative "masculine" model was also beginning to be promulgated in sites such as *Putnam's* and the *Atlantic*.[59] The gradual triumph of this competing masculinized model played a major part in the suppression of the domestic literacy narrative from "official" American literary history. But it did not prevent twentieth-century echoes of the genre from reverberating in some popular literature (such as inspirational-religious novels and much literature for young adults), as well as in some schoolteachers' moral approaches to literature instruction. To recover a clearer sense of American literature making as an evolving and still-contested role, the history of didactic genres like the domestic literacy narrative needs to be recovered.

Authorship as the paid profession it gradually became, by the end of the nineteenth century, was quite different from the "amateur" yet socially meaningful authorial identity dominant in earlier eras, when having one's work circulated in a community of peers, or seeing the influence of one's writing in others' lives, could serve as a measure of whether or not one was classified as an author and, equally important, whether or not one saw oneself in those terms. In this sense, nineteenth-century literature making was a task accessible to virtually any member of the American middle classes. For instance, letters to friends and family often took on a highly literary quality, anticipating shared reading by an appreciative audience. So, too, literary clubs, where women (and men) read their writing and circulated other cultural artifacts, also conveyed authorial power.[60] Accordingly, Stowe became an author for the Semicolon Club's ladies and gentlemen long before she wrote for pay, and in that supportive milieu she created an array of domestic, didactic narratives. This conception of authorship—working for communal influence at least as much as for pay—also helped guide the defining enactments of the domestic literacy genre that circulated in print texts for purchase. Ironically, it was just this conception of feminized literature as generously social that helped promote big sales for some of the most professionalized practitioners of the genre, who often presented themselves as "friends" of their readers, sharing a kind of virtual parlor literacy space. (See figure 2.) Equally important, rhetorically positioning domestic literacy narratives as home-oriented textual teaching encouraged recognition of this work as acceptable labor for genteel ladies. Women, "everyone" was saying, were meant to be teachers. So literature that depicted women's management of others' literacy became, figuratively, just another parlor or schoolroom for motherly teaching. And the literacy management genre would have been a particularly appealing vehicle for American women writers like Susanna Rowson, Lydia Sigourney, Harriet Beecher Stowe, and Frances Harper, all of whom, when they began careers as writers, already had a strong sense of themselves as teachers.

In this context, another step toward defining the place of domestic literacy narratives in literary history involves elucidating its educational goals. This step requires rehabilitation—or at least re-vision—of the term *didactic,* which has too often been used, in literary studies, only in a pejorative sense.[61] The negative view of "didactic" texts and "didactics" as an enterprise came about partly through attacks on sentimental, feminine, and overtly instructional fiction in such influential venues as high-culture periodicals and academic manifestos promulgating "aesthetic" values for literature.[62] Yet my own reading of numerous book reviews from a range of nineteenth-century periodicals has shown that, for much of the nineteenth century, the classifying term *didactic* was used as frequently to praise as it was to blame.

Along those lines, one 1835 author's discussion of his use of the term *didactics* serves as a reminder that today's dichotomy contrasting subtly "literary" writing with explicitly "didactic" texts should not be carried over uncritically into analyses of nineteenth-century works. Influential editor Robert Walsh chose the title *Didactics: Social, Literary, and Political* (1836) for an anthology of his writing. In his advertisement, Walsh presents "didactics" as a highly positive enterprise. He links his own collection with a view of literature as able to integrate the rational ("principles") with the emotional ("affections") so as to do "service to the American youth"—that is, to carry out a national teaching enterprise.[63] For Walsh (and, we might assume, for the middle-class readers of the periodicals he edited for several

Fig. 2. "Truly your friend, Sarah J. Hale." Portrait by W. G. Armstrong (ca. 1835). The Library Company of Philadelphia

decades), the work of "didactics" was "literary" in part *because* it was "social" and "political." As such, it represented a version of literature that comfortably embraced teaching as a primary goal.

Historicizing American literature as, in Walsh's terms, a social and political enterprise goes a long way toward accepting its didactic heritage. But we probably cannot fully appreciate the complex nature of that heritage until we have also recovered an informed understanding of nineteenth-century teaching. Work on this essential re-vision has, fortunately, already begun, thanks in part to Mariolina Salvatori's *Pedagogy: Disturbing History, 1819–1929*. Salvatori set out on a reclamation process to uncover the history of attitudes toward "pedagogy" in American culture, especially its eventual devaluation to something "nonscholarly, technocratic, implementational, and a- if not anti-theoretical."[64]

One historical pattern that Salvatori found was concentrations of discourse conveying different views of pedagogy in two distinct periods, around the 1840s–50s and the 1880s–90s. Intriguingly, Salvatori's two periods correspond generally to stages two and three of my rough chronology for the domestic literacy narrative's development (and to Barker's second and third stages of the domestication of politics in American culture, as outlined earlier). This chronology views the midcentury as a period of increasing emphasis on public intervention and theorization in teaching. For Salvatori, this stage included creation of public normal schools and the emergence of theories of pedagogy. For the domestic literacy narrative as an educational discourse, social intervention and theory making involved having motherly literacy managers (like Stowe and her sister Catharine Beecher) assertively address public, political issues via literature grounded in theories of empathy. In addition, both Salvatori and I see the period at the close of the nineteenth century as a time when science asserted a new influence. For Salvatori, this process often led to a false dichotomy between the art and the science of teaching, and to struggles to reconcile them; for my view of the domestic literacy narrative, it promoted increased hybridization, as authors struggled to integrate the feminized style of domesticated literacy management with a masculine, professionalized discourse of social science and scientific education. The increasing professionalization of the foreign mission movement's writing for periodicals and of settlement house narratives' reports on teaching in their neighborhoods represents one sign of this shift being played out in the domestic literacy genre.

Implicit in Salvatori's interpretation is a suggestion that our devaluing of the didactic in literature has been related to the devaluing of pedagogy in education sites and in scholarship. That being the case, we need to rearticulate connections between nineteenth-century contests over the goals for American literature and parallel debates about how best to educate the nation's citizenry. Useful work has already been done, of course, by Americanists like Richard Brodhead and Laura Wexler.[65] What *Managing Literacy, Mothering America* contributes to this larger agenda is evidence of one genre bringing together nineteenth-century debates about literature, literacy, and community-oriented teaching. Domestic literacy narratives simultaneously sought influence over literary writing practices and over education, while defining a social role for middle-class women based on their home-inflected teaching for the national welfare.

New England Authors and the Genre's Social Role

Let no mother feel perfectly at ease about her children, simply because they read, unless she knows the character of the books that engage their attention, and what use is made of the knowledge they impart.

(Lydia Sigourney, *Letters to Mothers*)

In the closing paragraph of her preface to *The Book for Girls*, Lydia Sigourney outlines her commitment to promoting literacy among readers to whom she was particularly devoted—"the young of [her] own sex." Although composed by one writer working in Hartford, Connecticut, in the 1830s, this characterization of her authorship delineates hallmarks of the domestic literary narrative *as* a genre—one already being championed by an array of writers as a source of feminized, nationwide teaching centered in the home. Like others helping to establish the form, Sigourney positions its work in relation to her own identity as a motherly educator and her readers' similar priorities for using literacy. "I have myself been a teacher," Sigourney explains. "Some of the happiest years of my life were thus spent. Henceforth, all teachers and all scholars are to be as friends." Imagining her book as addressing young American women in "the voice of a friend,"

Sigourney hopes it can "continue to speak words of instruction and love, long after the hand that prepared it [would] moulder in the grave."[1]

Lydia Sigourney carried out the role of teacher at home, in schools, and through print publication, but the type of instruction she most exalted was managing literacy by the fireside. Toward that end, she describes a compact between herself as a motherly teacher-writer and her anticipated female readers. In picturing this implied learning contract as a shared reading of printed texts, she links her own literary program to ideas about middle-class women's proper position in the young republic. By referring to "reading" as an "accomplishment," for instance, she situates her book and the female social role it advocates within a conservative Anglo-American tradition. This view casts genteel women as charming entertainers for their families. Accordingly, elsewhere in her preface she calls upon her audience to practice reading as a "graceful" "art" demanding effective "elocution," correct "emphasis," and appropriate "cadence"—thereby construing women's reading as depoliticized entertainment. Hence, Sigourney observes, "to read well is a high accomplishment," "mak[ing] the evening fireside delightful, or the wintry storm pass unheard." At the same time, such reading could embody a form of benevolence, to "comfort the sick, and cheer the darkness of the friend whose eye age has dimmed." Woven within this depiction of feminine literacy as a generous, pleasure-giving performance, however, Sigourney offers an equally insistent valuing of literacy as enabling the female reader "to impart . . . instruction." She indicates that reading to others will enable America's women to "instill into the unfolding mind lessons of wisdom." So, by accepting the book (and its author) as teacher, a young woman reader can become a teacher herself, prepared to manage others' home-based literacy. This idealized user of Sigourney's book will then achieve a noble balancing act: maintaining "sentiments that are feminine in their character" along with the "knowledge" needed to do "woman's duty." What Sigourney advocates in this description is a shared literacy network. And she implicitly portrays that community of mothers and mothers-in-training as defining the goals of the American domestic literacy narrative.[2]

Lessons for American Middle-Class Mothers

Besides Sigourney, numerous other New England writers, many of them prolific in a range of generic forms, contributed to the defining stage of the domestic literacy narrative, from the 1780s to the 1850s.[3] One figure highly involved in this process was Sarah Josepha Hale, whose editing of the *Ladies' Magazine* allowed her myriad opportunities to regulate others' writing and reading as well as to create her own educational narratives.[4] Meanwhile, Harriet Beecher Stowe's use of the genre moved during this era from marketing short didactic stories for magazines toward a direct intervention into politics via *Uncle Tom's Cabin.*[5] Even earlier, Judith Sargent Murray (*The Story of Margaretta* [1798]) and Hannah Foster (*The Boarding School* [1798]) had set out topics and strategies others would build upon. In the early 1800s, while teaching in her innovative academy for young ladies, British emigrant Susanna Rowson had helped distinguish American women's didactic writing from the literature of her former homeland. Rowson's texts affiliating with the emerging genre include *Reuben and Rachel: Tales of Old Times* (1798), *Sarah; or, The Exemplary Wife* (1813), and *Biblical Dialogues between a Father and His Family* (1822). Particularly in her prefaces, Rowson laid out a rationale for American women's teaching, learning, and literary production as aiding nation building.[6]

The foundational text of the American domestic literacy narrative, however, was actually a British publication that was repeatedly repackaged for U.S. readers through much of the nineteenth century, but especially in the decades around 1800. Anna Laetitia Barbauld set the pattern for the genre's basic plot and characterizations in her groundbreaking primer, *Lessons for Children.*[7] *Lessons* debuted in England in 1778 and began circulating in the new United States very quickly, often in pirated editions made possible by the lack of international copyright law.[8] Besides repeatedly editing *Lessons,* American women writers also combined Barbauld's work with appreciative biographies, as early as Mary Hughs's in 1826, shortly after Barbauld's death.[9] Taking a more appropriative stance, Sarah Hale incorporated some of Barbauld's texts into an 1840 anthology merging her own authorial identity with the British writer's: *Things by Their Right names, and Other Stories, Fables, and Moral Pieces, in Prose and Verse, Selected and Arranged From the Writings of Mrs. Barbauld, with a Sketch of Her Life, by Mrs. S. J. Hale . . .*

Initially marketed as an aid to home teaching, *Lessons* quickly found its way into American schoolrooms too, especially in the Northeast. An example of Barbauld's work becoming a textbook is evident in the pretitle page of the Hale-edited collection cited above, where a paragraph signed by the members of the "Board of Education of the State of Massachusetts" officially designates the book as "sanctioned" for its "School Library" series.[10] Gillian Avery reports that many of the textbooks generated to support the regularization of spelling in the United States through schoolhouse use were actually "gleanings" from *Lessons for Children,* renamed with titles like Hartford's *The Child's Spelling-book,* which both lifted directly from Barbauld and added new language "applicable to American schools."[11] Many New England schoolchildren memorized passages appropriated from Barbauld's *Lessons* without ever knowing the identity of the author.[12]

Several components of *Lessons for Children* proved especially influential—including organized, conversational pedagogy between a mother and child; language-supported interactions between the home and the outside world; and connections between literacy-based intellectual growth and the development of a strong moral sense. Barbauld's primer presents conversations between a mother and "little Charles," whose learning to read and to interpret the world around him are interrelated. While teaching Charles vocabulary, for example, the mother-son dialogues acculturate him to the responsibilities he will have as an adult and the tools his social status will provide for those duties. A discussion of different characters at work on different tasks also signals to Charles that his own adult role will be professional-managerial, not manual labor. Accordingly, Barbauld's primer played a notable part in the construction of middle-class identity—and its links to print consumption—in England at the turn into the nineteenth century.[13] Then the key traits of this ideology were transported to America through members of the gentry subclass identified earlier.

For both mother and child, a complicated balance between restraint and empowerment lies at the heart of Barbauld's teaching in her *Lessons,* as it would in later American domestic literacy narratives inspired by her work. In the opening dialogue, for instance, "Mamma" draws Charles to her side for instruction, then reminds him to take good care of his material possessions or be classified as "naughty." Like other scenes, this vignette insists that, to be a "good boy," Charles must study under his mother's guidance before he earns the right to "go and play." This paradoxical portrayal of education as initially constraining so as to be eventually liberating is further developed in other episodes. So, although Charles's reading instruction begins in Mamma's lap, by the opening of volume 2, he can sit on his own stool and is ready to take on more empowering "new lessons." Hence, he grows to understand that his humanity (i.e., what makes him better than his lively pet, Puss) is dependent upon literacy: he "can talk and read" while the cat can *only* play.[14]

Barbauld's controlled, incremental teaching through literacy management is extended throughout the several volumes of *Lessons,* each of which is composed for a reader of a particular age. Barbauld carefully sequences her content to move from the simplest, most concrete vocabulary in short sentences, to increased detail and complexity in word choice and sentence structure. For example, part 1 includes this introduction to the vocabulary of colors: "Ink is black, and papa's shoes are black. / Paper is white, and Charles' frock is white. / Grass is green. / The sky is blue" (C 1: 14). Part 2's lesson on seasons offers a portrait of February reinscribing some of these colors within a more complex context: "February is very cold too, but the days are longer, and there is yellow crocus coming up, and the mezereon tree is in blossom, and there are some white snow-drops peeking up their little heads. Pretty white snow-drop, with a green stalk!" (C 2: 15).

Like her work of managing language acquisition, the mother's responsibility to convey properly restrained morals to her son is suggested in virtually every scene in the primer, even some that appear, at first glance, to be focused solely on vocabulary or computation skills. At one point, for example, Mamma teaches Charles to count to ten by using a pile of raisins. Next, preaching generosity, she adds a directive for him to share the fruit with other children. Another exchange stresses the need to respect others' belongings. Parallel to his expanding vocabulary, the trajectory of Charles's adventures is an ever-widening one, but with a compasslike anchor. With his mother accompanying him, the young boy explores the world beyond the home but "reads" its meaning through the lens of his mother's managing questions. For example, one episode frequently published as a separate American "toy" book is Charles's journey to France, which starts with a description of the young boy's trip from home and moves to country road; to seaside boat-boarding; to channel-crossing; and, eventually, to a tour of another culture. In all these episodes, while "little Charles" is the active learner with whom young readers can identify, his mother's agency is clearly crucial, as conveyed in a guiding female voice. So whenever Mamma tells Charles a story about some other little boy's experience (whether a negative or positive example), she also serves as explicator.

Americanizing Barbauld's *Lessons*

A belief that literacy management practices Barbauld had modeled needed adapting for the American sociopolitical context encouraged some of the changes that packagers of her *Lessons* series made for U.S. editions. Other textual interventions were driven by market concerns or by a combination of ideological and monetary impulses. As suggested earlier, one technique in the Americanization of Barbauld's *Lessons* involved appropriation—such as using her name to market books, whether or not she was sole author. An equally notable approach, however, utilized what Vicki Tolar Collins dubs "rhetorical accretion," interpolating new material directly into *Lessons* editions.[15] Americanizing the narrative through accretion became a more prevalent practice as the nineteenth century progressed and the personal presence of Barbauld as author faded from cultural memory. As particular traits of the domestic literacy genre became more closely associated with the new nation's own identity, "rhetorical accretion" helped position Barbauld's *Lessons* more clearly within the context of America's own domestic literacy practices, gendered education systems, and beliefs about civic life's connections to home teaching. Along the way, accretion could wind up distorting the text.

One brand of accretion that carried significant ideological weight was in new illustrations for American editions. In adding pictures of teaching mothers, editors were also "selling" the lifestyle such images depicted. Thus, illustrations in many U.S.-made editions reinforced the idea of domestic literacy management as genteel yet public work. These representations of domestic literacy in action became highly coded. King and Smith's 1823 New York edition, for instance, used a color engraving of the Mamma figure preparing to teach. Sitting with hand outstretched, this gracefully dressed mother beckons her child to the fireside, decorated with an elaborate screen and mantel clock. Charles, book in hand, steps toward his mother, eager for his reading lessons. Variations on this illustration recur in countless other editions, promoting the ethos of maternal pedagogy.

To re-view the *Lessons* text in the context of these images is to sense how the cultural construction of the American middle-class maternal teacher was facilitated by Barbauld but also by "her" interactions with Americanized descendants—packagers of her texts who were also marketing a genre with its associated ideology. In particular, for the nineteenth-century audience, seeing recurring versions of the stereotypical home-based literacy scene eventually meant that the individual images were no longer strikingly distinct—that is, they were normalized. Meanwhile, the iconic quality of the gaze connecting mother and child to their reading, over time, constructed home literacy as collaborative. Brought together by looking at the book, neither mother nor child alone is the dominating subject. Bringing focus to a shared desire, reading the text together allows the mother-child relationship to become more reciprocally nurturing, as suggested by the ray of sunlight embracing mother, children, and book in the frontispiece illustration for one 1843 edition. (See figure 3.)

Furthermore, once the basic image of home-based mother and child reading together became so predictable, any slight variation(s) in the paradigm would have been notable. Thus, for instance, the wide-open doorway in the background of the 1825 Gilley issuing of the *Lessons* would have been a more significant symbol for a nineteenth-century reader than for us today. In a similar way, editions that added more illustrations of Charles's and Mamma's tours outside the home thereby highlighted maternal teaching's being extended outside the domestic sphere. For example, several antebellum editions used four illustrations in a progressive sequence of maternal pedagogy. The first scene shows Mamma in an enclosed room, near the fire, with a book in her lap. Charles steps toward her. The next engraving, in contrast, shows Mamma taking an older Charles for a walk outside. Her hand points to a loaded wagon—offering a "reading" of that text for her son, apparently explaining what it is and how it works. The third illustration reworks the first. Rather than reading *to* Charles now, she listens to him read, as he perches on a stool, holding his own book. She is seated again, in the same position and in the same room—except the door is now open, to reveal a meadow, trees, and a building. If the second and third illustrations portray Charles's increasing maturity—his ability to take on more responsibility and see more of the world—he nonetheless still needs a maternal guide. In fact, the final engraving, where a hare is being pursued by dogs, carries undercurrents of danger associated with the undomesticated world or with attempts to travel through it without maternal wisdom's support.

Along with such image-based accretions to the *Lessons* text, many editors made direct changes to Barbauld's language.[16] Simply substituting a word or phrase could make for substantial shifts in meaning. In a few editions, for example, "Charles" becomes Little Marrian. This gender switch in the main character may affirm U.S. reading audiences' increasing commitment to equity in female education. Perhaps this editor wanted young ladies to be able to imagine themselves as the mother-led student more literally than was possible when the child in the story was a boy. In this sense, "Little Marrian" moved the argument for equal (or at least improved) female education from the seminary and other school institutional sites down to the earliest point of possible inequity—during at-home literacy acquisition. Mrs. Barbauld is still named author in these editions, even though she herself had repeatedly insisted on the need to distinguish between the educational programs necessary for young boys and the more restricted opportunities appropriate for girls. And *Little Marrian* may represent an effort by Barbauld Americanizers to problematize gender roles in other social practices as well.[17] The frontispiece illustration shows Marrian

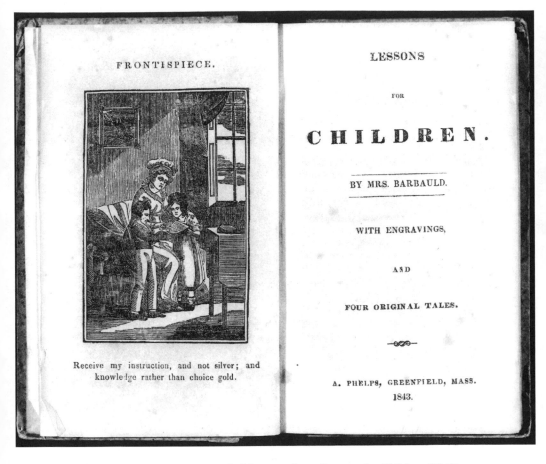

Fig. 3. Frontispiece image and title page from *Lessons for Children* (1843).
Historical Textbook Collection, Gutman Library Special Collections,
Harvard Graduate School of Education

reading a book, a boy in a sketch beside her painting a picture. What does it mean, in nineteenth-century America, to give Marrian the task and the power of reading the printed text, while her male companion is relegated to being a decorative artist?

Interpolations of longer passages could have an even more striking effect. For instance, in the 1850 Munroe and Francis *Lessons,* two entirely new scenes (involving a silly talking dog and advertisements for other books) are grafted directly into what had, up to that point in the narrative, been a reprinting of Barbauld's own text. The extra episode is abruptly tacked on after a very lyrical bedtime ending for one volume of the lessons, where the motherly voice speaks in rich images to Charles about the moon and sun. Suddenly, a chatty canine Flora tells the reading audience she can talk as well as the sun and moon. She belongs, she says, to some children "whose parents hired a cottage for the summer near a beautiful sea-beach, where they had a view of the waters of the Atlantic Ocean." Flora then names some animals they observed during their stay. Up to this point, although the rationally ordered sensory experiences of the original *Lessons* are diminished by the jabbering dog, importation of details about the Atlantic Ocean and American animals could be seen as a relatively innocuous reshaping of the English story to fit the anticipated audience. Yet the next shift is even more striking, as Mamma's voice suddenly reenters the text, but with a different role than anywhere else in Barbauld's own *Lessons*—to direct Charles's future reading by advertising book choices. "Now Charles," the mother-teacher voice declares, "I have got to the end of my little book, which I wrote for your instruction. Let me tell you of some other very pretty books, which I wish you to read, and one is called *Familiar Tales,* in which are as many as twenty-nine stories, just suited for you." Progressing quickly into a hawking of titles ranging from Edgeworth's *Frank, Henry and Lucy,* and *Parent's Assistant,* to Child's *Flowers for Children,* the new Mamma voice goes on for pages to advertise other home teaching books.[18]

Jolting as it is to read such an interpolation today, this speech does signal that, by 1850, publishers expected American readers to view Barbauld's text as part of a network of narratives on domestic literacy management. Such a clear sense of genre could promote additional reading of other books from the network. Like the Web site amazon.com's "recommendations for you," this added commentary invited readers to purchase other narratives of the same type, narratives about and for home-based teaching. If the advertisement seems remarkably crass, it does effectively remind us of the close relationship between the growth of the domestic literacy narrative and the rise of the American literary marketplace.

Besides the American editions of *Lessons for Children* and direct imitations of them, Barbauld's influence on the domestic literacy narrative is also evident through her impact on early American practitioners of the genre. Writers like Hale, Child, and Sigourney used gender- and class-based strategies to affiliate with Barbauld as a role model for women's writing and learning. Anna Barbauld herself was a product of an educational environment closely associated with the dissenting academies' moral ideals and middle-class practicality. Her own teaching, as her literary heirs' would be later in America, was decisively shaped by belonging to a subgroup within the larger middle class—Protestant leaders eager to provide intellectual and moral guidance for the larger culture. The academies' interactive, inquiring pedagogy—designed originally when dissenters were excluded from the elite British universities—also offered Barbauld a strategy for challenging gender boundaries. She had, like her brother, been given the education required of a minister, teacher, or other male professional, but her sex precluded her direct entry into those positions. Nonetheless, she gained indirect access to public work on multiple fronts, and in all those ways she would inspire American women authors. First, through the philosophy and teaching practices she developed for *Lessons,* Barbauld constructed the meaningful feminine social role of maternal teaching. Second, in the act of writing her primer and other publications of its ilk, she defined an even more influential role—motherly teacher-author with a middle-class audience of learners. Third, through her eventual marriage to a minister, Barbauld allied herself with a partner willing to share teaching duties at the innovative boarding school they founded. Anticipating in a number of ways the kind of intellectual and professional partnership Harriet Beecher would later form with Calvin Stowe, Barbauld developed as a teacher and a writer through avenues generally closed to women, partly because of her family's strong links to the ministerial social class. At the same time, her access to print production was supported by her membership in that subclass, whose commitment to teaching the larger society encouraged its members' facilitation of learning in their own families—including females as well as males. Along those lines, and like Barbauld's, Stowe's efforts to enter the literary marketplace would be aided by brotherly and paternal support.[19]

Though hardly a familiar figure today, in the first decades of the nineteenth century, Barbauld was a hot commodity in the U.S. literary marketplace, as shown in comments by Lydia Maria Child. In *The Mother's Book* (1831), her popular antebellum advice manual for women's parenting, Child included a section on selecting appropriate reading materials for at-home teaching. At the top of the list "for children from four to five years of age" is the following entry: "MRS. BARBAULD'S LESSONS FOR CHILDREN. All unite in cordially approving this lady's writings. Good sense is clothed in very attractive simplicity, and the thoughts are continually directed to God as the giver of all we enjoy."[20] Along similar lines, Sarah Josepha Hale printed this 1832 description of Barbauld's impact on home teaching: "Mrs. Barbauld was the first English female writer who attracted the attention of parents; and the test of forty years has not at all impaired the interest she imparted to her *Lessons for Children*. The child of the present generation reads her stories with as much interest as his parents did, and that for the twentieth time."[21] Hale included Barbauld in the *Woman's Record* (1855), touting the English writer-teacher for her contributions to "the cause of rational education" and for "her 'Early Lessons,' which still stands unrivalled among children's books."[22] Hale had already set Barbauld within a group of just four women whom she profiled for an 1830 article in the *Ladies' Magazine* where she identified "the best" women, who deserved credit for "influencing . . . the improvement of the world."[23]

Hale was certainly not alone in viewing Barbauld as a mentor. Besides specifically recommending *Lessons* in her *Mother's Book*, Lydia Maria Child placed her own "The Mysterious Pilgrimage" next to Barbauld's well-known "Life" poem in the *Looking Toward Sunset* anthology, setting up an interplay between the two entries. In the introduction to their paired texts, Child identifies Barbauld as "an English writer of great merit, extensively known as the author of the excellent *Hymns* and *Early Lessons for Children*."[24] Similarly, when praising a didactic book on the seasons written by Mary Anne Hooker for Sunday school classes, Lydia Sigourney compares the collection to "Mrs. Barbauld's Hymns in Prose."[25] In pointing to Barbauld's ability to write about home education as public work, and in naming her as an inspiration, Barbauld's American descendants showed how she had created a path for them to follow, as well as genre-based tools for them to use.

As one intensely personal example of this affiliation process in action, we can cite a letter composed by Catharine Maria Sedgwick in 1825 for her sister-in-law, Elizabeth: "Yesterday evening Harry told me he had sent a copy of Redwood to Mrs. Barbauld, and that he had a letter for me from her. No happiness that did not spring from my own family circle ever produced an emotion of such pure delight and gratitude. I would send the letter to you, that you might see the lines traced by her own venerable hand, but I can not bear to part with it, or expose it to any unnecessary risk."[26] And the words from Barbauld that had been so precious to Catharine Maria Sedgwick? After praising the novel *Redwood*, Barbauld had noted, "You Americans tread upon our heels in every path of literature," yet she nonetheless declared, "We will not be jealous of you, for you are our children, and it is the natural wish of parents that children should outstrip their parents in every thing good and lovely." Urging Sedgwick to visit "should you ever come to England," Barbauld opined, "You ought to," "this being your mother-country," and hoped for the chance "to pay my respects to you."

Barbauld died before Sedgwick could meet her in person. Nonetheless, the English author would remain a model for American women writers throughout the nineteenth century. Meanwhile, that Barbauld's *Lessons* continued to circulate in America in a wide variety of forms is testimony not only to the appeal of her particular text but also to the staying power and flexibility of the genre she had launched.[27]

Marketing Republican Motherhood and Maternal Authorship

The American women writers who made the most extensive contributions to the domestic literacy narrative's antebellum definition process were Catharine Maria Sedgwick, Lydia Maria Child, and Lydia Sigourney. As Mary P. Ryan observes, these three authors "molded the first stage of domestic literature."[28] To re-view their writing within the context of this particular genre, however, will expand our understanding of their oeuvres. Nina Baym has complained that Sigourney is known (and caricatured) "primarily as a poet of mortuary verse."[29] Child's career as a political activist for the disenfranchised (publisher of *The Freedmen's Book,* author of "Appeals" for Indians and African Americans) has fascinated more researchers than her literature for white middle-class mothers.[30] And Sedgwick's *Hope Leslie* was reissued before texts like *Live and Let Live* and *Married or Single?,* so we have tended to see her more as a historical novelist than as a promoter of domestic teaching.[31]

Sedgwick, Sigourney, and Child were celebrated, during their own time, as creators of the very didactic writing our literary histories have undervalued. Magazine reviews, in particular, exalted them as literary educators. The proliferation of such reviews in the 1830s, in fact, suggests that by then the outlines of their teaching agenda were already clear to middle-class readers. A July 1830 *Ladies' Magazine* review of Sedgwick's *Clarence; or, a Tale of Our Own Time* offers a case in point. Explaining that this new book exemplified a welcome trend, the reviewer declares, "The merit of this species of writing, when combining its prerogative of amusement with . . . instruction, is pretty universally acknowledged."[32] Having contrasted this American brand of female educative writing with "the licentious overflowings of the English press," the reviewer joins "national pride" in "our own talented writers" with the unique ability of women like Sedgwick to achieve gendered, didactic authorship. The report further praises Sedgwick's "moral" and opines, "Most assuredly we need such lessons."[33] An 1834 review situated Sigourney's *Sketches* in the same author-reader-text network while signaling her ability to educate the nation by supporting women's domestic work as teachers.[34]

A parallel review of Lydia Maria Child's *Good Wives* (1833) offers another example of a literary figure's ongoing construction as a national educator of domestic teachers. A revisiting of Child's career up to that date situates it in a larger framework that imagined "the prevalent rage for reading" as potentially beneficial for the nation—but only if more books like her recent one were published to train women for the "important duties of a wife and a mother."[35] Although Child's popularity in Europe is duly noted, the essay emphasizes the Americanness of her authorship. Thus, while admitting that earlier volumes of Child's Ladies' Family Library series included interesting portrayals of such continental luminaries as Madame de Staël and Madame Roland, the reviewer insists that such figures "are not examples for the daughters of republican America" (237). In contrast, the review praises the new volume's treatments of women like Mrs. Howard, Mrs. Fletcher, and Mrs. Winthrop as better suited to American tastes (238). Then the review invokes a scene of domestic instruction, with maternal education of the son closely linked to the mother's reading texts like Child's. Via a blurring of "they" pronouns that merges the identities of family members (presumably reading together) with the books themselves, the reviewer asserts the national educative value of this writing and its mother-guided use:

> We regard the writings of such women as Mrs. Child, as among the most valuable works now issued from the press. They are valuable, not only for the additional richness they must impart to the female mind, and the greater degree of enjoyment they throw around the domestic fireside, — but they have an important bearing on the well-being of our country. Where are we to look for the future good and great of our land? and on whom is their moral character in a great degree dependent? They are now around the family hearth, and a mother's love and a mother's voice now imparts to them the principles which shall govern their future conduct. . . . We hope the Ladies' Family Library is but the commencement of works of this description, and that they may increase till their influence shall reach every female in our happy land. (238–39)

To tease out the trajectory of the American domestic literacy narrative in this idealized national scenario, we must set these trends in the literary marketplace within the context of another antebellum development—the evolving conceptions of republican motherhood. Historians like Nancy Cott, Linda Kerber, and Mary Beth Norton have outlined the traits of a postcolonial American middle-class role for women—using moral influence to prepare male citizens for their duties in the new republic.[36] The explanatory power of the republican motherhood model, however, has sometimes obscured the fact that this role was neither immediately created nor uniformly enacted from the moment of the military victory at Yorktown or the proceedings of the Constitutional Convention. Rather, as Cott reminds us, republican motherhood, like other cultural developments in the postcolonial era, evolved over time, aided by the circulation of rhetoric in the literary marketplace.[37]

Norton's ongoing work on American white women's identities has, moreover, stressed the need to historicize concepts such as republican motherhood. In political terms, for instance, the Revolutionary War encouraged Americans to begin "a public dialogue on the subject of women and their proper roles," so that women's responsibilities increasingly focused on "civic education." In economic terms, Norton notes how republican motherhood helped to reunite the "state and family," which had begun to diverge during the eighteenth century with the growth of industrial capitalism. The political belief system playing out through the Revolution foregrounded the relationship between a "successful republic" and "virtuous families," thereby promoting mothers as reproducers and nurturers of civic virtue.[38]

Norton and other scholars indicate that the civic-education activity of republican motherhood was, at least initially, limited to the home itself and concerned chiefly with sons (and/or fathers, brothers). Still, the domestic setting did not truly confine the project's reach.[39] As Nina Baym remarks, "The home would seem to be an obvious site for [a] kind of public sphere, since from the earliest years of the republic men and women progressives defined it as the place where citizens and citizenship were produced, and they expanded traditional maternal duties to encompass instruction of the young not only in basic literacy (which had been part of women's work since the seventeenth century) but also in the rudiments of patriotism, republican values, and an understanding of civic virtue."[40] Baym's investigation of individual authors such as Elizabeth Peabody and Emma Willard follows this line. Baym argues, for example, that despite the general perception of Sarah Hale as "firmly committed to keeping women out of politics" and as using "the concept of women's sphere to further this goal," Hale was actually "a profoundly political writer throughout her career."[41]

The famous ladies' magazine Hale directed over many years provides compelling evidence of the idea that women's activities at home, especially their domestic teaching, would have a profound influence on the nation. As early as 1830, a Ladies' Magazine essay was already insisting that a "family is society in miniature," so that "whatever destroys its primary features must disturb the tranquillity of its joys," ultimately affecting "the whole community of which it forms a part."[42] Indeed, women's failing to carry out nurturing responsibilities would be disastrous for the nation. Thus, another antebellum *Ladies' Magazine* piece, "The Influence of Manners," compares the decline of Roman matrons' dedication to their home teaching during the imperial era with the serious danger to America that would ensue if a woman failed in "the instruction of her children and the regulation of her family."[43]

Such depictions of republican motherhood suggest that we should set antebellum maternal duties within a larger context of American civic life. Along those lines, Michael Schudson argues that citizenship itself was changing from an eighteenth-century emphasis on the personal role of rural, property-holding gentlemen (enacting a "politics of assent") to the nineteenth-century exercise of civic duty as interpersonal action through a more urbanized system of affiliations (often involving groups such as political parties). For Schudson, this sea change between 1800 and 1865 represented a "battle between deference and democracy" (or, initially, Federalists and Jeffersonians) that was fought "in all spheres of life," including the family.[44] Within this framework of what Schudson sees as a "broad and deep transformation," the early nineteenth century saw a shift in middle-class women's domestic work to educating citizens. Meanwhile, as historians such as Carl F. Kaestle and Robert H. Wiebe suggest, many antebellum Americans grew anxious about democratization, as access to the ballot box became more widespread.[45] These concerns encouraged calls from commentators like Judith Sargent Murray and Benjamin Rush for the nation to place increasing trust in genteel women's enlightened teaching of young citizens.[46]

Literacy management allowed middle-class women to gain cultural agency as nation builders. As Bruce Burgett demonstrates in interpreting the famous letter exchanges between John and Abigail Adams, women readers and writers could exploit "the egalitarian promise of the literary public sphere" even as they remained constrained by "the inegalitarian practices of the political public sphere."[47] And crucial to this construction of literacy participation and management as female avenues to sociopolitical power was the reconfiguration of literature making into a national enterprise. In the 1820s and 1830s, literary production in the United States was still primarily driven by loose networks of local readers and publishing houses rather than by a national mass market. However, the trend toward a national literary marketplace was already evident, especially in the Northeast. Writers like Sedgwick and Sigourney often had multiple editions of their texts published by affiliated printers in different cities, such as Boston, Philadelphia, and New York. Books produced in New England were already defining themselves as "American literature," sometimes matching the popularity of English imports and, at the very least, dominating the nation's reading in ways that books from other regions could not.[48] In addition, although many periodicals (like James T. Hall's *Western Magazine*) were aimed at relatively small audiences, others (like the *Ladies' Magazine*) were aggressively seeking broader circulation. Women played a major part in this transformation of the middle-class readership from scattered local audiences to larger regional and national ones. And, of course, the creation of a national reading audience facilitated authorship of *American* domestic literacy narratives.

Middle-class women were imagined as a national reading audience long before they were fully accepted as professional writers, however. The colonial era's gendering of literacy had assumed that women needed training in reading, partly, of course, to be able to teach their sons. In contrast, women's disempowered legal status limited their practical reasons for needing to learn to write.[49] This division in literacy instruction was reflected in the ways that the few women who were published (like Anne Bradstreet) felt compelled to apologize for their intrusion into the male world of print.[50] As the nation moved from a rural toward an urban economy, though, and shared farm labor gave way to a division of work between business and home, middle-class women assumed primary responsibility for educating their children, especially before sons were old enough for the town school or tutor. In addition, when some families migrated west, as several members of the Beecher clan did, another benefit of women's writing became clear—the ability to maintain links between separated families and friends. But women's access to publishing venues remained relatively limited.[51] Gradually, however, the ideology of home as the middle-class woman's domain promoted the belief that print texts designed to help them with domestic duties should be produced by other women.[52] Women-authored books for teaching children sold well. Lydia Maria Child's *The Mother's Book* (1831) and Lydia Sigourney's *The Child's Book* (1844) are just two examples.

Long before they welcomed female excursions into other literary forms, male cultural arbiters touted women writers' unique ability—even their responsibility—to write for children (and, by implication, for mothers). An

anonymous 1828 *Ladies' Magazine* essay praises Susanna Rowson, one of
the early practitioners of the domestic literacy narrative, in such terms:
"By far the greater proportion, both in number and usefulness, of the publications intended for the young, are the productions of the softer sex. Their
situation peculiarly fits them for the task. . . . Their keener vision enables
them to discern those nicer shades which are beyond the observation of our
own sex. . . . Their influence therefore upon the early mind as writers, is
second only to their agency as mothers, in pointing out the commendable
qualities of the heart, in teaching the tendency of natural bias, and in
warning the young of the dangers by which they are surrounded, from the
operations of feeling and passion."[53] The argument advanced here helped
women writers claim a special niche in the literary marketplace as domestic educators. Their very natures gave them unique access to "the earliest
development of character." Yet this celebration of women authors subordi-
nated their literary endeavors to "their agency as mothers." That is, motherhood was the identity that qualified these women for writing, in addition
to providing their subject and goals. By constituting their work as regula-
tory, the reviewer set up conservative boundaries around women's writing.
Within this empowering (if also constraining) model, then, individual authors like Sigourney, Child, and Sedgwick deployed a literary genre supporting mothers' astute management of domestic literacy and, hence, of
national civic values.[54] The central activity represented in these texts, accordingly, was a home-based literacy exchange between mother and child
that allowed the middle-class woman indirect yet significant access to social
influence.

Mother-Guided "Literacy Events"

A synthesis of Pierre Bourdieu's and John Guillory's views on cultural production, along with Shirley Brice Heath's conceptions of social literacy, can
serve as a framework for interpreting maternally managed instruction in
the domestic literacy narrative. Guillory's *Cultural Capital* draws on Bourdieu's ideas to propose that literary canon formation is grounded "in the
constitution and distribution of cultural capital, or more specifically, a
problem of access to the means of literary production and consumption."
Guillory views the "'means' in question [as] provided by the school, which
regulates and thus distributes cultural capital *unequally*," and he suggests
that the school's role in "the *reproduction* of the social order" is centered in
its work to "[regulate] access to literary production by regulating access to
literacy, to the practice of reading and writing." For Guillory, the "literary

syllabus is the institutional form by means of which knowledge is disseminated," and he argues that it "constitutes capital in two senses," linguistic
and symbolic. Guillory defines "*linguistic* capital" as "the means by which
one attains to a socially credentialed and therefore valued speech, otherwise known as 'Standard English,'" and he defines "*symbolic* capital" as "a
kind of knowledge-capital whose possession can be displayed upon request
and which thereby entitles its possessor to the cultural and material rewards of the well-educated person."[55]

Antebellum domestic literacy narratives operated within a home-based
literary-institutional milieu similar to the one outlined by Guillory, in that
the genre itself could be used (like the syllabus in Guillory's formulation) to
distribute capital to children in middle-class homes where the texts were
being read, discussed, and internalized. Through their work to manage linguistic and symbolic capital, the mothers in these narratives (and the real-
life mothers reading them with children) regulated home literacy and thus
the reproduction of the social order. However, middle-class mothers' guidance of literature use, as envisioned in this genre, was also different from
Guillory's concept of the school's control over cultural capital in the twentieth century. For one thing, the literature-assisted distribution of capital in
antebellum domestic literacy narratives was overtly tied to ideas about literary taste in that era and about women's unique ability to provide a moral
vision through which they could dispense an affect-inflected ethical capital.
In addition, the domestic literacy narrative and accompanying ideology for
mothers' reproductive roles were highly influenced by this instruction's taking place at home or in domesticated versions of other social spaces (such
as Sunday school).[56]

To understand the domestic literacy narrative's use in nineteenth-
century homes, a historicized application of Bourdieu's theories on art and
"taste" is a helpful complement to Guillory's concept of the syllabus as a
distributor of cultural capital. According to Derek Robbins, Bourdieu's
analysis of how educational institutions reinforce social class distinctions is
consistent with his study of how "museums and visitors to museums col-
luded in creating a myth of natural 'taste' which concealed the reality
which was that all taste had been socially acquired in the past and had
been handed down within the family context." Bourdieu, Robbins suggests,
recognized the discrepancy between such myths as objective standards for
aesthetic appreciation and the reality of these views being socially constructed in the family setting. Likewise, Robbins points to Bourdieu's analysis as unmasking related myths—such as "the mystique of 'talent' or 'innate

ability'"—which educational systems should be striving to undo. Instead, in failing to provide mechanisms for all students to learn what is "presented as 'natural'" (but is really a class-based construction), schools have reinforced class divisions and hierarchies.[57]

Writing from a nation with a highly centralized education system, Bourdieu has understandably stressed the close, mutually reinforcing relations between "the academic institution" and "the institution which holds a monopoly over legitimate *symbolic* violence, namely, the State."[58] However, to interpret the complex interactions among nation building, middle-class self-definitions, and systems for cultural reproduction in nineteenth-century America, where schooling was (and, to a great extent, still is) decentralized rather than nationalized, greater attention needs to be paid to the institution of the family and, specifically, to the role of mothers in educational work. Along those lines, recovering a sense of how middle-class social reading practices shaped the domestic literacy narrative's use is especially important. Historicizing nineteenth-century literature consumption, we can reconstruct the antebellum domestic literacy event, a writing-reading-conversation exchange that was then at the heart of both real-life maternal literacy management in middle-class New England homes and the narratives depicting such activities. In addition, we should note how domestic literacy narratives tended to depict such literacy events as recurring literacy practices, which gained social power in large part through their regular repetition.

The work of Shirley Brice Heath is useful in this recovery project. In her ethnographic study of several Piedmont South Carolina communities, Heath depicts literacy in action in various social class and racial groups. She describes a "literacy event" as an occasion when "talk revolves around a piece of writing."[59] Heath found that various subcommunities clustered around the Southern mill region used their reading and writing differently, in line with distinctive cultural practices and values. For example, in one group, individuals rarely read a bound book; instead, a literacy event typically encompassed lively, informal discussion of a piece of writing, like a letter from a friend, to construct meaning collaboratively. Heath shows how repeated enactment of such literacy events rendered these occasions into regular literacy practices, defined by an informal set of rules that would, in turn, reinforce social class identification.

While authors of antebellum domestic literacy narratives did not, of course, use such theoretical terminology, they did depict social scenes of reading and writing like those Heath observed in the twentieth-century

South. That is, they demonstrated ways in which home-based literacy events could become recurring literacy practices, managed by motherly domestic teachers to shape middle-class and, by extension, national values. So the authors creating printed tableaux of family literacy shared with their audiences a view of how community-building literacy happened, once genre-linked views of home reading coalesced.

A conversation between a maternal "Aunt Lottie" and her niece in Sedgwick's *The Poor Rich Man* (1836) limns just such a scene. When "little Ruth" declares that her family's recently having acquired a house reminds her of the "story about Aladdin's lamp," her aunt suggests that a better comparison would be to "those words in the Bible, 'The liberal man deviseth liberal things; and the good that he purposeth, that he doeth quickly.'" By attributing the family's rise in fortune to a reward for good deeds rather than a stroke of good luck, Aunt Lottie underscores the domestic literacy narrative's links to Christian moral values. Ruth then observes that her aunt is "always" able to "remember something in the Bible that seems to suit," and Lottie explains that this is so because she studies the Bible so often. By the end of this exchange, Ruth, Lottie—and Sedgwick—have alerted readers to the power of literacy events that are associated with regularized literacy practices. Lottie's "love" of the Bible, her continual oral sharing of knowledge about it, and the potential for reshaping lived experience through related literacy exchanges are cast as central to middle-class domestic literacy practices.[60]

Overall, among writers and readers of these texts, guided conversation (or what today's sociolinguists would term "oral literacy") was at least as valuable an avenue to learning as solitary, silent study of print text could be.[61] Indeed, the narratives frequently portray transcriptlike dialogues—what Sedgwick called "records" of conversations—between mothers and their children. In texts like her *Facts and Fancies* (1848) and *Stories for Young Persons* (1841), mother and child are shown *as* social readers discussing writing together.[62] These conversations teach the child correct language patterns (Guillory's linguistic capital), convey information about "real" middle-class life experience (symbolic capital), and provide guidance on ways of discriminating between right and wrong (what I would call moral or ethical capital).

The recurring internal elements in the genre's depictions of social literacy, in fact, highlight ways in which linguistic, symbolic, and moral capital are distributed through maternal management. To be more specific, modeling effective language use (linguistic capital), the mother also manages reproduction of symbolic capital as she directs the child's understanding of social scenes depicted in the print texts—information that will eventually provide access to class-appropriate employment and sociopolitical influence. At the same time, because a mother is controlling this conversational pedagogy and because her own major area of influence is ethics, the literature-centered literacy she purveys also distributes moral capital.

To inculcate broad moral concepts, authors of domestic literacy narratives employed rhetorical patterns closely associated with nineteenth-century ideas about feminine ways of thinking and learning. Women's minds were assumed "naturally" to privilege these ways of understanding the world and interacting with others: narrative (versus exposition), concrete examples (versus abstract ideas), and sensibility (versus explicit argument). Meanwhile, as Deborah Fitts points out, children (including young males) were viewed as hovering in an underdeveloped cognitive state and having only an imperfect sense of the mature, rational thought of adult men. In that context, since females were supposed to be inherently more emotional beings, they were increasingly being depicted as more skillful at feeling-based teaching of the young than men could be.[63] Therefore, some republican leaders argued, women (not men) should teach children and, through moral suasion and its gendered rhetorical tools, direct America's youth to their future roles—if girls, motherhood; if boys, extended schooling and the marketplace.

Lessons Without Books (1830), by Catharine Maria Sedgwick's sister-in-law Elizabeth, provides a case in point. As daughter Emily reads aloud to her brother, their mother presides over the domestic learning.[64] Emphasizing that a child's moral growth is dependent upon a mother's fostering language development, the scene also demonstrates how individual *literacy events* implicitly can argue for making such occasions regular, maternally managed *literacy practices* in the home.[65]

> Emily often read aloud to her mother, and Frank . . . would listen and try to understand what she read. Some passages from the life of Lord Nelson were one day selected for her, and among others, that in which his father says that in whatever situation Horatio might be placed, he would always get to the top of the tree. "Do you know what that means, Emily?" said [her mother].
>
> "Is it not figurative language, such as we were talking about the other day, mother?"
>
> "Yes, dear, but what does it mean?"
>
> "I don't think I can tell," said Emily.
>
> "Well I guess that I know," said Frank; "it means that no boy will ever beat him in climbing."

"You have come pretty near the meaning," said Mrs. Cleaveland, "though without understanding it. —Nelson's father intended to express . . . that whatever might be the occupation or profession of his son, he would be first in it. . . . Do you understand me, Frank?"

"O yes, mother; but I hope the tree that I have to climb, won't be as slippery as that pole in father's gymnasium."[66]

Simultaneously managing both Emily's reading to Frank and her children's interpretation of that oral text, Mrs. Cleaveland distributes linguistic, symbolic, and moral capital. While she models the idea that figurative language is not literally representative, this astute maternal literacy manager uses the event of shared reading to direct Frank's attention to a future time when he will take up an "occupation or profession"—an essential element in the ongoing reproduction of the middle class. Furthermore, by following up her explanation with a query to her son ("Do you understand me, Frank?"), she signals that part of his adult social role will be, as Guillory suggests, to display and circulate symbolic-knowledge capital.

Also embedded in Mrs. Cleaveland's explication of the figurative analogy is a more overtly moral lesson—that to be "first" is a goal worth striving for, one closely associated with positive role models. When Frank crafts a comparison between climbing to the top of the tree and reaching the top of "that pole in father's gymnasium," Sedgwick's own readers—especially mothers presumably teaching this text in their homes—could note ways to move their children, via shared literacy, to control of language, class-based knowledge, and ethics. Linguistically, Frank could construct his own example patterned on the diction and structure of the original text. Symbolically, he could translate the literary analogy to a scene from his own life. Morally, though Frank may still not fully understand the implications of his mother's story, his joke about "that pole in father's gymnasium" does suggest that he realizes being "first" may necessitate tackling "slippery" (i.e., complex) challenges in a man's world.[67]

Mrs. Cleaveland later encourages both children to tell some of their own favorite stories about Lord Nelson, and she comments that "this relating of anecdotes is a very useful exercise for you, as it accustoms you to the use of language and also to acquiring clear ideas of what you read; for unless they are first clear and distinct in your own conception, you cannot communicate them" (83). This emphasis on employing literacy for instruction that promotes interpretation ("conception") and redistribution of cultural capital elements ("communicate them") is one hallmark of domestic literacy narratives. The mother's careful use of language to shape her chil-

dren's literacy connects her home teaching—and therefore such authors' literary work—to forerunner domestic didactic texts like Anna Barbauld's
primers (where sequenced conversations taught words, behaviors, and values). And the social literacy practices at work in such scenes also link the
domestic literacy narrative to related social practices like Margaret Fuller's
conversaziones, family parlor reading, and the participatory text making of
literary clubs (e.g., at women's academies) that would flourish throughout
the nineteenth century.[68]

Integrating Multiple Literacy Practices

For mothers, narratives like Elizabeth Sedgwick's modeled not only what
but how to teach children by managing literacy. Undergirding these texts
was a belief that interrelated literacy practices could reinforce one another,
so that adept maternal management of print consumption involved integrating multiple modes of textual processing—that is, discussion and writing as well as reading. As Sigourney explained in her "Reading and Thinking" chapter of *Letters to Mothers,* simply providing one's child with books
was not enough: "'I have left my boy at his books,' says the parent, with a
self-complacent smile. Now, though it is far better to read than to do mischief, we cannot always be certain that reading is a defence [*sic*] from every
danger. A boy, if idle, may choose a book as a refuge from incumbent industry; or, if ill-disposed, may select an improper one; . . . let no mother feel
perfectly at ease about her children, simply because they read, unless she
knows the character of the books that engage their attention, and what use
is made of the knowledge they impart."[69]

How were mothers to ensure that both "the character of . . . books" and
their children's "use" of those texts were sound? Again and again, domestic
literacy narratives and their related literary forms (such as expository essays on child rearing) urged mother-teachers to integrate a range of reading, writing, and conversation activities. For instance, Child argued in *The
Mother's Book* that the "habit of having the different members of a family
take turns to read aloud, while the others [were] at work" could be "extremely beneficial" and enhanced by having "young people . . . give a
familiar account, in writing, of what they have read."[70] Similarly, Sigourney
recommended that mothers manage the daily literacy activities of their
children. Most importantly, she said, reading should be done *with* the
mother, who would constantly be "questioning [her children] respecting
[their book's] contents, and adding such illustrations, as the subject, or
their peculiar state of intellect and feeling, may render appropriate."

Sigourney further advised that these carefully guided literacy events should always be reinforced with the nightly practice of "recapitulati[ng] . . . the lessons of the day."[71]

Literacy, as espoused by these domestic teaching narratives, was not an array of decontextualized decoding skills but rather an integrated cluster of collaborative activities whose outcomes could be noted in both individual and social terms.[72] Meanwhile, literature's place in this network of familial literacy practices was primarily educative, with the middle-class mother acting as a domestic teacher attaining extended social influence. For instance, Sedgwick's "Ella" in *Stories for Young Persons* demonstrates the transportable influence of integrated literacy practices through a young girl's literacy-guided experiences away from home. Daughter of a poor yet refined physician with too many children, Ella agrees to spend a year with a relative of her mother's in New York. Before leaving home, Ella shows her mother all the little family treasures that she intends to take along. The most significant, they both agree, is the Book they had read so often together. "I am glad to see your little Bible among your treasures," Ella's mother observes. But she inquires about the "little paper marks in it." "Those I put in to mark the places where you have marked the verses with your pencil, so that I may turn to them at a minute's warning," Ella declares.[73] And indeed, when later "stung" by an unkind insult from her cousins, Ella retires to read by herself but not alone: "Wiping away her tears, she took her little Bible from its hiding-place in her basket, and opened it at one of her mother's marks. Her eyes fell on these words: 'In whatsoever state you are, learn therewith to be content.' 'The very words for me,' thought she; and she kissed them, and kissed the delicate trace of her mother's pencil beside them" (100–101). Ella's strength here derives from a maternally directed literacy that she reactivates by rereading and retracing the writing in her book. These interactions highlight the appeal the ideology of domestic literacy management had for women of an earlier century, with far more constricted social opportunities for females (even privileged ones) than in our own time. For Sedgwick's first readers, the image of Ella reinscribing her mother's gentle pencil markings asserted a means for middle-class women to extend their influence over children, and thus over society, beyond the domestic sphere.

Interestingly, this reading scenario is both similar to and different from that described by Michael Warner in *Letters of the Republic*. Warner argues that in late eighteenth-century America, "the traditional culture of print" changed, so that one could "imagine oneself, in the act of reading, becoming part of an arena of the national people that [could not] be realized except through such mediated imaginings." For Warner, this process involving "the textuality of print" and "the character of political culture" was "reciprocal," with the medium of print and republicanism interacting to alter "the identity of each."[74] While the (women) readers of domestic literacy narratives engaged in a similar class-forming imaginative process through their engagement with print, texts like Sedgwick's account of young Ella and her mother as collaboratively literate added an affective element to the class-constituting process Warner describes. In domestic literacy narratives, such learning was also guided by mothers' empathetic moral sense and often included the kind of bodily awareness represented in Ella's tracings on the page. So feminized readers were feeling as well as thinking themselves into a national class with enhanced social power.

This national class of middle-class teachers constituted itself, in theory at least, around appropriately *gendered* literacy practices, rather than around economic rank. Monetary wealth, in fact, was generally portrayed as a less significant factor in shaping "good" motherhood than properly literate behaviors. For instance, in *Letters to Young Ladies* (1837), Sigourney included the biography of a model republican mother whose home literacy management was complicated by a reversal of family fortunes and a migration from New England to the West.[75] Although this portrait acknowledges the mother's difficulty in leaving behind her beloved "mansion, . . . schoolhouse," and "white spire among the elms" for the "savage landscape" of her new habitation "of rough logs," Sigourney depicts this maternal paragon as domesticating the wilderness through transportation of integrated literacy practices to her new "dreary forest" home (224–26). From singing hymns to a sick child to sharing the "few books that she possessed," this representative American mother "instructed" her children in the evenings, after her long days of other work, "diligently pour[ing] into their minds, the knowledge which she had treasured up in her own" (225). Transferring values through literacy, her fireside teaching Americanized the West.

Educating and Honoring the Mother-Teacher

The intellectual rigor associated with motherly direction of family literature study was a recurring theme in domestic literacy narratives.[76] Such portrayals helped justify middle-class women's reliance on the physical labor of others and on the acquisition of domestic tools (such as improved kitchen technologies).[77] Equally important, depictions of domestic literacy management as intellectual work supported ongoing calls for improved women's education, since mothers could hardly be effective teachers unless they had been taught well themselves.[78]

Lydia Sigourney was a particularly enthusiastic purveyor of this justification, especially in such advice pieces as *Letters to Mothers* and *Letters to Young Ladies*. Her chapter entitled "On Female Education" in the latter text, in fact, offers a comprehensive argument for improving the training of mothers. She declares that, in America, the "intelligence and virtue of . . . every citizen have a heightened relative value," since the country's "safety may be interwoven with the destiny of those, whose birthplace is in obscurity" (12). Acknowledging here some middle-class anxiety over democracy's openness, Sigourney then urges that "teachers under such a form of government" are crucial to protecting the "heart of the nation." And no teacher, she insists, plays a more important part than the motherly home-based one: "Of what unspeakable importance then, is *her* education, who gives lessons before any other instruct[o]r—who pre-occupies the unwritten page of being—who produces impressions which only death can obliterate— and mingles with the cradle-dream what shall be read in Eternity. Well may statesmen and philosophers debate how *she* may be best educated, who is to educate all mankind" (13).

Such expository arguments favoring improved female education were so closely intertwined with the teaching agendas of domestic literacy narratives themselves that we can hardly understand the persistence of one literary form without examining the other. These two genres frequently appeared together, actually, in periodicals for middle-class parlor reading. A familiar example of this kind of hybrid publication was, of course, Sarah Hale's magazine, which drew from an array of genres in its ongoing campaign for improved female education. Along with stories lauding women's home-situated teaching, Hale published speeches by men and women supporting female education. She praised model curricula from women's institutions (like Emma Willard's Troy Female Seminary), published reviews of books on education, printed readers' correspondence favoring female education, and wrote her own pro-education editorials.[79]

Hale and other proponents of women's learning drew on English writers' arguments (such as Mary Wollstonecraft's *A Vindication of the Rights of Woman*) but stressed America's special need for enhanced female education. Whereas English supporters of female learning tended to tout women's equal mental capability, U.S. proponents emphasized the political needs of republican culture.[80] This accelerating campaign extended colonial New England's calls for women's learning for religious purposes, such as demands that mothers (and dame schoolteachers) be able to read to provide children with access to the Bible. Still, postcolonial pleas for improved female instruction advocated a Protestant religious foundation for both women's own education and their guidance of home learning. In that vein, an 1833 *Ladies' Magazine* essay, "Miss Fiske's School for Young Ladies," explains that the school was molding women for "our Republic" by stressing "Christian virtues."[81]

Meanwhile, like the concept of republican motherhood itself, the agenda for female education developed incrementally, with improvements in access and quality more uneven and local in practice than the "national" rhetoric writers like Hale used would suggest. The West and South lagged behind the Northeast—worth noting, given the tendency of New England writers to generalize their own experiences.[82] That said, retracing the three basic stages of antebellum arguments for female education can point to related shifts in the characterization of the teaching mother in domestic literacy narratives. While the arguments of any one period certainly recurred in later phases, different concerns tended to mark each phase.

In the first period (running into the early nineteenth century), apologists concentrated on establishing the right and need for women to be educated. This involved, in the first place, arguing that a mother's responsibility for molding the character of future citizens required that she be adequately taught. So Dr. Benjamin Rush urged, "Let the ladies of a country be educated properly and they will not only make and administer its laws [indirectly, of course], but form its manners and character."[83] However, these early proponents also stressed that the needle of housewifery could be quite compatible with the pen of female learning.

Susanna Rowson's collection of student exhibition dialogues, *A Present for Young Ladies* (1811), ably exemplifies this theme.[84] For its time, the curriculum at Rowson's academy was innovative, but her packaging of this text demonstrates the former actress's keen awareness that she was marketing female education to a potentially reluctant audience of paternal tuition payers. Although she included some of her own writing on education (such as "Sketches of Female Biography"), Rowson astutely had her students act as her primary advertisers in this volume just as they did at the annual academy exhibitions. She reprinted performances from the early 1800s, when various star students "debated" such topics as how to balance book-based learning with domestic duties. A typical dialogue depicts a conversation among three girls who consider what novels might be instructive rather than merely amusing. Singling out a cluster of English women writers (Fanny Burney, Maria Edgeworth, and Hannah More), Lucy, Caroline, and Ellen intertwine commentary on their own reading processes with affirmations of good literature's didactic capabilities. Acknowledging the blurred lines between home and academy by affirming the teacher-parent collaboration necessary for successful female education, this dialogue (certainly edited if not written by Rowson) underscores the continued maternal management of young ladies' literacy—even in the school setting. Along those lines, one speaker asserts that, if made aware of texts such as "Calebs in search of a wife," even her "severe" aunt would approve those "where nature speaks out, / And religion is honoured." And another agrees that such a novel "would be allowed by my mother" as "a lesson for me" (40).

The second stage of the female education campaign, around the 1820s through the mid-1830s, marked the shift from good wife to good mother as the primary role for middle-class women. Proponents moved from affirming the right of young girls to attend common schools and then seminaries, to debating what female education programs should include.[85] By January 1828, the first issue of the *Ladies' Magazine* could look backward and forward with some confidence about the place of female education in the United States.[86] "Had any one," Sarah Hale observed, "calculated on the improvements . . . in female education" made in the republic up to that time, he "would have been thought an extravagant visionary" (21). With the right to an education well established, Hale could focus on ways in which girls' learning could be improved. Her 1830s reprinting of one of Emma Willard's essays reiterated the lady editor's position as a supporter of female education only insofar as it would not "make ladies dissatisfied with their circle of domestic duties," but she joined Willard in arguing that, to be good mothers (versus mere husband catchers), women needed a solid education *beyond* the common school.[87]

Third-stage antebellum advocates continued to insist that home-based teaching of children was the primary role for middle-class women—a duty that necessitated their being thoroughly instructed.[88] However, from the mid-1830s through the 1850s, an increasing push for expanding the curriculum of women's education to include what had been male-only subjects emerged. Courses were justified based on their ability to enhance women's teaching in the domestic sphere. For instance, the need for mother-teachers to have strong characters themselves so as to cultivate a similar rigor in children might be cited as a reason for studying philosophy. Consistent with that view, by 1834 Mary Lyon and Zilpah Grant had added the following texts to their curriculum: William Sullivan's *Political Class Book,* Joseph Abercrombie's *Inquiries Concerning the Intellectual Powers,* William Paley's *Natural Theology,* and Joseph Butler's *Analogy of Natural and Revealed Religion.*[89] Meanwhile, signs of a hierarchy of need and ability became far more explicit than in the early republican discourse on women's learning. For example, an 1834 essay by "S. F. W." asks that a few females with unusual abilities receive advanced schooling, so as to "devote themselves to the education of their sex." This advocate declares, "a Willard, a Beecher, a Child, and a Sigourney, have done much to raise the standard of female attainments; but we want many others who shall tread in their footsteps, and *improve* upon their example."[90]

As claims for women's responsibilities for home teaching became more assertive, questions about competition between mothers' domestic instruction and schools needed to be resolved. One way that domestic literacy narratives approached this potentially thorny issue was in showing mothers' influence as complementing school learning. For instance, in Sigourney's narrative poem "Mother and Child," a young boy's school lesson directly affirms the important position his mother still held in his education. "Fretful and disobedient" before heading "away to school" for the day, he is unable to enjoy his walk, because "the spirit of naughtiness / Lay heavy at his heart."[91] Fortunately, when he "entered the school-room," his teacher "read a lesson" about the importance of mothers as educators: "Who smiled on your little plays, / And taught your little tongue its first words?" (9). As his classmates chant the answer, "It was our mother," the naughty child feels worse and worse (10–11), so as soon as he returns home, he eagerly seeks out his own mother:

> He kneeled down by her side,
> —He hid his face in her lap, and said,
> "I was naughty to you, and did not repent.
> I went to school and was unhappy.
> Mother, forgive me,—." (11)

Just after the printed poem in *The Pictorial Reader* edition (1844) comes an illustration of maternal guidance effectively restored by way of collaborative literacy, as the mother holds a book and reads it to her child by their fireside.

In images as well as words, domestic literacy narratives repeatedly proposed that school and home teaching could be mutually supportive because maternal guidance of literacy could bind the two educational sites together.

The presentation of this theme in one section from Anna Barbauld's *Lessons* became so popular that it led to numerous "toy" book editions excerpting only this episode, when little Charles leaves home for school, considers skipping, but reaffirms a commitment to go when he encounters numerous reminders of his mother's teaching as he walks along the path. An 1830s Lilly and Wait packaging of this popular episode used full-color illustrations for each page, with one especially striking image being the one where Charles prepares to step outside the yard of his home, while Mamma stands at the threshold, extending her arm to point the way. Positioning the teaching mother as neither inside nor outside the domestic space, yet in any case able to direct action beyond it, illustrations like this one helped reiterate a concept central to the domestic literacy genre—the public reach of home-based teaching. (See figure 4.)

A related rhetorical move downplayed the influence of school while insisting on the staying power of domesticated literacy—even for sons who moved away from home to study. In Elizabeth Sedgwick's *Lessons Without Books,* for example, Mrs. Cleaveland's older son, Henry, brings maternal teaching into the larger sociopolitical arena. Writing back and forth with his mother and his sister, Henry continues to use conversational techniques learned at home.[92] Henry asserts that the writing still being exchanged with his home-based feminine teachers is like "a parcel of 'talk,' folded up in paper." Then he offers an example of the extended reach of domestic instruction by describing his efforts to share a letter from his sister about the sad death of an African American servant with "one of the Southern boys," in hopes of "chang[ing] his opinion about the blacks being an inferior race" (266). By making Henry, his mother, and his sister all teachers attempting to reform "one of the Southern boys," Mrs. Sedgwick underscores the genre's vision of national governance as shared by both sexes through maternal literacy management that well-trained sons carried into the extradomestic arena. Also, in taking on, however tentatively, the volatile issue of slavery, Mrs. Sedgwick links this otherwise uncontroversial text with the more radical abolitionist versions of the domestic literacy narrative, a subgenre that would be further developed at midcentury by Stowe's *Uncle Tom's Cabin.*

Antebellum domestic literacy narratives that argued for the superiority of home-based teaching over schools tended to couch their pleas in rhetoric discounting the challenges associated with home instruction. Declares Sigourney at the opening of a *Letters to Mothers* chapter entitled "Domestic Education": "I am not without hope of persuading mothers to take charge

of the entire education of their children, during the earlier years of life"
(105). She then refutes each of the reasons mothers might give for assigning children's education to others (e.g., the press of housework, inadequate
learning by the mother). Sigourney urges that, if a mother is determined to
place her young children in school, she should "at least teach them herself
to read, ere she sends them there" (106). Sigourney's vagueness about the
precise age when youngsters might safely attend school may be seen as
leaving an opening for the middle-class mother to transfer educative duties,
at some point, to an extradomestic setting. But multiple anecdotes about
advanced content (including "Geography, and . . . the Natural Sciences"
[109]) being taught in the home indicate that the author's preference was
for American children's domestic education to extend well beyond basic
reading instruction.

Indeed, Sigourney's "The Only Son" overtly asserts the superiority of
domestic education, especially over boarding establishments. An ideal child
initially, Frank "went cheerfully to school" near his home every day, then
"came regularly home," where he always exhibited "good conduct."[93] But a
rich, "unmarried uncle, who was very fond of him" and intended to make
Frank his heir, avers, "I think you had better send Frank from home" to
continue his schooling (89). Frank's parents resist at first, although the uncle urges that boarding school could overcome Frank's excessively "childish" devotion to his mother. This insensitive uncle fears that "boys brought
up by women, are good for nothing"—that if Frank is not "sent from home,"
he will "never be a man" (90). In vain, Frank's mother protests that her
gentle, feminine teaching keeps him from "bad company" since "he studies
his lessons by our fireside, in the evening" (90). Juxtaposing the uncle's
denigration of maternal domestic education with a more "manly" alternative, the story eventually subverts this hierarchy, as Frank's experiences at
boarding school lead him through "vice" and dissipation to an early death.[94]

The Mother-Child Literacy Bond and Public Life

Although domestic literacy narratives continually stressed the mother's
role as home teacher, the typical plotline for the genre focused on the recipients of maternal pedagogy more than on the mother figure herself. (Anna
Barbauld, of course, had set this pattern by focusing on "little Charles" in
her *Lessons*.) One effect of foregrounding the young (often male) learner
was to downplay the authority the maternal teacher exercised—to stress
nurturance rather than political power as her goal.[95] Another was to emphasize the benefits to society of having middle-class women carry out this

THE morning was pleasant,
   And bright shone the sun:
Said Mamma, "My dear Charles,
   To school you must run;
How loud sing the birds,
   And how sweet smells the air,
Haste, love, to the school,
   You ought now to be there."
Then she tied on his hat,
   And told Charles to be good;
And watched her dear boy
   Till he got to the wood.

Fig. 4. From *Little Charles. Embellished with Coloured Engravings* (1833–34).
Courtesy, American Antiquarian Society

cultural work. This rhetorical stance also positioned readers as learners—a strategy that contributed to many of these stories being interpolated into Sunday and common school readers. At any rate, already evident in texts such as the dialogues Susanna Rowson's students performed and the pseudostudent letters Hannah Foster included in *The Boarding School*, this technique of highlighting the learner became a favorite of later writers such as Child, Sedgwick, and Sigourney.

Sedgwick's "The Bantem" opens with just such a scenario: "There was once a very little boy whose name was Willie. Willie's mother read the Bible to him before he could read himself, and when he did not understand she explained it to him. She talked to Willie about Jesus Christ, and Willie knew He came from God to teach men, and women, and little children, and that the oldest and the youngest ought to obey what He commanded. One of the first of Jesus's rules which Willie learned was, that *you should do to others what you would have others do to you.* When Willie first learned this golden rule from the Bible, he thought it would be very easy to obey it, but he soon found it was not so *very* easy."[96] The story then depicts Willie's learning, from the painful experience of losing a pet, that charity is easier to imagine than to carry out. Despite Willie's positioning as protagonist, his interpretation of his experience, like the story's stated moral, is directed by his mother, who poses apt questions through the lens of their reading and discussion. Such literacy-oriented ties between mother and child tapped into deep affections, with collaborative reading of literature at the core of their intense relationship. This was just one way that such texts interacted with the sentimental mode and with religious didactic literature. In that vein, Sigourney's "Hon. Stephen Van Rensselaer" recounts the worthy exploits of a colonial patrician turned enthusiastic republican but lauds the role his mother played in "the formation of his character," relating her influence to the "ardent" bond generated between mother and child through literacy.[97]

One recurring sentimental plot suggested that mothers could continue teaching from beyond the grave via children's memories of shared literacy.[98] A related storyline showed widows' literary pedagogy overcoming the loss of a father, even in spite of financial setbacks. For instance, in "The Widow Ellis and Her Son Willie," Sedgwick depicts a series of ethically challenging incidents whose meaning Willie interprets through Bible-based conversations with his mother.[99] She reminds him on one difficult occasion to "remember those texts you wrote off into the first leaf of your Bible-book" (19). So powerful, in fact, is this literacy-shaped moral sense that Willie is able to reform the "crusty" temper of his former nemesis, Captain Stout, thereby shaping the larger society beyond home.

In narratives like Sedgwick's, middle-class women's home-based teaching was continually being reinscribed as their primary role. Characterizing literacy-centered labor as carried out for the national welfare built a rhetorical foundation for women's eventual extensions of their teaching into public arenas.[100] In the meantime, they could already claim indirect access to politics through well-taught sons like Sedgwick's Willie. Just so, in the "Privileges of the Mother" chapter of her *Letters to Mothers,* Sigourney urges readers to recognize that motherhood gives them "an increase of power" by way of an "influence which is most truly valuable, . . . that of mind over mind." Declaring that "this dominion, over the unformed character of your infant" is "entire and perfect," Sigourney contrasts such influence with less achievable control over friends and servants, then explicitly yokes motherhood to educating children: "Wise men have said, and the world begins to believe, that it is the province of woman to teach. You then, as a mother, are advanced to the head of that profession. I congratulate you. You hold that license which authorizes you to teach always."[101]

The most popular antebellum figure of maternal instruction extending from the home into the new republic was the mother of George Washington.[102] In Sigourney's typical entry in *The Boy's Book,* a series of "interesting anecdotes of the early years of Washington" stresses his mother's influence, with conversations between Mrs. Washington and her son depicted as molding his character.[103] Certainly these celebrations of domestic education for the good of the country were also self-serving for their authors, who were themselves seeking to create a national class of regular readers for their work. So it is tempting to dismiss their constructions of the nation building resulting from literacy-oriented home teaching as "mere" rhetoric. However, the occasional male-written narrative participating in this ongoing process—constituting mother as literacy-managing teacher while constituting these stories as a genre—shows that, for some members of the middle class, this ideal represented actual experience.

One such validating text was Albert Bushnell's *My Mother,* which boasted the extra authorizing apparatus of poems and a preface by Sigourney.[104] Chapter 4, "Her Maternal Character and Influence," clearly represents a version of the antebellum domestic literacy narrative woven into a larger biographical text. Bushnell (a respected missionary to Africa) draws upon the by then familiar language of the genre to characterize his mother as his literacy-guiding teacher and, therefore, his character builder. Having reviewed his mother's youth and marriage, Bushnell moves on "to contemplate her in the most interesting and responsible station in life. A Christian mother" (75). Noting that this "sacred relation" carried "the most weighty responsibilities," Bushnell intones, "Perhaps no earthly influence is greater; and certainly no period in life is so favorable for exerting that influence, as the plastic state of childhood." Underscoring the power she exercised by praying with her children and discussing Bible stories or missionary newspapers with them, Bushnell places maternal literacy management at the center of the learning that led him to mission work (75, 83–87, 95).

Bushnell confirms the central tenet of the domestic literacy narrative: a middle-class woman's impact on the republic through her well-trained son. However, in his insistent linkage of her role with a Protestant religious agenda, Bushnell also accents an aspect of this ideology that was often more muted. In that context, today we must ask: to what extent was the nineteenth-century domestic literacy management ideal assuming a Protestant ethos as *the* Americanizing one? Repeated references to the Bible as the primary literature for literacy development helped situate women's domestic teaching in a tradition affirming believers' ability to access the Word directly.[105] Such patterns aligned this feminized teaching with a potentially empowering version of spiritual life for women that, to some extent at least, complicated the alliance between the male ministerial class and middle-class women, as articulated by Ann Douglas in *The Feminization of American Culture.*[106] (Ministers themselves, in fact, appear rarely in domestic literacy narratives, and when they do, they take on more of an advisory or collegial role than a leadership position.)[107] At the same time, however, the Protestant underpinnings of New England antebellum domestic literacy management that are so clear in Bushnell's narrative could disempower as well. For one thing, this emphasis made it very difficult for some "Others" (such as Irish Catholic immigrants or "pagan" Native Americans) to gain access to the social role of domestic literacy management. For another, binding literacy acquisition so tightly to religious training promoted the genre's view of successful learners as necessarily Christianized, as in the case of *Uncle Tom's Cabin,* at the potential expense of more secular versions of citizenship. Purportedly benign, literary educational programs that operated through a persistently Christian maternal focus could actually be used to justify control over potentially disruptive agents of resistance against white American middle-class values. With such trends in mind, and while examining social class and race relations, I will now explore the part that nineteenth-century women's domesticated teaching played in constituting one set of values—white, middle-class and Protestant—as *the* American way, and I will review how some members of "Other" groups responded to that social construction process by affirming, adapting, or resisting that vision of national republican life.

[3]

Cross-Class Teaching and Domesticated Instruction

*There was nothing in which she more delighted than to do good to chil-
dren. She assisted in the education of those, whose parents were in restricted circumstances, and distributed useful books to those who were
unable to purchase them.*

Lydia Sigourney, "Mrs. Jerusha Lathrop"

When antebellum American mothers defined their primary duty as literacy-
centered domestic education, they acquired social power that reached beyond the home and into the purportedly "separate" public sphere, especially
through their well-educated children. Lydia Maria Child affirmed her belief
in the national importance of this work by dedicating *The Mother's Book* "to
American Mothers, on whose intelligence and discretion the safety and
prosperity of our Republic So Much Depend."[1] Inclusive-sounding categories
like Child's undifferentiated bow to "American Mothers" ignored the reality
that class-based differences in daily domestic life (along with factors such as
race and ethnicity) actually limited the accessibility of this role. A cluster of
"benevolent" literacy management stories directly engaged such class distinctions among antebellum American mothers, however.

Writers like Sarah Josepha Hale, Lydia Sigourney, and Catharine Maria

74

Sedgwick justified their own class-connected privileges by defining "ladies" from their social group as having beneficent teaching responsibilities beyond their own homes. These writers used literary constructions of women and children from other, less privileged classes to distribute but also to monitor limited versions of domesticated literacy among lower-class Americans, thereby reinforcing middle-class women's position as educators for the nation. A related extension of the domestic literacy narrative's ideology claimed the role of schoolteacher for American women. The genre's arguments favoring women teachers over men were closely intertwined with several ongoing agendas among middle-class social leaders. These goals included defining an educative role for single middle-class women, exalting gender-based ways of teaching, and expanding the curriculum for female education.

"Enlightened and Benevolent"
Teachers of "Inferiors in Position"

Discursive interactions among members of today's middle, working, working-poor, and unemployed classes often reflect anxieties about the literacy-related construction of national identity. We see this pattern, on the one hand, in continuing discourse about "America's underachieving schools" and, on the other, in critical memoirs of working-class learners like Mike Rose, Richard Rodriguez, and Victor Villanueva.[2] But analogous narratives on women's cross-class literacy management from previous eras have not yet claimed a prominent place in historical studies of literacy or in the recovery efforts of scholars reforming the literary canon.[3] One reason for this omission may be the lack of attention paid to the role of white middle-class motherhood in national education during the nineteenth century. A related reason may be that the Americanizing mission originally addressed in this subgenre was long ago transferred to public schools (officially) and popular media (unofficially). Another problem may be that the classism and racism now evident in such texts make us uncomfortable today.[4] Such attitudes would not have appalled most members of their original reading audience, unfortunately. That audience—typically women involved in motherly, benevolent teaching themselves—would have found the subgenre's representations of the typical recipient of charity to be quite consistent with their ideas about class in nineteenth-century America.[5]

Recent attempts to synthesize a view of class as economic status with the interpretive frameworks provided by class stratification theory have emphasized the need to situate individuals and groups being analyzed within a social structure specific to their time and place.[6] With that in mind, I would argue that the privileged women publishing antebellum domestic literacy narratives about teaching those they termed their "inferiors in position" had to negotiate seemingly incompatible agendas—an impulse toward democratizing literacy and an equally powerful one toward reinforcing class status through constraint of some literacy practices.[7] Steven Mintz stresses that pre-1840s use of the term *class* in the United States involved plural middle classes, as well-educated nineteenth-century Americans had a highly conscious sense of differences among various middle-class groups. For his own study of several prominent Anglo-American families, Mintz concentrates on a small subset of the middle class that was dedicated "to ideals of public and communal service"; that shared a sense of "genteel status . . . on the basis of education and place in the local hierarchy of status and privilege"; and that demonstrated "acute concern with order, stability, and community."[8] Authors of benevolent domestic literacy narratives clearly belonged to, or at least aspired to join, the particular class Mintz describes. Accordingly, they simultaneously affirmed the social responsibilities of genteel public leaders and worried over threats to their group's influential position in society.[9] They were well aware of the power they could wield as a class (even more than as individuals) and therefore equally intent on distributing social practices related to their group-defined values throughout the population, while safeguarding their unique position as managers of those very values. As a community-conscious class, they were dedicated to literacy-centered benevolence for the good of the local and national community but also for their own group. They described themselves—in stories, essays, novels, speeches, pamphlets, and events they sponsored—as "enlightened and benevolent."[10]

This discourse community conceived of class in terms of social action more than economic well-being; or, in today's theoretical terms, through a Bourdieu/Weber lens more than a Marxist one. With market capitalism's volatility constantly making and unmaking familial wealth patterns, measuring social rank solely in monetary terms would have meant that women and children faced total loss of status if their husbands or fathers lost income due to personal injury or business fluctuations.[11] Instead, numerous American women authors proposed that a brand of middle-class status based on educated virtue could be maintained, even in the face of such adversity. Fiction reflecting this stance includes Susan Warner's *The Wide, Wide World* (1851). In Warner's novel, the genteel mother uses domestic literacy management to communicate to her young daughter, Ellen, that reading and writing can safeguard social worth despite the family's trying circumstances. A crucial element in this proposition involves Ellen's maternally managed acquisition of a Bible and writing instruments, along with directions for using them, just before the young heroine is sent away from her ill mother.[12]

At the same time, these would-be cultural arbiters hardly wanted to equate rise in income with rise in status. Frequent attacks on "women of fashion" in antebellum women's literature show that, for all the emphasis on accumulating wealth associated with nineteenth-century capitalism, these "enlightened and benevolent" guardians of American values strove, through literature, to link social status to educated behaviors and educational enterprises more than to wealth.[13] Women whose male family members worked in the ministry, teaching, or law, in particular, had a strong self-interest in promoting such a view over an economic hierarchy that could have positioned them below the more affluent wives of captains of industry. Thus, literary texts often included railings against the hedonism of those rich women who concentrated on consumerism rather than childrearing and charity.

Still, the fashionable class of women was perceived as far less dangerous to the well-educated middle-class mother-teacher than were the "inferiors in position" with whom she came in contact regularly as they worked in her home and with whom her children would have to interact after moving beyond her sensitive hearthside surveillance. So a primary target of middle-class women's efforts to safeguard America was the troublesome mass of native laborers and new immigrants, under- and unemployed citizens, their potentially disruptive children, and of course their wives. From the point of view of a member of the "enlightened and benevolent" class, managing the mores of these "inferiors in position" became more important than improving the lower classes' economic standing. A key to that process was controlling the degree and nature of their literacy. So anxieties about interclass relations—especially concerns about the negative impact that undereducated voters and the females who influenced them could have upon the republic—promoted adaptations of the domestic literacy narrative to expand motherly literacy management beyond the home for the good of the nation.

The 1830s and 1840s marked the defining period for the subgenre. Earlier in the nineteenth century, short stories for children had already constructed its basic premise: a motherly teacher-reformer does good works for the needy. Variations on its themes can be traced through scenes in hybrid texts published later, such as Charlotte Forten's writing about teaching in the 1860s Sea Islands and Jane Addams's *Twenty Years at Hull-House* accounts of her turn-of-the-century settlement program.[14] However, the subgenre's first full articulations can be located in the decades just before the Civil War. Then, as Mintz and others note, members of the privileged classes were struggling to reconcile the ideals of Jacksonian democracy with their commitment to republicanism. Two closely related plots associated with this goal developed in the 1830s: a storyline exalting the benevolent maternal teacher who extended her work beyond home and one concentrating on the programs of educative reform that she carried out. Lydia Sigourney's "Mrs. Jerusha Lathrop" and an article entitled "Infant Schools" in Sarah Hale's magazine exemplify these two basic types.

Lydia Sigourney's biography "Mrs. Jerusha Lathrop" in *The Girl's Reading Book* aptly conveys major goals of these class-oriented narratives: to affirm the literacy-directing benevolent work of privileged mothers and to encourage the formation of future middle-class maternal teachers in the same pattern. By profiling a New England woman from the 1700s, the daughter of one of Connecticut's colonial governors, Sigourney distances her model from the contemporary scene, with its fluid class positions and anxiety over some citizens' lack of self-control. Foregrounding domestic literacy as the heart of female education, Sigourney depicts Mrs. Lathrop as well prepared to support her husband's research and, more importantly, to educate their three sons.

The trajectory of Mrs. Lathrop's biography up to its halfway point positions her life story as a model for domestic teaching mothers, who devoted their main instructional energies to their own families. The second half of the narrative, however, turns to interclass relations. When all three of Mrs. Lathrop's sons died quite young from tragic illnesses, she sought solace from "the burden of her griefs" through educative service to "children of sorrow and poverty." Widowhood later prompted her to expand these instructional efforts still further: she "seemed to love the poor as if they were unfortunate members of her own family." As she "assisted in the education of those, whose parents were in restricted circumstances," Mrs. Lathrop "distributed useful books," collaborated with local common school teachers to finance scholarships for worthy poor children, and held her own domestic school "on Saturday afternoons, with the children of the neighborhood." Her curriculum included science and religion, as well as stories teaching sensitivity and generosity. Mrs. Lathrop herself benefited from this "venerated" life of "imparting happiness" to others through teaching the poor. This work "served to keep her mind unimpaired, and her feelings vivid" until she died serenely in 1805, almost ninety years old, but a role model for new-century Americans.[15]

The leather bindings, wide margins, and costly illustrations of *The Girl's Book* editions I have seen indicate that biographies like this one were read not so much by the needy whom Mrs. Lathrop served as by the middle-class women Sigourney hoped to form into print-made heirs of her New England heroine. These latter readers, after all, stood to gain the most from class-confirming reproduction of such icons. Meanwhile, the working-class and poor characters in these texts served primarily as props, illustrating the benevolence of their motherly teachers.

Like the role-model stories "Mrs. Jerusha Lathrop" exemplifies, reports on charity projects depended upon drawing cross-class distinctions. This strategy often entailed attacking the dangers of unregulated lower-class literacies, while affirming the adoption of middle-class literacy practices by "inferior" characters whose lives were transformed through that process. For example, the 1832 *Ladies' Magazine* article "Infant Schools" praises the generous middle-class women who were supporting four Boston schools for poor children. Portraying the work of the schools' "managers" as enlightened benevolence, this story terms infant schools one of the "bright spots on the earth," linking "sympathy with suffering."[16] To encourage readers' donations for the schools, the story describes the activities of the "few ladies" in charge as "fostering care over hundreds of poor children who would otherwise be left to roam the streets" (179). Avoiding direct criticism of the children and their own mothers while still associating their situation with threats needing to be faced, the *Ladies' Magazine* observes: "Such must necessarily be the condition of the children of the very poor even though they be worthy and industrious."[17] The article avers that infant schools make poor children "better, wise, happier," through instruction directed by the charitable ladies. The story closes by exalting the positive impact of such maternal literacy management on American society: "When all the children of the poor are educated in the Infant and Sabbath Schools[,] we may confidently expect that the vices of poverty . . . will be overcome. The dangers also which threaten society from the discontents and envyings of the poor would be averted as the continued and generous attention of the rich would inspire a respect for and a confidence in those whom Providence had favored with the means of doing good. . . . The general diffusion of knowledge, especially moral and religious sentiments among our poor, is one principal reason why we are more peaceful and happy than the nations of the old world" (182).

Texts like "Mrs. Jerusha Lathrop" and "Infant Schools" seem to present their aims in straightforward terms. However, we can recognize the rhetorical ingenuity of these narratives when we relate their publication to the core ideology of benevolent middle-class motherhood. In terms of the material conditions of publication, for instance, the subgenre tapped quite effectively into a growing network of periodicals and didactic handbooks seeking to build a regular readership among middle-class mother-teachers. In terms of social values, the narratives sought readers' conscious affiliation with civic duty. Through these stories, after all, managing "inferiors'" literacy became a self-affirming component of middle-class motherhood, comparable to Dana D. Nelson's configuration of male middle-class "civic management."[18] (The use of the term *managers* in "Infant Schools" is striking in this regard.) Thus, middle-class women's domestic management was extended to spaces (public life) and objects (others' children, institutions) that had not been clearly mandated within early visions of republican motherhood. With this agenda in mind, we can see that two major elements were inextricably connected in all benevolent literacy narratives—a national class of worthy middle-class mothers (both as audience and as major characters) and needy but salvageable recipients of their charitable instruction.

Creating Benevolent Mothers for the Nation

When Mrs. A. G. Whittelsey announced publication of the *Mother's Magazine* in 1833 from Utica, New York, this energetic editor identified her audience as the "ladies and gentlemen of the first respectability and talents."[19] Addressing the maternal readers they hoped to cultivate, the magazine's packagers presented a list of sixteen projected topics in this inaugural issue—subjects that would "bear upon a [white, middle-class] mother's office" and "the varieties of responsibility" she faced.[20] These "topics" imagined a national class of maternal reader-teachers—women who would purchase the *Mother's Magazine* and carry out its mandates.

For one thing, to invoke a shared ethos, the list sets a number of religion-based goals for the publication, including discussing "duties of Christian parents"; offering "biographical sketches of Christian females, and of pious children"; addressing the need for "Christian females" to avoid association with drinkers; and exploring ways mothers can have "every thing connected with the child, from its earliest infancy, tend to the formation of a high Christian character" (4–5). Significantly, the very nature of the audience's anticipated "Christian" educational work is emphasized through another variable—social status. Along those lines, the list constructs a maternal reading class for the magazine through identification of those the idealized Christian mother would teach. Predictably, one group is her children. But additional recipients of her maternal expertise help define this class of mother by what she is not—"female help" or "poor" (5).

By announcing that the *Mother's Magazine* would provide suggestions for "improvements in domestic economy," with a special focus "on the subject of female help," the topics inventory situates readers as members of a class whose home labor is more social, intellectual, and moral than physical. The periodical's audience, in other words, needs to know how to supervise housework more than how to do it. This topic implicitly links the motherly class being discursively constructed here with depictions of threats to her power that would appear in an array of popular-culture texts throughout the nineteenth century, ranging from Harriet Beecher Stowe's satirical depictions of homemakers struggling to direct their servants, to advertising cards' pictures of the complicated relations between middle-class women and their domestic workers.[21] Such an acknowledgment of the need to *manage* "female help" distances the "ladies" of the magazine's audience from their domestic workers but also joins those same groups through the anticipated supervision process.[22] Furthermore, the allusion to this supervisory need acknowledges a major threat to a lady-mother's ability to manage home and community benevolence effectively, since domestics could undermine that process either by failing to do their physical labor well (thereby misdirecting the mother's energy to corrective activity) or by corrupting the primary objects of maternal teaching (her middle-class children).

Moreover, as the *Mother's Magazine* indicates, while this persistent threat to maternal pedagogy existed inside the home in the form of "female help," another challenge that lay physically outside the domestic space might be even more dangerous. Since the central duty of the enlightened middle-class mother was to teach her children their (Christian) duties for the American republic, there was little to be gained from this literacy-centered home education program if the society that her children entered was debased by uneducated individuals. In this case, as in her interactions with domestic servants, the lady reader of the *Mother's Magazine* had a tenuous position to define for herself and for the potential extradomestic recipient of her benevolent guidance. If she attempted a complete takeover of the education of all children suffering through hard times, she might undermine another worthy mother's responsibility—a right central to her own gendered identity. However, if she left poor wives and children entirely unsupported, she ran grave risks for the character of the republic. Therefore, she needed to limit her efforts to take over maternal teaching duties to those who clearly could not do the work themselves, while in the meantime providing collateral support to those who might be attempting to climb the slippery slope between working poor and middle class.[23] Thus, the *Mother's Magazine* delineates degrees of poverty and need while suggesting varying appropriate responses from that superior class of mothers assigned the task of guiding education for the public good.[24] In that vein, while the periodical sets as one of its aims to "encourage efforts to ameliorate the condition of *poor* children, and to bring them under the direct influence of moral and religious cultivation," a qualification adds: "We mean the wretched poor" (5).

The partially veiled anxieties about class relations in this inventory from the *Mother's Magazine* reflect themes that Michael Argyle suggests recur across time and place in discourses about interclass relations. Arguing that social psychology can provide useful analytical tools for the study of class, Argyle points out that interpreting the language-based "attitudes and stereotypes" one class constructs around another can be particularly revealing.[25] Accordingly, he proposes that some of the analytical categories being used by social psychologists studying class could be productive for understanding literature's involvement in class formation and maintenance. To interpret benevolent domestic literacy narratives within their cultural milieu, two of Argyle's formulations seem especially salient—"social distance" and "social mobility." Argyle defines "social mobility" in positive terms as the degree to which individuals can move up in class rank. He argues that relationships and experiences such as in families and educational settings have historically played a notable part in determining social mobility (36). In contrast, Argyle casts "social distance" in negative terms, as "the perceived gap between classes, in terms of inequality of various kinds, the amount of deference or respect, or the unlikeliness of making friends or marrying between classes" (38). Argyle sees social distance as closely related to "power distance," which can be measured in several ways (including interactions between employer and employed) and which recognizes the need of one group to exercise authority over another.

Especially when coupled with historically situated considerations of class relations, both these concepts elucidate the specific ethos that promoted antebellum narratives depicting middle-class maternal management of lower-class literacy. If social mobility is an essential concept for a democracy, where any man supposedly can rise to be an officeholder, social distance may be equally essential for those members of a republic's elite, concerned about guarding some special rights of leadership for themselves (or, in the words of the *Mother's Magazine*, for the "ladies and gentlemen of the first respectability and talents"). Indeed, in the first half of the nineteenth century, when middle-class Americans were clearly struggling to balance those two not-synonymous governance models—democracy and republican-ism—cultural arbiters would have found both class-oriented concepts emi-nently usable. For instance, Argyle's "social mobility" formulation helps us understand the *Mother's Magazine*'s faith that "the condition of poor chil-dren" could be "ameliorate[d]" with "the direct influence of moral and reli-gious cultivation"—that such "wretched" children could be expected to rise in class through effective education and that American society would bene-fit from such a process. At the same time, however, we can read the maga-zine's move to hold "intemperate husbands" and their suffering wives at arm's length as signaling a need for social distance.[26] Calibrating the seem-ingly opposite yet equally necessary impulses of social mobility and social distance, in other words, remained one of the foremost aims of benevolent literacy narratives.

Lower-class female literacies, in fact, presented a growing challenge to (white) middle-class women's national dominance of domesticated reading and writing. Awareness of class distinctions among women during this an-tebellum period was constantly being heightened by differences in groups' literacy practices. For instance, growing Northeastern industrialization en-couraged distinctive versions of literacy associated with sites like the Low-ell mills, where female readers and writers explored topics and used pub-lishing venues sometimes different from middle-class-approved models.[27] Meanwhile, burgeoning immigration, especially by young Irish women, brought new inhabitants whose oral and written literacies resisted middle-class mothers' "American" ideals on religious as well as economic grounds.

Bruce C. Daniels's overview of Jacksonian-era class relations provides a specific historical context for using Argyle's conceptions of social mobility, distance, and power to interpret antebellum middle-class women's writing about lower-class females' potentially threatening (il)literacy. Daniels points out that, by the first half of the nineteenth century, a "cleavage between an ideology of increasing democracy" (similar to Argyle's "social mobility") and "a reality of increasing class distinctions" (similar to Argyle's "social distance") "reflect[ed] the ambiguity inherent in the definitions of equality and democracy." Noting that "the Jacksonian era solidified the American commitment to equality and democracy," so that "it was no longer politi-cally feasible to question either concept in public," Daniels nonetheless em-

phasizes that a "tension emerged . . . between those who interpreted equality and democracy to mean equal opportunity in the marketplace and political arena and those who interpreted the words to mean that some degree
of equality of condition ought to prevail in both politics and economics."
And he argues that the conflict between these two different visions of
equality continued to be played out through the "tension between mass society and elite rule."[28]

The authors of benevolent domestic literacy narratives—though initially
quite literally a small group of genteel, white, Christian New England
women—could define themselves and their readers as a *national* group of
mothers teaching for the republic in large part because of their shared vision of middle-class identity. This collaboratively constituted identity was,
in turn, reinforced through the literacy practices they carried out in their
homes and promoted in their publications, such as the *Mother's Magazine.*
By creating a subgenre that portrayed these educative literacy practices as
adoptable by lower-class women, these same writers could confirm their belief in a democratic vision of social mobility. This move strengthened their
claim that the literacy-based maternal teaching they had forged as their social role was truly exercised for the national welfare—what Daniels calls the
"mass society." At the same time, however, by designating a literacy-based
distance between themselves and the members of lower classes whom they
taught, these writers also reaffirmed the need, in Daniels's terms, for "elite
rule." Depicting management of others' literacy, in other words, became a
means for negotiating between the otherwise irreconcilable views of American sociopolitical life—equality of "opportunity" and rightful differences in
"condition" and responsibility.

Needy Objects of Maternal Teaching:
The Example of the Irish

Portrayals of Irish female domestic workers in narratives by writers such
as Lydia Sigourney, Catharine Maria Sedgwick, and Harriet Beecher Stowe
reflect the anxiety over social class—and its links to racial attitudes—that
these writers tried to contain rhetorically.[29] Michael Argyle's mandate to
examine linguistic constructions of one class by another is worth invoking
in this context. Characterizing the Irish domestic as illiterate, a middle-
class writer (and her reader) could enforce social distance, thus keeping
middle-class management of community literacy as a class-specific duty,
even while delegating the physical tasks of housework to hirelings. With
that aim in mind, the Irish domestic's purported stupidity about following

directions, along with the brogue marking her ineffectual attempts at standard English, were targets of satire closely linked to her assumed lack of appropriate maternal literacy training. (That the Catholic Irish did not read the Protestant Bible but relied instead on Popish priests' interpretations of the Word was one aspect of this stereotyping.) The badly educated Irish domestics' threat to Protestant middle-class children's literacy, and thus to their character formation, was often cited in women's literature, even though, as Hasia R. Diner reports, personal written "reminiscences of upper-middle-class life in nineteenth-century America" frequently include sentimental, "warm and tender" "memories of Irish servants" that would seem to belie such fears.[30]

In *Letters to Mothers,* an anecdote on the perils of exposing one's (Protestant) middle-class children to the unmanaged literacy of an Irish domestic exemplifies this social distancing. In one of her most heavily gender- and class-coded passages, Sigourney warns:

> I am confident that mothers are not sufficiently careful, with regard to the conversation of domestics, or other uneducated persons, who, in their absence, may undertake to amuse their children. "If the little girl cries, while I am gone," said a mother to an Irish domestic, recently hired, "tell her a story, and she will be quiet." Ah! and what kind of story? You will not be there to hear it. But the tender intellect . . . may imbibe foolish, or vulgar, or frightful images, and take their colouring, like soft wool, sinking in Tyrian purple. "Tell her a story!" Why that is the very aliment which her opening mind seizes with the greatest eagerness. And you are ignorant whether that aliment may not be mingled with corruption.[31]

Early on, the term "conversation" signals to readers that they are in the proactive maternal domain of domestic education exercised through shared literacy practices. But this enlightened teaching space has been severely compromised by the presence of an "uneducated" intruder. Sigourney's brief cautionary narrative stereotypes this American mother as well as the Irish servant, suggesting that the former is well on her way to that infamous category of irresponsibility, the "woman of fashion." But the traits assigned to the servant are even more threatening. The "Irish domestic," just "recently hired," is underprepared for middle-class home responsibilities, mainly because her literacy has not been properly shaped by American middle-class maternal guidance. Rather than knowing how to tell, dialogically, the right kind of stories—like those character-building exercises in narratives such as *The Child's Book*—Erin's uneducated domestic worker can invoke only "foolish, or vulgar, or frightful images" for her innocent charges. (The subtextual association of these images with Romish religious imagery would have been clear to Sigourney's contemporaries, I suspect.) In contrast, the American mother, provided she drew upon her own superior literacy training, could tell the kind of tale her child's "tender intellect" needed to hear. Though critiquing the recalcitrant mother's failure to teach her child up to now, Sigourney imagines her possible remediation—but not a change in status or ability for her Irish servant.

Catharine Maria Sedgwick's similar manual for middle-class females echoes Sigourney's depiction of the Irish domestic as representative of unregulated literacy and its perils for the republic. In *Means and Ends,* Sedgwick uses the negative example of an uneducated Irish girl to urge her readers to learn from their books so as to shape their own moral characters: "Think, my dear young friends, of the difference that is made in the character of a human being, simply by reading. Compare an Irish girl who comes to this country at fifteen or sixteen, who has never been taught to read, with one of your own countrywomen in the humblest condition, of the same age, who *loves to read,* and who has the books within her reach!"[32] Significantly, Sedgwick need not elaborate on this comparison; she stereotypes the "Irish girl" as illiterate and therefore of poor character, unlike a native-born American woman who, even if "in the humblest condition," would be able to read; inclined to love the many "books within her reach"; and, as a result, a true "human being."

By hinting that, in ways beneficial to the middle-class home, even illiterate Irish female domestic workers could become appropriately educated, some of these texts coupled social mobility with literacy acquisition yet still assigned continued control over that literacy to middle-class mothers. Hence, these writers constructed the enlightened teaching of middle-class motherhood as combining enablement with enforcement. (That is, they promoted some social mobility within the working-class ranks while maintaining social distance and set power relations across class lines). The real-life difficulty of negotiating this double-edged class-interaction model was easier to downplay in short anecdotes within extended advice essays, however, than in free-standing narratives, such as Sedgwick's "The Irish Girl," in her 1844 *Tales and Sketches.*

Although this story eschews the stereotyping evident in so many other portrayals of young Irish women during the antebellum era, the narrative's refusal to endow the appealing heroine, Margaret, with an "American" middle-class social role indicates just how persistent impulses of social distancing could be, even when a text was gesturing toward democratic inclusiveness. Margaret, whose brother James had been working on a nearby railroad-building project, is the young nurse-companion for Mrs. Ray, a kindly matron whose credentials as a middle-class domestic literacy manager are clearly established early in the story. (Mrs. Ray, like other New England benevolent mother figures in this subgenre, is cast as a national ideal of motherhood by virtue of both her regional and her native-born American status.) By opening with the motherly voice of Mrs. Ray urging her young protégée to "sit down, Margaret, child, and rest you—here by my bedside," Sedgwick undoes the typical employer-employee hierarchy of most texts depicting Irish girls in antebellum America.[33] This scene situates the dialogue within a tradition of mother-child conversational learning exchanges going back to Anna Laetitia Barbauld's *Lessons* and its early New England heirs. Having offered a series of stereotype-resisting compliments to Margaret's homemaking (a "teakettle . . . as clean as a china cup," "tidy ways," and a marked ability to participate in refined talk with Mrs. Ray), Sedgwick makes a more explicit connection between this tale and the familiar middle-class domestic literacy narrative.[34] She stresses Margaret's sweet praise of her beloved mentor as a "mother-like" teacher (192). Intertwining details about Margaret's cleanliness and good manners with Mrs. Ray's expressions of motherly affection, Sedgwick adeptly echoes other antebellum texts depicting mother-led character formation in children through oral literacy grounded in shared feeling. Then Sedgwick even hints at the possibility of social mobility for Margaret when Mrs. Ray tells of bragging about her to the richest woman in town: "Says I to Sister Maxwell, 'Margaret . . . can read handsomely—there's few can read like her'; says I, 'I wish the minister could read so'; says I, 'her reading sinks right down into the heart'" (192).

For a nineteenth-century middle-class reader schooled in the social codes of the domestic literacy narrative, this seemingly transparent description would have carried striking signals. For one thing, Irish domestics—especially recent immigrants—were regularly portrayed as illiterate, so to depict Margaret as able to read at all is noteworthy. Second, that Margaret's reading "sinks right down into the heart," better even than the local minister's, would have resonated as a decisive marker of social status. Interestingly, Sedgwick characterizes Margaret's astoundingly ladylike literacy as derived from lessons provided by a noblewoman back in Great Britain, thus positioning *this* Irish girl within what Daniels describes as a prior lineage of merit.

Sedgwick seems to be preparing her readers to affirm Margaret's wish to marry one of the local New England natives and to become a fully vested

American middle-class mother. Had the tale ended here, we might commend Sedgwick's resistance to Irish stereotyping and her affirmation of social mobility. Instead, however, the remainder of the story reinforces social distance. Though she thought she'd been wooed by the most eligible Anglo-Saxon village bachelor, the son of a wealthy landowner, Margaret discovers that young William Maxwell will never marry her. Rather, he gives in to his parents' wishes that he wed the American-born Protestant Belinda Anne, whom Mrs. Ray had earlier identified as no more "neat" and "pretty" than Margaret (200). As if settling the matter of cross-class (and cross-ethnic) marriage beyond a doubt, and thereby affirming Argyle's views on social distance, Sedgwick has Margaret drown herself, since the Irish girl is unable to achieve the position in American society to which she had (wrongly?) aspired.[35]

A telling displacement for antebellum readers would have been in the narrative's moving away from the exploration of Margaret's domesticated (and, literally, home-bound) middle-class literacy to her desperate wanderings over the countryside in search of young Maxwell, since the refusal of lower-class women to stay safely indoors with their middle-class literacy managers was a frequent theme in other popular-culture texts. This setting-related breakdown in generic structure shifts "The Irish Girl" from a relatively new subgenre to a more familiar and less optimistic one—the story of a naive maiden's seduction and downfall.[36] A partial restoration of both social class mobility and generic form occurs at the story's close, however. Margaret's brother James grows so incensed at old Mr. Maxwell's callous reaction to his sister's death (*"It's only a Paddy girl!"* [212]) that he is ready to commit murder. At that point, Sedgwick finally tips her hand as to the true heroine of the tale—Mrs. Ray. Persuading James to forego his wish for revenge and instead to choose a life of true American virtue, Mrs. Ray becomes even more efficaciously "mother-like" to him than she had been for the doomed Margaret (214). Collaborating with James's employer, Mrs. Ray dissuades the young male immigrant from committing the crime and sets him on a righteous path instead: "an end of cruelty and hate" and an acceptance that can "bind" the hearts of immigrants and native-born "together" for the good of the nation (214, 198–99). Here, in this fantasy consigning the immigrant woman to a watery grave but her brother to enlightened citizenship, the male figure turns out to be less threatening to class security than his sister. Whereas she had sought marriage with a New England man—a step that would have guaranteed social mobility, especially when she began to raise their children—her brother accepts benevolent literacy guidance without asking for any advancement. Separating limited political enfranchisement from full-fledged social participation, Sedgwick solves the "problem" of the Irish by turning a representative Irish man into a boy seeking motherly literacy management and by erasing his female counterpart from the national landscape.

Tracing Interclass Dependence and Resistance

In her novel-length benevolent literacy narratives *Live and Let Live* (1837) and *The Boy of Mount Rhigi* (1848), Catharine Maria Sedgwick crafted more optimistic plotlines than she did for Margaret in "The Irish Girl." Both Lucy Lee (*Live and Let Live*) and Clapham Dunn (*The Boy of Mount Rhigi*) successfully achieve middle-class status, in large part because they accept motherly mentoring based in enlightened literacy training. Affirming working-class uplift through Lucy's climb from "domestic service" to a home of her own in the West, and Clapham's escape from an abusive cycle of rural poverty to a proper New England home, Sedgwick clearly designed these texts with working-class uplift in mind. Highly popular in their own day, these books conveyed Sedgwick's strong conviction that middle-class women's cross-class teaching could benefit the nation. With appealing portraits of characters like Lucy and Clapham, Sedgwick invited women of her own privileged social group to support cross-class teaching, and she implicitly promised working-class readers material advancement if they would accept such literacy-based moral guidance. Despite their hopeful plot trajectories, however, these accounts certainly invite critique today. After all, however sincere their charitable agendas, these antebellum narratives retain a strong sense of noblesse oblige, ceding continuing social power to the managing class's maternal figures without questioning the limits of their lessons.[37]

Where were the counternarratives, written from the more critical perspective of working-class learners themselves and comparable to the assertive voices of Mike Rose, Victor Villanueva, and Richard Rodriguez in the late twentieth century?[38] For American women, in particular, the suppression of nineteenth-century working-class voices is hardly surprising, given the double bind of class and gender restricting their access to print publication.[39] On through the nineteenth century and into the twentieth, representation of working-class women's experiences with benevolent literacy remained in the hands of their middle-class "betters."

We can note some examples of empathetic cross-class identification, at least, in midcentury and post–Civil War writers like Louisa May Alcott and

Sara Parton. Indeed, in Elizabeth Stuart Phelps's *The Silent Partner* (1871) we find a forceful reconfiguration of benevolent literacy narratives in scenes of the middle-class reformer Perley Kelso opening her parlor to literacy events shared with local factory women like Sip Garth—collaborative readings, discussions of faulty press coverage of the mills, and celebrations of fine art.[40] Although "society" women like Miss Van Doozle condemn Perley's efforts to study and worship with the mill girls as "a fanatical benevolence" reeking more of "sheer morbidness" than true "Christianity" (237), Perley herself grows from the kind of naive purveyor of so-called charitable literacy evident in many narratives earlier in the nineteenth century to a community leader. She becomes so invested in her work that she firmly rejects opportunities for marriage and dedicates herself instead to a career of public teaching and social reform. Devoting as much energy to educating young women of her own social rank—like the sweet but uninformed "Fly"— as to uplift of abused workers like Sip, Perley eventually learns to appreciate the power of alternative, working-class literacies. Though she continues to sponsor domestic teaching events for her working-class friends, in the end Perley exalts the informal oral literacy of Sip over her own more middle-class and print-bound literacy practices: "I undertook to help her at the first, . . . but I was only *among* them at best; Sip is *of* them; she understands them and they understand her" (293). As a "little preacher" simply "bringing her hands together . . . and talking fast," Sip has "a style [that] can no more be caught on the point of a pen than the rustle of crisp leaves": she draws on the power of community-based oral performance, uplifting her working-class audiences with street preaching grounded in their own experiences.

As another example of a more insightful brand of uplift literacy narrative, when looking south at the turn into the next century, we find Grace MacGowan Cooke's 1909 *The Power and the Glory*. Here the heroine Johnnie Consadine's condemnation of the Uplift Club in her Appalachian mill town bursts from the page in righteous indignation. Finally moving a working-class character to center stage as a fully developed heroine, Cooke skewers supposed do-gooders like Miss Sessions and Mrs. Archbold, whose "patronizingly" dispensed lessons to the mill girls are designed more for middle-class self-gratification than for true outreach.[41]

But "bootstrapped" women seeking to tell their own stories continued to face barriers. For instance, the discourse spaces Progressive Era lady reformers sometimes shared with working-class women provide subtle evidence of cross-class tension around issues of literacy management. In the records of middle-class-sponsored clubs for working girls, in the working-class plays performed at settlement houses under the direction of lady organizers, and in the reports of the pioneer social service workers who gathered data in crowded urban neighborhoods, we can sometimes detect the traces of working-class women's resistance to middle-class literacy management. Accounts of the gatherings of working-class clubwomen affiliated with Hull-House, for instance, were reported in print by Jane Addams and her upper-middle-class colleagues, who prepared the settlement's monthly bulletin, not by the Jane Club members themselves. However sincere the motives of Addams and her fellow "residents," their continued control of the publications on Hull-House's domesticated literacy programs monitored both content and tone.[42] Yet the bulletin's veiled allusions to disagreements among club participants about the balance between social activities and book-based study hint at efforts by the settlement's working-class "neighbors" to manage their own literacy.

Significantly, in Addams's case, even when she did not apply constraints of her own, other cultural arbiters reinforced the dividing lines between the teacher-author of the settlement's benevolent education program and the learners studying there. Along those lines, when Hilda Satt Polacheck sought to publish a memoir about her experiences in the Hull-House community education program, she repeatedly met with rejection. Potential publishers demanded that she revise her narrative to focus not on her own perspective but on her interactions with the charismatic figure of Jane Addams. According to Polacheck's daughter Dena Polacheck Epstein, no editor would accept the narrative of "an obscure woman" unless it was revised to emphasize Addams's role as a generous, motherly mentor.[43]

A notable exception to this pattern of constrained storytelling is the career of Anzia Yezierska. Beginning with her early short stories (*Hungry Hearts* [1920]), and later in novels such as *Salome of the Tenements* (1923) and *Arrogant Beggar* (1927), Yezierska explicitly attacked middle-class women's control over lower-class literacy through benevolent domesticated teaching. Today, reading Yezierska's novels in tandem with Catharine Sedgwick's "The Irish Girl" or Jane Addams's *Twenty Years at Hull-House,* we can develop a more complete and complex picture of cross-class literacy relations than benevolent literacy authors (even liberals like Phelps and Cooke) provided for their readers.

From the outset, Delia Caparoso Konzett argues, Yezierska constructed dialogue, plot, and characterization in *Hungry Hearts* narratives like "The Free Vacation House" to critique philanthropic teaching's assault on immi-

grant working-class culture. Konzett sets that story's verbal exchanges between a native teacher and an immigrant mother in the context of Americanizers' fear that the "immigrant home under maternal authority represented a powerful threat to the assimilation process." Since those mothers
often "had little contact with reform agents and institutions," their "maternal influence had the potential to undo the work of teachers and other reformers," prompting middle-class women to try "to infiltrate the private
space of the home and weaken this influence" with programs like the purportedly "free" vacation of the story's title.[44] When we set Yezierska's dialogue in relation to the many mirror-opposite exchanges in benevolent domestic literacy narratives, we can affirm her rhetorical artistry. Read as a
counterpoint to didactic texts promoting middle-class literacy management,
the immigrant mother's rough speeches take on heightened resonance.

So too, in *Salome of the Tenements,* Yezierska has her heroine move beyond a romantic vision of the pedagogy at one New York settlement house
to an angry resistance. At first, Sonya avoids facing the shortcomings of
the settlement's various educational programs, because she is so infatuated
with its founder, John Manning. Ironically, however, after she has successfully leaped over an array of social barricades to marry Manning, and at
the very point when he is trying to transform her into a wealthy dispenser
of benevolence herself, Sonya takes a hard, critical look at the settlement's
classes in home economics, its constrained recreation activities (like a
tightly regulated dance class), and the negative attitudes of its middle-class
women managers toward those they ostensibly serve. Eavesdropping on
one lecture being given by a "rigid woman in a white starched collar" for
others being trained to carry out "friendly visiting" in the neighborhood,
Sonya confronts the social distance between these putatively generous activists and her own working-class values. Hence, she also confronts the gap
between her husband's naive ideals and her own experiences. Turning the
language of benevolent literacy narratives against the speaker (and, simultaneously, against such undemocratic practices as this settlement's), Yezierska has her lead character underscore the irony of terms like "worthy" being applied to poverty and of reformers intent on maintaining social
distance classifying themselves as "kind."[45]

Arrogant Beggar, published in 1927, offers an even more sustained critique of benevolent, class-oriented education programs. As Cara-Lynn Ungar shows, this novel mounts a stinging attack against "charity houses" like
the one where its heroine, Adele Lindner, initially seeks education for so-

cial uplift. Instead, as Ungar argues, Adele finds herself bound by the limits of reformers imposing "precepts of domesticity, moral guardianship, and sexual purity."[46] Adele gradually realizes that the chief donor (Mrs. Hellman) and the charity house's classes are providing only constrained opportunities for learning—such as housekeeping classes that will fit Adele only for domestic service. As Ungar points out, "the charity women teach the working-class women to recognize, but not to participate in, middle-class womanhood" (86). Eventually, however, after escaping the potential trap of the charity house's restrictive instruction, *Arrogant Beggar*'s Adele becomes an active agent constructing a counterprogram for community literacy. Adele's alternative is located in the coffeehouse she opens, where working-class patrons interact freely with creative artists in a new social space tied to the city's increasingly Bohemian values and social practices.[47] There Adele uses skills appropriated but reshaped from her charity schooling to re-form public domestic teaching.

From comparative study of benevolent literacy management texts, on the one hand, and responses like Yezierska's, on the other, a complex picture with practical and ideological implications emerges. Teachers, social workers, community volunteers, and other twenty-first-century professionals focusing on working-class literacy should examine ties between nineteenth-century literary representations of benevolent domesticated literacy and today's literacy uplift projects. In that vein, scholars operating from a variety of disciplinary perspectives have begun to take note of the persistent tendency among current literacy management initiatives to enforce social class distinctions through their language and teaching practices.[48] An increased awareness of such tendencies may encourage more critical responses to the recurring discourse depicting a "literacy crisis" among working-class youth and adults, both within and outside of schools; to the sometimes simplistically upbeat reports celebrating literacy outreach programs aimed at "saving" working-class populations; and to the lasting assumption that what the "worthy" poor need is a limited (and closely monitored) dose of middle-class literacy and associated social values.

Single Women as Motherly Teachers

Throughout the nineteenth century, on a parallel track to the ideology justifying middle-class women's cross-class charity programs, a campaign developed to promote women as paid teachers for America's schools. Perhaps unsurprisingly, therefore, as a counterpart to the subgenre of benevolent literacy narratives, another specialized form of the domestic literacy narrative supported efforts to claim the schoolhouse as a site of motherly pedagogy.

By many measures, this campaign for the classroom was a successful one. In America, unlike Britain, the professional teaching corps shifted from almost exclusively male to predominantly female. After a slow start early in the century, by the late 1860s, two-thirds of American teachers were women; twenty years later, women working in the schools outnumbered men three to one.[49] The 1830s and '40s were a pivotal period, as multiple arguments arose to back women's paid work in schools. We are quite accustomed today to thinking of teaching as a women's profession and to seeing some kinds of teaching as thoroughly feminized (such as elementary schools and secondary fields like English/language arts). But that attitude is mainly the result of our having lost sight of historical processes behind this pattern. So, as impressive as the statistics tracing the feminization of American schoolteaching are, Geraldine Joncich Clifford argues that it is the cultural developments gradually recasting "teaching as women's work" that cry for increased scholarly attention.[50] With Clifford's call in mind, we now turn to intersections between the domestic literacy narrative's construction of middle-class motherhood and the feminization of American schoolrooms. From the 1830s through the turn of the twentieth century, one subgenre of the domestic literacy narrative sought a usable "border" space for women's schoolteaching, while constituting schools themselves as domesticated domains.

One early contribution of the domestic literacy narrative to the trend feminizing teaching was its depiction of single, childless women as worthy domestic teachers. After all, before women could claim a gendered place in the district schoolroom or the urban common school, advocates had to show that women could ably enact maternal teaching even if they were not literally mothers—that their gendered ways of guiding literacy were more central to effective teaching of young children than was biological motherhood. Such founding figures of the American domestic literacy genre as Lydia Sigourney, Catharine Maria Sedgwick, and Lydia Maria Child touted single women's home-based literacy management, with Sedgwick exhibiting a special interest in this theme due to her own choice to remain unmarried. Actively engaged herself in the teaching of brothers, nieces, and nephews, Sedgwick crafted an appealing model of single women as home educators.[51] In *Means and Ends,* for instance, she portrays the productive domestic teaching of a brother by his sister. Invoking familiar republican motherhood arguments, Sedgwick declares that "the characters of men [were] formed, at home, by the mother, the first teacher," responsible for guiding their "moral basis" (270). But Sedgwick also assigns this task to the "sisters," as well as the "mothers" and "wives" of American men (271).

To exemplify her point, Sedgwick recounts the story of Mary and Raymond Bond, siblings whose "Platonic love" could easily have been based upon Sedgwick's close relationship with her own brothers. Positioning Mary's educational training and her eventual teaching along a fluid borderland, Sedgwick defines an intellectual and psychic space where the single woman teacher could serve the nation—a social location sustained by collaborative literacy exchanges. In Mary's case, this extension of domesticity is cast in terms of her learning experiences, capabilities, and attitudes rather than a literal exit from the home. Nonetheless, Sedgwick formulates the underpinnings for an argument that would eventually justify single women's extradomestic teaching for pay. She insists that "Mary was not confined to 'woman's sphere,'" since her brother shared his boarding school learning experiences with her: "Raymond, as far as was possible by the communication of letters, participated [in] his studies with her; and during his vacations, they studied and read together, and talked on those intellectual subjects that most interested him" (272). This ongoing learning exchange not only gives Mary access to extradomestic knowledge through Raymond; it also makes "home more attractive to him than any other place" (272), so that he is more inclined to seek an intelligent, refined wife (274). In the meantime, when their father faces death, Mr. Bond plans for Mary to help serve as "her mother's chief counsellor as to what is termed 'out-of-door business'" (273). Having been taught such skills as account keeping by Raymond, Mary can "supply the defects of her mother's education," so that Mr. Bond can leave his property "to the widow," trusting in her ability to manage with Mary's help. All along, Mary is also "most effectively aiding in the education of the younger children, teaching book-keeping to [Raymond's] brother, and various matters to the little ones," while still "preserving the sweetness and cheerfulness of her temper, the modesty and deference of her manners, and the unpretendingness of her conversation" (273).[52] Giving young ladies access to greater learning, this story indicates, will not undermine their femininity; instead, it will equip them to carry out a productive home teaching role while maintaining such feminine qualities as "modesty," "deference," and "unpretendingness." A maternal teacher without becoming a mother, Mary embodies an argument that would be reconfigured to support unmarried middle-class women's schoolteaching for the good of the nation, a move enabled partly by the advanced learning now available to them in the enlightened American republic.

That real-life versions of these teaching sisters existed is evident in women's memoirs from postcolonial, pre–Civil War America, both North and South. Lucy Larcom's tender portrait of her older sibling describes Emilie, "my most motherly sister," teaching Lucy to memorize hymn lyrics and, as a prize for progress, to write her "p's and q's" in cursive, in "a neat little writing-book," with a "goose quill" designed to make the young girl "proud and happy" in her own literacy acquisition.[53] For some older sisters, being the domestic teacher could actually become quite burdensome. North Carolinian Rachel Mordecai complained, earlier in the century, about having to care for and teach a growing brood of half-siblings when her father remarried after her mother's death: "Scarcely have the first years of infancy passed before the entire charge devolves on us, of forming the dispositions, improving the mind, even taking care of the apparel of each child in the family—this we must do, or see all neglected."[54] But Rachel also enjoyed the intellectual stimulation of trying out the English Edgeworths' pedagogical theories on her young sister, and she appreciated the ways this domestic teaching enhanced her work in the family-run seminary for young ladies, unusual in the region for its academic strengths.

Such social contributions of unmarried sisters could be used, in fact, to justify the cost of enhanced female education, as in Lydia Maria Child's *The Mother's Book:* "I have known young ladies, on whom a good deal had been expended, who more than repaid their parents by their assistance in educating younger branches of the family; and is not such a preparation likely to make the duties of a mother more pleasant and familiar to them? . . . The acquirements and industry of one branch of the family have served to educate and bring forward all the rest; is not such a power, well used, extremely conducive to kindness and benevolence?" (141).[55] Like Sedgwick, Child short-circuits potential resistance against her position by emphasizing that well-taught females could teach others in their family, and she carefully genders this work as female—"conducive to kindness and benevolence."

Child provides another case in point through multiple anecdotes of effective maternal domestic teaching carried out by women who had never, themselves, been biological mothers. Though Child does not present a single life as superior to a married one, she nonetheless insists on the special abilities unmarried women can have as maternal domestic literacy managers. In one of her "Unmarried Women" sketches, for example, Miss Susan Burleigh "read to her young friends [nieces and nephews] at stated times," told appealing stories from her "prodigious" personal collection, and "surrounded herself with choice books and pictures" that "would entertain and instruct young minds"—so that "no one could approach her sphere without being conscious of its vivifying influence."[56] Child exalts another of the "unmarried women" who "adopted the orphan sons of her brother, and reared them with more than parental wisdom and tenderness," including "guiding them in precept and example . . . , bestowing on them the highest intellectual culture, and studying all branches with them" (132). Repeatedly, Child characterizes the motherlike management of linguistic capital by these unmarried domestic teachers as a special kind of parenting, not an inferior imitation. For instance, she opines that in "the nursery, their labors, being voluntary, are less exhausting than a parent's," and she contrasts the "weary, fretted mother" who eventually "turns a deaf ear to the twenty-times-repeated question" with the single aunt or friend who can still give "a patient hearing and a kind response" (136). Laying the groundwork for arguments that would later be used by single professionals like Elizabeth Peabody, Child limns these maternal figures as sometimes being more motherly than biological maternal teachers.[57] Rather than bemoaning their having no children of their own, she praises their "hearts [that] seem to be too large to be confined to any one set of children" (136). Child also notes how these women extend their domestic pedagogy beyond the family circle by drawing others to their home teachings. For example, Child's Aunt Sarah Stetson uses careful study of English literature and history, as well as "flashing wit," to render her fireside a veritable literacy magnet: "all the intellectual people of the town sought her company with avidity," with everyone from the local "Unitarian minister and his family" to "the young people" flocking to "gather up her words of wisdom" (139–40).

If such stories of productive spinsterhood went a long way toward establishing a single woman's version of domestic maternal teaching, they still positioned this work as unpaid benevolence, whether within or across social classes. A more complicated maneuver exercised with greater frequency as the century progressed was to endorse a single woman's teaching for pay outside the home as worthy social service. For example, in a biography entitled "Margaret Mercer," Lydia Sigourney casts her subject as a "patriot" whose teaching of young ladies represents a form of republican motherhood. Sigourney frames that argument by explaining that if it "is to the mothers of her sons that every country looks for the impress that is to make them her great and good men," then the nation should honor "such women as Margaret Mercer," who teach those future maternal teachers.[58]

Along related lines, Sedgwick's story "Old Maids" in *Tales and Sketches by Miss Sedgwick* records a conversation between an appealing young character (Anne) and her motherly friend Mrs. Seton. Their discussion of the general desirability of marriage is tempered by Mrs. Seton's suggestion that, in some cases, deciding not to marry might prove wise. The climax of the talk comes in her story about two sisters, Agnes and Lizzy. Lizzy's bad marriage is mitigated by Agnes's teaching successfully for pay to support herself, Lizzy, and Lizzy's children, who otherwise would have suffered horribly due to the "unfaithful," "self-indulgent," and "intemperate" behavior of their dissipated father.[59] In setting up Agnes as a role model, after first seeming to cast her as an "old maid" object for pity, Mrs. Seton redirects the ideology of domestic literacy management to a public setting (the schoolroom) that remains intimately connected with the home. Agnes, though initially denied access to maternal teaching because of her spinsterhood, claims a superior version of the role by becoming both a successful schoolteacher and an educator of her sister's children. In the story's outer frame, through Anne's empathetic "tears" and Mrs. Seton's observation that the tale is "no fiction," Sedgwick projects her premise as applicable to other American women reading about Agnes's model.

"The Natural Instructor of Youth"

To get a sense of why the fictional Agnes's option of becoming a schoolteacher became so acceptable for genteel American women, we need to position texts like Sedgwick's "Old Maids" within a developing set of antebellum trends favoring female educators, especially for young children. One such argument, building on the tradition of colonial dame schools, asserted that women were especially able guides for early reading instruction. A second factor was the appeal that a domesticated teaching model held as a strategy for reproducing hierarchized social relations through the inexpensive labor of women, whose schoolteaching could be framed as such a "natural" extension of female benevolence that their salaries could remain low. A third factor cast schoolteaching as a mother-in-training activity. Yet another held that women's empathetic moral sense made them especially adept at teaching young children. Describing the part each of these related trends played in the process making schoolteaching middle-class single women's work can clarify how already accepted gender roles interacted with newer ideas about women's social responsibilities to create a national class of female cultural workers situated in the schoolhouse. Reviewing each of these trends can also highlight how the domestic literacy narrative, while evolving as a literary genre, contributed to historical movements in female teaching and learning.

In his study *Early New England Schools* (1914), Walter Herbert Small underscores the close connections between the "dame school" of colonial America and the "school dame" of the nineteenth century. Pointing out that many private dame schools made a transition between serving a very few families to serving village communities, Small's research into town financial records from the late seventeenth and eighteenth centuries reveals that communities often paid women teachers in cash or in barter for educating local youngsters in reading, spelling, and arithmetic. Although these records generally indicate that this schooling took place in the home of the teacher, her work was already being conceived as community-level (rather than individualized, private) service requiring a fair (if low) recompense. Building on Small's archival review, we should note the significance, by the early nineteenth century, of some New England towns' already voting increased appropriations to cover the cost of *women-run,* domesticated primary schools for children aged about four to about six or seven.[60] Small himself points to such nineteenth-century dame schools' domestic teaching as especially suited to the needs of young children, who sometimes had difficulty making the move directly from home to the formal setting of the (typically) male-run village school, with its overcrowded conditions and monotonous recitation-based instruction.

If unable to draw on adequate support from sisters, aunts, or domestic help so as to carry out the idealized domestic instruction programs described in advice literature by authors like Sigourney and Sedgwick, a New England mother could call upon these extensions of the colonial dame school model, thereby enhancing the trend constructing early education as a responsibility of female teachers. For example, in *A New England Girlhood,* Lucy Larcom describes Aunt Hannah's home school, which Larcom began attending when she was "about two years old, as other children about us did," since "mothers of those large families had to resort to some means of keeping their little ones out of mischief, while they attended to their domestic duties." Larcom describes learning her "letters in a few days," while standing at the knee of this "neighbor whom everybody called 'Aunt Hannah.'" Recalling more advanced lessons, Larcom notes, "Certain it is that a few passages in the Bible, whenever I read them now, do not fail to bring before me a vision" of Aunt Hannah's teaching.[61]

Meanwhile, in focusing the educational program of such schools on reading, while setting that teaching in a domestic, maternal tradition, local communities avoided placing their primary schools in competition with home-based instruction. Instead, such arrangements assumed cooperation between motherly teachers and actual mothers, who could address the same pedagogical content in complementary ways by the evening fireside.

A second antebellum trend promoting the use of female instructors had to do with women's purported ability to shape behavior to norms favored by middle-class social arbiters and to do so using skills so inherent to their identity that they hardly merited monetary recompense. As suggested in the discussion of the influence women brought to mixed-gender lyceums (see chapter 1), the ideology of domesticity encompassed a view of women as able to refine others through collaborative literacy. Especially in the charity school movement, this belief opened up education of the lower classes as a field where middle-class women needed to be involved for the good of the nation.[62] In providing women an entrée into schoolteaching, this reform work was an important step toward women's accessing a new career. Yet, by associating schoolteaching with charitable outreach, this argument also helped ensure that women teachers' salaries remained low. Understandably, being able to pay women much less than men made the feminization of the schoolroom increasingly attractive to male civic managers.[63] Women actually contributed propaganda to this rationale themselves, with Zilpah Grant and Mary Lyon just two examples of educators who faced financial struggles in their personal lives yet argued that women teachers needed less pay than men did.[64] One reason for this strategy was defensive: communities did not have to pay female teachers well, since there were hardly any other professional options open to them. (In that context, women teachers were typically more willing than men to accept seasonal employment; rural areas needing children for harvesting could count on a female teacher not to disappear in search of a better job.) Overall, female teachers were paid about a third to a half of a male salary, partly on the grounds that they did not have families to support.[65]

Characterizing teaching as a stepping-stone to motherhood was another strategy aimed at gaining women entry into the teaching profession without seeming to undermine conservative middle-class gender roles. Historian Averil McClelland suggests one way of describing the trend toward feminized schoolrooms: an "ideology of teaching daughters."[66] Observing this pattern in the mid-Atlantic as well as the New England states, McClelland relates the growing tendency to hire women to factors such as population increases leading to more schools; women who were better educated than their mothers wanting to share their knowledge; improved job opportunities for men in other fields; and an upward trajectory in the average marriage age, which left women with "a kind of 'window' of several years" when they needed something useful to do.[67] None of these factors conflicted with the assumption that the eventual goal for middle-class young ladies was marriage and motherhood. In fact, they helped constitute the paid teaching of young children as an apprenticeship in motherly management of children.

Shifting views of childhood and of the teaching act itself also contributed to women's ability to become teachers. In accord with antebellum psychological theories, educators looked for ways to provide instruction suited to the developmental level of younger students. Glenda Riley suggests that, for nineteenth-century Americans, the "prevailing view of children became less one of a miniature adult to be rescued from original sin and more one of a pliable and innocent being whose upbringing demanded specialized equipment, toys, and books."[68] Along with this reconceptualization of childhood identity, perceptions, and needs came a call for a more maternal brand of instruction. Teachers, rather than treating their young charges like rational adults and punishing them physically when they were naughty, it was urged, should be sensitive to their students' childlike natures.

As agents of sensibility, women were increasingly being promoted as teachers for very young children. An 1844 New York legislature report on education intoned: "In childhood the intellectual faculties are but partially developed—the affections more fully. At that early age the affections are the key to the whole being. The female teacher readily possesses herself of that key, and thus having access to the heart, the mind is soon reached and operated upon."[69] Females, supposedly, were naturally endowed with greater sensitivity and therefore better equipped than men to teach young children, who, regardless of their sex, were more emotional than rational, more susceptible to appeals of the heart than to correction directed toward the mind. Significantly, male advocates could be as enthusiastic as females in their advocacy of this position, as exemplified by "A Father" writing for the *Ladies' Magazine* in 1834: "Woman is constituted by the Creator [as] the natural instructor of youth. He has committed the child to her care from its birth; and he has poured into her heart an inexhaustible affection, a serene patience, a winning gentleness, which preeminently fit her for the management of children. In all these qualities she far surpasses man. She has more knowledge of the youthful heart, and more power to control it, not by force but by the . . . sway of love. I have little doubt, that if all our schools for young children were placed under the care of female instructors, they would be quite as well taught and better governed."[70]

As "A Father" suggests, closely related to the shifting perceptions of childhood and women's "natural" abilities to manage children were theories of feminized moral suasion. The growing lack of self-restraint in the country's young, it was often said, could be best addressed via the more gentle persuasion of feminine teaching than through the coercion of the rod, which was clearly at odds with republican values.[71] In particular, hiring women who would use moral suasion in teaching was seen as a possible way to curb Jacksonian rowdiness in young boys—especially on the frontier—without having to resort to undemocratic brute force. In that vein, "A Father" declared that, not only for "their own sex" but also for males, females were "the best teachers," whose "affections[,] . . . gentle, kind and amiable," could guide the "morals" of children (477).

The National Board, an organization training women educators for work in the West, emphasized their special governance abilities. Interestingly, many of the communities actually hiring National Board graduates were desperate for a teacher but uncertain about women's capacities for maintaining order. The Hartford Seminary's board-sponsored preparation course, therefore, stressed discipline. But, in accord with theories of the day, the course advocated moral appeal to students rather than physical force.[72] Bible readings and singing, for instance, were recommended for instilling positive discipline. An illustration of this theory working in practice is provided by Ellen Lee, daughter of a Princeton, Massachusetts, shoemaker. After National Board training, Lee migrated west and took over a log school of fifty-five pupils, aged fourteen to twenty-two. Though the group had acquired a reputation for being unruly, Lee succeeded by using moral suasion. In a letter to her own former teacher back east, Lee reported, "They thought, of course, if a man could not govern their boys, a woman could not . . . but I was allowed to take my course, and . . . by awakening their consciences to a sense of right and wrong . . . , I have succeeded much better."[73]

Popular culture's images of teaching reinforced these views throughout the century. Verbal and visual portraits of women at work in the classroom continued to depict them as motherly figures nurturing their students. Representative of this lingering trend is an appealing 1867 illustration from *Harper's Weekly,* designed for a short sketch entitled "The District Schoolteacher." Drawing on traditions first developed in domestic literacy narratives earlier in the century, illustrations like this one helped safeguard women's hold on schoolteaching as a career but also limited the likelihood that such highly feminized, "domestic" work would claim a well-paid professional status. (See figure 5.)

Upgrading Education for Future Teachers

As women became teachers of pupils studying more than the rudiments of knowledge, and as women became trainers of other teachers, the curriculum for female education clearly needed to expand. However, since reformers were always wary of conservative backlash, they tended to couch their polemics in an ethos still favoring domestic teaching as women's primary work. Interestingly, efforts to deemphasize "accomplishments" (such as singing and fancy needlework) and to make the curriculum more rigorous (i.e., comparable to that in male institutions) conflicted in some ways with simultaneous calls to feminize schoolrooms via a nurturing brand of instruction. Advocates of female teaching often tried to suppress this potential contradiction by divorcing instructional content from method. Whereas the move to reform women's learning focused mainly on *what* they studied, the efforts to domesticate schoolhouses focused on *how* they taught. Proponents were careful to draw distinctions between the masculine knowledge to which women now needed increased access and the appropriately feminine means lady teachers would use to impart it to their own students. This split between content and method would, of course, generate tensions in the developing education programs of female learning institutions, as well as both intellectual and psychological strains within women educators themselves. Before drawing from multiple domestic literacy narratives to illustrate negotiations of these strains in portrayals of women schoolteachers, I will survey a group of texts describing curricula over several different decades to illustrate the trajectory of American female education reform that was tied to preparing middle-class ladies for schoolteaching.

Hannah Foster's *The Boarding School* (1798) can serve as a baseline text, a reminder that the initial postcolonial stance of American women educators was grounded in an English tradition of female learning tied to preparation for the marriage market.[74] In the early republic, as noted earlier, calls for allowing women some educational opportunities were associated with their teaching of children for the national welfare. However, conservative views on middle-class woman's role as household manager and helpmate to her husband had great staying power. Accordingly, Foster's story of a boarding school for proper American young ladies still valued such feminine skills as entertaining one's spouse and guests. Her curriculum foregrounded "highly ornamental" aspects of female conversation ahead of the conversational teaching one might carry out with children.[75]

Despite modeling a nascent form of domestic literacy management, Foster's "preceptress," Mrs. Williams, frames her pupils' learning mainly as preparation for genteel housewifery:

> Look upon Elvira. . . . Her husband's business abroad prevents him for attending to domestic avocations; nor need he be anxious respecting the management of his household affairs. . . . The superintendence of her family, and the education of her children is her delight. Capable of instructing them in every needful branch of science, and of furnishing them with every requisite endowment, she is, at once, their guide, their example, and their friend. . . . In the entertainment of [family] friends, how distinguished a part she sustains! Her powers of mind have been so happily improved, that she is able to discuss every subject with ease and propriety. To an enlarged understanding and a cultivated taste, to an extensive knowledge of the world and an acquaintance with polite literature, she [adds] those amiable virtues, which give society its highest relish. (28)

The kind of "good education" that Foster's book advocates for model femininity like Elvira's is itself carried out in a domestic setting aimed at regulating young girl learners into a "useful and happy life" by way of "early infusion of virtuous principles into the docile mind" (3). For Mrs. Williams (Foster), the goal of this home-based teaching is to cultivate such traits as "charms of person and mind," "decorum and propriety," "piety, morality, benevolence, prudence and economy," rather than to teach disciplinary subjects (6–7). Hence, Mrs. Williams's half-dozen boarding students practice the refined middle-class housewifery they will eventually take on themselves. In other words, as Foster says, Mrs. Williams "particularly endeavoured to domesticate them" (7). Hours of careful "needle-work" last until lunchtime—with conversation directed by one girl's oral reading of Mrs. Williams's selection. After luncheon, the young ladies offer collaborative critique of a composition one of them has drafted. Then, the small group enjoys "amusement"—whether "dance," "sentimental song," or some other activity "consistent with the decorum of the sex" (10). Overall, this curriculum is grounded in "pleasing pursuits and enjoyments" providing a practice version of that era's ideal for middle-class married life.

How different are the goals outlined for American women's learning about twenty years later in Emma Willard's "Plan for Improving Female Education" (1819) and how intricately bound up, already, with visions of middle-class lady educators. Yet how cautiously did Willard position her re-

THE DISTRICT SCHOOL TEACHER.—Drawn by A. R. Waud.—[See next page.]

Fig. 5. "The District Schoolteacher." Drawing by A. R. Waud, *Harper's Weekly* (November 8, 1867). The Library Company of Philadelphia

form ideas within a tradition favoring mothers' domestic literacy management as the chief labor of middle-class women. Having begun her career in
1814 by operating a home school for girls, Willard was eager to convince
the state of New York to provide financial support for enhanced women's
education. However, Willard was careful to distinguish between the expanded content base American women now required in their curriculum
and the feminine ways in which they would continue to carry out their
home and school teaching tasks. Thus, Willard reassures the readers of her
proposal "that the seminary here recommended, will be as different from
those appropriated to the other sex, as the female character and duties are
from the male."[76] She argues that restricting female learning to "frivolous
acquirements" undermined women's ability to teach their own children,
even as she suggests that improved female seminaries "might be expected
to have important and happy effects, on common schools." Seminary graduates, with the proper training in advanced courses, could take on "the business of teaching children," thereby freeing up men, "whose services the
state wants in many other ways" (75, 79). Therefore, she urges that
women's course work include studying "the nature of the mind, so as to be
aware of the importance of those early impressions, which we make upon
the minds of our children" (75). Similarly, Willard proposes that science
and philosophy be taught to women, so that they could draw upon those
fields to teach children about "the causes of natural phenomena" (79).

Overall, Willard urges an expansion of the fields of study, but toward a
conservative aim—teaching American youth lessons for moral stability. She
posits that improving the education available to women in seminaries
would allow "the government [to] exercise an intimate, and most beneficial
control over common schools" (80). However, she balances this call for "a
class of individuals" (i.e., women teachers whose "ardour" would produce
"happy effects, on common schools") with repeated reminders that the masculine knowledge these teachers-in-training acquired would be used only for
appropriately feminine aims—gentle dissemination of morality and benevolence for the good of the nation. That is, she indicates that such educated
women would not attempt to use their knowledge for selfish, competitive,
or other more male-oriented enterprises; instead they would employ feminine "patience," "gentle arts of insinuation," and "quickness of invention"
to reshape masculine knowledge with feminine teaching methods, rendering it accessible to children's young minds yet harmless for women teachers
to possess (79).

Moving forward another decade from Willard's proposal to records of

Catharine Beecher's administration of the Hartford Female Seminary, we can note how far at least some American women's educational programs had progressed, if perhaps at a price. In the *Catalogue of the Officers, Teachers, and Pupils of the Hartford Female Seminary for the Summer Term of 1828,* Beecher describes a curriculum strikingly different from Foster's 1798 boarding school fare.[77] From the opening page, with its impressively long columns of 131 registrants (coming from as far away as Milledgeville, Georgia), the catalog reflects an increasing tendency to assume that middle-class young ladies needed the extended, extradomestic study with large groups of peers that their brothers had long ago claimed.[78] With the number of *teachers* (eight) greater than the number of *students* in Mrs. Williams's home-based school, Beecher's enterprise had clearly become a thriving business. The course of study, meanwhile, was markedly more demanding than anything Foster's Mrs. Williams would have provided, and in range of subjects it exceeded even Willard's proposed plan.[79] Geography, history, grammar, literature, and arithmetic were just a few of the "branches" everyone studied. Chemistry, rhetoric/logic, and geometry required students to carry out their own experiments, "draw their own diagrams on the black board," or "analyze the ideas . . . and arrangement" of verbal arguments—that is, to use complex literacy practices for analysis and synthesis (9–10). With a schedule including long hours of quiet study as well as formal recitation, the catalog delineates a shift away from the relaxed, domestic, conversational pedagogy of Foster's narrative to a formalized, rigorous, and assessment-oriented system of study. Along those lines, among the items listed in "Things Required" are to "study two hours out of school without speaking" and to arrive promptly in the hall for quiet review sessions (12). Among the items listed in "Things Forbidden" are to "speak without liberty" and to "eat in school hours"—quite a change from the chatty informality at Mrs. Williams's home school in Foster's text.

If we read only the formal catalogs for the late 1820s Hartford Seminary, we might well conclude that Beecher had gained access to a more rigorous curriculum for her students but sacrificed all of the more appealing aspects of feminized, domesticated learning along the way. But her *Suggestions Respecting Improvements in Education,* published in 1829 and directed toward fund-raising for the seminary, clarifies tensions embedded within her efforts to make the institution successful financially while, at the same time, continuing to position its curriculum within a nurturing maternal tradition.[80] In *Suggestions,* Beecher reveals ways her philosophy and practice still affirmed the ideology of domestic, feminized instruction, even to the point of actively resisting popular (and potentially more lucrative) masculine models. For example, in critiquing teacher preparation, Beecher urges a shift in emphasis from preparing educators to quiz for facts to training them to "teach children, to think, to reason correctly, to invent, to discover and to perform various mental operations . . . , [and] to communicate ideas" (13). Additionally, in advocating the teaching of "moral habits" among the young, she reaffirms motherly teaching's core goal of preparing dedicated, virtuous citizens, rather than focusing on memorization (10, 13).

Beecher's *Suggestions* text carefully justifies the need for additional staff at an institution that, for its time, had a remarkably large instructional team relative to the size of its student body. Beecher admits that, besides the eight full-fledged teachers, the seminary has ten advanced students assist with instruction. But she argues that even more staff is needed because the best kind of teaching is conversational, allowing "small" classes of students to work together with an instructor who has adequate time to prepare her lessons and a limited number of subjects to cover (21-25, 61). In addition, Beecher points out, teachers need to "mingle with pupils as companions," so as to "gain a thousand times more respect and influence than could be gained at the most elevated and imposing distance" (49). After all, she says, when "teachers have depended too much upon *authority*, and too little upon the *affections*, in guiding the objects of their care," students' moral progress is limited, since excessive "dignity and reserve" positions "their scholars at such a distance as prevents all assimilation of feeling and interest" (49). Drawing upon the language of feminine moral suasion, Beecher lobbies for resources to support feminized, conversational teaching.[81]

We may fail to note the courage behind Beecher's words if we lack awareness about the intense popularity, at that time, of systems of instruction claiming to handle much larger student bodies than Beecher was advocating. Specifically, the multiple success stories associated with the Lancasterian method—and with other monitorial systems that processed huge numbers of students via continuous, competitive recitation cycles—offered a rigidly hierarchized model quite at odds with Beecher's argument for family-like interaction among teachers and small groups of students.[82] Only when we set Beecher's plea for increased funding in the context of educational practices in her own day can we take full measure of the challenge she faced—defining a workable space for the Hartford Seminary in a contested, hybridized borderland between masculine and feminine middle-class learning models. She sometimes met this challenge by crossing back and forth between stances that were not fully compatible, leading to inconsistencies that may make her seem a self-serving opportunist today. But we need to realize that by juggling these recurring tensions, she found ways to provide a profession-building education for many American middle-class women, even if she was not always able to create as distinctively feminized a learning culture as she would have liked. Later in the century, as seminaries like Catharine Beecher's evolved into women's colleges, their curricula would continue to be tied to the construction of schoolteaching, charitable outreach, and maternal domestic education as middle-class women's primary social duties. Hence, educational leaders and their students would face ongoing difficulties in their efforts to balance gendered traditions with ongoing reform.[83]

Teaching along Shifting Borderlands

Similar to the rhetoric of Catharine Beecher's texts, the daily life of individual women schoolteachers was full of conflicts between the ideology of motherly teaching and the material conditions of schoolhouse labor. Surveying the tensions between ideal and actual as they recurred in nineteenth-century schoolteachers' experiences can help us better understand the polemical role domestic literacy narratives tried to play in negotiating such issues. Toward that end, we can use the lens of historical materialist standpoint theory. As Rosemary Hennessy indicates, analyzing how discourse helps shape hegemony involves showing how it brings together "elements from various contesting knowledges into an imaginary coherent conceptual framework."[84] In this case, I am taking the (eventually) hegemonic principle that American middle-class women were ideal, motherlike schoolteachers as an example of "an imaginary coherent conceptual framework" available as a map for individual women's lives. I have been building a foundation for arguing that women writers of domestic literacy narratives *helped create* this belief system and associated professional teaching practices through rhetoric guided by their own social standpoints. Their status as middle-class literary teachers made them complicit, on the one hand, in patriarchal efforts to control the maternal domestic role when it was situated in an extended social setting. However, this same status also made it possible for them, as Catharine Beecher's writing illustrates, to seek a space for oppositional activity grounded in gendered goals.[85] Thus, we can read individual narratives applauding domesticated schoolteaching as creating adaptable discursive versions of this identity. That is, viewing these texts through materialist standpoint theory emphasizes how representations of such a model provided a loose script that women could follow but also resist or adapt.[86] Analysis of key pressure points in the evolving social script for maternal schoolteaching demonstrates that, as Hennessy explains, actual "'women's lives' have a materiality . . . that exceeds their discursive construction," even though "the 'reality' of women's lives is only made possible through historically available knowledges" (145).

Tensions associated with efforts to domesticate the schoolroom were clustered around a number of points along the borderland between models for masculinized and feminized learning/teaching, with emerging ideologies tending to suppress these conflicts by casting female teaching in idealized "maternal" terms, even when daily instructional labor took on a very different form. These pressure points included women's motives for teaching, their qualifications and training, their methods of instruction, and their relationships to students and parents. Both historical research and narratives by schoolteachers reflect these inherent tensions and the multiple rhetorical strategies nineteenth-century writers used to contain them, so as to guide actual women's life choices.

Perhaps the most striking of these contradictions was between the idealized version of women's motivation for teaching—motherlike benevolence—and the reality that many individual women chose this career for other reasons. Jo Anne Preston's extensive study of writing by women's education advocates, school reformers, and female schoolteachers shows that, contrary to "the popular image of the female teacher as unaspiring, self-sacrificing, and emotionally driven," many "nineteenth-century female teachers were intellectually motivated and keenly interested in higher wages."[87] Indeed, a number of domestic literacy narratives about schoolteachers paint portraits partly in line with Preston's thesis, partly affiliated with the motherlike ideal of benevolent teaching, thereby suggesting that authors perceived a need to try to reconcile these opposing views. For example, the subject of Lydia Maria Child's "Louisa Preston" is a dedicated scholar who suffers extreme anxiety when her duties in support of a poor mother and siblings divert her attention from school. Once Louisa completes a scholarship-funded course of study at sixteen, she starts teaching, but more because she wishes to help her poor brother and mother than from a maternal wish to nurture students.[88] In this case, benevolence is a motive for teaching, but the objects of the heroine's generosity are family members rather than schoolchildren. Similarly, Lydia Sigourney's portrait of Ann Marie Hyde stresses a money-oriented impulse behind Miss Hyde's teaching but portrays her wish for a salary as growing out of a "noble principle, a desire to assist" the needs of a widowed sister and her children.[89] All in all, while some stories show benevolent teaching being donated to needy students, other texts seek to reconcile such unselfishness as the idealized motive for female teaching with the reality of many individuals' needing income themselves or seeking a life change, like Lucy Larcom.[90]

Intellectual motivation, meanwhile, could be even more complicated to negotiate rhetorically, since to paint the woman schoolteacher as overly dedicated to learning for its own sake risked turning her into a self-centered bluestocking. Lydia Sigourney developed apt strategies for countering this charge, as in her memoir of early professional teaching experiences, *Letters to My Pupils* (1856). Admitting that her years as a young student represented a "halcyon period" in her life, Sigourney recalls her pain at being withdrawn from school at age thirteen, despite her clear "proficiency in study," since her parents were convinced that she had "already more than sufficient [learning] for a woman" and that more "would create distaste for the duties that eventually devolve on our sex."[91] Though admitting disappointment at being excluded from advanced study, the memoir downplays her own scholarly aspirations and emphasizes instead her dedication to teaching others. Reading with an awareness of antebellum women writer-educators' need to mask their own intellectualism, however, we should draw upon Hennessy's advice about socially shaped standpoints grounded in historicizable material conditions. Then we can see how *Letters to My Pupils* values individual feminine learning while covering it beneath a cloak exalting maternal teaching. By depicting herself as already attracted to motherlike teaching when she was exiled as a student, Sigourney frames her first efforts as instructor in stereotypically feminine terms. Yet she was able to use teaching to regain access to scholarly study. (Sigourney's portraits of former students-become-teachers are particularly telling in this regard.)[92] Whereas her parents had not been willing to allow their bright daughter to continue her own studies, they were easily persuaded to "gratify" her gender-appropriate desire to serve others. Hence, they fit up a classroom in their home "with desks, benches, and hour-glass," where she taught two "fair young pupils, from the most respectable and wealthy families in the vicinity" (161). Spending six hours a day with her young charges, she maintained her connection to intellectual achievement by teaching at home.

Sigourney's next experience, coteaching with Ann Marie Hyde, provided an even more potent intellectual reward, as the two took turns assuming the roles of teacher and student. Sigourney explains that the one who stud-

ied "among the pupils" was actually "secretly guid[ing] them by her example," but this role-playing also gave both beginning teachers continued access to the student experience they clearly loved (164–65). Along those
lines, Sigourney's characterization of Hyde is probably consistent with
many teachers' perspectives then (and now). Terming Hyde "less deeply im-
bued by nature with the love of teaching, than the silent pleasures of intellectual pursuit," Sigourney offers an admission of women's efforts to use
schoolteaching as an avenue to continued intellectualism (170). Similarly,
writing by such intellectual schoolteachers as Charlotte Forten, Ida B.
Wells-Barnett, and Lucy Larcom later in the century would also struggle to
reconcile women's own aspirations for learning with the ideology of generous teaching.[93]

A similar tension in literacy narratives about nineteenth-century schoolteaching centered on conflicting views about the proper qualifications and
training for women to teach. As outlined earlier, supporters of female
schoolteaching often depicted women as perfectly suited to the job by their
very natures. Such a view implied that any woman could, at any time, walk
into a classroom, especially one serving young children, and immediately
succeed as a teacher, simply by enacting a version of the feminized teaching "naturally" going on in American homes. However, this view of instruction as inherently women's work ran up against conflicting practices of social class discrimination (rendering schoolteaching a field open only to
refined ladies rather than to all women) and increasing calls for special
training for teachers.

In the first case, domestic literacy narratives tried to negotiate the social class issue by portraying some poor or working-class women as acquiring the polish needed for teaching through managed interaction with sponsors. So, in Sedgwick's short story "Ella," one reason given for the
heroine's visit to her relatives' city dwelling is to gain social skills "she
[could not] get in the country" so that she could aid "her parents in the education of their family" by becoming an instructor herself—one qualified "to
teach the expensive branches called accomplishments."[94] Along similar
lines, in *Means and Ends*, Sedgwick includes a brief story entitled "Emma
Austen" about a "day-scholar" at a fashionable school who earns her tuition
by "keep[ing] the school-room in order," since, as "the eldest daughter of a
widow in reduced circumstances," she cannot pay her way. In fact, Emma's
schooling is intended to make her "qualified to be an instructress," and her
initial concern over not being able "to pay for expensive teaching" signals

how difficult it was then for young women who were not certifiably young *ladies* to aspire to schoolteaching (176).

Sedgwick explores this issue in even greater detail in "Self Education," the story of a young assistant teacher in "a fashionable school in one of our large cities." "Among the teachers in Mrs. Reed's school," Sedgwick explains, is Amy Sutton, "a graceful person" who had "overcome great obstacles in her career."[95] Being both "valued and respected by her employer" and also "beloved by her pupils," Miss Sutton seems, in the opening pages, to be the perfect model of feminized teaching. But a few of the less enlightened girls at the school classify her as "an 'upstart,'" and their gossiping soon undermines her position. One of the students declares it "scandalous in Mrs. Reed to put Amy Sutton over the daughters of gentlemen," since the interloper had originally been a "low-born, low-bred servant girl!" (122). But Sedgwick has Mrs. Reed recount Miss Sutton's past to the students to shame the snobs by emphasizing how the heroine used education (largely self-financed through dressmaking) to achieve a feminine gentility by working as an "under teacher" (126–31). Nonetheless, as seemingly accepting as the story might be of a lower-class girl's rise in rank through education and schoolteaching, the fashion-conscious pupils' resentment suggests such paths were not always easy. And the packing off of Miss Sutton "to be principal in a school in Mobile" for "a very handsome salary" could be read as a victory but also as an acknowledgment that such an upstart was more likely to be accepted outside of New England, despite Sedgwick's assertion of "merit" over "nobility" (135).

As the century progressed, the unstable social class borderland that some women had been crossing by way of apprentice schoolteaching became more, rather than less, daunting. Once advanced institutions for teachers were developed, they were conceived of as the key to ensuring high instructional quality, and they benefited countless American middle-class women by providing them access to even more rigorous curricula than teachers like Amy Sutton had mastered via on-the-job training.[96] However, they also tightened access to the teaching profession, especially for immigrants and native working-class girls who, earlier in the century, could pay for preparatory study in small, informal private schools by doing chores, then slowly work their way up to teacher. Negotiation of this rising barrier, then, became increasingly challenging, as seen in novels like Augusta Jane Evans's *Beulah* (1859) and Anzia Yezierska's *Bread Givers* (1925).[97]

At the other end of the social class spectrum, one side effect of the trend toward regulated training for women teachers was to make it less likely that young ladies from the upper echelons of society could obtain easy entrée to teaching, simply based on their rank. Thus, in her 1859 introduction for *Women and Work,* Sedgwick critiques the tendency among daughters of the well-to-do to view teaching as an easily claimed interlude between youth and marriage. Cataloging the academic preparation American teachers needed, by the late 1850s, as well as the special temperaments they should cultivate, Sedgwick sarcastically attacks "young ladies (*ladies par excellence*)" who thought themselves qualified to teach simply by virtue of their socioeconomic status.[98] Reviling "most of the young girls whom we have sent to boarding-schools, with huge trunks . . . and richly trimmed dresses," Sedgwick insists that insipid lessons aimed at simplistic lives in "luxurious homes" would not qualify these empty-headed fools for the "divine mission" of teaching, which required both extended study of disciplines and "calmness, gentleness, and patience" (4–5). With her sound rejection of fashionable accomplishments and status as qualifiers for American teaching, Sedgwick imagines a national professional identity formed by training rather than by birth.

Another ongoing conflict between ideology and experience evident in literacy narratives about teaching was associated with instructional method—particularly the use of moral suasion and affectionate conversational pedagogy. Although arguments favoring the hiring of women teachers stressed their skill with such instruction, Jo Anne Preston's research suggests that, "rather than expressions of maternal affection, female teachers' writings are replete with reports of punishment" (549). For every success story like Ellen Lee's account of gentle moral suasion winning over her students, it seems, Preston found pictures of women's enthusiastic use of corporal punishment. When reading stories of nurturing, feminized discipline, therefore, we need to remember that this gendered approach was far from universally adopted.

Nonetheless, the persistence of such domestic literacy narratives' moves to exalt gendered teaching methods testifies to their very real appeal among educators, parents, and students throughout the century. For instance, one recurring plotline involves worthy pupil-opponents being led to share academic prizes, as in Child's "Louisa Preston," rejecting masculine models of cutthroat competition. Such themes reaffirmed the heritage of republican motherhood's home-based teaching, extending it into schoolhouses to shape community morality as much as intellectual attainment. Accordingly, Elizabeth Sedgwick's teaching memoir advocates women educators' continued emphasis on moral instruction, along with methods based on true affection for students: "It is one thing to educate the mind, a far higher and more important office to educate the heart and the conscience. How shall this be done? . . . First of all, by loving [students], by manifesting a real sympathy with them, and by showing an earnest desire for their happiness and improvement. Here, again, the friend must be uppermost, and above the teacher. If this were so, in schools and colleges, the result would seem almost magical."[99] Complaining that too many teachers had forgotten to love their students as much as their fields of study, Elizabeth Sedgwick urges all educators (whether they worked at home or in schools, whether they were male or female) to affirm the maternal teaching model (79, 88, 91).

To extend this concept of the maternal, nurturing teacher beyond home and domesticated schoolrooms into more overtly political realms required another step in the domestic literacy narrative's development. Harriet Beecher Stowe's literary pedagogy carried the form to its fullest antebellum potential in *Uncle Tom's Cabin*. But this creative assertion of motherly teaching for the nation around the most volatile issue of the era—slavery—was made possible in large part by arguments more conservative practitioners of the genre had adapted to feminize schoolteaching and to celebrate education of children at home. Stowe herself, in fact, had worked enthusiastically as a schoolteacher and home-based educator long before composing her most politicized domestic literacy narrative. Recovering ways her integration of such feminized teaching agendas prepared her for authoring *Uncle Tom's Cabin* can help reposition her career within the cultural context of her own day, while illustrating, again, the flexible nature of the domestic literacy narrative genre. These are the subjects I will next address.

[4]

Uncle Tom's Cabin as a Domestic Literacy Narrative

I expect to . . . teach you what, perhaps, it will take you some time to learn, —how to use the rights I give you as freemen and women. I expect you to be good, and willing to learn; and I trust in God that I shall be faithful, and willing to teach.

George Shelby in Harriet Beecher Stowe's *Uncle Tom's Cabin*

Uncle Tom's Cabin, the publishing sensation of the mid–nineteenth century, acquires enhanced meaning for twenty-first-century readers when situated within a cultural history of the domestic literacy narrative.[1] That interpretive process can begin with a look at two seldom-read texts by Harriet Beecher Stowe, from just before and soon after her major antislavery book's vast circulation began—a letter to Sarah Josepha Hale and a guidebook for readers of the novel. When we set the writing of *Uncle Tom's Cabin* in this framework, we can outline tracings of Stowe's 1850s sense of her authorship as motherly teaching, managing her readers' literacy for the national welfare. We can also appreciate how the domestic literacy narrative genre provided a perfect vehicle for the argument of her best-selling publication. In other words, we can write a new history of the nineteenth

116

century's most famous book as a gendered, didactic participant in the evolving print culture of its own day.

First, Stowe's letter to Hale. In November 1851, when she was writing *Uncle Tom's Cabin* for initial circulation as a serial in the *National Era,* Stowe had already worked as a seminary and school teacher in Hartford and Cincinnati, as a home-based educator of her own children, as an author of didactic sketches, and as an instructor of escaped slaves' and free blacks' children.[2] Having experienced these numerous variations on the role of middle-class motherly teacher, Stowe nonetheless claimed to be surprised that she would be tapped for inclusion in Sarah Josepha Hale's then-projected compendium on important American women. When answering Hale's request for biographical information, Stowe replied:

> Dear Madam,
>
> I was quite amused I must say at your letter to me[,] wholly innocent as I am of any pretensions to rank among "distinguished women" —However I read it to my tribe of little folks assembled around the evening [center?] table to let them know what an unexpected honour had befallen their mamma. . . . But in sober sadness, —having reflected duly & truly on my past life, it is so thoroughly uneventful & uninteresting that I do not see how any thing can be done for me in the way of a sketch. My sister Catharine has lived much more of a life—& done more that can be told of than I whose course & employment have always been retired and domestic—
>
> The most I can think of is that I was born in Litchfield, Conn—was a teacher from my fifteenth year till my marriage[,] that I have been mother to seven children—six of whom are now living—& that the greater portion of my time and strength has been spent in the necessary but un-poetic duties of the family. —These details you can throw into two or three lines—as great a space as I should have any claim to occupy in such a company.[3]

Stowe's response to Hale's query reflects the now-famous author's sense of herself before the fame of *Uncle Tom's Cabin* changed her public identity and, at the same time, contributed to a shift in American society's view of women authors. A reading of the letter against the background of Stowe's life experience up to that time—and thus within the context of expectations for white, genteel women's social roles as motherly teachers—highlights rhetorical strategies from which she was drawing in her writing. Noting what Stowe said (and did not say) about herself here sets the stage for interpreting narrative-writing choices she was making for *Uncle Tom's Cabin.*

Opening her letter to Hale by describing herself as "wholly innocent . . .

of any pretensions to rank among 'distinguished women,'" Stowe characterizes herself as surprised by the proposal that she be included in the anthology. To justify her hesitancy about the honor, Stowe describes herself in
language that—considering her audience—conveys a proper level of feminine
modesty while also characterizing her day-to-day labor in terms Hale would
surely have admired. Accordingly, Stowe deems Hale's selecting her as "un-
expected" yet admits that she assembled all her children to announce the
"honour [that] had befallen their mamma," thereby depicting herself as carrying out just the kind of cultural work Hale had long claimed to value
most. Indeed, Stowe describes herself as providing home instruction to a
"tribe of little folks assembled around the evening . . . table," where she
read the letter that cast her motherhood in a public sphere. Significantly,
she suggests that, while her own experiences had been too "thoroughly un-
eventful & uninteresting" to merit a biographical piece, her sister Catharine had "lived much more of a life" and therefore would be a better subject.
She contrasts her own "retired and domestic" "course & employment" with
Catharine's. Hence, although by 1851 she had already published a number
of magazine stories and an anthology of sketches, Stowe implies that her
own hierarchizing of "distinguished" feminine work would place education
and writing about education above other literary endeavors.

Along those lines, she shifts in her second paragraph to presenting the
details of her life against an educational backdrop that would have been
highly positive to Hale. Stowe points out that she had been "a teacher from
[her] fifteenth year till [her] marriage." This detail sets her personal history in a pattern that would have resonated with middle-class women leaders like Hale, advocates of giving females opportunities for advanced learning and of making schoolteaching women's work. In other words, this
sequence progressing from youthful teacher to mother places Stowe's life
in a popular middle-class women's life script (see chapters 2 and 3). Even
though Stowe humbly declares that "the greater portion of [her] time and
strength [had] been spent in the necessary but unpoetic duties of the family," she could have counted on Hale to resist the avowal that mothering six
children hardly deserved "two or three lines" in the proposed collection.
Through Stowe's self-representation in this letter, we can see both her conscious membership in a mother-teacher class and her strategic use of defer-
ential rhetoric affiliated with that role.

If the letter to Hale suggests how Stowe was conceptualizing her own
authorship during the composition process for her most famous novel, the
text she marshaled later to explicate her blockbuster to readers of her own

day offers an even fuller testimony of how strongly she equated her writing with teaching. Explaining her rationale for preparing the *Key to Uncle Tom's Cabin,* in fact, Stowe distinguishes her didactic goals for the novel from aesthetic ones, while stressing its grounding in real life: "Artistically considered, it might not be best to point out in which quarry and from which region each fragment of the mosaic picture [in the narrative] had its original; and it is equally un-artistic to disentangle the glittering web of fiction, and show out of what real warp and woof it is woven, and with what real coloring dyed. But the book had a purpose entirely transcending the artistic one, and accordingly encounters, at the hands of the public, demands not usually made on fictitious works."[4]

Here and throughout the *Key,* Stowe positions her authorial self in the role of motherly teacher, though in this case addressing a larger public audience of learners than in her self-portrait for the Hale letter. She explains aspects of *Uncle Tom's Cabin* that some readers had failed to understand, including her educational goals and strategies, as well as her methods of research. For instance, she cites conversations with escaped slaves and writing by authors like Frederick Douglass to show that her accounts of slavery's cruelty are trustworthy—even understated (19, 66). Overall, the *Key* offers a morality-oriented interpretive framework for readers, guiding them through the novel with structured directions like those provided by motherly teachers in domestic literacy narratives when leading discussion of print texts. Taken together, the *Key* and the letter to Hale locate Stowe's authorship in a tradition of didactic writing. To reread *Uncle Tom's Cabin* within that tradition underscores how her novel represents a high point in the domestic literacy narrative's development, particularly through its moves to claim influence for white, middle-class women in American political life.

Such a reading requires separating Stowe as historically situated rhetor from the many various "Stowes" constructed in twentieth-century criticism. Stowe stands in today as a cultural marker for diverse, sometimes contradictory understandings of such wide-ranging topics as American women writers' literary value, white antislavery activism's impact on American culture, and sentimentalism in antebellum literature. Rich as associated literary interpretations of her novel have been, their very cumulative force has often obscured dimensions of her authorship that would have been far more recognizable (and appealing) to readers of her era than to critics in our own. Hence, this chapter seeks to retrieve a sense of the 1850s Stowe as a motherly teacher and *Uncle Tom's Cabin* as a domestic literacy narrative by combining literacy-oriented biography with genre-based discourse analysis.

"Stowe" as Author-Function, Stowe as Rhetor

My rereading of *Uncle Tom's Cabin* draws on a collection of Beecher family records of shared literacy experiences that would have facilitated Stowe's 1850s deployment of the domestic literacy genre. I place that archive in dialogue with *Uncle Tom's Cabin* itself and with the *Key*. Taken together, these three components form a map of relationships connecting Stowe's family and community literacy practices with her writing process, especially her invitations to readers to see her work within the context of Protestant maternal literacy management. This intertextual reading assumes that authors make historicizable discursive choices based on anticipated audience response but also on genre-related tools that are accessible through their past experiences as readers and writers. Though such a biographical-cum-rhetorical analysis might have limited validity for interpreting texts by writers working in a formalist tradition, its use in Stowe's case is productive for a number of reasons, including the mid–nineteenth century's assumptions about ties between women writers' personalities and their publications, as well as the era's penchant for didactic literature.

At first glance, the interpretation of Stowe's work that I am offering here may seem at odds with current views on authorship, particularly theories emphasizing the social construction of textual meaning and the so-called death of the author. But actually this recovery of *Uncle Tom's Cabin*'s composition history depends on postmodern concepts of writing and reading outlined by Roland Barthes in "The Death of the Author" and Michel Foucault in "What Is an Author?"[5]

First of all, in indicating ways that some twentieth-century interpreters have positioned *Uncle Tom's Cabin* within critical frameworks dominated by literary value systems different from those in Stowe's own day, I am echoing Barthes's contention that "a text is made of multiple writings, drawn from many cultures and entering into mutual relations of dialogue, parody, contestation" (171). Consistent with Barthes's emphasis on readers as meaning makers who can supercede authors, my review of various critical readings of *Uncle Tom's Cabin* will affirm his point that the "text is not a line of words releasing a single 'theological' meaning (the 'message' of the Author-God) but a multi-dimensional space in which a variety of writings, none of them original, blend and clash" (170). Similarly, my reading of the novel as a domestic literacy narrative that affiliates with multiple genres (such as antislavery writing) clarifies its elicitation of widely divergent responses, even in the 1850s. Located in "a multi-dimensional space" where numerous genres ("none of them original") come together, *Uncle Tom's Cabin,* from the beginning, has enabled multiple, often "clash[ing]" audience reactions.

To supplement twentieth-century critics' responses to *Uncle Tom's Cabin,* I want to showcase Stowe's own historicizable, sophisticated use of the domestic literacy narrative, blended with other genres such as the antislavery narrative, to the extent that it can be recovered by situating the text in relation to family and class-connected literacy practices. In filtering my analysis of the novel through the lens of the Beecher family's voluminous records of their own literacy development and distribution, I am building on Foucault's notion of the "author-function" to retrace some steps in the social construction of "Stowe" as an "author." Foucault argues that "these aspects of an individual which we designate as making him [or her] an author are only a projection, in more or less psychologizing terms, of the operations that we force texts to undergo, the connections that we make, the traits that we establish as pertinent, the continuities that we recognize, or the exclusions that we practice," and that "all these operations vary according to periods and types of discourse" (203). That is, my reading of *Uncle Tom's Cabin* within the context of other didactic writing by Stowe and her contemporaries facilitates recovery of one rhetorical aspect of her authorship that has been obscured by readings of "Stowe" led by values ("connections," "traits," and "continuities," as well as "exclusions") from other periods. Rather than considering such readings inaccurate, however, I would suggest that they have addressed different dimensions of *Uncle Tom's Cabin*'s "writing," as constituted by readers operating from diverse vantage points in time and social context.

This view of Stowe (or, more particularly, of variously constructed "Stowes") as containing a "plurality of self" through authorship also accommodates elements in the novel that often seem at odds—for example, abolitionist sympathy versus racist stereotyping—as well as readings of the narrative that have emphasized one or the other side of such contradictions. Stowe was, in Foucault's terms, "the author of much more than a book." "Stowe" as author-function has generated "theory, tradition," and practices (of sentimentalism, for instance; of divergent readings of the character "Uncle Tom"). "Stowe" has also generated "other books" (literally, like *Aunt Phillis' Cabin* and *Uncle Tom's Children,* but also figuratively) whose own "transdiscursive" qualities have been bound up with the staying power of the novel's multiple genre affiliations and of varying social constructions of "Stowe-as-author" herself.[6] As a supplement to such versions of "Stowe" (which have been culturally adaptable for different readers), I am arguing that one dimension of her hybrid text was guided by past teaching experiences and a wish to teach readers. To do so, I am drawing on a conception of her authorship as both rhetorically self-conscious and ideologically shaped—with both of these aspects of her writing influenced by a historical context that emphasized maternal literacy management.

As a member of the highly influential Beecher clan, Harriet Beecher Stowe was raised to cultivate an acute self-awareness of her potential as an educative agent for the national community. Consistent with the nature of class relations in antebellum America, the Beechers' writings to and about each other constantly depict ways in which their literacy garnered and distributed shared social power. For instance, anecdotes in letters and speeches frequently reference the family's New England heritage and its positive effects on the West (such as when they migrated to Cincinnati and participated in community building through seminary teaching and parlor literacy practices). Family texts also celebrate the Beechers' influence as religious role models through preaching and writing and the national impact of their educational work (especially Catharine's, father Lyman's, and Stowe's brothers'). The Beecher family's sense of their literacy practices as tools for nationwide influence was so strong, in fact, that they were accustomed to save copious written records of their own personal interactions, along with specific examples of how they used literacy for America's welfare.

As outlined earlier, historians Louise L. Stevenson, Steven Mintz, and Stow Persons have shown that the Beechers were certainly not unique in the antebellum era for having a clear feeling of Americanized noblesse oblige. All three describe a nineteenth-century social class that self-consciously assumed the responsibility for molding Americans' national identity and, more specifically, for ensuring that the systems of thought and behavior this social group most valued were distributed (but also regulated) throughout the population. Stevenson suggests that typical members of this civic-minded class were physicians, journalists, business leaders, and college professors committed to providing moral as well as intellectual education for the population. (The work of both Stowe's husband and her father as theology professors is relevant in this regard, as is the seminary teaching of Catharine and Harriet.) Mintz notes the group's close ties with the ministry, especially through American and British religious leaders affiliated with the Dissenting tradition and Scottish moral philosophy. The personal connections between British Dissenters and American Unitarians and Congregationalists were clearly significant in supporting their collective, trans-Atlantic mission of social guidance. For Stowe in particular, and with special reference to the early domestic literacy narrative's circulation, Anna Laetitia Barbauld's Dissenting heritage was bound to the Beecher clan through such connections as the Beechers' reading of books by Barbauld-trained teachers and students and their personal contacts with Harriet Martineau.[7]

Person-to-person connections aside, Mintz identifies common traits in the writing produced by this class on both sides of the Atlantic and calls attention to their shared belief in the efficacy of written language as a vehicle for community reform.[8] In particular, a groupwide commitment to educational writing's efficacy helped ensure that ideas about American authorship among members of this class would be inextricably joined with their aim to be prominent national leaders. As a member of this self-identifying group, Stowe, long before her writing of *Uncle Tom's Cabin,* had already internalized the social values and class-inflected educational mission that Mintz, Persons, and Stevenson describe.

Up to now, studies of Stowe's life have understandably emphasized her position as a prominent writer more than her role as a teacher (or even as a teacher-writer).[9] Knowing how prolific and renowned she was in the years after *Uncle Tom's Cabin,* and recognizing how many literary agendas she addressed, makes it difficult to see Stowe as anything but a highly successful author, in command of the literary marketplace. That is, the strength of Stowe's post-1850s social identity (or, in Foucault's terms, her author-function) has often precluded our ability to retrieve a sense of her working, on individual texts earlier in her career, as a rhetor with deeply engrained educational goals and argumentative methods, transcending (by today's standards) high-art literary aims. Indeed, as producer of numerous books, editor of various anthologies and magazine publications, and a well-known literary celebrity traveling abroad, Stowe herself cultivated the identity of professional writer in the decades after her blockbuster appeared.[10] Reexamining the formation of her social role up until the time of *Uncle Tom's Cabin,* however, allows another salient picture to emerge. Before her first novel burst onto the publishing scene, Stowe apparently saw herself more as an educator than as a literary luminary, partly because, in the early 1850s, American authorship itself had not firmly coalesced around ideas of professionalism but also because the social roles she had been fulfilling were more in line with "woman as motherly teacher" than "woman as literary figure."

One reason we have had difficulty retrieving Stowe's pre–*Uncle Tom's Cabin* professional identity is that, in our time, the preeminence of writing over teaching obscures our understanding of past eras' different valuations of educational work. Certainly, Stowe is not the only well-known American woman whose teaching career has faded into the background behind studies of her literary labors. And even when we do retrieve women writers' teaching experiences biographically, we still tend to deemphasize recovery of their didactic writing, favoring texts that fit our current views of literary merit.

In that context, like the emphasis in previous biographical studies of Stowe, critical readings of *Uncle Tom's Cabin* have sometimes been more consistent with twentieth-century views on literature than with those of the 1850s. American literature at that point was frequently a more unabashedly didactic enterprise than the aesthetics-oriented one it would become in the twentieth century.[11] Yet what most interpretations of *Uncle Tom's Cabin* have in common, besides their tendency to defend or attack the novel, is that each reading (including this one) tends to come out of its own literary-critical perspective and so may say as much about shifting values in scholarship in later periods as about the novel in its own time. Thus, dismissive New Critical readings have given way to enthusiastic reader-response or feminist readings. In particular, because they are often writing against guardians of the "traditional" canon of the American Renaissance, some defenders of Stowe's text continue to fight on a battleground of aesthetic "literary merit" as defined by competing paradigms.[12]

However, several others have charted a historically sensitive direction for reading Stowe's novel through its connections to antebellum ideologies of domesticity, religion, and education.[13] Such interpretations usefully situate *Uncle Tom's Cabin* within gendered, middle-class social life in nineteenth-century American culture. Nonetheless, some have occasionally promoted reductive conceptions of Stowe's family life and therefore of her conception and practice of a writing career. In that vein, studies depicting Stowe's literary domesticity as obsessively, tear-inducingly sentimental in its techniques, or assertively protofeminist in its themes, deemphasize the didactic strand in her work. Such readings minimize the intellectual dimensions of middle-class domestic motherhood during Stowe's day—particularly management of family and community literacy as shaping her writing.

Meanwhile, although a few steps have been taken to recover Stowe's career as a teacher before her marriage, a tendency to pigeonhole Catharine as the educator and Harriet as the literary lady minimizes overlaps in their professional and family roles, which were sometimes quite competitive.[14] So, for example, repetition of anecdotes about Catharine supportively doing the household chores so that Harriet could write a novel reifies their relationship into a model of sisterly support for divergent career paths. Yet Catharine's regular moves to limit Harriet's access to the teaching profession may have played an equally compelling part in encouraging the younger sister to write fiction. This pressure merits increased attention, especially since Stowe seems to have enjoyed the lively, intellectual interaction of the schoolroom far more than her older sister, who preferred being a rather detached administrator.[15] At the same time, depictions of Stowe as a frustrated would-be minister denied access to the pulpit because of her gender aptly acknowledge her (and her family's) firm recognition of the restrictions gender placed on women's work in the nineteenth century yet run the risk of oversimplifying her relationship with her father and brothers in a negative direction. In fact, both Harriet's father, Lyman, and her brother Henry Ward were especially supportive of her literary career, even though their ministerial celebrity probably did convey continual reminders of the gendered limits of her life choices.[16] Restraining and encouraging, the extended Beecher family played a complex role in guiding Stowe's authorial self-fashioning, primarily through the rich literacy practices Harriet developed with them and their larger social circle, then mined for her writing in the 1830s, 1840s, and beyond.[17]

Foregrounding the author's educational career to reread *Uncle Tom's Cabin* as a domestic literacy narrative can also create a mediating space between Ann Douglas's critique and Jane Tompkins's defense of the novel. Whereas Douglas's seminal treatment suggests that the "feminization" of culture like that represented by *Uncle Tom's Cabin* robbed New England–dominated American intellectual life of its vigor, I interpret Stowe's literary adaptation of moral suasion as a coherent intellectual stance associated with the feminization of the American teacher corps and the continuing social construction of the domestic middle-class mother-teacher.[18] And while Tompkins, as a necessary adjustment to readings like Douglas's, highlights the sentimental power of the novel, I think we are now ready to complicate further such familiar scenes as Eva reading the Bible to Tom by connecting them with the complex and often patronizing tradition of "benevolent" literacy instruction.[19] Overall, then, I am shifting the interpretation of *Uncle Tom's Cabin* from twentieth-century literary to nineteenth-century literacy concerns to emphasize how the novel presents domesticated Christian literacy as an education program to heal the American union.

Such an interpretation requires us to interweave texts from Beecher family literacy practices with important scenes from *Uncle Tom's Cabin.* While echoing Stowe's personal literacy experiences, these scenes also draw upon the heritage of the domestic literacy narrative. Analyzing such texts together foregrounds cultural forces that supported Stowe's assumption of a mother-teacher role over the years before the novel's initial publication in the *National Era.* To enact that role through her writing of *Uncle Tom's Cabin,* Stowe called upon a cluster of educational and literary themes that, by 1850, would have been easy for readers familiar with the domestic literacy narrative to recognize: domesticated literacy as an avenue to social power, enlightened feminine moral suasion as a beneficial teaching method, and the well-taught child as an inspiring teacher for society.

Domesticated Literacy and (Limited) Social Power

Records chronicling Stowe's acquisition of Beecher family literacy suggest that one factor shaping her development of the title character of *Uncle Tom's Cabin* was her own experience acquiring a highly capable yet simultaneously limited brand of literacy. One major source of this interpretation is the biography prepared by her son Charles, who depicted Stowe's literacy acquisition as closely connected to Beecher traditions of social action.

"Harriet is a genius," Lyman Beecher is supposed to have observed about his eight-year-old daughter. "I would give a hundred dollars if she was a boy."

Writing in the mid-1980s, what critic Thomas F. Gossett found most impressive about this family anecdote was the reported willingness of Harriet's father to pay one hundred dollars to change her gender—in a year when the New England minister typically made only eight hundred dollars, total.[20] For Harriet Beecher Stowe's son Charles, however, writing about his mother in the early twentieth century, this story was most meaningfully viewed as part of an extended account of her literacy acquisition, which Charles presented as simultaneously enabling and constraining.[21]

Certainly Harriet Beecher Stowe had conveyed to her son an appreciation of domestic literacy's ability to shape youthful intellectual growth, for his biography is full of examples of home teaching scenes showing his mother learning about herself and her place in the American community by reading, writing, and sharing family conversations. Along those lines, one of his mother's earliest memories, Charles indicates, was of a long visit to her grandmother's house soon after her mother's death. In a vignette placing her memory squarely in the tradition of domestic literacy narratives, he quotes his mother: "I can now remember . . . being brought into a large parlor where a cheerful wood-fire was crackling. . . . I was placed in the arms of an old lady, who held me close. . . . There was a little tea-table set out before the fire, and Uncle George came in from his farm-work, and sat down with grandma, and Aunt Harriet to tea. After supper I remember grandmother reading prayers, as was her custom, from a great prayer-book, which was her constant companion" (18–19). Though only five when her mother died in 1816, Stowe later told Charles that her "earliest recollections" were of maternally managed gardening and reading. In particular, she described her mother's "reading to the children, one evening, Miss Edgeworth's 'Frank,' which had just come out, . . . [and which] was exciting a great deal of interest in the educational circles of Litchfield" (3).[22] Mrs. Lyman Beecher, like many other American middle-class mothers, and like her own daughter Harriet years later, operated a small home-based school for the neighborhood, where she offered her own version of the nurturing teaching style Harriet also attributed to her maternal grandmother. As Stowe's son's biography shows, even at a young age, Harriet was learning the middle-class social role of mother-teacher through her own home-based schooling.[23]

Nonetheless, her literacy-oriented learning also transmitted the gender distinctions that would limit her future choices for meaningful cultural work. Young Harriet impressed those around her with the strength and acuity of a masculine-seeming mind. Her father and others praised her energy for all kinds of labor and, in particular, her eagerness to learn from the wide array of books in their home. Yet Harriet quickly realized that her gender was restricting her social interactions. Thus, her son writes that she would sometimes "throw aside her book or her needle and thread" to dress in "a little black coat which she thought made her look more like a boy," so as to join the others in tasks like chopping wood and the theological debates Lyman led to incorporate his sons' mental training with physical labor (9).

Though included in such conversations, Harriet was excluded from fishing trips and other occasions because she was a girl. She sought solace, then, in reading, since her father did allow her full use of his library, even while denying her access to more overtly boyish activities. In fact, notes Charles, "her father's study," was "one of Harriet's favorite haunts. . . . Its walls were set round from floor to ceiling with the quiet friendly faces of books, and there stood her father's study chair and his writing-table, on which always lay open before him his Cruden's Concordance and the Bible. Here Harriet loved to retreat and curl herself up in a quiet corner with her favorite books around her. Here she had a restful, sheltered feeling as she thus sat and watched her father at his sermon-writing, turning his books and speaking to himself from time to time in a loud and earnest whisper" (11). According to Charles, his mother met several of her lifelong favorite books "grouped along in sociable rows" on the shelves of her father's study, "where she first discovered texts that would become such friendly, oft-repeated readings as to be memorized." Besides *Pilgrim's Progress,* she especially loved Cotton Mather's *Magnalia* stories of the Pilgrim Fathers, which "filled her soul with a great eagerness to go forth and do some great and valiant deed for her God and her country" (12–13). Given her exclusion from so many of her brothers' games, Harriet was understandably careful to protect her access to the paternal library. Her recollections of reading there stress how she kept quiet so as not to disturb her father and how she treasured many of his books as if they were stolen gems.[24] (Years later, she would use a similar portrait of learning to read as acquiring a treasure in her portrayal of Uncle Tom's seeking solace through Bible study.) Meanwhile, watching Lyman Beecher at work on his sermons, she was already learning that, for her social class and especially for community leaders like her father, literacy was closely tied to professional labor and social influence.

All these experiences with literacy acquisition were entirely consistent with the evolving American ideology of domestic literacy management. Meanwhile, in a family constantly setting high goals for its young males, Harriet became increasingly aware that some ways of using literacy (such as preparing and delivering sermons) would be forever closed to her by virtue of her gender. This realization helped prepare her to believe that the options for literacy-associated uplift among America's blacks would also "naturally" be limited—in that case because of race rather than gender restrictions. Specifically, Charles Stowe's biography suggests that Harriet Beecher's own early experiences of literacy as both enabling and constraining could have encouraged similar conceptions of Uncle Tom's literacy later.

Despite its association today with stereotypes of unmanly acquiescence to suffering, some critics have noted that Stowe's characterization of Uncle Tom can be read as an idealization of Christian ministry enacted through feminized self-sacrifice.[25] This positive view of Tom's character is certainly in accord with seeing the novel as a domestic literacy narrative. Calling up the stories of Stowe's own early literacy development, we can trace a narrative line through *Uncle Tom's Cabin* that depicts Tom's gradual acquisition of literacy as preparing him for a saintly (if feminized and restricted) heroism. Like the children in so many of New England's antebellum domestic literacy narratives, Tom internalizes important ethical lessons while learning to read. Also like those earlier child-students, he acquires a brand of literacy that enforces conservative values even as it facilitates his own intellectual and moral growth. And like the motherly educators in stories by authors such as Lydia Sigourney, Lydia Maria Child, and Catharine Maria Sedgwick, Tom uses his own literacy to teach others, thereby serving as a Christian role model. Limited as this model is by today's standards, in Stowe's era, among white, middle-class women readers accustomed to domestic literacy narratives and to constraints on their own social action, this characterization could have been viewed in highly positive terms.

Stowe lays out a literacy-based narrative trajectory for her hero's growth from the earliest chapters of the novel. Significantly, the first time her readers see Uncle Tom, he is in the cabin of the novel's title, seated with George Shelby at a table "in front of the fire," in the midst of a reading and writing lesson.[26] A polished array of dishes, as well as a carefully laid cloth, predict "an approaching meal," but Tom seems oblivious to such familiar sights, sounds, and smells of domesticity all around him as Aunt Chloe's cooking or his older children's helping the baby's early steps. His attention is focused, instead, "on a slate lying before him." There, "he was carefully and slowly endeavoring to accomplish a copy of some letters," "overlooked by young Mas'r George, a smart, bright boy of thirteen, who appeared fully to realize the dignity of his position as instructor" (68). Although some critics have pointed to Tom's tentative use of written language here as a sign of inferiority, readers familiar with the sequential learning patterns of domestic literacy narratives going back to Anna Laetitia Barbauld's *Lessons* series would have recognized the scene's echoing of first-step learning in those foundational texts of the genre. Indeed, for those readers (who probably had taught domestic reading lessons themselves), as for informed primary school teachers today, Tom's "laboriously" practicing his *g*'s and *q*'s would have marked him as beginning to construct connections between written and spoken language, that is, as passing through an expected developmental stage in literacy acquisition.

This sense of the impact and "level" of Tom's literacy is clearly quite different from that espoused by some other readers of the novel. Hortense Spillers, for example, uses the same lesson scene I've described here as a way of characterizing Uncle Tom as "Stowe's dyslexic man" because he confuses his *g* and *q*.[27] However, just as Barbauld's "little Charles" and his literary descendents passed through progressive steps of learning letters and words to finding an active role in society, Tom's emergent literacy carries an implied promise of future personal development. Central to that promise, of course, is the relationship between Tom and his nurturing yet controlling teacher, George Shelby, in many ways the true hero of the scene. Stowe's pegging George's age at thirteen is significant in this regard. Just beginning adolescence, George is old enough to take his mother's lessons beyond their own fireside, but he has not yet acquired the full social power of adult white manhood. (Indeed, when Mr. Shelby sells Tom, George cannot prevent the transaction, but his tearful goodbye to Tom suggests that his mother's influence will make him a different man than his father in the future.)

This fireside teaching is clearly not the first literacy management session for George and Tom. Aunt Chloe, "pausing while she was greasing a griddle with a scrap of bacon," observes "young Master George with pride" and compliments him on the "way he can write, now! and read, too! and then to come out here evenings and read his lessons to us, —it's mighty interestin'!" (69). Chloe's description of George's work would have carried heightened meaning for Stowe's contemporaries. "To come out here [in the] evenings and read his lessons," her readers would have recognized, positions George as an idealized figure, in domestic literacy narratives' terms, extending his own learning by teaching others. Surrounded as George and Tom are by what, for Stowe's nineteenth-century middle-class audience, would have been traditional emblems of home-based literacy management (fireside, children, and chores in progress), George's careful instructions echo the domestic teaching practiced in antebellum home primers. Yet this lesson is more radical, because in this case white, middle-class literacy is extended into a slave cabin.

Juxtaposition of Stowe's opening scene with Lydia Sigourney's parallel treatment of would-be pedagogy in *The Faded Hope* is quite telling in this regard. As outlined earlier, Sigourney's text, a biography of her son, is based on her own family life in the antebellum North. Significantly, in that case, the narrator-mother judges her son Andrew's impulse to teach their African American servant more humorous than practical. In contrast, Stowe imagines a Southern plantation where the young master himself is teaching a slave, and, from this opening scene, she shows benefits accruing to Tom and his family through his literacy acquisition.

George's assumption of the domestic teaching role is, on one level, a logical extension of republican motherhood's mandate to educate the young male for enlightened sociopolitical leadership. Teaching the slave is, in moral terms, an indication that George Shelby has learned republican virtues well enough to apply them. Still, though this eager "Master" himself may be more aware of "the dignity of his position as instructor" than the subversive quality of his actions, a white, American, middle-class reader of the 1850s would have recognized the revolutionary nature of Stowe's re-designed domestic teaching occasion. After all, in most Southern states in the 1850s, teaching a black man to read and write was a crime.[28] So Stowe's cross-race teaching scene is, at the least, more radical than many so-called benevolent literacy narratives' treatment of cross-class teaching.

Barbara Finkelstein notes that, for Southern slaves, even the desire to read and write was "vigorously and forcefully punished, especially after 1835, when the last of the prohibitions on literacy were made into law. . . . Being sold away for reading and writing apparently was not regarded as an idle gesture," so that slave "narratives are suffused with the fear of literacy detection."[29] In that vein, Stowe in her *Key* quotes Frederick Douglass's memory of his owner's anger over the master's naive young bride teaching Douglass to read.[30] "Learning," the master fumes, "will *spoil* the best Nigger in the world. Now . . . if you teach that nigger [Douglass] how to read, there would be no keeping him. It would forever unfit him to be a slave. He would at once become unmanageable, and of no value to his master. As to himself, it could do him no good. . . . It would make him discontented and unhappy" (17). So too, Josiah Henson, whom Stowe identifies in the *Key* as one of the models for her Tom character, reported that, at thirteen, he "nearly lost [his] life because [he] made an effort to gain this kind of knowl-edge." Beaten severely by his master for being caught with a speller, Hen-son had his book and his courage taken away: he told of not trying to read again until he was over forty.[31] Small wonder, then, that slave literacy was so often portrayed as a secret, stolen treasure. In contrast, Stowe's intro-ducing her hero during a reading and writing lesson given in a plantation-owned cabin by the master's own son underscores immediately both an en-nobling element in Tom's character and the novel's radical border blurring between private and public, domestic and political, feminine and masculine, literacy and literary power.

Scattered throughout *A Key to Uncle Tom's Cabin*, in fact, are interpretations of why slave literacy was fearful for masters to contemplate, necessary for them to suppress—and, not incidentally, appealing to Stowe as a crucial theme for her novel. Having been accused of exaggeration in the novel's depiction of slave life, she admits in the follow-up *Key* that some masters were "kindly" enough to treat their slaves well, perhaps even to set them free. A complementary decision, according to Stowe, could involve a caring master's wish to "teach the slave to read and write" and to "build school-houses for his children" (110). Nevertheless, she argues throughout her defense of the novel, the reality of some masters' individual humanitarian impulses (which are represented in *Uncle Tom's Cabin*, after all, by characters like Augustine St. Clare) could not overcome the larger reality of cruelty. On the contrary, Stowe insists in the *Key*, however much a "generous man" might wish to "raise up" slaves by providing them with such benefits as "the power of reading the written Word," cultural practices protecting the institution of slavery could easily undermine his efforts (110). For example, whatever good intentions St. Clare may have had to free Tom, the legal system made the man into disposable property for Marie after her husband's death.

Overall, Stowe theorizes in the *Key*, statutes forbidding the schooling of slaves were consistent, from the proslavery point of view, with a wish to maintain the status quo: "It has been foreseen that the result of education would be general intelligence; that the result of intelligence would be a knowledge of personal rights; and that an inquiry into the doctrine of personal rights would be fatal to the system. It has been foreseen, also, that the example of disinterestedness and generosity, in emancipation, might carry with it a generous contagion, until it should become universal; that the example of educated and emancipated slaves would prove a dangerous excitement of those still in bondage" (110–11). A black man, either educated or emancipated, could be "contagio[us]"—leading others to agitate for "personal rights"; a black man who somehow became both literate and free would be truly "dangerous," however childlike he might appear to be (110).

Given the announced role of the *Key* as explicator of *Uncle Tom's Cabin*, this passage contrasting the victimized, illiterate slave with the empowered, literate free man presents the novel's narrative in capsule form. Like Frederick Douglass, from Stowe's perspective, Tom is transformed through literacy acquisition. By giving him access to the Bible, the reading skills he learns eventually also gain him spiritual freedom and enable him to teach, uplifting the lives of others.[32] Thus, only during a brief period when Legree's abuse temporarily leaves him "in utter exhaustion" and unable "to commune with anybody" by sharing stories and songs does Tom find "that the religious peace and trust, which had upborne him hitherto, . . . [gave] way to tossings of soul and despondent darkness" (552–53). Stowe's emphasis on Tom's having "very little communion" with Cassy and Emmeline during this time of despair is significant, since it affirms her depiction throughout the novel of his literacy as social—as being most empowering when shared. In fact, even the Bible, when read alone, could prove an insufficient source of strength. (See figure 6.) When Tom, while isolated on Legree's plantation, tries to recover the supportive experience of his hearthside study with George Shelby and his subsequent Bible study with little Eva, the missing elements of community leave him stymied:

> One evening, he was sitting, in utter dejection and prostration, by a few decaying brands, where his coarse supper was baking. He put a few bits of brushwood on the fire, and strove to raise the light, and then drew his worn Bible from his pocket. There were all the marked passages, which had thrilled his soul so often, —words of patriarchs and seers, poets and sages, who from early time had spoken courage to man, —voices from the great cloud of witnesses who ever surround us in the race of life. Had the word lost its power, or could the failing eye and weary sense no longer answer to the touch of that mighty inspiration? Heavily sighing, he put it in his pocket. A coarse laugh roused him; he looked up, —Legree was standing opposite him. (553)

But Legree, despite this momentary triumph, does not win the final battle over Tom. Soon, revitalized by Bible phrases recalled from earlier social exchanges, Tom takes on the Christlike role of religious teacher to the other slaves, sharing with them the Bible stories he had tried unsuccessfully before to read in solitude and leading the singing of Methodist hymns that further infuriate Legree but strengthen the slaves (557–59). For Stowe, such literacy, carried out in a Christian community, would have been truly empowering.[33] That Stowe herself had such a paradigm in mind for Uncle Tom is clear in her discussion of his characterization in the *Key*. Allying her literary figure with a slave from Baltimore who was repeatedly punished for reading the Bible "with other servants," Stowe describes how this brave teacher continued his community-building literacy practices even after being sold south (23). Stowe also compares Tom with Josiah Henson, who, after escaping to Canada, "learned to read, and, by his superior talent and capacity for management, laid the foundation for the fugitive settlement of Dawn" (27).

This view of social literacy enabling community leadership is more consistent with ideals for nineteenth-century middle-class *motherhood,* however, than with more recent models for American manhood, whether black or white—hence the intense twentieth-century resistance to Uncle Tom, especially among many African American male readers, who understandably reject the feminized qualities associated with his brand of indirect influence through literacy management.[34] In contrast, white middle-class women readers of the 1850s would have been quite well prepared to see Tom as moving from acquiring his own Bible-oriented literacy to sharing that knowledge with others and, finally, managing the moral direction of his community.[35] His trajectory of increasing, if still inherently limited, social power would have mirrored their own idealized experiences as domestic literacy managers—patient teachers guiding others' behavior through discussion of print texts and shaping the larger community through others, despite their political disenfranchisement. Nineteenth-century white male readers, meanwhile, could affirm Tom's saintly moral guidance in much the same way that they accepted female influence in their own homes—without any danger to their own masculinity. In that sense, Tom's extended conversations with Augustine St. Clare mimic middle-class women's nonthreatening efforts to persuade their husbands toward morality—whether to sign a temperance pledge, to embrace Christian self-improvement, or to oppose slavery. (In this regard, we might note ways in which Tom's persuasive conversations with St. Clare echo the scene where the Ohio senator's wife calls on Bible-based literacy to enlist his help for Eliza.)

If we remember that Stowe wrote her major antislavery novel for middle-class whites and not, as has often been observed, for Uncle Tom, we can appreciate his characterization as one rhetorically sophisticated element in her adaptation of a flexible literary genre for her own first audience. Doing so should in no way blind us, of course, to the racism inherent in her willingness to consign Tom first to childlike and then feminized social status. However accessible these choices made his character for her original audience, they have left behind a troubling legacy, particularly for readers unfamiliar with the literary traditions she was using in her own time. Associating Tom with white children like George Shelby (and later little Eva) echoed the implied promise of future leadership embedded in so many other domestic literacy narratives' portrayals of learners in training. (That white women in the novel's anticipated readership tapped into just such a view is evidenced in Jacqueline Jones's reporting how, throughout the reports of early American Missionary Association [AMA] missionary teachers working in the South, the "image of the black man as a Christian

TOM READING HIS BIBLE.

Fig. 6. "Tom Reading His Bible," from *Uncle Tom's Cabin* (1852 London edition). This illustration is signed by G. Cruickshank,
who also illustrated many of Charles Dickens's texts.
The Library Company of Philadelphia.

child permeated" their language, even to the point of "striking resemblance to that projected in Harriet Beecher Stowe's *Uncle Tom's Cabin*, which many of them had apparently read.")[36] Similarly, Stowe's white women readers would have been able to identify with his indirect exercise of influence over Augustine St. Clare and the slave community at Legree's plantation through literacy-based learning from George and Eva. But basing Tom's claim to social agency in this highly gendered model also paved the way for future representations of his character (e.g., in plays, illustrations, and statuettes) as weak at best—particularly since the efficacious aspects of the feminized literacy manager role became less familiar to American readers over time, as domestic literacy narratives' discursive patterns and ideology faded from cultural memory.

Perhaps one way to help today's readers access *Uncle Tom's Cabin* in its own cultural context is to expand our focus beyond Tom to other characters marked by Stowe's adoption of the domestic literacy narrative. One of these is Mrs. Shelby, on stage for brief periods but ideologically significant, given the novel's generic heritage. Working indirectly through her son George, Mrs. Shelby can be seen as another of Tom's motherly teachers and, like Tom, a motherly teacher for the reader. Also like Tom, Mrs. Shelby is quite limited in her own access to social agency and must stake her best hope for a more moral society in the "rising generation" represented by George. As Stowe explains in her *Key*, although technically a member of the plantation class, Mrs. Shelby tries to resist its misplaced values. Stowe pointedly credits her commitment to morality-linked education, to the extent possible in a constrained situation. And just in case the novel's first audience had missed the sympathetic components of the character, Stowe describes Mrs. Shelby in the *Key* as

of the very best class of Southern women; and while the evils of the institution [of slavery] are felt and deplored, and while the world looks with just indignation on the national support and patronage which is given to it, and on the men who ... deliberately make efforts to perpetuate and extend it, it is but justice ... [to] bear in mind the virtues of such persons. Many of them, surrounded by circumstances over which they can have no control, perplexed by domestic cares of which women in free states can have very little conception, loaded down by duties and responsibilities which wear upon the very springs of life, still go on bravely and patiently from day to day, doing all they can to alleviate what they cannot prevent and, as far as the sphere of their own immediate power extends, rescuing those who are dependent upon them from the evils of the system. (12)

In limning Mrs. Shelby as typical of the best Southern mothers who are "doing all they can to alleviate what they cannot prevent," Stowe excuses them from some blame for slavery based on an argument underscoring cross-regional difference ("domestic cares of which women in free states can have very little conception"). Simultaneously, Stowe invites an affiliation through gender to override her readers' awareness of those very regional differences. This rhetoric of identification emphasizes traits in Mrs. Shelby that, consistent with the ideology of domestic literacy management, would be affirmed in Northern mother-teachers as well: she is one of the "good" Southern mothers who want "to teach [slaves] what is right" and who, whether or not they are able to set their "slaves at liberty," try to provide education more enlightened than most men of either region—North or South—seem willing to accord to black Americans (12). In Mrs. Shelby's case, credit is due not only for her own generous impulses (e.g., her ruse to help Eliza escape) but also for the more sustained role she has evidently played in training her son George for moral citizenship. Her teaching has prepared him to offer Tom the first steps to literacy and, later, to free the Shelby slaves. Linked to Stowe's praise for Mrs. Shelby in the *Key*, like her characterization in the novel, is a condemnation of the worst sinners behind slavery—white males of the South *and* North, the "men who, knowing [slavery's] nature," still "perpetuate and extend it," making it a "national" rather than merely a regional source of shame (12). Implicit though submerged within this critique, of course, is a question Stowe addresses later in the novel. If America's men—those fully empowered with the enfranchised citizen's rights—have failed to eradicate slavery, how are they to be won over to a more enlightened view? Said another way, what up-to-now inadequate lessons on civic virtue need to be reconfigured, and how can the motherly teachers of the American nation be reformed, themselves, to provide the needed instruction toward a nationwide moral healing?

Moral Suasion in Motherly Teaching: Remaking Ophelia

Stowe, like Frederick Douglass and other free black leaders, perceived literacy development as crucial to the uplift of slaves and former slaves, so both her novel and the *Key* repeatedly emphasize the necessity for all African Americans to have access to education. Similarly, as suggested above, she was highly invested in a core premise behind the ideology of maternal teaching—that middle-class women needed to teach middle-class children and men proper moral values. With both those goals in mind, while her depiction of Mrs. Shelby sought to have Northern women readers empathizing with their counterpart's constrained circumstances, Stowe's more pointed development of the Yankee schoolteacher character Miss Ophelia used a different affiliation strategy—one encouraging guilt among her Northern readers for what they had failed to do, along with a sense of commitment to future education of Southern blacks and white Northern political leaders.

Appearing in the section of the novel in which Tom resides with the kindly but weak Augustine St. Clare and his saintly daughter Eva, Ophelia might seem at first glance to be a healthy New England antidote to the flighty Marie St. Clare. In contrast with the serious Ophelia, Marie is clearly cast as a perverted version of American motherhood who abrogates her rightful home teaching role to concentrate instead on selfish materialism, like the infamous "women of fashion" in earlier domestic literacy narratives. Interestingly, though, Stowe sets up a more complex relationship between these two women than simple contrast. While Marie is purposefully overdrawn as a static character and villainess, the spinster Ophelia begins as a caricature of a Yankee schoolmarm and progresses to a deeper awareness of herself as motherly teacher and of Northern society as responsible for national education, especially of black Americans. Ultimately, Ophelia transforms herself into a role model consistent with the antebellum ideology of motherly teaching, which had already been extended to include unmarried middle-class women (see chapter 3).

Although Stowe's focus on educational methods in the Ophelia and Topsy episode has received insightful attention, the heightened force this narrative strand would have carried for nineteenth-century readers of the domestic literacy genre has not been fully articulated.[37] To underscore the likely appeal of genre-based elements in this episode for readers in the 1850s, I will turn first to records of Beecher family literacy in action. Specifically, in divergent attitudes toward teaching expressed over the years by Harriet and her elder sister Catharine, we can trace the possible ingredients for an initial satirical skewering of Catharine in the *Uncle Tom's Cabin* figure of Ophelia, followed by a celebration of the character's eventual adoption of moral suasion. Indeed, Stowe's own teaching under Catharine's direction could easily have helped inspire the novel's use of the reformed Yankee schoolmarm character to support this didactic message.

Already in the 1820s, Harriet had become an instructor at Catharine's Hartford Female Seminary. Despite Harriet's perennial enthusiasm, her work in Hartford remained firmly under Catharine's control—at least according to Catharine's record of this period.[38] Even when Catharine took an extended break from administration and turned the institution, for all intents and purposes, over to Harriet's dedicated care, the elder sister never seems to have considered making any official transfer of authority. Catharine's reluctance in this regard is especially striking given that Harriet clearly excelled at her expanded responsibilities. Catharine's 1874 *Educational Reminiscences and Suggestions* includes her version of the fall 1829 period, when young Harriet collaborated with teacher colleagues to run the seminary during her elder sister's health-related absence. Printing letters she received from Harriet but framing them with commentary to depict herself in the best possible light, Catharine credits herself with the formation of an "emergency" plan for shared governance of the institution and ignores Harriet's enthusiastic reports on the implications of students and teachers beginning to share responsibilities through a system of "circles." Reading against the grain of Catharine's self-assured presentation, however, we can foreground examples of Harriet's efforts to formulate her own philosophy for teaching and for leading the other teachers with a cooperative approach anticipating the moral suasion model that was just emerging in writing on feminized education during that period.

Harriet's December 1829 letters written home to share and sort out her new thinking about teaching methods brim with energy. Though Catharine became known as an advocate of women's teaching through moral influence, her actual instructional practice had been dominated, up until this time at least, by less creative, patriarchally inspired instructional strategies.[39] Harriet's letters, in contrast, discuss efforts to share authority with students, to encourage good behavior via personal influence, and to affirm reciprocal moral uplift: "Dear Sister. . . . I feel as if we are holding the helm, and can turn the vessel the right way. The force of *moral influence* seems equal to that of *authority,* and even stronger. When the girls wish what is against my opinion they say, 'Do, Miss Beecher, allow just this.' '*Allow* you?' I say. 'I have not the power; you can do so if you think best.' Now, they cannot ask me to give up my opinion and belief of right and wrong, and they are unwilling to act against it."[40]

In her own exposition of the letters, Catharine never responds directly to Harriet's ideas about teaching through gentle, loving persuasion. By declaring that "this republican organization" for the seminary was "only fitted to that special emergency," Catharine rejects the opportunity to support her sister's feminized model for teaching (75). Only at the end of the episode does Catharine finally, though indirectly, acknowledge Harriet's role in the seminary's success, noting that "in after life Mrs. Stowe wrote to me, 'There never was such a school as that! We did not half know how good it was; what a pity we had to give it up!'" (75).

Significantly, the sisters' deciding "to give it up" was actually the result of a plan concocted by Lyman Beecher and Catharine to immigrate to Cincinnati. Charles Stowe's biography of his mother portrays the choice as based on Lyman's "desire to hold the West for Protestantism" (66). And Charles records part of a letter Catharine wrote to Harriet about the great potential for their opening a school there.[41] This then-private letter makes clear use of the plural when characterizing the sisters' projected effort, thereby affirming Harriet's pivotal role in the anticipated enterprise in a way the public *Educational Reminiscences* would not several decades later: "The folks are very anxious to have a school on our plan set on foot here," Catharine declares in her letter. "We can have fine rooms in the city college building, which is now unoccupied, and everybody is ready to lend a helping hand" (68). The tone and perspective here contrast sharply with Catharine's more self-centered representation of the same period in her *Reminiscences*. In that later text, she speaks of using "the college plan of co-equal teachers" but does so within a paragraph full of first-person pronouns and verbs emphasizing her own leadership. In addition, rather than describing her exploratory visit with Lyman to stir up local support, she depicts herself as being importuned by the Cincinnati citizenry: "*I* finally *consented* to provide superior teachers for a school, and to do *myself* all *I* safely could to sustain it. . . . *I secured* four of my former teachers and pupils. . . . *I* then rented a fine building" (82, emphasis added). Portraying herself as a highly organized visionary, Catharine relegates the other teachers, including Harriet, to a subsidiary role.

Harriet's own chatty letter to her friend Georgiana May, quoted in Charles Stowe's biography, excitedly outlines still another version of the story: "We mean to turn over the West by means of model schools in this its capital [Cincinnati]. We mean to have a young ladies' school of about fifty or sixty, a primary school of little girls to the same amount, and then a primary school for boys. We have come to the conclusion that the work of teaching will never be rightly done till it comes into female hands" (66–67). Harriet's letter goes on to describe the plans in detail, and her comments evoke arguments favoring women teachers that were circulating during the antebellum era. She explains, for instance, that female teachers are especially adept at using "moral influence" for teaching boys; that the few males who do have such abilities are understandably drawn to other professions (such as the ministry); and that men require higher salaries than women, regardless. Most tellingly, though, she insists that women are far more likely to have the "patience" and "gentleness" needed to guide character formation: "To govern boys by moral influence requires . . . the same division of labor that female education does. But men of tact, versatility, talent, and piety will not devote their lives to teaching. They must be ministers, and missionaries, and all that. . . . As for division of labor, men must have salaries that can support wife and family. . . . Then, if men have more knowledge they have less talent in communicating it, nor have they the patience, the long-suffering, and the gentleness necessary to superintend the formation of character. We intend to make these principles understood, and ourselves to set the example of what females can do in this way" (67–68).

Read as a prelude to her portrayal of the initially ineffectual New England teacher Ophelia in *Uncle Tom's Cabin*, Harriet Beecher's 1830s description of the ideal female educator anticipates one of the major themes embedded in her 1850s novel—that the best way to teach, the approach most clearly aligned with ideals of American motherhood, is to guide through loving influence. Building upon her positive experiment with moral suasion as an instructional tool during her sister's absence from the Hartford Seminary, by the time she took up teaching again in Cincinnati, Harriet Beecher had an even more detailed vision of the contributions gendered pedagogy could make to the nation and of the need for that teaching to be grounded in "the patience, the long-suffering, and the gentleness" already being celebrated in domestic literacy narratives.

Additional written records from her 1830s personal writing about teaching suggest that Harriet would have been quite content to remain in the schoolroom.[42] That the younger Beecher sister favored potentially influential interaction with students over administration and education-oriented publishing is evident in her willingness for Catharine to receive sole credit for an 1833 textbook Harriet actually wrote.[43] Even after her marriage to Calvin Stowe, she regularly operated an in-home school for the children of servants, neighbors, and her own family. Her letters to her husband often included animated anecdotes about her students' progress.[44] As late as 1844, she was still attracted by the idea of operating a school for young ladies. Writing to Calvin from Indianapolis, where she was visiting her brother Henry Ward Beecher, she reported: "I am seriously thinking of . . . coming here to I[ndianapolis] to take a class of young ladies & so influence the state. Such pretty girls as they have & so uncultivated. I really long to do something for them, teach them to be *women* & not men corrupters & destroyers. Female education is at a low ebb. . . . Henry says he wants only the woman & can move the whole state for her."[45] Although Harriet never did found a school to be "the centre of female influence" in Indiana, her enthusiasm for the proposal indicates that, even after marriage, she maintained a strong sense of teaching as a worthwhile venue for her talents. With its echo of her earlier statements about feminine nurturance, this 1844 letter demonstrates that her core philosophy of teaching remained consistently rooted in the concepts she had originally explored in the late 1820s.

Clearly, Stowe's *Uncle Tom's Cabin* treatment of the single woman teacher Ophelia as motherly wielder of moral influence builds upon the author's own teaching experiences and educational philosophy, as well as familiar domestic literacy narratives of the time.[46] Stowe's version of the motherly schoolteacher subgenre is particularly distinctive in the deft caricature of Ophelia—a rhetorically sensitive choice allowing her to critique middle-class Northern women's inadequate responses to slavery without alienating her readers through a too self-righteous tone. Besides serving as a Dickensian counterpoint to the heavily emotional subplot leading to Eva's death, the initially comical interchanges between the schoolmarmlike Ophelia and her incorrigible charge Topsy eventually lead the St. Clares' New England relative to a truly enlightened pedagogy.[47] In this highly gendered subplot, Stowe reiterates her novel's emphasis on maternal literacy management as a tool supporting national healing of the slavery conflict. Through Ophelia, she advocates a strategy for public influence—enlightened teaching in the home—that any Northern woman could carry out, should she so choose.

Given her straitlaced self-confidence, her firm mannerisms, and her clear wish to avoid excessive interpersonal contact, it is tempting to dub the version of Ophelia that Stowe presents at first as a satirical portrait of the elder Beecher sister, Catharine.[48] Like Ophelia, after all, Catharine enjoyed theorizing about education more than actual teaching. Like Ophelia, Catharine was more dedicated to supporting distant missions and causes (such as organizing petitions against the Cherokee Removal) than to the messy work of day-to-day, person-to-person teaching. Like Ophelia, the elder Beecher sister advocated a curriculum with regimented hours and constantly monitored activity.[49] Like Ophelia, Catharine was a well-educated, unmarried New England lady who journeyed to another region of the country with the hope of encouraging reform of its customs through her own intervention in its cultural life. Like Ophelia, Catharine was apparently hesitant to show the kind of loving affection in instruction that Harriet had been promoting for decades.

Whether or not she was based directly on Catharine, Ophelia certainly represents what Stowe and other practitioners of the domestic literacy narrative's ideology would have viewed as an inappropriate instructional model for a midcentury society best guided by motherly nurturance at home and in school:

> Miss Ophelia's ideas of education, like all her other ideas, were very set and definite; and of the kind that prevailed in New England a century ago, and which are still preserved in some very retired and unsophisticated parts, where there are no railroads. As nearly as could be expressed, they could be comprised in very few words: to teach them to mind when they were spoken to; to teach them catechism, sewing, and reading; and to whip them if they told lies. And though, of course, in the flood of light that is now poured on education, these are left far away in the rear, yet it is an undisputed fact that our grandmothers raised some tolerably fair men and women under this regime, as many of us can remember and testify. At all events, Miss Ophelia knew of nothing else to do; and, therefore, applied her mind to her heathen [Topsy] with the best diligence she could command. (357)

By ascribing to Ophelia beliefs about teaching that dominated New England culture "a century ago," Stowe relegates her theories to a prerepublican mindset that, even if it "raised some tolerably fair men and women," was now inadequate for the American nation. Stowe leavens her critique with good-natured satire (such as attributing the continued use of uninformed teaching approaches to areas of the country "where there are no railroads"), but she nonetheless contends that ideas like Ophelia's need to be "left far away in the rear" if the nation is to progress.

In line with this description of her views, Ophelia starts out trying to teach Topsy with the very methods Deborah Fitts says had already been discredited in informed educational circles of the era. Faced with Topsy's ongoing mischief, Ophelia declares, "I don't see . . . how I'm going to manage that child without whipping her" (362). Trying "to manage" Topsy with punishments, Ophelia advocates an approach that Augustine St. Clare maintains has been proven ineffectual, even for a "specimen" like Topsy, upon whom "a poker," a "shovel or tongs," had already been tried. In St. Clare's probing analysis, Ophelia's recommended whippings for children—Northern as well as Southern—become little better than a slave owner's assaults. By extension, whipping children to teach them implicates unenlightened teachers—in whatever American region they are—in the national shame of slavery.

As important to Stowe's message as her attack on corporal punishment, meanwhile, are the lighter but still telling jabs at Ophelia's "benevolent" projects, such as her self-affirming donations to faraway missions. Satirizing well-to-do ladies' tendency to distance themselves from true charity by giving dollars rather than their own involvement, Stowe (via St. Clare) demands: "Why, if your Gospel is not strong enough to save one heathen child, that you can have at home here, all to yourself, what's the use of sending one or two poor missionaries off with it among thousands of just such? I suppose this child is about a fair sample of what thousands of your heathen are" (408). Stowe's critique of this long-distance missionary motherhood proposes that women like Ophelia devote their primary energies to individual children in America. She uses St. Clare's question to suggest that failure to become actively, directly involved in teaching at least "one heathen [black] child" at home indicates an abdication of responsibility, a sin of omission that helps perpetuate the evils of slavery.

Ophelia eventually accepts the challenge to teach Topsy to read the Bible, and thereby to shape her character. She aims to carry her student beyond mere parroting of words to an ability to live by their deeper meanings. (In this, as in other areas, she joins educational theorists of her day and authors like Barbauld's heirs, who viewed mastery over linguistic capital as a step toward moral development.) But only when she learns from Eva how to teach with a more feminized, caring approach does Ophelia fully reform Topsy and, in the process, transform herself. Though at first viewed by Ophelia as the mere animal "specimen" Augustine had ironically dubbed her, Topsy is only unreachable as long as Ophelia persists in trying to instruct through masculinist techniques of coercion rather than through shared feelings. As Richard H. Brodhead notes, Ophelia is quite ready, at first, to resort to the patriarchal whip as instructional tool. Ultimately, however, she learns to nurture Topsy instead. Once she allows love to guide their interactions, Ophelia's relationship with Topsy changes, and the formerly cold spinster "acquire[s] an influence over the mind of the destitute child" (432).

Later, having reconceptualized her own teaching, Ophelia struggles to replicate the lesson for Marie. When the widow St. Clare decides to "teach" Rosa by sending her to the whipping house, Ophelia tries desperately to dissuade Marie (461–62). By having Ophelia fail, by having the selfish Marie remain as coldhearted as ever, Stowe reminds her readers that being a true mother-teacher involves far more than simply being female. In line with other antebellum domestic literacy narratives' assertion of single women as idealized mothers, the spinster Ophelia has become a more genuinely maternal figure than Marie. Accordingly, as a sensitive manager of domestic literacy practices fostering feminine influence, Ophelia writes to the Shelbys when Tom is sold off, because she hopes to help him finally return home (466).

Ophelia's letter arrives in Kentucky too late to save Tom, but her increasingly maternal teaching of Topsy succeeds, at least in terms consistent with other "benevolent" literacy narratives. One clear sign of the change in Topsy is her deep sorrow over Eva's death. As a token of her loss, Topsy treasures a little book that Eva had given her, and Ophelia capitalizes on St. Clare's reaction to that revelation to ask for Topsy's freedom. Eager to take the young girl back to New England, and far now from viewing her as the mere object of an instructional experiment, Ophelia imagines a day when others will take on the role she was slow to learn but eventually achieved—a Christian surrogate motherhood for America. Prompting Ophelia's reiteration of her commitment to Topsy and her wish to convert other Northerners to her reformed attitude, St. Clare addresses his cousin one last time and, through her, Stowe's readers: "If we emancipate, are you willing to educate? How many families, in your town, would take in a negro man and woman, teach them, bear with them, and seek to make them Christians?" (452).

Though Ophelia stops short of demanding support from others, she is ready now to admit that the "unchristian prejudice of the north is an oppressor almost equally severe" as the slaveholding institution itself.[50] Having acquired a strong sense of loving "duty," she has become a maternal role model for Stowe's Northern white readers, to whom the author pointedly assigns the major responsibility for educating the South's slavery-scarred black Americans. With the reformed Ophelia standing in as a symbol for an enlightened, committed North, Stowe envisions a postslavery America guided by a feminized educational system.

Teaching by the Well-Taught Child

The transformation of Miss Ophelia into an idealized motherly teacher, along with her suggestion that others in the North can be "taught" to follow her lead, seems at first to affirm that St. Clare's impassioned plea for help addressing the heritage of slavery can be met. But his untimely death pulls this vision of North-South pedagogical cooperation up short, leaving the challenge of teaching freed slaves unresolved, for another generation to address. This new generation, in fact, claimed Stowe's most extensive investment in the discourse of domestic literacy management for *Uncle Tom's Cabin.* Although the literacy-based influence of both Uncle Tom and Ophelia is limited in the end, Stowe invites her readers to look to a brighter future when figures like Eva St. Clare and George Shelby will assume virtuous leadership of the nation. In pinning her hopes for her country's remediation on well-taught youth, Stowe was following a pattern already established in domestic literacy narratives, which often looked ahead to "the rising generation" as America's best resource.

We can trace her confident belief in this ideal through writing that circulated within the Beecher family before and after the publication of her first novel. Stowe grew up in a home that constantly endorsed children's literacy-based examination of moral questions, with Bible study, group discussions, and writing all used as tools to help formulate a strong Christian vision. Her early schooling reinforced this view, which she would replicate later in teaching her own children and in writing about family life as bound to the national welfare. One clear sign that Stowe saw herself as having been explicitly trained, even while a young child, to become involved in major social issues appears in her writing about her favorite teacher at Miss Pierce's school. Catharine and Harriet both attended the famous school in Litchfield in the years before opening their own seminary in Hartford. At Litchfield, Harriet studied with John Brace, whose teaching remained, throughout her life, an influential model. Brace was known for using a nurturing approach, which apparently endeared him to his students.

Stowe's reminiscences about Brace's influence appeared originally in a biography of Lyman Beecher that his children wrote collaboratively in the 1860s. Years later, several details from Stowe's commentary, which link Brace and her father as caring mentors using similar teaching methods, reappeared in a speech her sister Isabella Beecher Hooker gave to honor Brace at an 1892 reunion for the Hartford Female Seminary, where Brace taught later in his career.[51] The majority of Hooker's talk was actually a reading of Mrs. Stowe's comments, stressing how Brace helped young Harriet Beecher acquire confidence that, though still a child, she could analyze complex moral issues, potentially even guiding adults' ideas with her own.

Harriet's learning from Mr. Brace was enhanced by the fact that her teacher and his wife lived as boarders in the Beecher home while he was working at Miss Pierce's. With such public/private, professional/personal border-crossing quite common then, there was a tendency for the emerging

American female educational institutions to be "domesticated," to absorb some of the comfortable characteristics of fireside literacy. With teachers and students often spending their evenings together in local homes, the hierarchized power relationships that would later become typical in public day schools, private boarding schools, and colleges with barrackslike dormitories were partially undermined in an institution like Miss Pierce's. In such a milieu, a teaching style more in tune with enabling parlor talk than with the stiffness of formal examinations would have seemed quite appropriate. Indeed, in Hooker's speech, the metaphor unifying Stowe's praise of Brace depicted his teaching as based more in "constant conversation" than recitation or lecture (27). Stressing his ability to build on shared talk about topics of interest, Stowe praised Brace's particular talent of "teaching composition" in ways that encouraged students to explore important moral issues (28). She described two of her own successful papers, written when she was only nine and twelve, as apt examples of *his* nurturing instruction.

Stowe vowed that the first paper, "The Difference between the Natural and the Moral Sublime," was not too difficult to write, despite its highly abstract subject, since "the discussions which he held with the class not only made me understand the subject as thoroughly as I do now, but so excited me that I felt sure I had something to say upon it" (29). For Stowe, then, the best of school literacy was not too different from the brand practiced in the Beechers' home—shared "discussions" as a step toward greater individual understanding, which, in turn, could be further elaborated via writing. In this conception of collaborative learning, the role of the teacher was not to dole out knowledge for the students to accept uncritically. Rather, consistent with domestic literacy narratives' portrayals of educating through integrated literacy practices, the teacher became a facilitator in the search for socially constructed knowledge. Students—even very young ones like the nine-year-old Harriet Beecher in this anecdote—could make meaningful, if tentative, contributions to this social brand of knowledge.

Stowe's characterization of a second compelling piece of writing she recalled from her young student days extended this idea of the well-taught child being able to use literacy in ways that could even enlighten adults. The second paper was a negative response to the question, "Can the immortality of the soul be proved by the light of Nature?" (29–30). In outlining the history of her own student writing experience, Stowe described the affirming moment when her father, attending the exhibition at which her paper was read, evinced clear interest in the essay before knowing that she was its author. Sensitively willing to be instructed by a child's composition,

Lyman must have been especially touched to discover that the writer was his own daughter. Stowe herself, even in the 1860s, when she first wrote of this memory, well after the astounding phenomenon of *Uncle Tom's Cabin* had made her famous above the other members of her well-known family, still classified this as "the proudest moment of [her] life": "There was no mistaking father's face when he was pleased," Stowe explained, "and to have interested him was past all juvenile triumphs" (30). It was, in fact, so notable a victory precisely because she had succeeded, though still a child, in teaching her own paternal teacher.

Lyman's place in this anecdote is crucial, of course, underscoring Harriet's self-representation as a child able to teach a wise and good adult. Though photographs of Lyman at the head of the imposing Beecher clan conjure up images of staid patriarchal authority, anecdotes in the biography emphasize his loving kindness as much as his intellect. Known for his unusual ability to empathize, Lyman was sometimes depicted as having a woman's caring sensibility. And in no other way was that quality more obvious than in his eagerness to listen to and learn from his children.

For Harriet, responding to a child's virtuous example remained an aim of her teaching, in person and in writing. This goal, grounded in personal experience, was fully consistent with the ideology behind the domestic literacy narratives she was writing in the 1830s and 1840s, including those penned originally just for family readers. Two letters to Calvin in the spring of 1844, for instance, reflect her willingness to be instructed by her daughter Hatty, as she would later depict St. Clare and others being taught by the saintly child Eva. The first letter includes a description of a typical day in Harriet's home school, reminiscent of scenes in Sigourney's *Letters to Mothers* or Sedgwick's *Means and Ends:*

> 1/2 past nine call the children into school, sing a hymn, pray with them and give them a bible lesson half an hour long. . . . They are very much interested. They then spend a half an hour on their texts & bible lessons for Sunday. Then read in a class & then sew till dinner time. . . . Today little Eliza by dint of frisking and figuring about, instead of learning her lesson, continued to lose her dinner privileges & to have only bread & water in her own apartment. After dinner I noticed Hatty gliding very quietly up stairs with her own saucer full of custard which she had saved up for Eliza. The child is always doing such things & yet strangers suppose she is not nearly so affectionate as Eliza.[52]

Here Stowe the home-based schoolteacher accepts the lesson within her exemplary daughter's forgiving, loving behavior. Rather than correct Hatty for undermining parental authority, Stowe praises her. Further, by attaching appealing feminine images to her description of Hatty's mission of mercy ("gliding," "affectionate," "quietly") and juxtaposing them with her own more masculine-seeming, inept efforts at correction (allowing "only bread & water"), Stowe implies that she perceived Hatty's feminine Christian values as worth emulating.

Another letter from the same time period uses vivid pictures of Stowe learning from Hatty. In this account of a shared talk, echoing Sigourney's "Rainy Day" narrative poem from the same time period, Stowe emphasizes Hatty's ability to interpret the Bible: "As it was raining & her health has been so poor she, poor child, was detained at home. So to comfort her I told her about Christ. I was telling her about the scene in the garden when the men came to take Christ & she said 'I am He & they went backwards & fell to the ground.' I told her that Jesus looked at them with his glorious eyes and they were afraid. She seemed quite excited & her little form quivered as she said earnestly 'Was it not because there was a spirit in his eyes?' Yes she continued it was the spirit in him that made them afraid—they thought he was a spirit." Discussing a print text together, as in scenes from so many domestic literacy narratives of the 1830s and early 1840s, Stowe and her daughter enact a reciprocal pedagogy. To report on how Hatty described Christ's power, Stowe proudly observes: "Hatty is a creature of imagination & feelings. In all the common acquisitions of children she is backward but full of thoughts & emotion. The other night she was looking at the lightening [*sic*] & she said, 'Seems to me the sky cracks open & shows a little piece of heaven.' She will keep these things & ponder them in her heart & they will come out in some new crystallizations by and bye."[53]

This role-reversing image of the young child teaching the adult—as Hatty taught Harriet, as Harriet had taught her father—resurfaces in some of the most memorable scenes about Eva in *Uncle Tom's Cabin*. Like Hatty, Eva is unlike other children. Like Hatty, she is both innocent and wise. Like Hatty too, she is a remarkable teacher—particularly in her ability to read the Bible collaboratively with others, then enact and impart its deepest lessons—especially to her father and Uncle Tom. For Stowe's friend Annie Fields, in fact, Eva's shared reading with Tom was at the heart of the novel: "The child reading the Bible on the knees of the slave, dreaming over its mysteries and enjoying them in her exceptional maturity."[54]

The rhetorical sophistication of Stowe's novel, in fact, is especially evident in her strategic application of the child-teaches-adult motif that was already well-known to readers of domestic literacy narratives and clearly in line with theories of feminized instruction in her day. As Deborah Fitts points out, one of the arguments antebellum proponents of hiring women teachers employed most effectively was the theory that feminine sensibility made women teachers better able to interact with young students. Psychological principles constructing the male mind as rational and the female as emotional were encouraging a reconceptualization of childhood away from the idea of young children as being miniature adults to a view of them as being "born with innate but undeveloped faculties" of reason and emotion. Since emotion was thought to develop first, women were the best teachers for young children. Crucial to this argument was the notion that emotional interaction and the development of the moral sense that accompanied it were "at least as important as intellectual development, if not more so."[55] Using literacy management to tap into her child's natural emotions, a mother could encourage moral vision, which the child could then share with others.

What Stowe designed in the Eva/Tom relationship, therefore, was an accessible adaptation of the learning-through-feminine-sensibility paradigm, which depended upon readers being able to accept both Eva and Tom as childlike yet accomplished teachers developing and communicating a heightened moral sense through their Bible-based literacy. Along those lines, Eva and Tom constantly teach each other, especially through their Bible readings and discussions. Their collaborative learning recalls the account in Harriet's letters to Calvin about her teaching and learning with young Hatty.

A carefully sequenced set of literacy experiences between Tom and Eva, in fact, leads the little girl to propose to her mother: "Why don't we teach our servants to read?" (385). Marie's response that "people never do" because "it is no use for them to read" is, of course, inaccurate on many levels (385). Tom, for one, can read, and he was taught by his former master's son. Shared perusal of a letter from George, in fact, had started Eva and Tom into the habit of Bible reading together.[56] Tom, who thought George's letter "the most wonderful specimen of composition that had appeared in modern times," "held a council with Eva on the expediency of getting it framed" for his room (379). Bible story readings and discussions ensued, followed by Eva's talk with Marie about teaching the other slaves to read. Significantly, Tom and Eva's collaborative Bible study takes him beyond the basic literacy instruction George Shelby provided for him and prepares this still-childlike hero for Bible-based teaching of other slaves on Legree's plantation, where he will demonstrate Stowe's appreciation of community-oriented oral literacy practices.

Though unsuccessful at reaching her mother through the normally feminine route of sensibility, Eva achieves better results with her father and, eventually, with her aunt Ophelia and Topsy. Even after her death, in fact, Eva continues to exercise moral influence that Stowe, invoking earlier domestic literacy narratives, attributes to shared literacy practices associated with Eva's memory.[57] So Tom uses a discussion of Bible texts he had studied in the past with Eva to try to reignite her father's religious convictions.[58] Requesting that St. Clare read from the Bible as Eva had so often done, Tom poignantly observes, "Don't get no readin', hardly, now Miss Eva's gone" (437). In acceding to Tom's wishes, St. Clare simultaneously places Tom and Eva in a collaborative teaching position, which leads the bereaved father to recall "the raising of Lazarus" as he "read [the text] aloud, often pausing to wrestle down feelings which were roused by the pathos of the story." Noting Tom's modeling of "absorbed . . . love, trust, and adoration" as he listens, St. Clare marvels that the narrative seems "real" to his slave, and Tom concurs that he could "jest fairly *see* it, Mas'r." In longing to have "your eyes, Tom," St. Clare expresses a wish for the moral vision Tom had gained through literacy practices shared with Eva. After querying Tom as to the strength of his faith, and suggesting that the slave might not "know" as much as his cynical master, St. Clare accepts Tom's childlike, gentle rebuke, also based in Eva-nurtured Bible literacy: "O Mas'r, haven't you jest read how He hides from the wise and prudent, and reveals unto babes?"[59] With his well-timed reference to God's revealing the deepest truths "unto babes," Tom reminds St. Clare (and Stowe's readers) of the need to welcome literacy-based lessons like Eva's and Tom's, however childlike the teacher might seem to be.

In succeeding days, collaborative Bible study also leads St. Clare back to an imaginative reunion with his mother, whose Christian literacy management he can finally recall. For instance, on one occasion, after "read[ing] to Tom" from the Bible (447), St. Clare rummages in a parlor drawer for "an old music-book whose leaves were yellow with age" (448). Explaining to Ophelia that "this was one of [his] mother's books" and pointing to "her handwriting," St. Clare begins to sing one of his mother's favorite songs, a Christian hymn (448–49). Meanwhile, even as "he attache[s] himself to Tom more and more, every day," and through that bond is "remind[ed] . . . so much of Eva," St. Clare becomes, "in many respects, another man. He reads his little Eva's Bible seriously and honestly," eventually vowing to set Tom free.

St. Clare's own death, unfortunately, follows too soon after his daughter's, before he has fulfilled the noble impulses spurred on by his literacy-guided exchanges with Tom. On one level, St. Clare's failure to act on his emerging convictions acknowledges that, however ennobling the spiritual vision a child like Eva might embody, her power to effect political change is inherently limited. At the same time, though, from Stowe's own religious perspective, Eva's literacy-oriented influence on Tom—her strengthening of his moral sense—can be credited with preparing him for the ultimate triumph of working as a religious teacher among his own people on Legree's plantation, then willingly dying as a martyr to help save others. Though Tom's embracing death on these terms may well be unacceptable to us today, we should still recognize the appeal his transformation would have had for Stowe and many of her readers. Being assigned a death as holy as Eva's grants Tom religious equality with his idealized young teacher and reaffirms the efficacy of her youthful but motherly teaching.

To the survivors from Eva's generation, meanwhile, in both the novel's narrative line and the politics of its day, slavery remained a challenge to be met. Ironically, in Stowe's final resolutions for the characters representing that generation—George Shelby, Topsy, and Harry Harris—the author reveals both the energy and the limits of her own moral vision, with comments in her *Key* providing revealing elaborations of the positions she set forth in the novel.

The narrative trajectory Stowe constructed for George Shelby, scion of white, middle-class leadership, follows a pattern that would have been both familiar and affirming to readers of other domestic literacy narratives. Guided by maternal instruction that he had begun to extend to the larger society, young George ends the novel ready to assume the mantle of benevolent citizenship. Although he has arrived at the Legree plantation too late to rescue Tom, George carries an uplifting lesson home from their final meeting. As if on cue, then, Stowe's audience would find in "The Liberator," the closing chapter of *Uncle Tom's Cabin,* a scene straight out of the most traditional domestic literacy management stories: "Mrs. Shelby was seated in her comfortable parlor, where a cheerful hickory fire was dispelling the chill of the late autumn evening. A supper-table, glittering with plate and cut glass, was set out, on whose arrangements our former friend, old Chloe, was presiding" (613).

Reiterating the pattern of a well-taught child grown up to teach others, George outlines the story of his final interactions with Tom. Though he "had written to his mother ... stating the day she might expect him," he has not yet revealed the hard news of Tom's death. When he does tell the assembled family, Chloe is devastated. But George tries to comfort her by repeating the final lesson of Tom's spiritual victory, recounting "with simple pathos" "the triumphant scene of her husband's death, and his last messages of love" (616). More important, suggesting he has embraced a transportable moral from the text of Tom's life, George calls together "all the servants of the Shelby estate" a month later for a ceremony. He presents them with "a bundle of papers . . . containing a certificate of freedom to every one on the place, which he read successively, and presented" to all (616). Indicating his understanding that simply to bestow freedom will not ensure his former slaves productive lives, George grants their request to stay on as paid workers, but he also promises: "I expect to carry on the estate, and to teach you what, perhaps, it will take you some time to learn, — how to use the rights I give you as freemen and women. I expect you to be good, and willing to learn; and I trust in God that I shall be faithful, and willing to teach" (616).

While Stowe herself clearly intends for George's actions in this final chapter to be highly commendable—a model, in fact, for her white, middle-class readers—we should take note today of his leadership's important limits. Concentrating on the religious dimensions of Tom's death, George downplays Chloe's loss. Granting legal freedom, he retains material control over his former slaves' futures. Like the purportedly charitable teachers of "benevolent" literacy narratives, he will decide the nature of the educational program that will be provided to these former slaves, so that the "rights" they are receiving "as freemen and women" remain tied to their "willing[ness] to learn" on his terms. How liberatory will his literacy management be? Imagining a civic pedagogy far more controlling than the "critical consciousness" models Paulo Freire would frame in the next century, this "Liberator" continues to set the agenda for literacy management himself, firmly tying his program to middle-class, white Christian values like those of his creator Stowe.[60] (Significantly, in this regard, whereas Stowe has Tom reach a level of moral perfection that will assure him an honorable heavenly reward, Freire's literacy program would seek redress and reform in this life.)

In the end, George Shelby's position in relation to his former slaves is clearly framed as one of patriarchal leadership for childlike dependents. Though "freeing" them, he retains (and plans to exercise) continued control over their destiny. While he projects his future guidance as beneficent, we must note the long-term effects of purportedly liberal education programs like the one Stowe envisions here, which reinscribe the need for white control over black learning. Along those lines, it is crucial for us to examine such markers of this ideology's lingering legacy as a twentieth-century illustration for the George-teaches-Tom reading episode discussed earlier. (See figure 7.) By recasting the thirteen-year-old George of Stowe's text into a more adult figure and arranging its components to focus on Shelby as towering over Tom, James Daugherty's 1929 portrait suggests which elements of the domestic literacy narrative's "benevolent" race-relations scenario carried over most forcefully from *Uncle Tom's Cabin* into twentieth-century culture. The White Man remains indisputably in charge.

The fate of the "Other" George offers more evidence that Stowe herself was not yet willing, in the early 1850s at least, to grant full citizenship to African Americans. Like her depiction of the freed slaves on the Shelby plantation, her choice to withhold educational and political opportunities from the Harris family would both reflect and shape American cross-race relations for decades to come. In the chapter just before "The Liberator," she seems first to locate George Harris's family within the middle-class ideal of domesticated literacy as an avenue to empowered civic life. Then she closes off the option of true enfranchisement. Describing the Harris home in Montreal in terms consistent with domestic literacy narratives' ideology, Stowe pictures the father, George, near the fire and tea table (staples of white middle-class America), studying a print text. She describes Eliza as "matronly" and "contented" (604). She even places their son, Harry, "a fine bright boy," in "a good school" (603). Nonetheless, as several critics have noted, though affording the Harrises a reunion with their relatives Cassy and Emmeline, Stowe cannot imagine their reentry into the United States and, instead, sends the family off to Liberia. However sincere her choice, however "wholly" she sees George Harris "given" to this service, migration removes the best-educated black males in her novel (Harris and his son) from America's future.[61] Through this displacement, she also symbolically leaves the white male George Shelby in sole charge of the future learning, and thus the degree of access to civic life, for those African Americans still within the United States.

Stowe's continuing to deny free blacks control over their own education and related access to political agency in the United States is also evident in her resolution of the Topsy storyline. Like the narrative arc she constructed for George Shelby, the Topsy plot reiterates elements familiar from other antebellum domestic literacy management texts. In this case, Stowe draws directly upon the narratives depicting cross-caste instruction by lady teachers transforming poor heathens into worthy Christians. Ac-

"Uncle Tom was intent on a slate lying before him."

Fig. 7. "Uncle Tom was intent on a slate lying before him," from
Uncle Tom's Cabin (1929). Image secured from Special Collections and Archives, Robert
W. Woodruff Library, Emory University; Illustration by James Daugherty, from
UNCLE TOM'S CABIN by Harriet Beecher Stowe, copyright 1929 by Coward-McCann, Inc.
Used by permission of Coward-McCann, Inc., a division of Penguin Group (USA) Inc.

cordingly, after describing "deliberative" New Englanders as being initially put off by Topsy, Stowe credits Ophelia's "conscientious" teaching with eventually leading "the child" to salvation and good "favor with the family and neighborhood." Having been "baptized" "by her own request" upon attaining "the age of womanhood" (612), Topsy represents the triumph of a single woman's motherly domestic instruction. Indeed, Stowe could have counted on her first readers, in tune as they were with such plotlines on "benevolent" outreach, to applaud the dedication of Topsy's adult life to missionary teaching in "one of the stations in Africa." Yet, in sending Topsy there, Stowe reverses the idealized teaching pattern she had constructed for Ophelia, whom she had positioned as best off when doing missionary-like teaching "at home" in the United States. By suggesting that Topsy's teaching "home" must be in Africa, Stowe denies the former slave any claim to American civic identity, as in Harry Harris's case. The novel fails, through this plot choice, to fulfill the mandate advanced in the question St. Clare had addressed earlier to Ophelia: "Suppose we should rise up to-morrow and emancipate, who would educate these millions, and teach them how to use their freedom? . . . and tell me, now, is there enough Christian philanthropy, among all your northern states, to bear with the process of their education and elevation?" (452).

It would remain for African American authors—notably Frances E. W. Harper—to create literary enactments of collaborative educational uplift programs *for* blacks *by* blacks *within* the United States, and more specifically in the postbellum South. Envisioning motherly teaching led by educated members of the black community, and dedicated to claiming that community's full participation in American culture, Harper would appropriate the very literary genre Stowe and other white women authors had used in their controlling versions of "benevolent" motherly teaching for the nation. Thus, although Harper would affiliate with some of the gendered ideals in the domestic literacy narrative genre, she would simultaneously remake the form to address pressing questions about educational and civic equity in postbellum American culture—questions still deserving our attention today.

Frances Harper's Literacy Program for Racial Uplift

I am now going to have a private meeting with the women of this place if they will come out. I am going to talk with them about their daughters, and about things connected with the welfare of the race. Now is the time for our women to begin to try to lift up their heads and plant the roots of progress under the hearthstone.

Frances Harper, letter from Greenville,

Georgia, March 1870

Throughout the nineteenth century, the basic plotline of the American domestic literacy narrative involved three interconnected elements: the motherly teacher whose enlightened direction of literacy helped sustain her community; the learner who was acquiring abilities facilitating civic participation; and a storytelling text whose shared use by the mother-teacher and child(like) learner joined them to each other and to a nation-building enterprise. Within the individual middle-class home, this text was a story told by the mother to the child, either by reading a print text together or by discussing print-based narrative knowledge the mother had already acquired. In feminized schoolrooms, the storytelling text was the curriculum, a "story" about socially significant content and values that America delivered through a motherly teacher to her students, future leaders of the polis.

For both home and school settings after the Civil War, the participation of African Americans in this recurring narrative line was highly contested in multiple arenas, including government documents and decision making, education systems, and mass-market publications. After all, when applied to African Americans, each of the ideology's three key elements—the motherly teacher, the learner-becoming-citizen, and the social text celebrating literacy's promotion of public community—posed significant challenges to white, middle-class views of blacks, especially the recently freed slaves of the Southern states. In this regard, the questions about postslavery communal outreach posed by Harriet Beecher Stowe's Augustine St. Clare to the would-be teacher Miss Ophelia were prescient indeed.

My review of contests swirling around postbellum African Americans' attempts to claim social roles associated with the domestic literacy narrative will highlight one influential author, Frances E. W. Harper. Harper's sophisticated appropriations of the genre—in *Minnie's Sacrifice* (1869), *Trial and Triumph* (1888–89), *Iola Leroy* (1892), and shorter sketches and speeches—addressed a variety of audiences, particularly African Americans committed to uplift through education.[1] I will focus here on the first of her novel-length narratives, *Minnie's Sacrifice*, published at a watershed moment in her authorship and in U.S. history—Reconstruction. Situating this single work from Harper's long career within a network of related publications emphasizes how her writing capitalized on gendered genre elements to claim *and* resist affiliation with white, middle-class American educational practices. Such an intertextual reading shows how Harper appropriated the domestic literacy narrative to fulfill a race-based agenda for using literature to guide the nation.[2]

Harper was far from alone in using domestic literacy narratives to address questions about African Americans' place in postbellum national culture. Besides other women writers, both black and white, white *male* authors also adapted elements from the genre for "solving" (or at least interrogating) the complex social issues swirling around former slaves' position in the reunified United States. One 1866 pictorial narrative published in *Harper's Weekly*, entitled "'Uncle Tom' and His Grandchild," embodies just such an effort. (See figure 8.) When we read this illustration and its accompanying print text today, we get at least a tentative sense of the historical context into which Harper would insert her own program for African American education—a context still dominated by white manage-

"UNCLE TOM" AND HIS GRANDCHILD.—[See Page 690.]

Fig. 8. "Uncle Tom and His Grandchild." *Harper's Weekly*
(November 3, 1866). The Library Company of Philadelphia

ment of black literacy, even in such purportedly benign settings as Northern periodicals.

The illustration itself is in many ways typical of the work then appearing each week in *Harper's*. Casting artists in a visual reporting role similar to today's photojournalists, the periodical's popular drawings seemed to provide readers a firsthand look at otherwise inaccessible events, thereby contributing to shared community (in the North and potentially nationwide). Even more so than with the new field of photography, however, illustrations like those in *Harper's* allowed for a wide range of interpretive decision making, especially when conjoined hypertextually (as in this case) with editorial narrative. Therefore, we should read this two-part text as more rhetorical than documentary—as a step toward staking out the ideological territory for Northern whites to "manage" postwar life.

The extended caption accompanying the illustration identifies its location as "on the road from Columbus to Macon," in a state Frances Harper would later be visiting during her educational tour through the South. The *Harper's* editors explain that their "artist, Mr. Ward," had come upon the scene "by the road-side, on the outskirts of a Georgia plantation." However authentic Mr. Ward's rendering of the literacy exchange he witnessed, the portrait would carry added force for *Harper's* Northern, middle-class readers because of its strong connection with—but also its striking reconfiguration of—familiar elements from domestic literacy narratives. In that vein, the editors explain the brief story:

> A little child, almost white, and very beautiful, is teaching her grandfather—a pure Negro—to read. The little girl is just from school, as appears from the satchel hanging on the chair. We did not know or ask the names of either the old man or the child: but from an affection for "Uncle Tom" and its gifted authoress we have adopted the title subjoined to our engraving. The picture, as we saw it, seemed to tell at the same time a very sad and a very hopeful story. The contrast of color, almost violent in those so near of kin, told the history of a great wrong. This little girl, with far more of "Southern chivalry" in her veins than of Negro blood, was, or had been for all that, a slave—a thing to be bought and sold, to be insolently loved or insolently hated; to whose children she must become a curse, as they would be a curse to her. But this sad fate had in her case been averted. She was now free; and her present occupation spoke of a new era for the Negro race. So that, on the whole, the picture was a hopeful one. In it seemed to us to be concentrated the great moral of our civil war.[3]

For readers familiar with domestic literacy narratives, the image of "the child" teaching "her grandfather" to read would have recalled but revised countless scenes of domestic literacy management where maternal figures instructed their children. Like white mothers and their children in prior domestic literacy narratives, the "Uncle Tom" figure and his grandchild share a print text, with the girl positioned physically in this sketch just as learners were in antecedent illustrations from the genre—kneeling beside the adult who holds the book. At the same time, the allusion to *Uncle Tom's Cabin* would have called up parallel scenes of Eva teaching the novel's title character. By assigning the child in this image-and-print narrative the role of Eva in Stowe's well-known book, the artist and editors certainly imagine a scenario for freed slaves that is more "hopeful" than in the 1850s. Indeed, this child's ability to teach her "Uncle Tom" is presented (through the editors' explanation about "the satchel hanging on the chair") as based in sanctioned school attendance. Along related lines, the narrative celebrates the child's "free" status, contrasting her current situation of teaching her "kin" with the horrors of a system that relegated her to being "bought and sold" despite her other evident blood ties—to "Southern chivalry" (here invoked with stinging irony). With its veiled condemnation of racial mixing achieved through "violent" means, the editorial interpretation of Ward's illustration further distances *Harper's* readers from the unnamed but cruel villains of the back story—white Southern slaveholders, especially male masters. Incapable of doing the kind of "great wrong" embodied in the "contrast of color" between the "little child" and "her grandfather," *Harper's* Northern middle-class audience is instead asked to celebrate "the great moral of our civil war," which, via cross-generational literacy acquisition, promises "a new era for the Negro race."

Appealing as the editors' reading of the illustration is on the surface, we should also note the narrative's occasional pressure points—those slippages in discourse where challenges that postbellum African Americans would face in their interactions with Northern whites subtly emerge. In spite of its righteous censure of the forced encounter presumably behind the young girl's "sad" racial identity, the text still classifies her as "almost white, and very beautiful," a marker of racial preference that establishes a greater distance between the periodical's readers and the "pure Negro" so significantly named "Uncle Tom." The two-part text's representation of its new version of Uncle Tom is, in fact, particularly striking. Far more frail than Stowe's strong, middle-aged hero, this newspaper character provides one example of an ongoing "reconstruction" process that would render "Uncle Tom," well before the twentieth century, into a nonthreatening old man. Furthermore, the gender swapping behind the adult and child identities in this remade portrait of domestic literacy management is significant. Making the young member of the "rising generation" (always a central element in domestic literacy narratives) into a vulnerable, attractive figure with shoulders clearly bared is at least as suggestive of whites' continued ability to "manage" American blacks as is the move to turn the teaching adult into a frail old man who needs to be taught. All in all, like many "white" texts from the Reconstruction period, and in line with Homi K. Bhabha's conceptions of colonial mimicry, this purportedly sentimental image and story may well say as much about Northern white efforts to contain African Americans in controllable stereotypes as about any genuine desire for a "new era" for blacks.[4] Thus, a central premise of this chapter is that we may more fully appreciate black "alternative" domestic literacy narratives like Frances Harper's when we read them in dialogue with texts like the *Harper's* illustration and story. The nonthreatening characters *Harper's* constructs here may seem a far cry from the "savagery" that Toni Morrison says white American literature often attributes to blacks. But the approach she describes white writers as using to claim self-affirming identity by staging their "difference" from blacks is actually quite similar to the visual and print rhetoric of "'Uncle Tom' and His Grandchild"—another side to the same coin.[5] While texts I will discuss later fit Morrison's description more explicitly, I want to argue that even seemingly gentler stereotypes like the lovely young mulatta and the kindly old "uncle" have served a comparable function, especially when, as here, linked to familiar social scripts like the domestic literacy genre.

Narratives of Constraint and Resistance

Understanding both the white reshapings of domestic literacy narratives used to "situate" blacks in postbellum America and the resistant writing of black authors like Frances Harper requires a look backward to whites' pre–Civil War ideas about African American literacy. Among Southern middle-class whites, each of the major elements in the recurring storyline of the domestic literacy narrative had long been identified as "naturally" inaccessible to African Americans. Counterscripts based on racist stereotypes had regularly been employed by Southern aristocrats to justify their dominance over slaves as necessary, due to the purported impossibility of blacks' becoming civilized.[6] Certainly, Northern cultural arbiters had used similar discursive strategies to claim national leadership by distancing themselves from the undesirable "illiterate" behaviors of Others (see chapter 3), whether cast in terms of ethnicity (as in immigrant groups like the

Irish) or class (as in poor manual laborers). That both these Northern and Southern containment techniques involved constraining literacy acquisition is worth noting. But we must also acknowledge the important distinction between systematic *outlawing* of literacy for slaves in the South (see chapter 4) and less extreme moves aimed at limiting the literacy available to non-WASP, working-class Americans in the North.[7]

Legacies from the legal constraints on slave literacy obviously carried over for generations after the Civil War. Signs of that heritage were evident in postbellum representations of African American women as still unworthy of being republican mothers; of African American (male) learners as incapable or dangerous when allowed access to white, middle-class domesticated literacy; and of the curriculum for African American students as therefore needing to be grounded in practical, nonthreatening industry. The lingering traces of these attitudes in public discourse about African Americans' education today point to the need for additional study of links between such literature from the nineteenth century and current depictions of black (il)literacy.[8]

As one contribution to that worthwhile larger project, and within the context of this book's genre history, Foucauldian theory can highlight how a wide array of discursive strategies were employed by white cultural arbiters of the South *and* the North to limit educational opportunity for freed people during and after Reconstruction. As Houston A. Baker Jr. shows, Foucault's concepts of institutional control effectively elucidate how (purportedly beneficial) educational institutions and practices have been used to constrain black Americans, especially in the South.[9] Adding the perspective of Rosemary Hennessy's materialist feminist stance brings us closer to the central goal of this chapter: to contrast Reconstruction-era verbal enactments of some whites' containment impulse with Frances Harper's canny resistance, a gendered rhetorical strategy she affiliated with the domestic literacy narrative.

In *Discipline and Punish*, Foucault focuses on the development of prisons and associated "'carceral' mechanisms" and institutions to reveal how they were "applied not [just] to transgressions against a 'central' law" but to "a whole multiplicity of illegalities" and challenges to the dominant power systems of eighteenth- and nineteenth-century Europe. At the close of *Discipline and Punish*, Foucault points out that, in the suppression of "bodies and forces" via multiple "mechanisms" and "discourses," "institutions of repression, rejection, exclusion, [and] marginalization" such as the prison and the school have been supported by the "unavowable petty cruelties, small acts of cunning, calculated methods, techniques, 'sciences' that permit the fabrication of the disciplinary individual." And he points ahead to other work that is necessary to study "the power of normalization" so often exercised in modern communities to restrict those on the margins of society.[10] What Foucault describes as European leaders' purposeful "fabrication" of the criminal and the insane surely has a parallel in constructions of the freedman as savage, the freed mother as immoral, and both as requiring disciplinary restraint. Significant sociopolitical power accrued to whites through such discourse, while the effects these "methods, techniques, [and] 'sciences'" had on blacks were often masked in pseudoscientific or journalistic rhetoric. So, starting with the Foucauldian assumption that social subjugation can be effectively enacted and thereby reinforced in public discourse, I will explicate recurring textual strategies white sociopolitical leaders used to represent black mothers, black postbellum students, and the curriculum for freed slaves. These discursive patterns set blacks outside the boundaries of an idealized American community achieved, for whites, through education models to which African Americans were being denied full access.

My reading of this suppressive discourse will also be guided by feminist rewritings of Foucault, however. Rosemary Hennessy's materialist feminism, in particular, extends Foucault's views on how discourses of power operate in very specific material contexts. Hennessy values Foucault's positioning of discursive practice in local social fields, such as, in this case, debates associated with education of the freedmen in the South. But she also critiques Foucault's "theory of power" (articulated in *Discipline and Punish* and elsewhere) as inadequate for developing frameworks for "understanding relations among discourses hierarchically." Hennessy feels that, in positioning "power along with its complement, resistance," as "everywhere," Foucault prevents our establishing "the distinctive political force of some discourses over others." A closely related problem, she argues, is the inability of Foucauldian analysis "to imagine how discursively constructed subjects could effect radical social change."[11]

In line with Hennessy's sense that discourse often strives to construct a hierarchy of political power, I will emphasize the consistency evident in efforts to set white control of postbellum education over black aspirations and to justify that control by stereotyped portrayals of white and black mothers and children, instructors and students, teaching and learning. In contrast, I will cite Frances Harper's writing to address Hennessy's mandate to identify instances of individual agency resisting coercive social power. Specifically, Harper appropriated the domestic literacy narrative to counter the discourse aimed at restricting African American citizenship by denying blacks access to national education and political participation as imagined in white versions of the genre.[12]

A Tradition of Resistance

I single out Frances Harper's resistant rhetoric from an extensive tradition in black women's American literature because of the unusually large body of writing she created over a long authorial career, the close ties between her fiction writing and her educational agenda, and recent scholarship's emphasis on her important position among black woman authors of the postbellum era.[13] Certainly, she was not unique in her determined engagement with race issues through resistant rhetoric. As Jacqueline Jones Royster points out in an analysis of authorial careers ranging from Maria W. Stewart's to Ida B. Wells-Barnett's and Anna Julia Cooper's, nineteenth-century African American women regularly and self-consciously used their writing for strategic resistance, much of it carried out "in acts of literacy that have yielded remarkable rewards for themselves and for others."[14] Even during the era of slavery, as a number of recent interpretations have indicated, Harriet Jacobs capitalized on her white, middle-class audience's genre-based reading schema to resist characterizations in *Incidents in the Life of a Slave Girl* that could otherwise have associated her with stereotypes of black slave women's immorality.[15] Elizabeth Keckley's 1868 memoir chronicled one woman's move from slavery to working as a seamstress for Mary Todd Lincoln, thus impressively positioning a black woman in *the* White House.[16] Ellen Craft's compelling testimony in an 1870s Boston courtroom did not win her husband William's difficult legal case, but, as Dorothy Sterling observes, Craft was his "best defense." She described their work at a school near Savannah in terms so impressive that one Massachusetts newspaper praised her "plain, straightforward manner, the strength of which the cross-examination did not appear to weaken," and declared, "It certainly seemed that she was a ministering angel to the people of her race."[17] Near the turn of the century, black women forged a carefully orchestrated, collaborative response to John W. Jacks's infamous 1890s letter vilifying African American women's morals. Both Josephine Ruffin's call to clubwomen to unite in reaction and Victoria Earle Matthews's pointed speech on "The Value of Race Literature" exemplified strategies of rhetorical appropriation.[18] Given this rich context, Harper's Reconstruction-era domestic literacy narrative may be productively viewed within a tradition of nineteenth-century African

American rhetoric adapting gendered writing to particular historical moments yet consistently recognizing the need to resist white discourse and beliefs about black women.

Even the particular approach of affiliating with white, middle-class norms for domesticated teaching (while marking distinctions associated with racial difference) did not originate or end with Harper. Other African American women writers had already published narratives making strategic use of the domestic literacy genre well before *Minnie's Sacrifice* appeared. In her *Incidents in the Life* narrative, for instance, Harriet Jacobs alludes indirectly to the genre's ideology by emphasizing her inability to carry out its ideals for maternal teaching: she associates the denial of her rights with being unable to teach her own children because she was separated from them.[19] In more explicit, extended applications of the genre's plot and characterization tools within hybrid texts, both Susan Paul's 1835 *Memoir of James Jackson* and Charlotte Forten's 1864 essays in the *Atlantic Monthly* on her Port Royal teaching depict African American women carrying out the mandate for single women's motherly teaching that was also being touted by white women educators. Thus, Harper's late 1860s version of the domestic literacy narrative had black as well as white forerunners.

Distinguishing between Forten's and Paul's adaptations of the genre underscores the artistic complexity and rhetorical force of Harper's. While Forten's reports from the Sea Islands exhibit some ambivalence toward her students and an uncertainty about her own social position as a teacher of contrabands, Paul's narrative more closely anticipates Harper's 1860s concept of African American women's communal teaching as blending the white, middle-class model of maternal teaching with a race-based heritage of community action.

Carla L. Peterson emphasizes the intense feelings of "cultural alterity" that Forten experienced at Port Royal in the early 1860s and shows that this sense of ambivalence left its mark on Forten's writing. Peterson pays particular attention to the diary (from which Forten drew for the *Atlantic Monthly* articles and for two letters published in the *Liberator*). In many of these diary entries, Peterson finds signs that "for the entire period that Forten spent on Saint Helena, she remained ambiguously poised between the two social groups"—the Northern teaching corps and Southern ex-slaves—feeling "unassimilable" into either. This tenuous social position made it difficult for Forten to enact on Saint Helena a class- and gender-based model for motherly schoolteaching consistent with domestic literacy narratives on feminized education, which she had previously internalized while living in New England. More specifically, she struggled to carry out the high ideals for feminized teaching that she had inscribed abstractly in writing like "A Parting Hymn." Whereas that poem celebrates the gendered work she anticipated for Salem normal school graduates like herself—benevolently educating the young—her own in-between status as the only mixed-race teacher in Port Royal meant that her role as motherly educator was unstable.[20] Perhaps unsurprisingly, then, Forten's depictions of her teaching vacillate between enthusiasm for her work, on the one hand, and frustration over the challenges she encountered, on the other.[21] Ultimately, while Forten's published accounts and her diary both affirm the importance of the Port Royal experiment, her 1860s reports about her Southern teaching never achieve the kind of unified vision for uplift that Harper would reach in *Minnie's Sacrifice*.

Nonetheless, it appears likely that Harper drew upon Forten's writing, specifically the two *Atlantic Monthly* essays, to stress the positive qualities of the South's freed people. Unlike white male accounts (outlined later in this chapter), Forten's descriptions of her experiences with ex-slaves in St. Helena are consistent with Harper's letters and articles about her travels through the South after the war. Harper's mention in an 1870s speech of a "Miss Foster" as having "written for the *Atlantic Monthly*" suggests that, despite confusion (or a possible typographical error) associated with Forten's name, Harper was familiar with the two-part series.[22] If she did read the 1864 essays, Harper would have found material for her own Reconstruction narratives, including Forten's use of shadow and light imagery to contrast slavery with freedom and confidence in freed slaves' eagerness to learn.[23] As Peterson notes, much of Forten's analysis emphasizes "the moral nature of the newly freed people," particularly "traits highly valued by the dominant culture: the industriousness of their labor force, the courage of black conscripts in the Union army, the willingness of many to accept the Christian rituals of baptism and marriage." At the same time, as Peterson points out, "Forten was also highly appreciative of a variety of folkways derived from African culture that had given the freed people the strength to endure and survive slavery" (191). She exalted their courteous attitudes, their vibrant dress, and their songs, which she valued above the Christian hymns she was teaching them. All in all, if Forten's characterizations of the freed people did not form a direct source for Harper's depictions in *Minnie's Sacrifice* several years later, they do correspond closely enough to suggest the two authors were accessing related traditions, including their similar experiences with abolitionist discourse.

Like Forten's work, Susan Paul's account of feminized teaching certainly merits attention as a forerunner of *Minnie's Sacrifice, Trial and Triumph,* and *Iola Leroy.* While I have uncovered no direct evidence of Harper's familiarity with Paul's story of an "attentive and obedient scholar,"
the portrayal of Paul's motherly teaching and James Jackson's learning at
the very least affirms an antebellum tradition of community-building education among African Americans—a heritage that also informed Harper's
writing after the Civil War. Paul's text is equally noteworthy for its depiction of an alternative to the hierarchized, patronizing, cross-class literacy
management seen in so many white women's stories about their educational "outreach" to the poor.

Published in Boston in 1835 but only recently rediscovered by Lois
Brown, Paul's *Memoir of James Jackson* merges two reconfigured narrative
forms: the celebratory biography of a young male American (as seen in
countless portraits of George Washington) and the "benevolent" domestic
literacy narrative.[24] Lauding the remarkable learning career of James Jackson, who until his death was a student in Miss Paul's primary school, the
memoir addresses multiple audiences. One audience, according to Lois
Brown, was sympathetic white cultural arbiters, who might be convinced,
through James's story, that African American children were capable of
spiritual-minded learning and that their literacy acquisition was therefore
worthy of support. Another audience was African American children, for
whom James could serve as a role model.[25] Still another, Brown explains,
was African American parents and influential leaders of the Boston black
community, whom she hoped to encourage "to invest in their children"
through religious education (25). Particularly for African American mothers, Paul casts James's literacy development in spiritual terms, repeatedly
stressing how his studies at school interacted productively with his learning at home.

The collaborative nature of James's literacy development anticipates
Harper's communal vision of African American education in *Minnie's Sacrifice* even as it sets the memoir apart from most white women's contemporary writing about benevolent literacy management.[26] Susan Paul herself
was, in many respects, a member of the esteemed social class to which Lydia Sigourney and Catharine Maria Sedgwick also belonged.[27] The daughter
of a highly successful minister and an esteemed educator (Catherine Paul),
Susan Paul had already gained renown as a teacher when she wrote the
memoir. With her status including membership in such genteel social
groups as the mixed-race Boston Female Anti-Slavery Society (BFASS) and

the African American Ladies Temperance Society, Susan Paul was an admired figure in her community. As such, she could have represented an African American version of the "enlightened and benevolent" class that, for white readers, was producing so many narratives about managing working-class literacies. Yet, drawing upon ideals for community-oriented education associated more with her race than with her social class, the memoir of James Jackson limns her ambitious management of his education as cooperating with (and actively supporting) the home teaching provided by his working-class mother.

Paul's portrayal of James Jackson's mother is, in fact, the narrative's most forceful sign of an alternative version of cross-class benevolence. Although Susan Paul stresses that James's mother always "had a great deal of work to do," the memoir shows how Mrs. Jackson contributed to his learning by discussing, at home, what he was learning in Miss Paul's school (84). In anecdotes anticipating Harper's valuing of the experience-based knowledge among ex-slave mothers, Paul offers repeated examples of James's mother astutely building on his school lessons by adding moral guidance from her own daily life to complement the more scholarly knowledge of Susan Paul. For instance, when James "went home" from a lesson about "the poor slaves," whose masters "did not want [them] to know any thing about reading the Bible" and who therefore were being "kept . . . from school," Mrs. Jackson urged him to craft his own prayer based on "what you think they need." The resulting text, prompted both by Miss Paul and by Mrs. Jackson, exemplifies their joint direction of James's literacy to shape him into a moral American: "O Lord, pity the poor slaves, and let them be free, that they may have their liberty, and be happy as I am, —and may they have good teachers to learn them to read, as I have, and make them all very good. Amen" (89).

In multiple anecdotes like this one, Paul portrays collaborative management of James's literacy. At the same time, she underscores how both motherly teachers share his affection, with neither usurping devotion from the other. Thus, while "his attachment to his mother [is] strengthened with his mind and body," his teacher's "attachment" to him grows "stronger and stronger" as well. Sharing maternal feelings for James as they share instructional duties, Susan Paul and Mrs. Jackson exemplify a reciprocal benevolence growing out of collaborative literacy management (92). As a result, James is able to teach his mother things she otherwise would not have known. At the same time, through his remarkable advances in scholarship, his schoolteacher is learning as well.

Interestingly, Susan Paul attempted to circulate her narrative about reciprocal cross-class literacy in a venue that would have allowed white middle-class women ready access to this model and therefore might have encouraged their commitment to less hierarchical educational agendas. However, her submission to the American Sunday School Union was rejected, probably, Lois Brown speculates, based on the organization's wish to avoid endorsing black schooling during a period when Nat Turner's rebellion had led so many whites to fear "African American literacy . . . as a stepping-stone to civil disobedience."[28] Despite its relatively limited circulation in the 1830s, the recent recovery of Susan Paul's narrative underscores a tradition of collaborative, spiritually oriented, and community-building education among nineteenth-century blacks—a heritage with which *Minnie's Sacrifice* would have connected, especially through its publication in the *Christian Recorder.*

Reading *Minnie's Sacrifice* as a domestic literacy narrative also enables us to see it as a significant step in the development of Frances Harper's own project of racial uplift. Following Frances Foster's lead, I see Harper's writing after the Civil War as falling loosely into three periods, each addressing distinctive challenges to her race.[29] In the decade just after the war, Harper concentrated on immediate issues associated with the education of the freedmen, especially in the South, where she traveled extensively on speaking tours. Harper countered propaganda about the inability of former slave mothers and their children to participate in white, middle-class versions of domestic literacy by proposing an alternative model drawing upon the experiences of slavery itself as a source of knowledge and leadership. In *Minnie's Sacrifice* and in the Chloe poem sequence of *Southern Sketches,* she adapted two different narrative forms (the serial novel and the poetry sequence) into domestic literacy narratives for two different audiences (black readers of the *Christian Recorder* and the mixed-race audience of her poems). In both cases, she ranked oral tradition *with* print text as a powerful source of learning, while asserting the capability of former slaves to exercise American citizenship.

During the post-Reconstruction era, Harper's writing faced what could have been a debilitating dilemma: calls to limit blacks' educational opportunities to industrial training and a weakening commitment to African Americans evident in Northerners' growing accommodation of the South. In speeches like "A Factor in Human Progress" and in her *Trial and Triumph* narrative, Harper encourages members of her race to adopt domesticated learning practices and educational goals for women that had been touted, earlier in the century, by white, middle-class women writers like Catharine Maria Sedgwick, Lydia Sigourney, and Lydia Maria Child, and that were being rechanneled in women's organizations like upper-middle-class study clubs. But she simultaneously shows that those approaches would need to be reconfigured to address the issues facing black women and men because of race and class prejudice. So Harper's writing during this period reasserts gendered, moral learning goals for African American middle-class women in the context of male-led debates about practical versus intellectual/cultural programs of study for her race. Therefore, *Trial and Triumph* represents a particularly astute use of the domestic literacy narrative to counter constrained education models for blacks being advocated (and managed) by paternalistic white leaders like the Slater and Peabody funds' agents.[30]

Finally, in the 1890s, Harper could see encouraging signs in the growth of a black middle class, especially in urban areas. Yet she also recognized the continued power of racism. On specific occasions such as the 1893 Columbian Exposition, in ongoing practices such as lynching, and in the ambivalence white women leaders of the suffrage and temperance movements showed toward their black counterparts, Harper and her contemporaries like Ida B. Wells-Barnett confronted racism's persistent menace. Signaling her full awareness of the difficulties inherent in black-white race relations, Harper's speeches during this period and her masterpiece narrative *Iola Leroy* encouraged African American women to claim expanded, race-oriented access to the social role of motherhood that had been articulated so often for whites in domestic literacy narratives throughout the century. As a synthesis of her proactive views on gendered teaching and learning, *Iola Leroy* stands as her most sustained appropriation of the literary genre that, before her vigorous interventions, had been dominated by white writers.[31] But she laid the foundation for that final novel in her earlier serials *Minnie's Sacrifice* and *Trial and Triumph*.[32]

Our appreciation of Harper's rhetoric in all these texts can be greatly enhanced by positioning her writing within each respective historical moment's public debate about African Americans' place in the national community. Critics have already done important work on *Iola Leroy*.[33] *Minnie's Sacrifice* and *Trial and Triumph* are just beginning to generate such detailed analyses, however, following Frances Smith Foster's groundbreaking expansion of Harper's available oeuvre.[34] While addressing specific 1860s contingencies through a race-based tradition of literary teaching, *Minnie's Sacrifice* resisted discourse being produced by white male writers who sought to limit freedmen's access to active citizenship. An analysis of the interplay between such writers' texts and Harper's 1860s serial addresses the goals in Hennessy's feminist adaptation of Foucault, underscoring white discursive efforts to reinforce social hierarchy but also Harper's efforts to "effect radical social change" through "oppositional discourses and the subjects [she] [re]constructed" imaginatively there.

Reconstructing African American Literacy: Conflicting Visions

Historian Eric Foner notes: "Perhaps the most striking illustration of the freedmen's quest for self-improvement was their seemingly unquenchable thirst for education." Although many slaves, like Frederick Douglass and Josiah Henson, sought literacy in spite of the state laws against instructing blacks, Foner points out that "over ninety percent of the South's adult black population was illiterate in 1860." Since newly freed blacks perceived "access to education for themselves and their children" as "central to the meaning of freedom," "adults as well as children thronged the schools" opened by white Northern benevolent groups in cooperation with the Freedmen's Bureau.[35] At the same time, Southern blacks often worked to open their own schools in cities like Savannah and New Orleans. And African American teachers from the North—such as Charlotte Forten, Harriet Jacobs, and William and Ellen Craft—journeyed south to aid in the education effort. Frances Harper was one leader in this initiative.

During the first years after the Civil War, Harper traveled throughout the South lecturing on education-supported racial uplift, both to mixed audiences and to freed slaves, including groups of mothers like herself.[36] While it is regrettable that no complete archive of those speeches exists, we can nonetheless use the letters she wrote to her mentor, William Still, and her articles for publications like the *National Anti-Slavery Standard* to draw inferences about the impact she had on her audiences and about the influence they had on her writing.[37] Certainly, she was well aware of the difficulties the South's freed people faced. But she often looked beyond those problems toward activist intervention. Referencing her 1870 speaking tour in Alabama, for example, she observed, "Men talk about missionary work among the heathen, but if any lover of Christ wants a field for civilizing work, here is a field" (*Brighter Coming Day*, 130).[38] Yet in the same letter, she positioned herself as part of the community she was trying to serve and insisted, "I am not discouraged, if I will only be faithful, and in spite of suspicion and distrust, I will work on; the deeper our degradation, the louder our call for redemption" (130). Writing in the next calendar year from the same state, Harper noted "that the improvement in some of the cabins was not very much in advance of what it was in Slavery," but she contrasted such rough living conditions with a seemingly natural refinement in people she met, since even amid those "lowly homes I met with hospitality" (*Brighter Coming Day*, 133). She admitted that, in South Carolina, she had to "listen to heart-saddening stories of grievous old wrongs, for the shadows of the past have not been fully lifted from the minds of the former victims of slavery" (*Brighter Coming Day*, 124). But she also promised that "the shadows bear the promise of a brighter coming day; and in fact, so far as the colored man is concerned, I do not feel particularly uneasy about his future. With his breadth of physical organization, his fund of mental endurance, and his former discipline in the school of toil and privation, I think he will be able to force his way upward and win his recognition even in the South" (124).

By proposing that the painful experience of slavery had endowed the freedmen with unique strengths, Harper began articulating an argument that she would develop further in her longer postbellum narratives—attributing the progress of members of her race as much to their own hard work and admirable character as to the Yankee missionaries carrying versions of New England domesticated teaching into Southern schoolhouses.[39] She invoked examples of former slaves whose condition was now superior to their masters', with "one of our new citizens" especially notable for having purchased his master's home, while the former slave owner was reduced to living "in the poor-house." In the same letter, she praised a woman who had used freedom's "opportunity for work and wages" to secure "some education" and then a chance at "teaching school"—that is, to reach a situation where "her former mistress has been to her for help." Overall, Harper attributed setbacks among the freed people to conditions beyond their control—especially the American government—while asserting that their potential for uplift was tied to a nobility forged through suffering.[40]

While Harper was supporting idealistic goals for Reconstruction education at no small cost to her personal comfort and safety, others were, in Foucault's terms, laboring to "fabricate" alternative versions of shiftless black motherhood, irredeemable black childhood, and deranged black manhood as threatening the South and the nation as a whole. Closely associated with these negative stereotypes were portraits of Reconstruction teaching and schools that questioned the very efficacy of such initiatives, given the "savage" traits of the Negro race. Significantly, some of the venues for this discursive construction process were locations where African American leaders like Harper might have expected to find unwavering confidence in their race. For instance, in the official reports of the Freedmen's Bureau, charged with facilitating education of the South's former slaves, and in the pages of the Northeast's then-premiere literary-political magazine, the *Atlantic Monthly*, we can point to striking examples of the negative racial discourse that Harper, on returning north after her Southern tour, would surely have felt compelled to resist.[41]

When we read 1860s Freedmen's Bureau reports today, racist stereotypes leap off the same pages where scientific-looking charts and statistics-laden prose document education's gradual progress in the postwar South. Full of internal contradictions along those lines, J. W. Alvord's *Fourth Semi-Annual Report on Schools for Freedmen* (1867–68) frequently celebrates improvements in the schools serving the "colored people" but (unlike Harper) attributes success to white Northern influence more than to the local freedmen themselves. While praising the determination of freed slaves to have their children educated, Bureau reports often underscore learning handicaps related to having been enslaved.[42] Typical characterizations read like this: "The causes of irregularity in attendance are found in the shiftlessness of old, servile habits" on the part of the students and only more rarely "in a lack of energy and interest on the part of the teachers" (14). Distancing the freedmen from a commendable noblesse oblige among Northern educators, Alvord's 1867 introduction declares, "It is enough to know that an ignorant people are seeking knowledge; degraded, yet susceptible of improvement, and that past injuries inflicted devolve upon us a special obligation" (1). Alvord's stance here represents a notable inverse of Harper's perspective toward the Southern freedmen in many of her letters.[43] Setting their rhetorical choices side by side, we can see how the antebellum domestic literacy narratives' most familiar discursive elements—such as the learner in training and the enlightened, benevolent teacher—could be adapted quite differently later in the century, depending upon audience and purpose.

But Alvord's view was nonetheless far more positive than a contemporary evaluation provided by J. W. DeForest in his 1868 *Atlantic Monthly* account of Freedmen's Bureau work in South Carolina. Discounting the likelihood that the schools opening all over the South would really be able to re-form freedmen's children, DeForest declares:

It is a mooted point whether colored children are as quick at learning as white children. . . . Certainly those whom I saw could not compare with the Caucasian youngster of ten or twelve. . . . They are inferior to him, not only in knowledge but in the facility of acquisition. In their favor it must be remembered, that they lack the forcing elements of highly educated competition and of a refined home influence. A white lad gets much bookishness and many advanced ideas from the daily converse of his family. Moreover, ancestral intelligence, trained through generations of study, just tell. . . . The negro, as he is, no matter how educated, is not the mental equal of the European. Whether he is not a man, but merely, as "Ariel" and Dr. Cartwright would have us believe, "a living creature," is quite another question. . . . Human or not, there he is in our midst, four millions strong: and if he is not educated mentally and morally, he will make us trouble.[44]

A number of narratives published in the *Atlantic Monthly* during Reconstruction—among them DeForest's two-part "The Man and Brother" series in September and October of 1868—echoed the most pessimistic assessments of Freedmen's Bureau administrative records.[45] Coming from a regular *Atlantic* contributor who had served as a Bureau superintendent in South Carolina, DeForest's accounts carried potent authority. Furthermore, appearing in a magazine closely associated with J. G. Whittier and other liberals, the essays would have easily claimed the attention of Northern middle-class readers long accustomed to reading positive visions of African Americans.[46] DeForest did include a few stories that cast the freed people in a positive light, and he reminded readers that, in his administrative role, he was more likely to encounter the problems than the successes of former slaves. Nonetheless, the tone of his narrative, and the anecdotes he chose, present a far more pessimistic view than had Charlotte Forten's 1864 two-part *Atlantic* series about her teaching in the same state.

The dominant theme of DeForest's first essay offers a callous vision of the freedmen as "first savages, then slaves" who have little hope of making progress toward informed citizenship.[47] Repeatedly suggesting that their enslavement might best be viewed as a step up in status, DeForest cites anecdote after anecdote to illustrate racial traits that would make improvement through education unlikely (even impossible?) for the freed people to achieve.[48] While commenting on black sharecroppers' inability to make a living, for instance, DeForest attributes their problems not to inequities within the system but to their constantly going on "day huntings and night frolics" when they should be working in the fields—a tendency he connects to a natural inability to calculate how much work is really required to produce a harvest. DeForest similarly describes the freedmen's involvement with religion and political associations as grounded more in inherent raucousness than in serious motives. Complaining that "the negroes waste much of their time in amusement," he observes, "What with trapping rabbits by day and treeing 'possums by night, dances which last till morning, and prayer-meetings which are little better than frolics, they contrive to be happier than they have 'any call to be,' considering their chances of starving to death" (I, 342). Similarly, though satirizing the "delightful fervor" of an ex-Confederate planter who sat near him on a railroad car, DeForest repeats the old man's grumbling assessment of the entire "breed, seed, and generation of niggers" as "the meanest, triflingest creeturs agoin'," with "no good side to 'em." Quoting the old planter's equation of a negro with "a no-account creetur," DeForest seems to affirm this striking generalization: "All the men are thieves, and all the women are prostitutes. It's their nature to be that way, and they never 'll be no other way. They ain't worth the land they cover. They ought to be improved off the face of the earth" (I, 342).

In both parts of his series DeForest expresses particular concern about freedwomen, especially mothers. He indicates that one reason refined white missionary schoolmarms had trouble with their charges was the unfeminized disciplinary approaches being employed by black mothers at home. Having opined that, "if the negro younglings are well loved, they are also well whipped," he then recounts the story of one frustrated Bureau-supported teacher whose efforts to import New England's moral suasion approaches for domesticated teaching encountered angry resistance from a former slave mother. According to DeForest, when the teacher turned a young girl away from class "for bad behavior, the mother appeared to remonstrate. 'What you turn her out for?' she demanded, 'Ef she's naughty, why don' you whip her?'" When the kindly teacher explained that she didn't "approve of whipping children," the freed mother's reaction was swift, decisive, and, for nineteenth-century Northern readers of the *Atlantic*, a clear sign that she was incapable of the nurturing instruction portrayed in domestic literacy narratives: "'It's your business,' screamed the mother,—'it's your business to whip 'em. That's what you's sont here for'" (II, 416).[49]

DeForest argues that the middle-class feminine traits that freedwomen of the South were trying to acquire were the wrong ones. Although he deems it "almost ludicrous to find the 'woman question'" posed about those "whom we have been accustomed to hear of as a 'nigger,'" DeForest sarcastically points to "a growing disinclination to marriage among the young freedmen, because the girls are learning to shirk out-of-door work, to demand nice dresses and furniture, and, in short, to be fine ladies" (II, 425). To emphasize the hopelessly lax morals of South Carolina's freedwomen, DeForest declares that a "large proportion of the colored applicants for Bureau rations were young women with three or four children, and without the pretence of a husband, —this, although bigamy is fearfully frequent" since "the average woman is apt to marry again if her 'old man' is absent for a year" (I, 343). Convinced as he was of the uncivilized nature of freedwomen, DeForest could understand a former plantation owner's explanation of why whipping was a logical choice for disciplining a slave woman. So, even as DeForest admits that the punishment may have been ineffectual, he intones, "Whether [her] morals would have been in better hands than [her master's], had her forefathers remained in Africa, is a question . . . which must probably be decided in the negative" (I, 343).

We might dismiss such crude stereotyping as DeForest's more easily today if we could ascribe it to a fanatical former Rebel rather than an administrator of the Freedmen's Bureau. We might even struggle to find irony in some of his complaints and thereby decide that ex-Confederates were the true targets of his criticisms—not so much former slaves. However, seeing his language echoed in official Bureau documents makes arguing such a position difficult. Along those lines, we must consider the stark implications of J. W. Alvord's characterization of freedwomen in a report he filed in 1868, one year after the document already examined.

Alvord's 1868 report would have been especially troubling to Harper, particularly in light of the appreciation she had gained for Southern rural freedwomen's admirable qualities by living among them during her lecture tours.[50] Alvord's section entitled "Female Education" claims to identify a danger associated with the character of black female students. Although allowing that an intense educational program might alleviate the threat eventually, his emphasis on the "degradation" inherent in the group belies any idea that they might contribute to the nation's Reconstruction:

> The effect of slavery on female character has been fearful. Both sexes were bereft of all true culture—cultured rather in whatever could corrupt and demoralize—but womanly virtues were wholly ignored; the female as a slave was crushed literally. She was driven from domestic life to the fields, to bear burdens fit only for the beast. She was bereft of social position, and abandoned to become the subject and victim of grossest passion. Every surrounding influence forced her back to the stupor and brutality of the savage state. There was no binding matrimony, no family sacredness, nothing which could be called home in slavery; and the wonder is, that after two hundred years of such influence, any trace of femi-

nine delicacy remains, or that girls, the offspring and imitators of such mothers, are aught but degraded. (75)

Besides drawing upon familiar abolitionist arguments about slavery's cruelty to women and families, Alvord's hybrid text is also ironically dependent upon the belief system central to domestic literacy narratives, whose images of motherhood, family teaching, and associated moral development are all recast into a degraded model. Former slave women, Alvord insists, have lost any claim on the "true culture" of "female character" and "womanly virtues." Having been forced by slavery "back to the stupor and brutality of the savage state," they cannot be expected to fulfill the social role assigned to white middle-class women: enlightened motherhood. Instead, they are doomed to replicate their flaws in their children, who, as "imitators of such mothers," can be "aught but degraded."

However difficult it is to read such racist passages today, we should recognize their arguments as a revealing context for Harper's writing about African American women's role in Reconstruction. Having created her own professional identity by extending domestic teaching to cast herself as a maternal teacher for her race, Harper would have been interested in making versions of that mission available to black women and acceptable to white allies.[51] Therefore, she would have paid attention to texts like Alvord's, interrogating the place of black womanhood in American culture, however far removed his ideas were from her own. As Hennessy's reading of Foucault suggests, a rhetorician like Harper could have turned such discourse back upon itself by reformulating it to meet her own educational goals. Hence, commentary like this from Alvord's 1868 text provides a useful prelude to reading *Minnie's Sacrifice:*

> Now that freedom has come, we must, with a just appreciation of the causes of this ruin, lay plans of recovery. . . . Mothers, sisters, daughters—chaste and refined—must circle round happy firesides, filling the abode with those elements of civilization peculiar to the family institution, and which schools alone can never furnish. Indeed, schools are even now greatly hindered by the counter teaching of vicious home life. Six hours of daily public training in books . . . will not overcome the degrading drill of the remaining eighteen at home. The current of depraved habit eddies back to its old channels too quickly, and the most faithful teacher is often discouraged by this sad drawback upon her labors. (75–76)

Interestingly, even as he offers up a race-oriented version of the social distancing familiar from benevolent literacy narratives earlier in the century, on one level Alvord's prescription here for improved African American womanhood and a reformed national family is quite consistent with Harper's own agenda. Writing from Greenville, Georgia, in 1870, she would affirm his call for developing women's home leadership as a crucial avenue toward racial uplift: "I am now going to have a private meeting with the women of this place if they will come out. I am going to talk with them about their daughters, and about things connected with the welfare of the race. Now is the time for our women to begin to try to lift up their heads and plant the roots of progress under the hearthstone" (*Brighter Coming Day*, 127). Certainly, she was well aware of the debilitating effects that slavery had on motherhood. But, having traveled extensively in the South and having met many former slaves, by the late 1860s Harper had developed a clear understanding of ways in which women had coped with slavery's assault on female identity and family. Part of her work in *Minnie's Sacrifice*, then, was to counter the stereotype of female slave degradation that was being pushed in white male Reconstruction narratives to its extreme—to blaming the victim and assigning to her a depravity more fairly attributable to slavery itself. To reclaim motherhood and its teaching role, Harper would revise the model of the moral American mother who directed her children's preparation for civic participation by managing their literacy to accommodate the experiences of the very Southern freedwomen white male writers like Alvord and DeForest were demonizing as incapable of recuperation. In *Minnie's Sacrifice*, she would celebrate the motherhood of women whose teaching texts were grounded in folk culture rather than merely in the printed word; she would demonstrate the efficacy of collaborative, communal teaching to complement the white, middle-class model of single-family-centered domestic pedagogy; and she would imagine ways for synthesizing knowledge gained from experience with school-based learning to train new generations of her race for full participation in American life.

Minnie's Sacrifice as Counternarrative

Minnie's Sacrifice appeared as a serial in the *Christian Recorder* between March and September of 1869.[52] Placing the novel in that venue signaled Harper's choice to write specifically to her own race in a location especially appropriate for her goals. By addressing a serious, well-educated audience, the *Christian Recorder* was seeking to establish itself as a black counterpart to white publications like the *Atlantic*.[53] Thus, using the *Christian Recorder* to revise the kinds of portraits DeForest and other *Atlantic*-type writers had painted of the freed people was a way of meeting those critiques on comparable ground. Furthermore, the *Christian Recorder* was the official publication of the A.M.E. Church, with a tradition firmly established, by the time *Minnie's Sacrifice* appeared, of combining official church materials with imaginative writing aimed at moral uplift of the race. As Frances Smith Foster points out, the periodical explicitly included on its masthead a goal of "Dissemination of Religion, Morality, Literature and Science," thereby conjoining religious doctrine, aesthetics, and moral instruction in a way difficult to appreciate in today's literary landscape.[54] Since this connection between the literary and the didactic had also been a key part of the domestic literacy narrative's tradition, Harper's choice of venue was particularly astute.

At the same time, in adapting the genre to the exigencies of Reconstruction, Harper faced challenges. She had overcome her own background as an orphan to construct herself as a maternal teacher for her community, through public speaking and writing consistent with domestic literacy narratives' valuing of performative literacy and activist motherhood. In addition, having worked as a teacher after being trained at her uncle's school, she was fully aware of the potential benefits to her race of adapting the New England educational tradition. Thus, she would not have wanted to reject out of hand the teaching program being enacted by Yankee schoolmarms for the freedmen, closely linked as it was to the idea of achieving moral worth and sociopolitical access through literacy development. Yet her extensive Southern travels had introduced her to alternative versions of communal motherhood. She now understood that folk culture's oral literacy practices of storytelling had been as important a factor in maintaining black Southern communities as print text had been to New England home-based teaching led by republican mothers.[55] Part of the genius of *Minnie's Sacrifice*, therefore, is Harper's synthesis of disparate literacy traditions. This process can be made particularly clear by looking at a representative, pivotal scene in the 1869 serial. Here and throughout the novel, Harper promotes a hybrid American motherhood, communal learning practices, and an expansive vision of the proper kinds of texts African Americans could use for racial uplift.

The archetypal scene in New England antebellum domestic literacy narratives is the teaching occasion when the white middle-class mother-teacher uses her enlightened explication of a print text to mold the character and thus direct the civic participation of her child. Harper's validation and simultaneous reformulation of that touchstone moment and its faith in motherly education's power are especially apparent in an exchange near the close of *Minnie's Sacrifice,* when Minnie's mother, Ellen, tells a story about a noble slave woman so as to guide her daughter's teaching of freed slaves. One level of the novel's structure up to this point has been dedicated to the familiar abolitionist tactic of critiquing slavery's oppression of motherhood. For instance, as the first episode begins, the hero Louis's mother, Agnes, has just died in childbirth, a victim of what Harper calls the "old story" (3). Agnes's baby is, of course, unlikely to be recognized by his father, their master. Furthermore, Louis's grandmother seems at first glance to be ill equipped to help him. Having lost the last of her three children in Agnes, Miriam is "painfully rocking her body to and fro," as if overcome by this latest "great sorrow" in her life (3). However, despite such discouraging odds, Harper shows how slave women did enact an enlightened motherhood and how Reconstruction-era America could benefit from their experience-based knowledge. The last conversation between Ellen and her daughter, Minnie, conveys perhaps the fullest representation of this theme.

With her husband, Louis, having just left on one of his own teaching missions, Minnie confides that she is nervous for her family's safety, and she asks if her mother ever feels "bitter towards these people, who have treated [her] so unkindly" (82). Admitting that she "used to," Ellen explains that she has "learned to cast [her] burden on the Lord," so that her "misery [has] all passed away": she has placed herself "at the foot of the cross" and "felt that [her] feet were planted on a rock" (82). Already sensing the underlying theme of her mother's lesson, Minnie responds with an observation about the nobility of learning through suffering—a cornerstone of Harper's contention that former slaves, and especially slave mothers, were worthy teachers for their race and, by extension, for the nation. Noting that "these suffering people have drawn to God," Minnie anticipates the specific illustrative story that her mother then tells to seal the issue—an oral text whose moral power prepares Minnie to embrace her responsibility, and her gift, of teaching her "scholars" for a better life (82–83). To underscore the idea that suffering can promote godliness, Ellen narrates the experience of Milly, "a colored woman to whom [her owners] were real mean and cruel," but whose faith eventually gave her freedom. A feminized parable, Ellen's story is clearly designed to teach her daughter the slave mother's virtues, as represented in Milly's decision to wait, rather than flee in search of freedom, after having been "beat[en] . . . to keep her from running away." With her clothes packed, "she kneeled down and prayed, and asked what she should do, and something reasoned with her," encouraging her not to leave.

Then, according to Ellen's purposeful gloss, "the best part of it was this, Milly's son had been away, and he came back and brought with him money enough to buy his mother . . . and so Milly got free" (83).

Straightforward as Ellen's tale seems, for Harper's *Christian Recorder* readers it would have been useful for recuperating the character of freed Southern women being excoriated in white publications and thereby coming to productive terms with a part of their racial history. The story also offered a key to educating themselves for the future. Ellen presents Milly's choice *not* to flee as worthwhile in this case. This decision produces an eventual victory over Milly's unjust masters, whose cruelty has prompted her prayers, which in turn lead to her being reunited her with her son. Besides arguing that "God's robe of love and light" supported slave women like Milly, Ellen's story proposes "that some things they see clearer through their tears," that this very crucible of slavery created unique knowledge now available to the whole race. Minnie's next comment, that she "will visit some of [her] scholars," reinforces a connection between the painful, experiential learning of slavery and the teaching needed during Reconstruction, for Minnie observes that her students—former slave women—teach her as much as they learn. "I often feel strengthened," she declares, "after visiting some of these good old souls, and getting glimpses into their inner life." Noting how they are constantly affirming "the power of God," Minnie associates their religious faith with a folk wisdom that can now help lead an uplift movement for the race.

Minnie's visit to the "lowly cabins" of her "scholars," just after talking with her mother, reiterates the reconstructed pattern of maternal teaching first presented in the exchange between Ellen and her daughter. Ellen's story of Milly has provided the kind of moral lesson New England's white domestic literacy narratives typically generated through shared consumption of print text. Now the brief tales the former slave mothers tell Minnie reassert both their right to a new version of the republican mother role and the efficacy, for their race and nation, of their assuming that responsibility. Hearing about one woman's kind adoption of orphans, another's loss of her child during slavery, and a third's ability to help her husband endure enslavement by trusting in God's eventual justice, Minnie "returned calmer than she had left," endowed with a "holy peace" uniting "high and low, rich and poor" (84). Having seen how "these people in their ignorance and simplicity had learned to look upon God as a friend," Minnie realizes that she cannot "teach these people religion" but instead "must learn from them" (84).

For Harper's anticipated readers, Ellen's oral story and Minnie's "reading" of it, followed by Minnie's hearing the freedwomen's tales, would have provided multilayered delineations of a new American motherhood, expanded to include the freedwomen of the South and the heritage of their slavery experience.[56] Harper carried out this creative appropriation within the narrative structure of the scene, reminiscent of white middle-class domestic literacy exchanges but also strikingly different: Ellen, an unschooled former slave, teaches her well-educated daughter, Minnie, via a new kind of domestic literacy management. By extension, Harper invites her own audience to imagine repetition of parallel learning scenes in real-life dialogues outside the printed publication site where *Minnie's Sacrifice* was appearing—in the postwar domestic settings where the author could envision African American families sharing her narrative with each other. That Harper indeed imagined just such communal reading experiences is clear, in fact, from the didactic maternal voice she assumes in her conclusion, where, like Harriet Beecher Stowe in *Uncle Tom's Cabin*, she speaks directly to her audience. Posing her argument as a rhetorical question, she says, "May I not modestly ask that the lesson of Minnie shall have its place among the educational ideas for the advancement of our race?" (90). Harper hoped that, through social reading of her serial, her audience would reenact the storytelling mother-child scene in *Minnie's Sacrifice*, drawing not only upon the white, middle-class model of processing print text collaboratively to generate social meaning but also the alternative model seen in Ellen and Minnie's celebration of oral folk culture.[57] Synthesizing maternally led learning approaches from two traditions, Harper's readers could enact a new kind of literature- *and* experience-centered literacy to reconstruct African American family life and the nation.

This new model of domesticated literacy carried out for the whole community is attained incrementally within the *Minnie's Sacrifice* narrative itself, as the paired characters of Minnie and Louis gradually recognize that their mixed-race identities can be beneficial to themselves and to others. Some have criticized Harper for seeming to exalt mulatto characters over others in *Iola Leroy,* and certainly her approach here might be seen as having similar limitations.[58] However, reading *Minnie's Sacrifice* as a reformulation of the domestic literacy narrative to resist racist stereotypes highlights the special contribution that a mixed-race hero and heroine could make to Harper's argument about African Americans' rightful place in society. In a number of white writers' attacks during Reconstruction, mulattos were singled out for special opprobrium. For example, H. S. Shaler's 1870

Atlantic essay, "An Ex-Southerner in South Carolina," claims that the "mixed races" represented a roadblock to a reunited America, since they were "peculiarly inflammable material," being more "quick-witted, but generally more unfitted and indisposed to hard labor than the pure blacks."[59] According to Shaler, the mulatto acquired disastrous traits from both sides: "From the white he inherits a refinement unfitting him for all work which has not a certain delicacy about it; from the black, a laxity of morals which, whether it be the result of innate incapacity . . . or the result of an utter want of training . . . , is still unquestionably a negro characteristic" (57). Unsalvageable as a worker and immoral besides, the mulatto, according to Shaler, had nothing to offer to society.

For Harper, in contrast, textually recuperating the mulatto would logically go hand in hand with expanding the model of American motherhood to include white as well as African American nurturing traditions for civic teaching.[60] In direct opposition to Shaler's views, Harper's heroine Minnie takes on an uplift agenda grounded in a flawless moral sense—teaching the people of her mother's race and seeing this work as an opportunity for greatness that would not have been available to her as a white woman (72). As she explains to Louis's sister, the choice of living as a black woman was not initially easy, but became a blessing. Having spent the "first years of [her] life . . . without . . . knowing" the truth of her identity, Minnie at first feared "social ostracism" when her mother revealed herself. But Minnie gradually becomes "reconciled to the change" and realizes that "there are lessons of life that we never learn in the bowers of ease. They must be learned in the fire" (72). For Minnie, affiliating with her mother's race eventually means achieving a distinctive purity, allowing her to recognize "that any society, however cultivated, wealthy or refined, would not be a social gain to me, if my color and not my character must be my passport to admission" (72). In an era when attacks like Shaler's were pervasive, for Harper's African American readers to see this mulatto character, who could have passed for white, decide instead on teaching her mother's race would have been more inspiring than to have a "pure" black presented as a role model of maternal citizenship.[61]

Harper also made a significant choice by portraying two mulatto characters—one from each gender—learning about civic responsibility. The doubling move of having Louis and Minnie both working as dedicated teachers merges the educational responsibilities of mothers and fathers in African American communities and the larger society. At the same time, by having Minnie insist that "the negro woman's hour" has surely arrived, that she

merits "as many rights and claims as the negro man" (78), Harper emphasizes equal political enfranchisement for both genders as a goal central to
the needs of the race. Accordingly, Louis freely accepts Minnie's suggestion
that a government truly grounded in "our common humanity" will be
achieved only when "entrench[ed] . . . in the hearts of both men and
women." In their brief married life, Harper depicts the possibility of an androgynous teacher-citizen, with equality embodied in the give-and-take,
male-and-female parlor "conversations upon the topics of the day" in their
home, as well as their commitment to shared participation in political life
outside the domestic setting (79).[62] In the androgynous ideal represented in
the community-oriented marriage of her two mulatto characters, not only
does Harper counteract the explicitly racist stereotypes in writing like De-
Forest's and the Freedmen's Bureau reports; she also offers a far more useful model for literacy-based uplift than the sentimental but inadequate
image of the *Harper's Weekly* narrative from Georgia described at the beginning of this chapter.

In that context, having Minnie, rather than Louis, be the victim of Klan
murderers is painfully shocking at first, but this plot twist is consistent
both with the historical record of the period and with Harper's move to
blur gendered social roles for postbellum African Americans. On the one
hand, as Eric Foner points out, "gender offered no protection" from white
Southerners' violence against the black community in the years immediately after the war.[63] On the other, Harper's choice reinforces her suggestion that the so-called separate-sphere divisions of labor did not apply to
the race-based social situation she was addressing.[64] Indeed, by the end of
the narrative, Louis could represent a new ideal synthesizing gender as
well as racial identities, carrying out as he does the same work of nurturance that Harper associates throughout the novel with the former slave
mothers of the South. For Louis, as for other would-be "mothers" of the
race, Harper proposes that patient communal labor will be as essential as
bold courage: "to labor and to wait until peace like bright dew should de-
scend where carnage had spread ruin around, and freedom and justice, like
glorified angels, should reign triumphant where violence and slavery had
held their fearful carnival of shame and crime for angels" (90). A civic
leader whose agenda offers a striking revision of Stowe's George Shelby,
Louis is also given access to political leadership avenues denied to George
Harris.

Both Louis and Minnie reach their idealized maternal status through
gradual learning over the course of the serial. Harper underscores the hy-

brid quality of their status by revealing the limits of both white and black individual maternal mentors, while suggesting that collaborative mothering by women from both races could create a new model for American motherhood. Thus, Harper celebrates the benefits of her main characters' exposure to white, middle-class educational models but underscores the inadequacy of those same models, acting alone, for meeting the needs of postwar blacks. Similarly, she recuperates the maternal commitment of black slave mothers but also acknowledges the white-influenced learning needed for full incorporation of African Americans into the national polity.

In the first case, Minnie's adoptive mother, Anna, is an appealing role model of white American motherhood—but also a sign of its limits. Some of what Minnie eventually teaches her Southern students, she acquires through Anna's instruction. Specifically, Minnie "learned from Anna those womanly arts that give beauty, strength and grace to the fireside, and it was her earnest desire to teach [the freed people] how to make their homes bright and happy" (74). On its own, however, Anna's example is not sufficient to meet the challenges facing the race Minnie chooses to serve. Anna's circumscribed life experiences restrict her ability to provide Minnie with accessible, concrete examples of Christian courage. For example, when Minnie, while still in the North, hears a sad story about the prejudice encountered by a "very interesting and intelligent" former slave, she speculates that "it must be dreadful to be colored." Anna's quiet advice that "God never makes any mistakes" stops well short of leading the young girl to face her true identity (46–48).[65] Only through her biological slave mother, Ellen, does Minnie come to accept her mixed-race identity and her rightful teaching mission.

Just as she complicates the portrait of white motherhood in Anna, Harper depicts Louis's surrogate white mother (and actual half-sister), Camilla, as both admirable and inadequate. In the gradual development of Camilla's motherhood, Harper limns both the limits of the white middle-class ideal and the potential benefits to the nation that a new model, incorporating the knowledge of the black freed people, could provide to a reunited American society. Already loving and empathetic in the serial's opening scenes, Camilla recalls the version of motherhood long associated with middle-class authors like Lydia Sigourney, Lydia Maria Child, and Catharine Maria Sedgwick. But living motherless in a Southern home corrupted by slavery, Camilla does not have the firmly grounded moral sense to lead Louis to full American manhood on her own. Camilla sentimentally identifies with Louis from the moment when she first sees him as an orphaned infant, and she lobbies her father to "adopt" the child she naively fails to recognize as already her sibling. Drawing upon her reading of the Bible's Moses story for inspiration, she constitutes herself as Louis's replacement mother, intent on saving him from the perils of slavery. She also sponsors his education in the North by persuading her father to send the young man there. Furthermore, like Anna, Camilla has a refined taste, appealingly reflected in her housekeeping, especially in her flower-filled New Orleans home after the war (70).

Significantly, though, Camilla's deepest understanding of the nurturing mother role comes not from white tutelage but from her daily interaction with the plantation's slaves, whose life stories teach her true moral values. Harper's *Christian Recorder* readers would have appreciated the irony of Camilla's father, who had corrupted Louis's innocent mother, Agnes, "superintend[ing] the education of his daughter" by having her "reading only from the best authors, both ancient and modern," so that she "was growing up with very little knowledge of the world, except what she learned from books" (10). What she does discover about the world, and ultimately what she learns of right and wrong, comes through contact with her father's slaves, especially Miriam and Agnes, and from her keen observation of race issues during travel in the North.[66] Listening to life stories told by blacks, she begins to reform her own tenuous, white Southern vision of morality. Turning the tables in scenes inverting the domestic literacy narrative staple of adult teaching child, she tries to shape the actions of her parent, who is clearly no moral compass himself. Thus, she uses her influence to curb rough overseers and even argues with Mr. Le Croix about slavery, basing her opposition on stories of oppression she has heard the slaves tell (14–15).

But Camilla is not able to escape the corrupting influence of her environment entirely, at least not in the first two-thirds of the narrative. Although she supports the Union cause, Camilla does not free her slaves before or during the war. After the conflict, she is unable to accept the idea of "social equality" outright, despite her personal connection to Louis, and so is hesitant initially about accepting a "colored" sister-in-law.[67] "She had," Harper tells us, "great kindness and compassion for the race, but as far as social equality was concerned, though she had her strong personal likings, yet, except with Louis, neither custom nor education had reconciled her to the maintenance of any equal, social relations with them" (69). Only when she sees Minnie's refined behavior firsthand is Camilla able to take the final step toward viewing the black race as equal to the white. Harper marks this crucial change in perspective not only by Camilla's "unfeigned admiration" upon seeing Minnie but also by the words used to summon Miriam: "Tell Miriam . . . to come; that her boy Louis is here" (70). Naming Miriam as Louis's true mother by designating him as "her boy," Camilla cedes maternal rights to the former slave grandmother, whom she now recognizes as Louis's rightful guide.

Until this important turning point, Miriam's position in the Le Croix home had remained tenuous, even after her relationship to Louis and his racial identity were revealed to prevent him from fighting for the Confederacy (59). Although he accepted the proof Miriam provided by showing him their "free papers," and therefore determined that he could "never raise a hand against [his] mother's race," Louis did not embrace Miriam as his grandmother on hearing the news; instead, he "arose like one in a dream, walked slowly to the door and left the room" (60). When Louis agreed to try escaping to the North, he followed the sage advice Miriam offered that he seek the help "of the colored people" along the way. But Harper gives no indication of his affirming his connection to the woman he probably still viewed more as a kindly house servant than as a member of his own family (62). Later, having learned about the true nobility of his race from the courage slaves showed in aiding his escape and from coming to love Minnie, Louis finally names Miriam as "my grandmother" when he introduces her to his wife (70).

Harper's audience, however, could have noted Miriam's strengths as a mother long before Louis did. For example, careful reading of Camilla's discussion with Miriam about the possibility of adopting baby Louis reveals ways in which the older woman *manages* their talk to encourage the younger's generous impulse. Similarly, when Louis realizes he will need to flee the South to avoid prosecution as a deserter, "Camilla called Miriam" for a "consultation," unhesitatingly giving over direction of his journey to his grandmother. Later, the moment of "proud satisfaction" when Louis fully celebrates their family bond represents a complex turning point for Miriam (71). Although Miriam's educative abilities will still be valued, as suggested by Minnie's attitude toward her "scholars," Miriam and the racial subgroup she symbolizes will now need to collaborate with others who have already benefited from exposure to the Northern, white, middle-class education model being carried into the South during Reconstruction.

In her adept ability to draw from life experience, as well as her eagerness to benefit from the new order, Miriam anticipates the remarkable central character of Harper's *Southern Sketches,* a collection of narrative poems centered on "Aunt Chloe," a freedwoman whose morally sound folk wisdom confirms the strengths former slaves could bring to community governance.[68] In depicting Aunt Chloe's excitement over learning to read, her linkage of literacy with uplift, her understanding of the importance of the vote—her astute analysis, in fact, of the whole national political landscape— Harper created a mother figure whose strong sense of agency would surely have been impressive to both the blacks and the whites who typically read her poetry. Chloe's seeming loss of the motherhood role when her children are sold away would have echoed the plotline of many an abolitionist narrative. But Harper's suggestion, in later poems of the sequence, that the *Sketches* heroine could now serve as a powerful, enlightened mother for the nation would have indicated a new order in American literature and politics.[69]

Harper might seem, at first glance, to deny Miriam a similar victory, since this now-free folk mother steps into the background during the final episodes of the serial novel. One reason for this seeming discrepancy may have to do with audience and purpose: aimed at a mixed readership, and using a poem series rather than an extended prose narrative, *Southern Sketches*, in its focus on the single character of Chloe, matches the rhetorical needs of a different publication context.[70] Still, if we note parallels between Harper's portrayal of Minnie's scholars, in the closing scenes, and her depictions of both Miriam and Chloe, we can see that, in all three cases, the emphasis is actually more on community than individual uplift.

To stress her concept of communal motherhood, Harper draws in voices of freedwomen to celebrate Minnie's life at the funeral. Taking over the motherly teacher position that Miriam, and then Minnie, had held in the narrative, these former slave mothers reiterate the important contributions each model—Miriam's folk mother and Minnie's educated schoolteacher— could make to the race now. Harper sets up two parallel anecdotes—one from a mourning "Aunt Susan" who repeats a personal story she had told Minnie and another from a woman who describes Minnie's reading and interpreting of a Bible story. Having Louis listen attentively to both accounts, Harper first promotes a valuing of folk culture's lessons from the past through Aunt Susan's narrative about her "darter Amy" *and* about Minnie's empathetic, uplifting reaction to that story of undeserved suffering. Implying a connection between her own daughter's martyrdom and Minnie's, Aunt Susan imagines a reunion with both saintly figures "on de sunny banks of deliberance" (88).[71] Through the second short narrative by another freedwoman, Harper indicates that having the newly educated generation of blacks teach the old through print-based learning will be as important to the uplift of the race as having grandmother figures like Miriam and Aunt Susan provide stories in the oral tradition. Accordingly, Harper's second celebrant of communal literacy describes Minnie's reading from "de Bible, . . . wid dat sweet voice of hers," and then interprets that text as a Reconstruction parable: "When de old eagle wanted her young to fly she broked up de next [nest], and de little eagles didn't . . . feel so cumfertable, 'cause de little twigs and sticks stuck in 'em, and den dey would work dere wings, and dat was de way she said we must do; de ole nest of slavery was broke up, but she said we mus'n't get discouraged, but we must plume our wings for higher flying" (79–80). Although she bemoans not being able to "say it like [Minnie] did," this second interpreter of Minnie's influence is also a teacher for Louis and the other mourners. This freedwoman's skill at glossing both the Bible story and the meaning of Minnie's response highlights the ability of Southern freedwomen to learn from print texts, even when being read to rather than reading.[72]

By setting up these paired memorials to Minnie—one a description of her respectful listening before teaching, the second an account of her reading a print text and interpreting it for another—Harper validates both Southern blacks' oral learning grounded in folk culture and the imported Northern model of print-based study then becoming available to the freed slaves. In both examples of this new race-oriented approach to national literacy development, the mother-teacher's (Minnie's) pedagogy is depicted as part of an ongoing community culture, with her work drawing from and contributing to that community. By showing Minnie's students already able to reenact her teaching efforts, in this case to comfort and guide a collective of mourners, Harper emphasizes the potential benefits of black American maternal teaching serving a whole community rather than centering on a single child or individual family. In that context, when Louis and Minnie had earlier outlined their teaching goals, they described a "new community of interests arising from freedom" (74). Harper thus reenvisions domestic literacy management to include all members of her race as potential teachers and leaders. Overall, in appropriating and reconstructing the domestic literacy narrative, *Minnie's Sacrifice* expands the ideal of national motherhood by breaking down white/black, male/female, North/South, middle-class/rural poor, print/oral, and teacher/learner hierarchies to generate a more inclusive, interactive educational model promoting communal citizenship.

Maintaining a Moral Agenda

Harper would build upon the program for racial uplift she had outlined in *Minnie's Sacrifice*, not only in her later domestic literacy novels but also in lecturing and nonfiction writing. Her ideas on race education continued to emphasize maternal pedagogy. For example, in an 1878 speech, "The Coloured Women of America," she argued that "mothers are the levers which move in education" (*Brighter Coming Day*, 271). For Harper, motherly teaching remained, as it had been in *Minnie's Sacrifice*, a role that could be prepared for and enacted outside the home as well as in it. Offering multiple examples of female scholarship and industry supporting race progress, Harper described such role models as an African American woman who overcame poverty by studying and teaching at Oberlin, later becoming the esteemed "principal of the Coloured High School in Philadelphia" (*Brighter Coming Day*, 273–74).[73]

Harper's continued emphasis on intellectual preparation blended with moral education set her apart from some other black leaders of the 1880s and 1890s. As historian Linda M. Perkins notes, numerous articles in African American publications in the last decades of the nineteenth century invoked "a conservative view of women reminiscent of . . . antebellum New England" in their focus on domestic teaching of sons, along with an unrealistic promotion of separate spheres ideology imagining "that the black woman's [only] place was in the home."[74] Harper certainly maintained her commitment to mothers' education of children as vital to the race, but she also spurred black women (and men) to high career aspirations outside the home, since such work could serve the larger race community. Whatever the setting, paramount for Harper from her earlier writing to the close of the century was a focus on moral teaching and learning as the highest calling, of most significance to racial uplift. Thus, in "A Factor in Human Progress," published in the *AME Church Review* in 1885, she declared:

> The education of the intellect and the training of the morals should go hand-in-hand. The devising brain and the feeling heart should never be divorced, and the question worth asking is not simply, What will education do for us? But, What will it help us do for others? Do you point me with pride to your son, and tell me the best college in the country is his alma mater; that he has passed triumphantly through its curriculum; that he is well versed in ancient lore and modern learning, and that his mind is an arsenal of well-stored facts, fully equipping him for the battle of life? I ask, in reply, Is he noble and upright? Does he prefer integrity to gold,

principle to ease, true manhood to self-indulgence? . . . If not, I answer, his education is unfinished. (*Brighter Coming Day*, 276)

Still committed to a race-inflected version of domesticated literacy, she welcomed the growing access blacks had to higher education but resisted efforts to limit such programs to intellectual *or* vocational training only, while continuing to promote moral education as crucial. In confronting the growing tendency of white philanthropists to construct black education as preparation for work in the trades, Harper entered into a contested terrain that would eventually be dominated by a dichotomizing of W. E. B. DuBois and Booker T. Washington. Her own engagement with this issue would maintain a gendered perspective, touting moral education as home based yet community oriented. So in 1892, even as her final novel, *Iola Leroy*, was being published, Harper delivered a touchstone address to the Brooklyn Literary Society: "Enlightened Motherhood." Having declared that she could not provide "an exhaustive analysis of all that a mother should learn and of all she should teach," Harper nonetheless insisted that mothers' "interest in the welfare of the home" was closely linked to "the good of society," making her educative work "grandly constructive" (*Brighter Coming Day*, 287). In the face of male debates about industrial versus classical education models, Harper reasserted a gendered model for domesticated community governance: "The school may instruct and the church may teach, but the home is an institution older than the church and antedates school, and that is the place where children should be trained for useful citizenship on earth and a hope of holy companionship in heaven" (*Brighter Coming Day*, 285–86).

For much of the twentieth century, Harper's writing on educational issues garnered relatively limited attention. Hopefully, recovering the significant position of *Minnie's Sacrifice* in the development of the domestic literacy narrative may also contribute to enhanced appreciation of Harpers's crucial role in American literary history. Still, important work remains to be done to retrieve a fuller understanding of her impressive body of writing on education. Harper's impact on African American women later in the century (e.g., writers like Anna Julia Cooper and Victoria Matthews, turn-of-the-century clubwomen) is gaining increased attention. But we also need to explore her educational program's influence on African American schoolteachers, both in earlier periods and today. That work will be particularly challenging, since the very accessibility of Harper's ideas on teaching for community uplift led her views to become so tightly woven into the fabric of many educators' value systems and classroom practices that the intellectual connections between their work and her influence may be difficult to retrieve. This step in the recovery process for Harper's career would be worthwhile, though, especially in the face of continued assaults—ranging from punitive standardized testing models to factory-like (and sometimes even prisonlike) schools—on nurturing, inclusive traditions for instruction. In Harper's own acts of teaching, both personal and discursive, and in stories of how her vision of motherly pedagogy still guides the learning in some homes and classrooms, we could find useful resources for future reconstructions of American education.

Missionary Motherhood

*Dear Friends of Woman's Work:—No matter where the work may be, I
never read our dear little magazine without feeling that those who write
for it are near and dear friends, and many a time I have felt so interested that I thought I must sit right down and write to you about my little corner in this wonderful work-room.*

Mrs. Shaw, "China—Tung-Chow"

Writing in 1877 for *Woman's Work for Woman,* one of the numerous publications aimed at affiliates of the women's foreign mission movement, an
overseas worker, Mrs. Shaw, described her ongoing activities for the cause.
Metaphorically she equated her station in China with one "little corner in
this wonderful work-room" of gendered missionary labor, and she stressed
the role that their "dear little magazine" played in supporting the "women's
work" she shared with so many "friends."[1] For Mrs. Shaw, other women in
the movement were colleagues to whom she was bound by reading and writing as well as by religious commitment. At the heart of this print-based exchange of feelings was a highly specialized brand of the domestic literacy
narrative. This late nineteenth- and early twentieth-century version of the
genre was strategically adapted to the particular needs, interests, and aims
of the women participating in the American women's foreign mission movement. Writers crafting domestic literacy narratives in this overtly religious

context reframed domesticity, literacy, and narrative itself into internationalized yet still Americanized maternal terms. Readers, meanwhile, participated imaginatively in an enthusiastic enterprise of missionary motherhood by affiliating with faraway counterparts through shared consumption of print.

These narratives' recurring portrayals of how domestic literacy management promoted missionary work reflect the multidimensional activities of women dedicated to the movement in the United States and abroad: laboring alongside preaching husbands or, increasingly, as single women missionary teachers; organizing networks of women within the United States to provide financial support for colleagues abroad; training young people to serve as future missionaries; and studying the exotic locations where the gospel was being spread. All these endeavors were cast in publications like Shaw's *Woman's Work for Woman* story as motherly community building consistent with the ideology of domestic literacy management.

In light of those connections, my analysis of women's missionary writing will show that the domestic literacy narrative made a significant contribution to the American foreign mission movement during the turn into the twentieth century. To point out continuities in the history of the genre, I will highlight rhetorical elements affiliating these texts with traditional versions of the form (see chapter 2), with techniques for "benevolent" literacy management and for constructing schoolteaching as maternal literacy management (see chapter 3), and with ideals for politicized teaching (see chapters 4 and 5). At the same time, however, by demonstrating ways in which mission-movement authors reconfigured the domestic literacy narrative to meet their community's special needs, I will emphasize my view of the genre as a flexible, culturally responsive form.

The lively communications circuit of the American women's foreign mission movement was rife with the complexities of "contact zone" relationships, as characterized by Mary Louise Pratt.[2] Nonetheless, countless now-unfamiliar authors productively negotiated this complicated space through writings in line with Fredric Jameson's conception of narrative as a socially symbolic act and of genres as flexible "literary *institutions,* or social contracts between a writer and a specific public, whose function is to specify the proper use of a particular cultural artifact."[3] Accordingly, an analysis of the foreign mission movement's *use* of the domestic literacy narrative genre is in line with Jameson's call for a "historically reflexive" interpretation of generic categories (107). Jameson advises attention to both "the play of structural norm and textual deviation" (145) but also to the influ-

ence of the historical moment, as represented in such elements as "the se-
mantic raw materials of social life and language, the constraints of determinate social contradictions, the conjunctures of social class, the historicity of
structures of feeling and perception and ultimately of bodily experience, the
constitution of the psyche or subject, and the dynamics and specific temporal rhythms of historicity" (147). Following Jameson, I will situate the writing of women like Mrs. Shaw within a framework of relations, demonstrating ways in which their narratives connect with traditions established for
the domestic literacy narrative earlier in the century, while also extending
those models. To suggest why both the traditional structures and new devi-
ations were necessary to this particular body of writing, I will explore this
subgenre's relationships with the "social life and language" of the foreign
mission movement, including its "determinate social contradictions" (such
as doing [purportedly] nurturing spiritual work in an imperial era) and its
promotion of "structures of feeling and perception" among users of its textual network, so closely linked to the "bodily experience" of international
travel. Thus, I will suggest how these applications of the domestic literacy
narrative tapped into new "rhythms" of national history, as perceived by
women who imagined themselves "mothering" Others into a gendered,
Protestant American culture.

Stories of domesticated teaching represent only one genre strand evident in the hybrid texts circulating in the American women's foreign mission movement, which also produced detailed financial reports, curricula
for study at home, travel stories, advice for organizing mission support
groups, and more. Yet this enormous body of writing has not yet garnered
much scholarly attention *as* gendered writing. Perhaps in part because feminist scholarship has tended more toward critique of organized religion's
constraining effects on women than toward interpretation of its enabling
ones, the important role that literature linked to religious movements (e.g.,
temperance) has played in American social life has often been underanalyzed. Fortunately, though, recent scholarship has suggested how fruitful
such inquiry can be.[4]

To focus, as here, on one literary genre's role in the mission movement
will emphasize links between the development of gendered organizational
communities in late nineteenth-century American culture and evolving
ideas about the social role of American literature. In an increasingly print-
rich culture, shifting visions of American womanhood—especially white,
middle-class motherhood—shaped and were shaped by this body of writing.
At the same time, exploring how the particular writers and readers of mis-

sion literature configured the domestic literacy narrative to meet their unique needs will emphasize a view of literary genre as rhetorical—adapting in response to changing community forces while also serving as a tool writers can use to influence society.[5] In addition, appreciating the sophistication and the cultural capital represented by these texts requires situating them in their own historical context, as Jameson's formulations for genre study indicate. Such historical analysis, in turn, promotes a remapping of the social landscape that we typically associate with middle-class women's lives in the late nineteenth century—leading us to reconceptualize the relationship between American home-based literacy and international religious politics during this era.

Practically and philosophically, the domestic literacy narratives circulating as part of the Protestant women's missionary movement imagined and created a border-crossing network of motherly educators allied to each other and to a tradition of American literary pedagogy grounded in the "enlightened" maternal management of (others') literacy practices. The epitome of the domestic teaching narrative during its early stage of development in antebellum New England is the story of a single mother teaching her son by the fireside, simultaneously preparing him for enlightened citizenship and providing his maternal teacher with enhanced access to public life. The parallel vision inscribed in this late nineteenth-century adaptation of the genre portrays a faraway maternal teacher carrying the ideals of American middle-class Christian life to foreign children and childlike learners or a U.S.-based motherly supporter and her children/peers using literacy to participate imaginatively in that enterprise.[6]

Border-Crossing by Missionary Mothers

The American women's foreign mission movement represents just one example of the nineteenth-century penchant for organized social activity that Anne Firor Scott incisively describes in *Natural Allies*.[7] Like parallel enterprises such as the abolitionist and temperance crusades, foreign mission organizations sought to carry American women's moral influence into the public sphere beyond the home. Similar to the clubwomen's movement chronicled by Anne Ruggles Gere, foreign mission associations linked social reform with women's self-improvement through collaborative study, writing, and discussion.[8] Despite its overlap with other organizational activities, however, the American women's foreign mission movement was unique in its activist engagement in international affairs, especially its overseas extension of a Protestant religious mandate through published versions of domesticated teaching. Meanwhile, as Patricia R. Hill shows, the phenomenal impact the enterprise had on evangelism overseas was closely tied to "the hold that foreign missions had on the female imagination" and the "changing cultural paradigms of ideal womanhood in America."[9]

Part of what made the movement so powerful was its sustained conjunction of charismatic women laboring in faraway places (like Lottie Moon) with faithful counterparts, often themselves charismatic, working at home (like Mrs. Russell Sage and Miss Fannie Heck) to make those foreign initiatives possible. This alliance gave the enterprise both a never-ending body of new experiences of great interest to its burgeoning literacy community and significant material resources.[10] With each half of the community gaining sophistication about how to use their literacy to stay connected, the movement grew steadily from its nascent, disorganized antebellum days to an apex in participation and influence around the turn of the twentieth century.

For social historian Dana L. Robert, the 1910–11 Woman's Missionary Jubilee and its hallmark publication, Helen Montgomery's *Western Women in Eastern Lands,* marked a milestone in the movement's development.[11] As Robert indicates, the Jubilee "gathered thousands of women for celebrations in forty-eight major cities" and smaller towns for "a series of meetings that reflected the grassroots character of American women's missionary involvement."[12] But even well before the 1910–11 Jubilee, the movement had passed momentous benchmarks. For instance, an 1879 editorial in *Woman's Work for Woman* proudly trumpeted the success of the General Assembly held at Saratoga that May, when representatives from sixteen states confidently set the annual fund-raising goal of one hundred thousand dollars for their Presbyterian missionary society.[13] Using the Women's Missionary Union of the North Carolina Baptist State Convention as a state-level example, we can document remarkable growth in figures reported by the *Raleigh News and Observer* in 1915: "The [state's mission] Union has grown from seventeen societies giving less than five hundred dollars a year [in the 1880s] to more than twelve hundred with an annual contribution of nearly fifty thousand dollars. It has also developed into a complete mission organization with branches for young women, girls, boys, and children."[14] Nationally, as Patricia R. Hill observes, by "1915, there were more than three million women on the membership rolls of some forty denominational female missionary societies," and interdenominational involvement in the movement "was substantially larger than [in] any of the other mass [women's] movements of the nineteenth century."[15]

Throughout this steady organizational expansion, the foreign mission movement interacted with a range of other communities, such as women's secular clubs and political organizations—forging bonds that often enhanced its material resources while helping maintain the vitality of its message and membership. Perhaps foremost among these alliances was the movement's connection to supporters of women's education.[16] Seminaries and early women's colleges provided fertile recruiting ground—both for foreign missionaries and for home support groups. Dana L. Robert argues that ideals embodied in the earliest mission wives' work can often be traced back to their study of religion in places like the Hartford Female Seminary. Carrying their own learning into missionary endeavors, and spreading it to native women and children as well as correspondents at home, antebellum missionary wives established links between American women's education and the foreign mission movement that were strengthened and formalized as the century progressed.[17] Politically, the arguments made to justify women's accompanying their husbands to foreign missions in the antebellum era, then going as missionary workers in their own right later in the century, replicated the pattern of persuasion that was used to claim advanced educational opportunities for females, first as supporters of others' instruction (as republican mothers or sisters) and later as contributors to the larger society through responsibilities tied to enhanced training (for schoolteaching and social reform work).[18] Philosophically, much of the content of the movement's agenda—whether abroad or at home—grew out of the curricula of those same seminaries and colleges. Logistically, the experience many women had as instructors for common schools carried over into the work they did for foreign missions, helping ensure that teaching would become an accepted (or even expected) activity for missionary wives and, later, for single female missionaries.

No other women's educational institution had more influence on the nineteenth-century American women's foreign mission movement than Mary Lyon's Mount Holyoke. Amanda Porterfield provides striking quantitative evidence of what might be termed the Holyoke missionary outreach, even in the decades when women missionaries were very few in number: "When Lyon died in 1849, twenty-seven alumnae had become missionaries in foreign countries, and eight had become missionaries to American Indian communities. The next year, the total rose to forty. In 1859, the American Board of Commissioners for Foreign Missions listed sixty Mount Holyoke alumnae on its rolls. . . . In 1887, fifty years after Mount Holyoke's founding, one-fifth of all women then serving as American Board missionaries were Holyoke alumnae."[19] In qualitative terms, the close connections between learning at Mount Holyoke and teaching by American women's foreign mission–movement leaders are obvious in the pages of publications like *Woman's Work for Woman.* Writing in January of 1882, for example, Maria T. True reveled in the opening of her new school for girls in Japan: "It seems likely to be 'a city set on a hill,'" she crowed. "I see visions of such precious fruit as Mt. Holyoke has brought forth."[20] In July of the same year, the lead article in *Woman's Work* described in more detail the "history of the founding of [a] Mount Holyoke of South Africa" by borrowing an account that had earlier appeared in *Life and Light,* a similar publication.[21] In this case, a male missionary (Reverend Andrew Murray, pastor of a Dutch Reformed Church in Wellington, South Africa) and his wife had read a biography of Mary Lyon, then contacted Mount Holyoke in 1873 to request missionary teachers for a projected "Christian school" where daughters of the colonists could be taught. Abbie P. Ferguson and Anna E. Bliss volunteered—at which point the reverend successfully raised money in his congregation to bring the two to Cape Town, where they soon delivered "devoted Christian teaching, not only for America, but for the world," through a curriculum "much the same as that of Mt. Holyoke Seminary" (218–20).

If the movement's links to American women's education served as a source for much of its utopian energy, its ties to imperialism (especially British colonialism in a number of locales) often provided tangible support in foreign fields but also undermined its position as a moral crusade. Because my treatment of women's missionary writing here focuses on how "insider" members of a subgenre's discourse community used their literacy for their own needs, I will not develop a detailed critique of their texts' colonialist features. Nonetheless, even this first-step analysis—while recognizing the belief these women held that Christianizing the world was worthwhile—needs to acknowledge the complex links between their work and the ongoing imperial enterprise. In economic terms, particularly in China and India but in other stations as well, American women missionaries benefited from English merchants' presence, which made many desirable goods and services available. Meanwhile, English missionaries, often on the scene before contingents from the United States arrived, could provide an appealing social base for American missionary families.[22] Political and military officials of the British Empire were sometimes part of this same collegial network. Particularly for families stationed in coastal cities dominated by European merchants, the social scene could become a major focus for mission wives, as they worried over how housekeeping and fashion choices might either reflect poorly on their husbands or gain them increased respect in the community. Women who had grown up in modest surroundings at home often found themselves able to afford servants and welcome in colonials' clubs.[23] At the least, such social alliances with colonizers could complicate missionaries' relations with local populations. At worst, adopting imperialist agents' attitudes and behaviors toward the natives could wreck the very foundation of the mission movement's spiritual agenda.

In some foreign mission settings, the European imperial presence offered a measure of safety. (Until the 1890s, the U.S. government was reluctant to protect missionaries, even when they complained about abuse by local populations.)[24] In other situations, though, missionaries themselves were perceived as a potent threat to colonial control, as in West Africa at the turn of the twentieth century, where schools established by American Congregationalists were burned down because allies of the ruling Portuguese feared that literacy would make the natives harder to recruit for the colonial contract labor that was really a form of enslavement. With their own country's leaders wavering between visions of empire and a realization that suppressing others was inconsistent with democratic national ideals, many American missionaries had an ambivalent attitude toward imperialism and its connections to their work. Indeed, as Jane Hunter indicates, American women missionaries often distanced themselves (rhetorically and personally) from the ideals of Old World colonialism and criticized English "authoritarianism, rigidity, and arrogance" while touting U.S. democracy and seeking to foster an egalitarian, if not an overtly *anti*colonial, Christianity.[25]

Nonetheless, the daily practices of empire building all around them could elicit negative feelings (at the least) from native populations, who sometimes equated American missionaries' religious education initiatives with ongoing incursions by British military leaders, politicians, and businessmen. For example, American women missionaries' visible interactions with European colonizers meant purportedly altruistic efforts like teaching local populations English—an effort the missionaries themselves promoted as enabling Bible study—could also be perceived as political suppression of local values and social practices. One way numerous American missionaries mitigated this issue was by learning the local language, sometimes well enough to write translations of the Bible and other religious materials for natives to study in their own tongue.[26] However, evangelistic goals were not the only reason for learning a local language; especially in the years before

they were encouraged to become active participants in missionary work itself, mission wives sometimes perceived their acquisition of native language
in the kind of controlling terms that postcolonial theory has recently underscored.[27] For example, Irwin T. Hyatt Jr. reports that Julia Mateer, one of
the first generation of mission wives in China, urged her peers "to learn
the Chinese language, if only to be aware of what one's houseboy was teaching her children."[28] And the first text mission wife Martha Crawford produced after learning Chinese in 1866 was a household guidebook with hundreds of recipes and tips, including how to make Tuscaloosa beef and
fritters and how to disinfect long underwear, so that local servants could
provide mission families with appropriately Americanized food and services.[29]

Among the most liberal missionary women, in contrast, concerns about
becoming caught up in the un-Christian dimensions of the imperial agenda
led authors to dissociate their writing from political issues as much as possible. One sign of their efforts to *contain* the complex social interactions
between missionary work and politics within a moral framework was American women missionary writers' longstanding tendency to focus on conver-
sions of individuals rather than on the movement's broader social impact.[30]
Generally, whereas a British missionary woman's narrative might portray
her labors within a "white (wo)man's burden" ideology, an American's text,
especially if written before the late 1890s, was more likely to mute larger
political implications of her teaching and instead to emphasize the progress
of model religious converts through literacy acquisition (i.e., reading the
Bible, telling Bible stories to other locals).[31]

Overall, nineteenth- and early twentieth-century missionary authors exhibited an inconsistent stance toward colonialism in their domestic literacy
texts. Women who lived in the same foreign setting for an extended time
did tend to develop a deeper understanding of the local community, so
their narratives were less inclined to stigmatize native cultural practices.[32]
Similarly, serious, comparative study of foreign cultures sometimes led
mission-movement participants in the United States to take an enlightened
stand toward such issues as Chinese immigration.[33] Still, a sense of white
Protestant Americans' innate superiority over other populations suffused
much of the movement's writing, from its earliest days onward.

Internationalizing an American Genre

The vast scope of American women's foreign mission endeavors countered
conservative assumptions about women's role in society. Claiming "the

world at large" as a rightful site for Christian maternal influence logically validated the presence of American women as missionary workers overseas.[34] So too, by blurring many of the lines that could have been drawn between "home" and "foreign" missions, the movement undercut ideological distinctions between private and public spheres. Understandably, therefore, the rhetoric developed for this subgenre of the domestic literacy narrative concentrated on ways in which American women's didactic Christian evangelism was extending their social influence through international networking. As one example, the Presbyterian periodical *Woman's Work for Woman* consistently embodied this goal both in its worldwide readership and in its carefully designed interweaving of reports from overseas and from home-based sites of foreign mission activities.[35]

By equating the work overseas with women's movement-linked teaching in the United States, domestic literacy narratives in publications like *Woman's Work for Woman* simultaneously validated the efforts of faraway motherly heroines and affirmed religious instruction in American homes as socially, even internationally, significant. So, Mrs. Murray Mitchell praised a station she visited in India by extolling the domesticated teaching going on there. Mitchell offered a portrait of instruction that her American readers would surely recognize—one also supporting their own literacy management practices.[36] Relating her missionary friend's successful progress in reaching local women to a technique of reading and discussing the Bible with them, Mrs. Mitchell praised "the questions they asked and the conversation which always followed" in terms reminiscent of the literature for teaching mothers first generated by New England authors like Sigourney, Sedgwick, and Child (116). With stories about home study of mission work using the same plotlines, characterizations, and vocabulary as those in accounts of foreign mission teaching, the movement's magazines, ephemeral literature, and books constantly reiterated this parallel.[37] Narrative reports on well-attended national meetings echoed the point, with the term *missionary mothers* used to identify both foreign and home-based workers. Those directing "auxiliary society meetings" in the United States were presented in speakers' papers as directly parallel to those engaging in the educational "Mothers' Work in Missions" far away.[38]

Consistent with this linkage strategy, mission publications printed stories from women posted overseas who credited their successes to the donations of American supporters. Reading such pieces, in turn, encouraged donors to feel their giving was virtually the equivalent of going to the foreign fields. The feelings of dedication expressed on both sides of the exchange in such print stories further strengthened the cause: "If my part of the work be successful," Miss Esther E. Patton wrote from India for *Woman's Work*, "my success is yours, because you have held up my hands and inspired me by your sympathy expressed in words and generous deeds."[39]

Another rhetorical technique associated with the movement's blurring of home/foreign boundaries involved writers imaginatively situating themselves *with* readers. Domestic literacy narratives often portrayed a gendered discursive space emphasizing how shared literacy events could bind distant locations together. Some foreign missionary women became especially adept at presenting themselves in an overlapping time/space geography, carrying out their motherly teaching duties at their stations far from home while vividly imagining themselves still closely connected with friends and family through social practices tied to maternal literacy management. Mrs. Helen Nevius, for instance, described keeping her watch on American as well as Chinese time.[40] Mrs. Henrietta Shuck, the first American missionary to China, wrote from the ship carrying her across the Pacific that she still felt present at the prayer meeting she knew would be going on that day at home in Richmond.[41] Decades later, Laura Haygood used a related rhetorical device, often placing dual headings above her letters, with one indicating the day and time at her foreign station, the other giving the corresponding information for her home in Atlanta.[42]

From the beginning of her many years in China, in fact, Haygood's letters emphasized ways her Shanghai station had been Americanized with literacy practices that gave her a palpable sense of connection to home. Soon after reaching her mission, for instance, she wrote: "I wish that I could gather you all about me in my study—the one bit of home to me in all China. Here are my books and my pictures[:] many of the dear home faces, my home, Trinity Church, the High School, the Class of 1883, many love-tokens from dear friends at home. Here I read my letters, the 'good news from a far country,' which is indeed better than 'water to a thirsty soul.' Here my heart and pen talk to the loved ones across the seas. . . . Here I read and study, here I feel often times the presence of 'Him who is invisible.'"[43]

Haygood's description of herself in her "study" at first understatedly characterizes that setting as just "one bit of home," and thus her wish to "gather you all about me" seems a poignant yet limited one. But the details she accumulates in describing objects on her desk—"my books and my pictures"—suggest how she used literacy to summon her readers imaginatively by invoking items to identify herself as a product of the same domesticated literacy training she knew they would have experienced: progressing from her "home" to "Trinity Church" and to "the High School" where she had worked as a teacher before becoming a missionary. Limning herself as eagerly reading letters from home, so precious as to be "water to a thirsty soul," she asserts the power of the ongoing literacy exchange. Their crisscrossing literacy practices will, Haygood notes, bear her own writing back "to the loved ones across the seas," allowing her "pen" to "talk" with them. Finally, she links God's presence in her work to the very literacy that also binds her to her friends and family through their letter exchanges and shared reading.

The literacy-based interactions among those committed to the women's foreign mission movement, like other community-building acts associated with domestic literacy narratives, fostered the kind of group identification process Michael Warner attributes to print consumption in the early Republic.[44] Two elements unique to the mission-oriented adaptations of the domestic literacy narrative genre were especially important tools for blurring the boundaries between American maternal teaching and women's foreign missionary work. First, the powerful affiliations at the core of the movement's literacy network clearly depended upon the figure of the maternal missionary teacher successfully reconciling potentially conflicting agendas—border-crossing travel and traditional home-based teaching. Second, and in a complementary way, domestic literacy narratives adapted for mission literature insistently depicted the process of textual exchange itself as essential to the movement's discourse community and its goals.

Constituting American Missionary Motherhood

The figure of the motherly, teaching missionary who worked in a distant land was the linchpin of the American women's foreign mission movement. She was a primary focus of fund-raising, a conduit of information, and the dominant model of behavior and feeling for all other women active in the venture. Therefore, tracking the shifting strategies the domestic literacy narrative used for representing her can help us recover important connections between this genre's ongoing development and the evolving missionary community itself.

The image of the motherly missionary at a foreign station maintained ideals of American middle-class maternal domesticity even as she crossed multiple boundaries. Achieving this crucial balance between movement and stability was possible in part because individual women themselves could and did cross back and forth between the role of foreign missionary teacher and U.S.-based supporter. Movement leaders living in the United States sometimes visited foreign stations to learn about the activities there first-hand, as the Southern Methodist board secretary Mrs. Trueheart did via an ambitious trip to China. In addition, a number of women who started out participating in "home missions" (e.g., running schools and charity centers for the poor in America) eventually made the transition to doing foreign mission work overseas. Meanwhile, missionaries took furloughs back to the United States to restore their health or to drum up resources for a foreign project. While at home, these women joined in fund-raising, including giving speeches in hometown parlors, churches, and schools—even in large public auditoriums. Often missionaries who never returned home themselves sent their children back to the United States for schooling. Sometimes those children later recrossed the ocean—grown, educated, and ready for foreign fieldwork themselves. Ships bearing new missionaries on their first trip abroad frequently carried veterans on their way back to a foreign station. Once arrived overseas, missionaries seldom stayed at one station permanently: initial postings to port cities were frequently followed by assignments to establish inland stations; extended illnesses could prompt journeys to other locations for a restful stay. A few women missionaries even became itinerant agents for their boards, traveling constantly to other stations to provide advice and evaluate progress. All in all, travel was a regular part of an American woman missionary's life, a constant activity that regularly exposed her to new ideas, challenges, and opportunities, even as the ideology of the foreign mission movement dictated that she maintain her core identity as a maternal domestic teacher.

Before they could fully enact this border-crossing brand of domestic literacy management, however, foreign missionary women had to claim a gendered evangelical role for themselves, distinguishing their work from male missionaries' labors. The progressive shift in the lived experience of American women missionaries from serving as supporters of male preaching to enacting their own maternal mission teaching is traceable through parallel changes in biographies adopting the domestic literacy narrative form. From antebellum depictions of mothers teaching future male missionaries and wives faithfully accompanying their husbands into foreign fields, women's missionary biographies evolved, by the close of the nineteenth century, into celebratory accounts of single women who trained native Bible women, built schools, taught native children, guided newcomer missionaries, and (eventually) administered large-scale community enterprises (including corporate-like fund-raising campaigns). The literary figure of the missionary woman as mother-teacher was gradually established around the 1850s, then adjusted over the final third of the century to reflect her enhanced authority and responsibilities—all of which still remained tied to an ideology of domesticated teaching. An increasingly professional leader moving more and more confidently across multiple borders—geographic, social, and psychic— she still embodied the traditional role of domestic literacy manager, thereby marking the polemically stable nature of American national values for women's work in new international contexts. To track that blend of evolution and stability, I will juxtapose the biography of Henrietta Shuck, from the early phase of the American women's missionary movement, with that of Laura Haygood, from the height of its influence. First, though, I will describe key traits that developed in this specialized domestic literacy narrative—the "missionary-mother" biography.

Early biographies of missionary women already depended upon a familiar argument about those being taught—whether children in a mission wife's home school or "heathen" adults in need of salvation—benefiting from the moral guidance of motherly teaching, which was closely bound to literacy governance. Illustrating both the flexibility and the resilience of the genre, these texts ranged from short narrative anecdotes embedded within longer biographies of male "star" missionaries; to mixed-genre accounts of women with broad social reform agendas (e.g., temperance as well as foreign mission work); to full-fledged, book-length treatments like Albert Bushnell's 1848 biography of his mother.

Maternal-influence stories such as Bushnell's credit mothers' home literacy training as the source of male missionaries' religious inspiration and the continuing guide for their ministries. With a preface by one of the domestic literacy narrative's founding authors, Lydia Sigourney, Bushnell's text underscores his subject's enactment of "the most interesting and responsible station in life. A Christian mother."[45] In insisting that "no earthly influence is greater," he characterizes ways in which her teaching from printed missionary articles led him to become an evangelist in Africa: "She used to take the missionary papers, and read illustrations of heathen scenes, and explain them, till our young hearts would break with sympathy for the heathen. . . . She would add, 'How shall they believe on Him of whom they have not heard, and how can they hear without a preacher? Will you go, my children, and tell them of a Savior's dying love, and point them to Calvary and heaven?'" (84–85).

Like so many antebellum domestic literacy narratives, Bushnell's story imagines a motherly figure whose own access to literacy enables her to teach her children about their upcoming duties and opportunities "outside" the domestic realm. As in other iterations of literacy-oriented republican motherhood in the antebellum era, both mother and child are empowered through the projected social activity of the son (Bushnell), who has been prepared for civic (in this case, religious) leadership by his mother's management of reading and writing. Already in this early version of the *missionary* domestic literacy narrative, however, a crucial element is introduced, one that would become more important for the subgenre as the century progressed: the "heathen" who must be taught to be Christian.

The incorporation of a "heathen" character would necessitate maternal teaching's taking on increasingly political dimensions, which the narratives themselves would represent in ways that masked this cultural work's potentially disruptive nature. As seen, for example, in Stowe's *Uncle Tom's Cabin,* one version of this configuration could follow the well-trained child into scenes where the potentially dangerous "Other" was Christianized and thus accommodated (if not enfranchised) within the American national social framework, as George Shelby and little Eva try to do for Uncle Tom. Anticipating the biographies that would cast women missionaries as the maternal saviors of heathens overseas, Lydia Sigourney's *Lucy Howard's Journal* includes an extended episode depicting the enlightened heroine's motherly teaching of a young American Indian girl after the Howards' migration to the American West, and *Uncle Tom's Cabin* constructs a teaching-to-Christianize-the-heathen sequence in Ophelia's education of Topsy, followed later by Topsy's missionary teaching in Africa.[46]

In the first half of the nineteenth century, however, narratives about foreign missionary work generally highlighted the role of a male preacher like Bushnell, rather than a female teacher. One obvious reason for this tendency was that, until the final decades of the century, single women were forcefully discouraged from becoming foreign missionaries on their own, whereas accompanying a male minister was enthusiastically sanctioned.[47] The Civil War marked a major turning point in the gendering of missionary work, however, in part because many women who discovered their leadership abilities through organized activity during the conflict were unwilling to retreat into an enclosed domestic sphere afterward, especially since the number of middle-class men killed in the war had made the ideal of married life less accessible to a whole generation of well-educated women. By the turn of the twentieth century, as Patricia R. Hill documents, fully 60 percent of foreign missionaries were single women, mostly recruited and funded by the women's foreign missionary movement.[48] Still, missionary literature of the late nineteenth and early twentieth centuries would continue to situate the labors of those women within the rhetorical framework established during the antebellum era, representing female missionary activity as a version of domestic teaching. For one thing, this trend built upon earlier texts depicting married women missionaries as teaching in their homes or homelike schools so as to support their spouses' (more important) preaching.[49] (These portrayals were, of course, both factually accurate and ideologically acceptable to middle-class readers at home in the United States.) For another, this pattern of extending the role of domestic teacher from married women to single ones had already been developed in antebellum narratives about New England schoolteachers. We can clearly see the continuity linking portraits of single lady missionaries at the turn of the twentieth century with domestic teaching narratives composed in New England decades earlier through what might usefully be called "bridge narratives"—accounts of married women missionaries composed between the 1840s and 1860s, when Protestant foreign ministry was typically a husband-wife enterprise. In such antebellum biographies, the female contribution is generally framed as a helpmate's role, even in cases when this womanly work was already being carried out as teaching distinctive from a husband's preaching. So, for instance, Helen S. C. Nevius's 1860s *Our Life in China* continually stresses Reverend Nevius's preeminent administrative and pastoral influence on the various missions where the couple actually labored together, whereas the narrative writing Mrs. Nevius did for *Woman's Work for Woman* later in the century places her own maternal instructional efforts more at center stage.[50] Earlier on, books such as *Memoirs of Mrs. Harriet Newell, Wife of the Rev. S. Newell, American Missionary to India* and *The Three Mrs. Judsons, and Other Daughters of the Cross* had set the pattern for subsequent missionary-mother biographies by positioning their subjects as part of "a galaxy" of wives faithfully bolstering their spouses' ministries.[51]

Even the earliest narratives about American women's *own* labor in foreign missions underscored links between spiritual uplift work and ideals of national middle-class motherhood, with literacy instruction as its touchstone. In depicting such values as traveling, through the missionary mother herself, to foreign locales, this subgenre of domestic literacy narratives remapped national culture to Christianize and thus to Americanize the world. Significantly, the missionary biographies of Southern women both before and after the Civil War maintained generic consistency with texts about their counterparts from other regions of the United States. Thus, we can see how this gendered literary form was working to preserve cross-regional connections among American Christian women across many decades, despite political divisions over slavery and other issues. This implicit elision of regional difference was easiest to achieve in narratives about mission work in the Far East, because the ongoing battle over slavery back home could be finessed more easily in these texts, as compared to narratives set in Africa. Indeed, as they often rallied women readers to oppose oppression based on gender in Eastern cultures (e.g., foot binding, arranged marriages, and killing of unwanted girl babies), narratives about missionary enterprises in China and India, in particular, could sidestep the potentially divisive issue of race to sustain affiliative relationships between Northern and Southern Christian women in the United States. With that context in mind, we can develop a clearer sense of the internationalized yet self-consciously American brand of motherhood central to the U.S. foreign mission movement through an examination of the book-length biographies of two Far East missionaries from the American South, Henrietta Shuck and Laura Haygood. These texts will serve as a reminder that this literary genre, which originated in New England–based "Americanizations" of a British publication (Anna Laetitia Barbauld's *Lessons for Children*), crossed many other geographical borders over the course of its history, while still maintaining gender as a unifying marker contributing to a nation-building agenda.

An Antebellum Missionary Mother

The 1846 *Memoir of Mrs. Henrietta Shuck* demonstrates the genre's evolving strategies for reconciling ideals of American middle-class motherhood with the realities of missionary women's unusual position in a foreign culture. In the Shuck biography, we can recognize how narratives from the formative antebellum period helped establish the rhetorical patterns that missionary domestic literacy narratives would refine later in the century.

A major step in adapting the genre established the female missionary as a transplanted version of American motherhood. In that regard, the biography of Henrietta Shuck frames her life as a socially constructed model for gendered religious service.[52] The preface casts the memoir itself as a project carried out collaboratively by members of the China Mission. This group, the biography explains, passed a resolution shortly after Mrs. Shuck's death to create a record of her "character, and the circumstances attending [her] life," one quite "interesting and instructive" and likely "to aid the cause of missions generally" (v). Thus, the U.S.–based Reverend J.

B. Jeter resolutely presents himself as "the compiler" rather than the author of the memoir (vi). Supplementing "extracts from Mrs. Shuck's letters" and personal journal notes with others' characterizations of her mission activity, he describes the publication as inviting readers to "pursue the narrative of [the] trials, anxieties, and vicissitudes" she faced while trying "to perform, with fidelity and diligence, the duties of her humble, but not unimportant station" (111). To create an extended parable from the experiences of his young parishioner's life, Reverend Jeter continually downplays his own editorial choices and foregrounds her writing itself to emphasize the combined influence of her family and other missionaries on her religious work.[53] Simultaneously exalting her and insisting that she was (merely) enacting the normal role of middle-class motherhood, this biography repeatedly suggests that other women can construct themselves to be like Mrs. Shuck.[54] Thus, Jeter remarks, "Whether we contemplate her as a lady, gracing the social circle—as a mother, sedulously training her children for heaven—as a Christian, meekly and faithfully copying the bright example of her Saviour—or as a missionary, laboriously fulfilling the duties of her important station, we cannot but approve and admire her character" (250-51).

Central to presenting Henrietta Shuck as a Christian role model for American women readers is the narrative's consistent valuing of class-based elements in her youthful training and her later evangelizing, with her specific social group designated as being Protestant, white, and well educated. Sorting through the experiences of her premissionary life, the "compiler" stresses details that would have resonated for any American middle-class reader of domestic literacy narratives, who would have been used to biographies of notable women cataloging the morality-shaping elements in their education while touting their resulting aptitude for middle-class maternal home instruction. So, for instance, Jeter chooses details to show Henrietta's lady schoolteacher delivering a program affirming "the importance of combining religious with literary instructions, and doing all to the glory of God" (17), a description clearly in line with American middle-class women's education programs being advocated in texts by authors like Sarah Josepha Hale (see chapter 2). Similarly, Jeter describes fourteen-year-old Henrietta as confidently taking over the "maternal oversight of her little brothers and sisters" upon the death of her mother (19), thereby echoing celebrations of elder sisters as motherly teachers in other domestic literacy narratives. Most important, the biography repeatedly signals a continuity across the stages of Henrietta's learning and teaching experiences, from her mother's nurturing home instruction; to her training at the refined school of Mrs. Little; to her enlightened teaching of her siblings; to her motherly work at a local Sunday school; and eventually to her inspirational mission school far away, where she transplanted educational practices linked to her socioeconomic status, religious affiliation, and national identity.[55]

American motherhood, in fact, was the imported ideal around which Mrs. Shuck organized the entire work of her life in China, according to the memoir. In particular, the biography portrays Mrs. Shuck's domestic literacy management as the foundation for her being a successful lady missionary. Besides teaching her own children, Mrs. Shuck gradually brought others into her home for Christian training, a move that her biographer presents as consistent with conservative American maternal values. Echoing suggestions by Lydia Sigourney that middle-class mothers living in the United States should adopt and instruct poor neighborhood children, Mrs. Shuck took in an abandoned child soon after arriving in China and quickly began "teaching him the English alphabet" (95–96).[56] Adopting another boy in short order, she associated her efforts to teach both children English with giving them transformative "knowledge of the adorable Saviour" (96). Before long, she had also rescued and begun teaching an orphan girl (105). She gradually built up her home school to serve as many as thirty-two children (130, 209). Like many educators in America, Mrs. Shuck eventually expanded her goals beyond teaching young boys to providing high-quality education for young women. Since so "little has heretofore been done for the females," she explained, she longed "to exert [her] little influence wholly on them" (168), and she prided herself that the girls she was instructing "read as well as most children of their ages in America" (167–68). In the last year of her life, writing to her sister Susan about a typical day's motherly labors, she described herself as engaged in domesticated teaching of "ten Chinese lads, and my own two boys [birth sons], my two girls, and three European children, soldiers' daughters"—a diverse group of students, all assembled in her home, where she integrated motherhood and missionary work (201).

Narratives like the Shuck biography—circulating during the period when evangelists' supportive wives were being replaced by proactive "missionary mothers" as the dominant paradigm—naturally emphasize continuities between the experiences of maternal teachers at home and their counterparts at foreign mission stations. However, these same texts do acknowledge the demanding differences between carrying out the role in the United States and transplanting it to faraway cultures. Handling the financial responsibilities for a broadened home base (e.g., having ever more children to sponsor) and facing dilemmas associated with educating one's own children in a foreign land were just two of the mission-associated domestic problems American mothers living at foreign stations had to manage. The Shuck biography's depiction of one young mother's efforts to face these challenges provided both a compelling personal story and an implicit suggestion of how reading about such experiences could allow women living within the United States to expand their own horizons. Readers were cast as participating in a movement simultaneously accessible (through its ties to domestic ideology) and expansive (through its extension of women's experience into the larger world and new roles).

Mrs. Shuck's anecdotes about financing her teaching offer a case in point. As the number of students in her home-based school grew, so did the need for sponsors, because she had to feed and clothe the children as well as teach them to read and write (139). When Mrs. Shuck confronted this economic reality, she realized that she must expand her educational enterprise "by degrees" (130). Although hoping to attract enough students eventually to have "a large school," she paced her expansion to match her fundraising. For instance, in the same letter to her father where she praised the progress of "one little boy" and a native girl now renamed "Jane Maria," she pointed out that the first was receiving adequate financial support from "Bro. Hume (of Portsmouth, Va.)," whereas the funds being sent by Mrs. Keeling and Mrs. Sinton for the second had "not [been] sufficient" (130).

Juxtaposing such ruminations on finances with Henrietta Shuck's letters written to supporters to extol particular students' progress, we see how women missionaries' teaching success stories served a practical purpose. While that awareness should not make us discount entirely an enthusiastic recitation about some worthy student's learning, it should, at the least, make us appreciate that this literary subgenre was highly implicated in a social enterprise as dependent on border-crossing money as the more overtly mercantile incursions of capitalist businesses into other lands. Authors of missionary teaching narratives were clearly cognizant of this unavoidable (yet potentially troubling) fact. Along those lines, an 1839 letter Mrs. Shuck sent to her stepmother admitted to discomfort with having "to write home and beg for money." Still, she insisted, "without money we can do nothing for the heathen," and, she therefore explained, her writing must continue to emphasize successful teaching, encouraging women in America to "open their hearts, and give to the needy" (139).

Even as she was developing rhetorical techniques to connect fundraising to domestic teaching, Henrietta Shuck was also using her writing to address another challenge associated with working in a foreign field—questions about how and where to educate her own children. According to both Reverend Jeter and Mrs. Shuck herself, American women missionaries were well aware that their own children had been consigned to a marginalized space, far removed from America's benefits yet never fully at home in their parents' foreign field. Not surprisingly, then, Mrs. Shuck wrote to relatives when her first son was only two years old that she was considering sending him eventually to "some Seminary in the United States" to acquire "a first-rate education" that could prepare him to "return to aid us in our work." In the same letter, though, she asked her parents where they thought Lewis should be educated: "with his parents in a heathen land, and receive such an education as they can give; or be sent from them, to be reared by others?" (128). Other epistles outline Mrs. Shuck's ultimate choice to keep her children in China, where she continually sought to be a mother-educator consistent with American middle-class ideals while accommodating cultural differences inherent in missionary life. Thus, she accepted the fact that "Chinese really seem[ed] to be [Lewis's] mother tongue" (130), even as she confided that hearing him use that language in his first attempt to join in family prayers felt unnatural. Countering such results of living permanently in a foreign land, however, Mrs. Shuck repeatedly wrote about her literacy-oriented efforts to build within Lewis (and his siblings) a strong affiliation with America, which the Shucks still viewed as their home.

As the memoir indicates, maintaining those ties was dependent upon an active literacy network. Ships traveling between the United States and China facilitated textual exchanges. In personal anecdotes anticipating the more formal and extensive circuit of mission periodicals later in the century, Mrs. Shuck's narrative makes constant references to particular "American vessel[s]" arriving and departing and to her excitement whenever they brought family letters (117, 119, 124, 146). While the time lag between the writing of a letter on one side of the exchange and its receipt at the other end often lasted more than a year (136, 175, 217), Mrs. Shuck's authorial voice always attempts to strike a conversational tone, rhetorically erasing the "distance and time" between herself and her American connections (122). That her correspondents evidently made similar efforts is clear from her description of one typical domestic literacy event she shared with young Lewis—reading a "very deeply interesting epistle" from her dear friend Mrs. Keeling. After noting that "every line in your letters, and also in those of dear brother K., is perused with peculiar delight, by my dear Lewis and myself," Mrs. Shuck especially commends her friend's ability to write in such an "affectionate and motherly manner," one seeming actually to "speak" to her and her child. Sharing the management of her son's literacy development with a friend back home helped Henrietta Shuck maintain her hold on her identity as an *American* mother. By choosing to include such anecdotes in his biography, Reverend Jeter affirms both that personal goal for Mrs. Shuck and its implications for American culture.

Mrs. Shuck admitted that her "dear boys" were especially "enraptured" when gifts arrived: "Every thing American is of great consequence with them" (174). She herself felt linked to her home via written texts, especially through the ability they gave her to do some long-distance mothering of her siblings in Virginia. From urging her sisters to take greater advantage of their schooling (103–4, 162–63) to begging that they declare their faith in formal conversion (123, 158–59), Mrs. Shuck constantly references the need for her family to stay connected through their letters and through their shared (i.e., imagined as simultaneous) Bible study. Attempting to manage her Virginia relatives' literacy practices by writing from afar, Henrietta Shuck echoes the mandate for domestic literacy then being outlined by authors like Sedgwick, Sigourney, and Child, who originally cast such teaching as a stay-at-home enterprise. Reprinted in the biography that depicts her as transplanting this teaching ideal into a foreign setting, these personal letters between Shuck and her family reaffirm the core values of the domestic literacy narrative's maternal role and the adaptability of the genre itself to an internationalized version of Protestant American culture.

Missionary Motherhood as Profession

Writing an 1898 article for the *Woman's Missionary Advocate*, Laura Haygood, herself already a renowned missionary to China, reported on the Jubilee Conference held in Shanghai that November. Haygood's narrative focuses on the conference's tribute to a maternal missionary from an earlier generation—Mrs. Lambuth, who had been a leader in the movement for over forty-four years. Stressing the familiar links between Lambuth's decades of service in China (1854–86) and the still-dominant ideal of women missionaries as maternal teachers, Haygood describes Lambuth's reunion with some grateful converts from a previous era: "It was beautiful to see many of the older Christians, " Haygood writes, "who had come to know Christ through her ministry and that of her now sainted husband, gather around her as children about a mother."[57] Haygood marvels that her colleague Mrs. Lambuth, returning for this visit years after retirement in the United States, found a fifty-fold increase in the number of native women working for the Methodist Episcopal church there over the number in place when Lambuth first arrived at her mission station so long ago. Accordingly, Haygood praises both her forerunner's influence on the foreign mission movement and the staying power of the gendered value system that had guided both of their ministries.[58]

Despite such emphasis on the continuity in their work, however, second- and third-generation foreign mission leaders like Laura Haygood were also well aware of the ways in which their positions had changed with the times. Between the period when loyal wives like Mrs. Shuck gladly accepted a role subservient to their husbands' evangelism, and Haygood's own foreign missionary labors, a gradual progression paralleling developments in women's work back in the United States—such as gaining access to professions like medicine and acquiring opportunities for higher education—had transformed the foreign mission role for American women from serving as an unpaid spousal adjunct to operating as a full-fledged single professional.

That Haygood herself understood the implications of this metamorphosis is clear from a report she sent home in 1897, when her own duties had already shifted from domesticated teaching in a single mission station to serving as sole, official agent for the Southern Methodist Episcopal board, responsible for regularly visiting several other stations scattered around one region of China. On this trip to Sung-Kiang station, meeting with longtime resident Mrs. Burke, she encountered an example of the "old-fashioned" model for American women's foreign mission labor, with this dedicated wife limiting her work to running a small school in her husband's parish, leading local women's study meetings, and guiding the activities of a few Bible women. Ambitious as such an agenda might have been in Mrs. Shuck's day, for Haygood (whose report did praise the dedication of her colleague) it marked the limits of an earlier approach. Hence Haygood's recommendation to the board was that a single lady—a paid professional who could "give her whole time to the work"—be sent to facilitate a more extensive educational program for the station than could be provided by a spouse who also had to manage her own family.[59]

Haygood's evaluation of the 1890s program in Sung-Kiang grew out of her own experiences in the Shanghai area, where she had, among other things, administered several major schools; led fund-raising campaigns to build others; and established a large, active network of local itinerant Bible women. Perhaps unsurprisingly, therefore, if the epistolary biography of Henrietta Shuck (1846) embodies and promotes missionary motherhood in one stage of the movement's development, the comparable *Life and Letters of Laura Askew Haygood* (1904) exhibits both points of continuity and signs of change in the American women's foreign mission movement.[60] The Haygood biography, like Shuck's, presents itself as providing an attainable maternal role model, but for a different time. While depicting its worthy subject as adeptly responding to challenges like those Shuck had encountered in travel and life abroad, the later narrative's portrayal of Haygood's different approaches to those duties marks significant shifts in maternal missionary labor and, therefore, in ways the genre was used to represent missionary motherhood.

Like the earlier Shuck biography, the Haygood narrative was collaboratively created to aid the mission endeavor by recording a model success story. The preface describes *Life and Letters* as "undertaken by the writers at the request of Mrs. S. C. Trueheart on behalf of the Woman's Board of Foreign Missions of the Methodist Episcopal Church, South" (v). Hoping that their book will advance the "noble work" of the board, Oswald Eugene Brown and Anna Muse Brown, who had long worked with Miss Haygood in China, deem their publishing task a "sacred trust" (vi, v). The Browns stress the gratitude they feel for the "very cordial help which [they] have received in [their] work from a large circle of friends" and from movement resources such as "the files of the *Missionary Advocate*" (v). As Reverend Jeter had in characterizing his labors on the Shuck manuscript, the Browns emphasize that one factor making their preparation of the volume relatively easy was the great writing skill of Miss Haygood herself: her letters, they say, "required very little editing," so the predominant voice in the text is "Miss Haygood's own" (v). Much like Reverend Jeter's, this preface describes a self-consciously social process constructing a role model represented in familiar rhetorical patterns and made accessible by Haygood herself. She was, after all, according to the Browns, both a public figure and a familial one—"a friend" who "had come to fill a place in [their] lives more like that of a mother" (v).

Another sign of the continuity in American missionary writing's use of the domestic literacy narrative is in the similarities between Jeter's depiction of Mrs. Shuck's pre–foreign mission education and the Browns' treatment of Laura Haygood's. As in the first text, the Browns establish Haygood's credentials as a maternal teacher by retracing the steps in her own home training, through early schooling, to her first position as an Atlanta educator at a girls' school and her leadership of home mission initiatives.[61] The Browns move slowly, almost lovingly, through a series of letters and anecdotes highlighting home lessons given by Haygood's mother (so thorough that their heroine "was enabled to graduate [from Wesleyan college] within two years" of her enrollment [3]), her grandmother's penchant for teaching the four Haygood children Bible stories (10), and the whole family's tendency to cultivate "literary taste" as an aide to spiritual values (12).[62] Like many a character in antebellum domestic literacy narratives, the Browns indicate, Laura formed an especially close bond with her brothers, William and Atticus. Soon after Atticus proudly helped teach her the alphabet at age four, for example, these two young Haygoods embarked on a lifetime of shared reading, often exploring "the same books and periodicals" (11).[63]

Similarly, the biography underscores Laura's early exposure to practices linking schoolteaching to maternal domestic pedagogy. The text describes how her mother, in the 1850s, "opened a school in her own house" to teach high school girls (4). Additionally, in stressing that Mrs. Haygood always "bound her pupils to her by the strongest ties of affection and appreciation," the Browns situate the ancestry of Laura Haygood's instructional program in the ideology of sentimental nurturance long associated with domestic literacy narratives (4). With detailed references to the maternal teaching ideal allied with this literary genre, the biographers build a framework for interpreting Haygood's international missionary teaching long before their epistolary plot takes her abroad: "From her mother, especially, she had that fine trait of thoroughgoing sympathy, and that quick, unerring insight of love which is best described by her brother William as 'universal motherhood'" (14). Thus, they intimate, Haygood's status as a single woman did not preclude her from carrying out the role of motherly teacher, since the "early lessons" at home in Georgia "helped her to be such a happy home-maker in China" (15).

Despite such signs of continuity, the advanced educational and occupational opportunities Haygood enjoyed before her time in China indicate generational differences between her situation and Mrs. Shuck's. The Browns' portrayal of Miss Haygood's Atlanta schoolteaching constructs a seemingly logical progression for her career in a post–Civil War South context, when Southern ladies of her social class had far more limited options for marriage than in Henrietta Shuck's day. Having successfully opened "a private school for girls" in 1872, Haygood moved to a larger school and by 1877 had become principal. In all these settings, despite her single status, she enacted the familiar role of motherly teacher. To foreground this point, Haygood's biographers quote one of her longtime Atlanta friends: "Mothers sought counsel of her in the management of their children. . . . Her pupils— and former pupils—and women of all ages sat at her feet and learned of Jesus. . . . All grades of society met in that big soul and felt at home" (86). And, foreshadowing her gentle yet inspiring supervision of missionary colleagues in China, Haygood also taught fellow women teachers in Atlanta, taking on a normal school class for the Atlanta public schools while also mentoring her colleagues at the Girls' High School.

Perhaps even more significantly, beginning in the early 1880s, Haygood helped lead Atlanta's then-fledgling Trinity Home Mission Society, a church outreach program aimed at serving the local poor, "without distinction of race" (87). As the Browns' biography carefully records, Haygood was elected president of the society and quickly took on tasks that would later serve her well in China. To promote interest in the home mission, she started writing stories for the *Wesleyan Christian Advocate*. To raise cash for Trinity House programs, she organized a sewing school where young girls made garments that were then sold for just enough to generate good salaries for the seamstresses (72–73). And, according to the Browns, she reveled in a favorite community literacy project—distributing Bibles throughout poor neighborhoods and organizing instructional programs led by apprentice teachers, thereby introducing them to the middle-class maternal literacy management role (79).

With a personal history of education and professional employment far beyond what had been available to Henrietta Shuck decades earlier, Laura Haygood arrived in China, her biography emphasizes, ready to enact a domestic teaching program far more public than her predecessor's. Along those lines, whereas Shuck had slowly built a small group of scholars for her in-home teaching, when Haygood first reached her Shanghai station, the Clopton Boarding School for girls was already operating with over twenty students. Haygood could also take advantage of young local women's having been trained at Clopton by having them teach at four day schools, each of which soon boasted an enrollment of about twenty children. One local school that Haygood opened in 1892 with nine pupils had ninety-nine on the rolls by 1903, not long after her death. All in all, as the biography stresses, Haygood maintained the domestic literacy management responsibilities of her missionary forerunners by teaching classes (especially for young girls) throughout her overseas career. But, like others of her day, she expanded her responsibilities to include training other teachers; visiting local homes with Bible women her schools had prepared; and, increasingly, managing the work of colleagues.

Reflecting this extension of maternal missionary teaching into more public arenas with heightened professional power, the Browns' early twentieth-century narrative repeatedly highlights the enhanced scope of Haygood's duties, while still depicting them as consistent with longstanding traditions of motherly teaching. For instance, the biography prints an 1896 letter to a Georgia friend, Mollie Stevens, with this administrative-oriented description of Haygood's ongoing activities: "My chief work at Soochow this week is to help in locating Mrs. G's new school for women, and to make a contract for its erection" (378). Similarly, when choosing excerpts from another letter to Stevens in the same year, the Browns first present Haygood's report of her multiday training session for "sixty or more missionary teachers." However, they then share her view that taking over classes for a sick colleague at McTyeire School was a blessing, since it reconnected her with the students there. And they reiterate her unwavering commitment to leading a Sunday school class of Chinese "Christian women" (372–73). Along related lines, when reporting on the glorious service held in Shanghai after her 1900 death, the Browns reassert the gendered aspects of her foreign mission career by including a lengthy salute from Mrs. Waung, "one of the Bible women" whom Haygood had mentored for years. With its loving description of how, even after her official board duties became primarily administrative, Haygood continued to lead Bible lessons for local women, Mrs. Waung's tribute echoes the language and the value system of the most traditional domestic literacy narratives from antebellum New England decades before.

Another clear point of both continuity and contrast between the Shuck and Haygood mission literacy narratives involves parallel depictions of the women's concerns about finances. Whereas Shuck's letters reflect her wish to foster a personal bond between potential donors and the Chinese they might support, by Haygood's day such one-to-one fund-raising practices seemed to have outlived their usefulness. Indeed, the Browns' treatment of Haygood's financial management casts it in a far broader administrative framework and underscores her attempts to discourage what had come to be known as "specials." They print Haygood's enthusiastic endorsement of an article she had read in *Life and Light,* where unrestricted donations in place of "specials" are advocated. Haygood argues that trying to match gifts to an individual student created numerous problems for the ever-expanding mission operation: "ladies and Sunday schools at home," Haygood opines, would be most helpful to the movement by giving "to the *cause* and not to the *person*" (447).

As such details in her biography reveal, fund-raising for the foreign mission movement, by Haygood's day, had become a large-scale administrative enterprise, calling for professional more than personal tactics. To illustrate this principle, Haygood's biography offers extensive coverage of the high point in her long, successful career—an elaborate and businesslike campaign to raise money for her pet project, the McTyeire School and home for missionaries. While an earlier-generation lady missionary like Mrs. Shuck would have limited herself to a genteel personal solicitation letter (if she became involved at all), that element made up only one component in this 1880s campaign. Haygood also created an impressive "general circular to the auxiliaries" at home and sold shares (with impressive printed stock certificates) in the school, which was built in 1890 and opened in 1892.

Whereas Henrietta Shuck had worried about providing her children with the most American education possible, Laura Haygood's overriding concern about cross-cultural learning was how best to select, train, and monitor the other women missionaries being sent to her region. As her own stature increased, Haygood became more pointed in her recommendations to officials at home. Her increasingly directive stance dominates a series of 1890s letters to Mrs. Trueheart, who by then was serving as the paid director of the board's activities and hence, nominally at least, as Haygood's supervisor. While reporting on one of her itinerant evaluations in an 1896 letter, Haygood demonstrates her growing commitment to developing site-based, specialized training for lady missionaries, even as she argues that their guiding beliefs should still be grounded in a traditional Christian home upbringing. Although she urges Mrs. Trueheart to send a "lady physician as soon as possible" for the new hospital in Soochow, Haygood cautions that some attributes essential to womanly missionary work cannot be taught after a newcomer arrives: "Do not ever let any exigency of the work lead you to send any woman to a heathen land to witness for Christ, unless she herself knows Him as a personal Saviour, and finds in His constraining love the highest motive for coming" (369–70). Yet at the same time as she stresses that missionaries need a preexisting religious value system nurtured by Christian home training, Haygood stakes out a different stance toward the issue of how potential colleagues can best learn to do their day-to-day work. Consistent with the increasing professionalization of mission labor, Haygood pushes for extended training—an acculturation step that had been unnecessary as long as women missionaries were merely sympathetic, informal supporters of male evangelism rather than experts delivering complex social programs in tune with a local culture's needs. Insisting that recruits should be fully "tested upon the field," Haygood recommends that a probation period be imposed and that newcomers be expected to learn tasks useful to their assigned station, rather than arriving "expecting a specific work" (370). Like her previous efforts to create a kind of halfway house for newcomer lady missionaries to learn about their adopted home, Haygood's turn-of-the-century strategy for addressing the educational challenges implicit in the increasing specialization of mission labor drew upon her commitment to both the movement's gendered traditions (honoring the feminine heart guided by Christian love) and its growing professionalization (assuming the need for trained expertise to do particular tasks).

In the Browns' detailed recording of such correspondence with Mrs. Trueheart, we see signs of how substantially the missionary version of the domestic literacy narrative changed over time, since the managerial tone and administrative detail in these 1890s letters clearly distance them from Shuck's correspondence on cross-cultural learning. Ironically, however, also woven into Haygood's more bureaucratic strategy is a framework for thinking and action that still positions her work as maternal teaching. Both in this letter sequence and throughout her missionary writing, the rhetoric she uses to designate her less experienced missionary colleagues (as well as her native students) portrays them as children benefiting from her motherly instruction, which is constantly associated with her enlightened literacy management. Thus, as evidenced by her disciples' consistent depiction of her as their "spiritual mother," however professional her ministry came to be, it remained, at its core, a maternal teaching endeavor.[64]

This same interplay between professionalizing women's missionary labor and maintaining its roots in domestic teaching is reflected in the contrasting rhetoric Shuck and Haygood used to characterize their international communications networks as maintaining their ties to American literacy practices. Whereas Shuck's literacy support system was limited, for the most part, to letter exchanges with her family in Virginia, by Haygood's day an ever-widening range of print publications built bridges between foreign missionaries and their supporters. That Haygood and women like her knew the value of this network is clear in the comments she makes about using it effectively with others. For instance, Haygood frequently indicates, in personal letters, that she is refraining from reporting on a particular event because a printed version of her analysis will soon be available in a mission newsletter or periodical. Thus, writing to her friend Mollie Stevens in May 1897, Haygood observes: "I have written a long letter for Mrs. Butler [a Methodist journal editor] about the school [at Soochow] which, sooner or later, you will see, so I must not take the time for it here" (387).[65]

Similarly, her letters often describe her own reaction to reading books and bulletins, then direct her correspondents' selection and interpretation of the same material. For instance, she urges one friend at home to study specific pages of the devotional publication that she had been using to teach a Chinese prayer group: "Take your 'Daily Light' and see the wonderful lesson to which we turned when we gathered around the table" (459). Offering a powerful connection based on shared reading and writing, this transoceanic literacy network, Haygood indicates, could grant her friends at home a window into her faraway world—and therefore a deeper understanding of her work. Along those lines, the Browns chose letter excerpts to show Haygood constantly making long-distance reading assignments for her correspondents, as when she recommends the "two St. Johns of the New Testament" and "Mackay's 'In Far Formosa'" as "delightful" choices for a "mission library" (386, 375). Sometimes she even makes distinctions between what her friends should use for teaching "the young people" at home (e.g., "Elsie Marshall") and what they should study themselves (e.g., the biography of a missionary couple "beautiful in their devotion" [383–84]), thereby suggesting that she viewed some correspondents as both teaching colleagues and students learning from her example. While these efforts at long-distance literacy management were exercised in part to maintain personal ties with friends at home, Haygood's ongoing textual moves across the various nodes in the mission movement's wide communications network also underscore her determination to extend her maternal teaching into fluid discursive spaces, belying geographic and temporal distance to instruct supporters at home. One letter to Mattie Nunnally aptly embodies these twin impulses: "Do you remember . . . the 'Memorials of Frances Havergal'? . . . If you have not read the book recently, give a Sunday afternoon to it. I wish that we might have it together—but we shall, shall we not? Little differences in time and place need not matter (405–6).

Recalling that we can read about this textual exchange today only because of the Browns' choice to include such letters in their printed biography, we get a sense of how pervasive appreciation of the mission movement's turn-of-the-century literacy network must have been among its many affiliates. That Haygood herself always valued its potential power is obvious, particularly in her continuing to write her home correspondents and preparing narrative reports for the board, even in the last weeks of her life. That her colleagues also recognized such literacy exchanges' importance is clear in the impressive array of testimonials created soon after her death, sent in both China/America directions and printed in a range of mission publications. Like the biography as a whole, and like the photo portrait of Haygood included in the Browns' book (figure 9), these tributes celebrate both the maternal dedication embodied in her long teaching career and the professional quality of her work. In their pervasiveness and their enthusiasm, these print texts show how circulating such domestic literacy narratives could, in and of itself, bolster the movement while reasserting its goals. Small wonder, then, that Haygood's biographers chose to reprint the assessment of one speaker at Georgia's first public celebration of her life. While casting Laura Haygood as a traditional "spiritual mother," Mrs. Pattillo, a representative of the missionary board, declared that this model missionary "belonged not only to Atlanta but to the world" (493).

Guiding Mission Literacy Networks

From its earliest days, the domestic literacy narrative's authors had depicted specific *ways* of reading they hoped their audiences would adopt. They frequently presented "how-to" accounts for carrying out specific literacy practices—such as discussing the Bible with children—to build character or achieve reformative goals. Many antebellum domestic literacy narratives located these accounts (whether model anecdotes or listlike advisories) in a literal home setting, concentrating on mothers' interactions with their own children. So, in texts like Elizabeth Sedgwick's *Lessons Without Books* and Catharine Maria Sedgwick's "Ella" (in *Stories for Young Persons*), as well as in anecdotes embedded within advice books like Lydia Maria Child's *The Mother's Book* and Lydia Sigourney's *Letters to Mothers,* writers touted specific techniques for directing literacy. Even in the earliest and most home-based narratives, however, such activities were presented as having implications well beyond the domestic sphere, both in the public actions of learners and through the construction of a national teaching class constituted through shared reading and writing (see chapter 2).

Once domestic literacy narratives had been reconfigured to promote a benevolent, extradomestic dimension for middle-class women's teaching (see chapter 3), the groundwork was laid for rhetoric to be adapted by foreign mission–movement members for their specialized needs. Texts such as Sigourney's biography "Mrs. Jerusha Lathrop" and her charitable advice

Fig. 9. Miss Haygood (1895), from *Life and Letters of Laura Askew Haygood* (1904). Courtesy Robert W. Woodruff Library, Emory University

pieces in *Letters to Young Ladies,* like the "how-to" anecdotes in Sedgwick's *Means and Ends* and the social reform project reports in Sarah Hale's *Ladies' Magazine,* had descendants among stories in mission-movement periodicals such as *Woman's Work for Woman, Mission Studies, Missionary Herald,* and *Royal Service.* In conceptual terms, one element the "how-to" literacy management texts in turn-of-the-century mission literature have in common with earlier benevolent literacy narratives is a strong sense of the mother figure's "enlightened" status and her consequent Christian duty to regulate the literacy development of Others. Both bodies of texts assume that skills for effective literacy management could be learned from reading about them. Employing those skills for the good of society would, in turn, solidify middle-class women's membership in a social group doing significant, nation-building work, whether that literacy management was happening in a "home mission" at a charity school in the United States, at a remote mission station overseas, or in an American parlor where participants could study accounts of both teaching scenarios.

There is one notable difference between the antebellum benevolent texts and those under review here, however. Partly because they needed to situate women readers' literacy management in a transnational as well as a local/national context, the "how-to" narratives of the later mission movement make many more direct references to the actual publication network connecting the women doing this instructional labor. Domestic literacy narratives written in the heyday of the women's foreign mission movement, in other words, often underscore their material position within a circuit of interactive texts. In these narratives, so dependent upon specialized structures of literacy exchange (such as transoceanic deliveries of letters and periodicals), the very processes of textual production and circulation become one major subject of the stories being told. Readers are encouraged not only to reenact literacy practices as inscribed in the texts but also to help sustain the very dissemination network that gave them access to the narratives in the first place. Hence, this subgenre of domestic literacy narratives regularly highlights the interactive relationships binding other forms of social text production (e.g., study-group discussions) to the printed stories themselves. When depicting such literacy activities as writing letters about mission work or giving talks at meetings, these narratives emphasize how textual exchange was creating communal knowledge. This cultural capital could be shared repeatedly to further strengthen the discourse community, as group members recirculated their print texts orally at home and at larger public events.

While full-length books such as the Shuck and Haygood biographies portray the mission movement's circulation network in action, periodicals, stressing their relative immediacy, paid even more attention to this subject. Along those lines, "Conducting a Ladies' Prayer Meeting," in an 1879 issue of *Woman's Work for Woman,* issued a call for assistance: "One of our readers and workers writes asking for the best method of conducting a ladies' prayer meeting, and says that she 'would very much like to know the experience of others in this matter.' Will not some of our readers send us their experience, and thus help many who are interested in the subject?" (54).[66] Offering audience members two reasons to stay connected with the periodical—to find suggestions for improving their own literacy practices and to give expertise to others—this brief article rhetorically positions the magazine's readers in a caring community, self-sustaining because of its ability to share knowledge in print.

Along similar lines, an 1883 story, "A Suggestive Incident," shows readers how they might use literacy to develop ties to the entire global mission community. Describing a genteel social event sponsored by a "minister's wife," this narrative lauds her move to assemble a "circle of guests" from near and far whose connection was their commitment to the movement. While some had only "pen-and-paper acquaintance" up to then, the hostess "adroitly grouped the ladies" and suggested such topics of common interest as "children's missionary organizations." With everyone able to draw upon this shared background, the "social 'catalysis' was wonderful to see and hear. There was an immediate loosening of tongues, . . . a practical discussion widening throughout the whole circle of missionary interests, and those who had no local ground in common found themselves very near together upon this broad standing-place of world-wide sympathy and service."[67]

Although stories like this one about the minister's wife took an indirect approach, the trend in mission publications was to present more explicit, detailed advice to readers about their literacy as the century progressed and the mission movement increasingly used formal organization structures. In 1879, for instance, *Woman's Work* provided a plethora of very explicit stories demonstrating how to develop movement-oriented literacy practices. In May, "From Home Letters" printed a narrative from "Salem, N.J.," where the local auxiliary had developed a system for assigning readings about different mission locations, designating a set of topics with a prescribed sequence (e.g., "the geography of the country; its manners and customs; the progress of missions") and having members write reports that others could study.[68] In July, a similar piece offered a lady reader's detailed narration of how her prayer group had developed a new strategy for weekly discussions: first choosing a topic from those "in the leaflets of the bible Reading and Prayer Alliance"; next having all members prepare responses to assigned questions; then discussing the text together at a meeting (which also included songs and prayers); and finally designating the next week's leader.[69] Along similar lines, the August issue described a whole collection of literacy-based "methods for enlisting Christian women" in the movement, including a "missionary social," which would integrate written texts presented by participants with songs and prayers so as to stimulate "interest among the members of [the] congregation." "For this social," the author, Mrs. Niles, suggested, "a poem may be written, an essay prepared, an article containing valuable information may be condensed, and all these interspersed with beautiful selections of appropriate hymns sung . . . and a period of free social intercourse . . . enjoyed with great pleasure and profit by all."[70] Combining compositions of their own with writing done in response to mission literature, women attending such an event would, according to Niles, find their ability to contribute to the movement strengthened.

While these detailed "how-to" stories may seem uncompelling today, we should appreciate the benefits accruing to their original readers. Learning specific skills for literacy leadership, the audience for these advisory pieces also became more aware of their connections to a venture of international proportions. For instance, a woman who might otherwise feel isolated at a foreign mission station could reaffirm her membership in a gendered American community by knowing she was reading, writing, and discussing texts in the same ways as her counterparts at home. Perhaps even more important, in using such domestic literacy narratives to ally themselves with mission workers overseas, women involved in home-based study could themselves become maternal teachers in a global context.

One author and leader of U.S.-based mission supporters, Fannie Heck, was particularly well-known in the late decades of the movement's heyday for her ability to link various sites of writing—including ephemera, magazines, and an influential book—with narratives serving the movement by celebrating the power of its literacy network. Heck gave hundreds of public addresses in support of mission work, frequently revising her typed copies of oral presentations for publication in newsletters, tracts, or pamphlet form. A skillful crafter of the memorable anecdote, she was also an astute financial manager, ably leading the Southern regional Baptist women's missionary union as president for multiple terms in the 1890s and the early twentieth century, while steadily increasing its budget.[71] The twin responsibilities of inspirer and financial manager provided a major impetus for much of Heck's writing, which effectively blended uplifting tales of evangelical success grounded in literacy learning with persistent (and sometimes quite overt) calls for cash.

Heck's booklet on the May 1900 Ecumenical Conference in New York City and her pamphlet story "The Things That . . . Remain" together demonstrate her rhetorical skill in adapting the domestic literacy narrative to mission-movement needs. The first of these, "A Great Event," directly attributes her ability to report on her valuable learning at the conference to "a sum of money" being "unexpectedly placed in [her] hands"—the implication being that, without this generous donation, the compelling history of domesticated mission work that she derived from the conference and narrated in the pamphlet would never have been recorded.[72] The second (a tiny, four-page fold-over tract) much more subtly suggests the role that well-managed literacy could play in evangelizing by contrasting the welcomes that two different women—one a generous donor and the other a limited supporter of the movement's literacy programs—received in Heaven; according to Heck, only the first was credited with having saved numerous heathen souls, who gratefully celebrated their salvation with her.[73]

In the many eulogies circulated after her death in 1915, representations of Heck and her career credited much of her success to her management of interlocking publication venues. The *Raleigh News and Observer*, for example, cataloged her "many tracts and leaflets," classifying "her literary efforts" as "extensive" and "valuable."[74] Citing her editing of the *Biblical Recorder*, the *Foreign Mission Journal*, and the *Baptist Sunday School Teacher*, this obituary also praised her editing of the influential periodical *Our Mission Fields* and her 1913 book on the history of the movement, *In Royal Service*. Mission-movement colleagues composed even more effusive tributes, emphasizing the contribution Heck's publications made to Baptist women mission workers throughout the South. An editorial in the September 1915 *Biblical Recorder*, for instance, characterized her as "richly gifted with both tongue and pen."[75] This mission journal's obituary described her writing as having "a charm of thought and expression that won for her a wide circle of readers." Another eulogizer cited statistics on the circulation of the journals she edited as evidence of her broad impact; praised her *In Royal Service* mission history as "already [having] been studied with its

15000 copies as has been no other [mission-movement] book"; and predicted her narratives would be read for generations to come.[76] All in all,
though positioning her work in the South, memorials to Heck stressed her
national-level role in the mission movement. Thus, like Laura Haygood,
Heck seems to have contributed to a reassertion of American middle-class
women's cross-regional and even transnational unity in the decades after
the Civil War.

And yet, however extensive her publishing of leaflets and delivering of
mission addresses had been, however profitable her fund-raising prowess,
the guardians of Heck's legacy still insisted that her work for the mission
movement maintained its roots in conservative American domestic teaching. In this regard, several years after her death, Heck's relative Susie M.
Heck Smith crafted this telling picture of Fannie's managing the literature
committee of the missionary union: "All the literature was sent out from
Miss Heck's home. . . . Every chick and child was pressed into service and
instructed in the art of neatly folding the letters and report blanks, [and]
the leaflets. . . . Miss Heck, seated at the roomy colonial desk at which this
portrait of her is written, saw that each package was as carefully prepared
as if it were a personal message to a queen."[77]

Smith's narrative about Heck's management of this gendered literacy
enterprise stresses its links to maternal domesticity more than its effi-
ciency as a fund-raising machine. Pointing out that "the literature" was
"sent out from Miss Heck's home," Smith casts the collaborative labor of
"neatly folding the letters and report blanks" as a "service" for which the
children in the home were "instructed," not a business activity with monetary compensation involved. Furthermore, she describes Miss Heck as
"seated at [a] roomy colonial desk," ensuring that each package was treated
as "a personal message," thereby emphasizing the distribution process's
link to traditional images of American domestic literacy. Meanwhile, by saying she was writing this sketch at the same desk where Fannie Heck had
created so many mission texts, Smith suggests that the very network her
mentor had developed would be sustained by literary descendants like
Smith herself, well versed since childhood in the foreign mission movement's ways of domestic literacy management.

The adaptations of the domestic literacy narrative created by leaders of
the women's foreign mission movement, such as Laura Haygood, Fannie
Heck, and their heirs, marked more than the apex of this gendered social
group's efforts to influence American social life. This era also marked the

genre's most geographically far-flung, ideologically complex enactments. And intriguingly, in the same decades that the foreign mission movement's organizational reach and spiritual energy declined, the narrative form that had served these and other American women so well for over a century began to fade from the literary scene.

Conclusion

Jane Addams, Oprah Winfrey, and Schoolteachers' Stories

If my family could only give me an hour a week, I would be able to use it as my therapy and I [could] be a better mom.

A member of Oprah's Book Club, July 6, 2001

As her classmates settled into their cross-legged positions on the floor, Susie glanced down at her papers. . . .

"Why don't you read the beginning of each draft so we can hear your revisions[?]" her teacher suggested. The children pulled closer as Susie began to read.

Lucy McCormick Calkins, *Lessons from a Child*

In the early twentieth century, the domestic literacy narrative faded from its former prominence on the American literary landscape. Even among gendered groups such as middle-class clubwomen, who presumably still would have been drawn to the genre's vision, a number of forces combined to assert formal and technical approaches to learning management over motherly direction of acculturation through shared literacy use.[1] At the same time, the emphasis on affect and moral growth so central to domestic literacy narratives was being set in the background of many schools' curric-

232

ula, which increasingly foregrounded observable behavioral objectives and quantifiable indicators of learning progress instead. Standardized tests became the dominant measure of schooling's success or failure, as the brand of literacy schools were asked to provide for children became more and more focused on discreet skills rather than exploratory linguistic practices.[2] Stories about motherly guides managing literacy development in domestic settings had far less cultural currency than in the past. Squeezed out both by "aesthetic," high-culture ideals for literature and by "scientific" approaches to teaching, the domestic literacy narrative gradually lost its mandate for doing important cultural work.

One publishing site where we can point to the narrative's decline during the early twentieth century is in the specialty literature associated with the women's foreign mission movement (see chapter 6). Another place reflecting the genre's gradually losing force is in settlement house teaching stories. For instance, Jane Addams's writing on Hull-House exemplifies a gradual shift away from rhetoric touting domestic literacy management toward new intellectual systems guiding her work in urban education and social reform.[3] A woman whose teaching career overlapped two different centuries, Addams went from writing as a student and somewhat tentative settlement founder to being the well-known author of numerous books and a regular contributor to mass-market magazines. Noting the continuities and changes in Addams's portrayal of her Hull-House project can help us understand both the relative staying power of the domestic literacy narrative and the decreasing tendency of American women writers to embrace its ideology fully.

As I argue elsewhere, the writing Addams did at Rockford College established a traditional domestic foundation for her settlement's education program.[4] As a student, in publications ranging from essays for her seminary newspaper to debate notes, from letters to her graduation speech, Addams continually invoked rhetoric typical of domestic literacy narratives to describe her aspirations for contributing to American society. Similarly, during the early years at Hull-House, Addams regularly made use of the genre's tropes to direct press coverage of the settlement. Whether crafting an apt quote for a story in a Christian periodical or for an article in a Chicago newspaper, Addams carefully chose vocabulary casting herself as a motherly teacher. At the same time, these early publicity pieces tended to depict her settlement clients as childlike learners in need of benevolent guidance (which she often framed as Christian missionary outreach) and their shared activities as domestic literacy practices.[5] Indeed, traces of this rhetoric—and of the social literacy it celebrated—are still evident in 1910's *Twenty Years at Hull-House*, showing that the genre remained useful to Addams on into the twentieth century. For instance, her portrayal of the "social atmosphere [combined] with serious study" that she cultivated for immigrant neighbors' clubs during the early days of the settlement invokes ideals reminiscent of antebellum authors like Sedgwick, Sigourney, and Hale.[6] Similarly, images circulated to publicize Hull-House programs situate its work in the tradition of domesticated, "benevolent" teaching, as in photographs of the settlement's kindergarten. (See figure 10.)

However, Addams's twentieth-century Hull-House writing also exhibits transitions in her thinking about her teaching's cultural work. For *Twenty Years at Hull-House* and in texts such as *Democracy and Social Ethics* (1902), Addams increasingly based her arguments in academic disciplines. In that vein, feminist scholarship has shown that Addams and her contemporaries perceived her writing as making major contributions to sociological theory as well as to the more practical field of social work—allying itself with the professional (masculine) discipline as much as with a feminine tradition of benevolent housekeeping.[7] Similarly, Addams's influence on John Dewey and George Herbert Mead is rightfully gaining increased attention from scholars studying the history of education and pragmatist philosophy, leading to a view of her Hull-House agenda as self-consciously tied to university culture.[8]

Closely associated with these trends was Addams's access to avenues of action that had not been available to earlier generations of middle-class American women.[9] We see this shift even in the opening "Earliest Impressions" and "Influence of Lincoln" chapters of *Twenty Years*, where Addams discusses her early, home-based learning. Although she describes her domestic instruction as based firmly on "affection" and "moral" lessons—ideals her first readers would easily associate with the female-gendered domestic literacy narrative—Addams identifies "the dominant influence" in those years as her father, and she retrieves her "first memories" through a "single cord" connected to a paternal rather than a maternal guide (3–4). Conversations with him fill the initial scenes of the memoir. In place of Anna Laetitia Barbauld's walks around the neighborhood with her son Charles, we find Addams's father leading his daughter on a tour of a mill he owned in town. In addition, Addams proudly describes her father's impressive Sunday school teaching. By affiliating his influence over her with this community-education commitment, she feminizes his social identity but also suggests that teaching based in nurturance—the brand of education

Fig. 10. Hull-House Kindergarten. Jane Addams Memorial Collection (JAMC neg. 227), Special Collections, The University Library, University of Illinois at Chicago

she would eventually carry out at Hull-House—could acquire a stature usually associated with masculine leaders. Later, by attributing her eventual skill in the political arena to her father's training, Addams's Lincoln chapter associates her work with a masculine model of civic power as much as with indirect, feminine approaches to persuasion.[10] Here, as elsewhere in the memoir, Addams blends goals and practices from the domestic literacy narrative with claims for a more masculine form of civic leadership.[11] Based on such details from Addams's writing (and texts like Laura Haygood's), I see the domestic literacy narrative's rhetorical patterns being reformulated in the early twentieth century and then fading from the literary scene around 1920. Perhaps American middle-class women, having gained some access to higher education, professional careers, and voting rights, no longer needed the indirect route to sociopolitical influence provided by the genre.

Domestic literacy narratives did not disappear entirely, however. In fact, they seem to have made a brief comeback in the late twentieth century in two seemingly disparate yet generically related specialty forms—narratives by motherly teachers (especially elementary school educators) using a "whole-language" approach for literacy instruction; and discourse (on the Web, in television shows) associated with Oprah Winfrey's book club. In the first case, authors like Lucy McCormick Calkins and Nancie Atwell have used rhetoric consistent with nineteenth-century domestic literacy narratives to advocate homelike teaching that stresses social language use and nurturing attitudes toward students' efforts to learn reading and writing.[12] In the second, Winfrey positioned her original book club's reading practices in a sentimental tradition emphasizing affective responses and moral lessons as crucial to literary appreciation. In both cases, however, the feminized discourse of domestic literacy management has come under fire.

Opponents of whole-language pedagogy and its narrative accounts have attacked the approach for lack of scientific rigor and "objective" standards. Yet, as Constance Weaver, one active defender, observes, whole language is not "a prepackaged program" but a flexible set of teaching practices. Its philosophy evolves in individual teachers' classrooms consistent with research "from a variety of perspectives and disciplines—among them language acquisition and emergent literacy, psycholinguistics and sociolinguistics, cognitive and developmental psychology, anthropology, and education." (In placing these fields within the setting of elementary school classrooms, where virtually all teachers are women, of course, whole language feminizes them.) Since, as Weaver notes, whole language "is also based upon the successful practices of teachers," many of its techniques grow out of their "own insights and observations of how children learn."[13] As she might also have said, whole language is based on establishing a domestic-like environment in the classroom and providing opportunities for language use in an authentic context—a context more consistent with the ideology of domestic literacy management than with more masculine, "scientific" models aimed at teaching and testing decontextualized skills and measuring student success against quantitative models.

In Oprah's case, despite her unparalleled success at generating hype for specific texts, and despite her championing of such well-regarded figures as Ernest Gaines and Toni Morrison, opponents criticized (and often caricatured) the original book club.[14] The brouhaha over her naming Jonathan Franzen's *The Corrections* as a choice, and Franzen's negative reaction, invoked highly gendered arguments about her rightful position as a manager of cultural capital.[15] Commentators repeatedly pointed to the high-culture/low-culture elements in the ensuing debate and suggested that, while Oprah deserved credit for pushing up book sales, she was having a troubling impact on the *kinds* of books people were reading.[16] In addition, Oprah books tended to be aimed mainly at women readers (one reason for Franzen's discomfort at having his book selected), and the strategies for reading that she encouraged were also highly gendered (even domesticated). For example, the original book club broadcasts featured small-group discussions on a set designed to mimic Oprah's own living room, and her guidance of the talk (which she often dominated) urged the audience to "read" the book in relation to their own daily home lives.

Intriguingly, the *Corrections*-associated complaints about Winfrey's influence through her book club were followed by a silencing, as Oprah sent the club into hiatus soon after the Franzen flap. Although Winfrey did not cite direct connections between the episode and her decision to end the regular schedule for the club, it is tempting to see *The Corrections* as having "corrected" her perception of her place in literary culture.[17] When we set the demise of Oprah's more "motherly" book club in the context of this cultural history of the domestic literacy narrative, recurring characteristics in her book selections and in the domesticated reading approach she encouraged take on a heightened resonance. Oprah's insistence on a feminized didactic dimension for her first set of books was in accord with the ideology of nineteenth-century domestic literacy management, as were her strategies for using emotional channels (such as affective language and tear-inducing video imagery) to reach those who "enrolled" in the club by watching her show or reading the books with friends. So too, the on-line discussions that Oprah's Book Club facilitated through its Web site eschewed academic-style formalist analysis and instead encouraged a sentimental reading stance tied to a feminine emphasis on life lessons and feelings. That the designated "managers" of those discussions had to undergo training to prepare for facilitating others' reading suggests a link between Oprah's Web site administration techniques and the feminized guidebooks for literacy instruction created by early purveyors of domestic literacy instruction, such as Catharine Maria Sedgwick.[18]

Might there be some unexamined connections between the demise of Oprah's Book Club (as originally conceived) and many Americans' reluctance to embrace whole-language pedagogy in the schools? How do both these cultural pressure points relate to shifts in middle-class women's domestic identities? Specifically, consider some of the implications, for domestic literacy, of so many middle-class women apparently having abandoned (or having been forced to give up) home-based education of children as their chief social role. Patterns of middle-class American women's employment in the late twentieth century would suggest that some, indeed, have rejected that position by choice. In the majority of two-parent families, both mother and father work outside the home, with neither partner focusing full-time on domesticated nurturance of children.[19] Of course, in families where a mother is the sole parent, and in numerous two-parent families, economic necessity—not choice—sends mothers into the paid workforce. Perhaps an ideology of republican motherhood (or parenthood) is possible only when it is economically feasible. Indeed, as a matter of public policy, ongoing efforts by Congress to reform welfare have placed increasing emphasis on encouraging—some might say forcing—poor single mothers to work ever more hours or to lose all welfare support. In 1996, as the economy was booming, Congress passed the Personal Responsibility and Work Opportunity Reconciliation Act, which required that "after two years on assistance," almost all welfare recipients, including single mothers, would have to work an increasing number of hours per week in order to maintain benefits. Specifically, the law declared, "Single parents must participate for at least 20 hours per week the first year, increasing to at least 30 hours per week by FY 2000."[20] As noted by Wisconsin Democratic congressman Ron Kind, who supported that bill, the 1996 act did provide "states with the resources they needed for job training, counseling, and child care." But several years later, Congress moved, in Kind's words, "drastically [to] increase the number of hours that mothers with young children will be required to work, without a corresponding increase in child care funds."[21] At a time when unemployment was on the rise, women's advocate and single mother Pamela Cave pointed out, President George W. Bush was "push[ing] more people from public assistance into work . . . without increasing funding for the child care necessary for the children of the mothers moving from thirty to forty hours each week," so that, "as a practical matter, children of struggling, single mothers" would "be put at risk of being left improperly or unattended for up to ten hours a week."[22]

In today's social climate, domestic literacy narratives advocating time-intensive literacy instruction of children at home may not be welcome, since such a mandate would inspire intense feelings of guilt in numerous American families. Indeed, while Oprah's management of women's home literacy emphasized several qualities associated with nineteenth-century versions of the genre, for her club members, the goal of reading itself was *not* to instruct others. Sometimes, in fact, similar to the women's romance reading investigated by Janice Radway, Oprah readers were overtly encouraged to read to *escape* from maternal responsibility, not to fulfill it.[23] Thus, one fan justified her participation in the club as a personal respite: "If my family could only give me an hour a week," she explained, "I would be able to use it as my therapy and I [could] be a better mom."[24] When Oprah and her book club fans described "a lightbulb moment" from their reading, the realization in question was internally rather than outwardly focused—aimed at nurturing the self rather than others.

By constructing goals in personal more than social terms, Oprah's Book Club, unlike the literacy in nineteenth-century versions of the genre, separated the construction of the reader from the national welfare. The lack of a nation-building agenda in a domestic reading program may seem more realistic than unfortunate. However, as Amy Kaplan has shown, the domestic space cannot be held unaccountable for the practical and moral choices being made "beyond" its sphere.[25] In this sense, politicians' calls for "family values" do have merit, whether the larger social space in question be neighborhood, hometown, region, nation, or an international community. When domestic literacy is divorced from the shaping of community life, the importance of language, reading, and writing to proactive community building is dangerously obscured. Along related lines, for two-career families or single parents, sending children off to school for professionalized, skills-based instruction that makes minimal demands for parental involvement in literacy instruction can have great appeal.[26] In contrast, today's "working mother" (or father) may well feel frustrated when a child's whole-language teacher makes unstructured but principled calls upon home-literacy "managers" to offer multiple, diverse, and interactive opportunities for reading and writing to complement the school program.

Surely, however, even the busiest of twenty-first-century parents can become more effective "domestic literacy managers" for their children, provided they understand the crucial nature of language learning and the potential benefits of guided social literacy. For mothers *and* fathers, such a commitment involves more than simply setting aside their own "book club" private reading (or television show); it also requires thoughtful consideration of how to read with children—with what texts and for what purposes.

After a talk I gave a few years ago to the "mothers' club" at an elementary school in a well-to-do neighborhood, a young woman stepped up for a postsession chat. She introduced me to her toddler and thanked me for my suggestions about carefully "managing" children's language acquisition at home to lay groundwork for their social interactions in school and the "outside" world.

"I never realized," she told me, "that what I'm saying in the car when I take them to soccer practice really matters. And I never understood that 'Read to them' was about teaching much more than the words on the page. I'll do better with the little one now than I've done with his older brothers. And I have lots of catch-up to do with them."[27]

Authors like Lydia Sigourney and Harriet Beecher Stowe have been easy targets for attacks on American literature written and read more for didactic than for aesthetic purposes. Even in an era of feminist recovery, they have deserved sharp critique for failings such as class and race bias. But the framers and users of nineteenth-century domestic literacy narratives knew some "obvious" things that have become inaccessible to many members of our fragile American community today—that parenting is serious work with implications far beyond the home; that print culture can exercise a powerful influence for good or ill in readers' lives; and, more specifically, that individuals' guided, domestic(ated) literacy can have a major impact on the larger society.

Notes

Introduction

1. Child's table of contents aptly signals key differences between compartmentalized, hierarchical views of American literature and the more inclusive vision typical of the genre under review in this study. She freely blended writers from England and the United States in the anthology. (Alongside authors like Oliver Wendell Holmes, William Cullen Bryant, and Harriet Beecher Stowe, Child included Charles Dickens, William Wordsworth, Anna Laetitia Barbauld, and Mrs. Gaskell.) Also, she made no distinction between "children's literature" and other texts in her anthology. Nine of the seventy-five selections of prose and poetry are by Child herself, with a number of those typical of what, in the nineteenth century, would have been seen more as "family" than juvenile texts. See *Looking Toward Sunset* (Boston: Ticknor and Fields, 1865), preface.

2. In the case of Child's oeuvre, happy exceptions to this lack of attention are Carolyn Karcher's *The First Woman in the Republic: A Cultural Biography of Lydia Maria Child* (Durham: Duke University Press, 1994), which provides readings of a number of Child's juvenile texts, and her *Lydia Maria Child Reader* (Durham: Duke University Press, 1997), which includes children's literature.

3. "Books and Authors," *Ladies' Magazine* 7 (Jan. 1834): 42.

4. In this sense, as Michael Warner points out, the print text being consumed by a reader allowed for self-identification with others who were actually far removed. See *The Letters of the Republic: Publication and the Public Sphere in Eighteenth-Century America* (Cambridge: Harvard University Press, 1990). In the domestic literacy narrative, writers could be viewed as supporting readers' literacy through group identification with characters carrying out the very social acts of reading, writing, and discussion being advocated.

5. The opening sentence of the text describes Andrew, "the youngest child of Charles Sigourney, Esq., and Lydia Huntley Sigourney," as having been "born at Hartford, Conn., on Sunday, July 11, 1830." See *The Faded Hope* (New York: Robert Carter & Brothers, 1853), n.p.

6. Sigourney's role as mentor, guiding but ultimately benefiting from her son's literacy, recalls the "sponsors" of literacy that Deborah Brandt has studied in contemporary U.S. culture. See "Sponsors of Literacy," *CCC: College Composition and Communication* 49 (May 1998): 165–85.

Chapter 1

1. Stephen Greenblatt observes, "Cultural analysis . . . is not by definition an extrinsic analysis, as opposed to an internal formal analysis of works of art," but it "must be opposed on principle to the rigid distinction between that which is within a text and that which lies outside" (227). See "Culture," in *Critical Terms*

for Literary Study, ed. Frank Lentricchia and Thomas McLaughlin, 2d ed., 225–
32 (Chicago: University of Chicago Press, 1995).

2. See M. M. Bakhtin, *The Dialogic Imagination,* ed. and trans. Michael
Holquist (Austin: University of Texas Press, 1981), especially "Discourse in the
Novel." See also Amy J. Devitt, "Integrating Rhetorical and Literary Theories of
Genre," *College English* 62 (July 2000): 696–718; Fiona Paton, "Beyond Bakhtin:
Towards a Cultural Stylistics," *College English* 63 (Nov. 2000): 166–93.

3. See David D. Hall, *Cultures of Print: Essays in the History of the Book*
(Amherst: University of Massachusetts Press, 1996). Hall observes that "between
the 1770s and the 1850s," "a major transformation of print culture was occur-
ring"—one moving "from scarcity to abundance" (37). He suggests this process
promoted development of new genres, changing the relationship between print
texts and their increasing readership (37–38).

4. Calls for integrating gender with other categories of analysis have emphasized careful, historicized use of the terms *female, feminine,* and *feminist.* For example, Toril Moi recommends the following distinctions: using "'feminism' as a
political position, 'femaleness' as a matter of biology and 'femininity' as a set of
culturally defined characteristics" (117). *Female,* then, would be used when discussing matters of nature, but *feminine* when treating matters of nurture (122). I
will employ Moi's distinctions when writing in my own voice in current context
but will leave nineteenth-century texts unchanged when quoting their use of such
terms as *female* and *feminine.* See "Feminist, Females, Feminine," in *The Feminist
Reader: Essays in Gender and the Politics of Literary Criticism,* ed. Catherine
Belsey and Jane Moore, 117–32 (Cambridge: Blackwell, 1989).

5. See Donna Landry, "Figures of the Feminine: An Amazonian Revolution in
Feminist Literary History?" in *The Uses of Literary History,* ed. Marshall Brown,
107–28 (Durham: Duke University Press, 1995).

6. See "Comparative Intellect of the Sexes," *Ladies Magazine* 7 (June 1834):
242–43. Like much writing about gender during this period, this essay, signed
"L. H. S." of "Hartford, Conn." (Lydia Sigourney?), hints at a radical perspective
on male/female social roles, then pulls back. So, the text imagines: "Man might
be initiated into the varieties and mysteries of needlework; taught to have patience with the feebleness and waywardness of infancy, and to steal with noise-
less step about the chamber of the sick; and woman might be instructed to con-
tend for the palm of science; to pour forth eloquence in senates, or to 'wade
through fields of slaughter to a throne.' Yet revoltings of the soul would attend
this violence to nature; this abuse of physical and intellectual energy; while the
beauty of social order would be defaced, and the fountains of earth's felicity bro-
ken up" (244).

7. See Janet Carey Eldred and Peter Mortensen, "Monitoring Columbia's
Daughters: Writing as Gendered Conduct," *Rhetoric Society Quarterly* 23 (Summer–Fall 1993): 46–69. See also Janet Carey Eldred and Peter Mortensen, "'Persuasion Dwelt on Her Tongue': Female Civic Rhetoric in Early America," *College
English* 60 (Feb. 1998): 173–88.

8. This framework responds to Fredric Jameson's assertion of "the priority of
the political interpretation of literary text." Jameson "conceives of the political
perspective not as some supplementary method, not as an optional auxiliary to
other interpretive methods current today—the psychoanalytic or the myth-critical,
the stylistic, the ethical, the structural—but rather as the absolute horizon of all
reading and interpretation" (17). See *The Political Unconscious: Narrative as a
Socially Symbolic Act* (Ithaca: Cornell University Press, 1981). Focusing particularly on the "early national period," Larzer Ziff notes that "literary had not yet

separated from political culture," and he emphasizes that "to distinguish certain writings as 'literature,' let alone to assert that within that category a relative few are aesthetically superior, is to affirm a position of cultural elitism and so of political conservatism" (193). See *Writing in the New Nation: Prose, Print, and Politics in the Early United States* (New Haven: Yale University Press, 1991).

9. Paula Barker, "The Domestication of Politics: Women and American Political Society, 1780–1920," *American Historical Review* 89 (June 1984): 593–619.

10. See Miles Myers, *Changing Our Minds: Negotiating English and Literacy* (Urbana: NCTE, 1996), especially "Shifting Social Needs: From Clocks to Thermostats," 8, 13. See also Myers's discussion of the "school-as-factory model" and the connections between that model and supposedly "'objective,' bias-free centralized approaches to assessment" (96–97).

11. Catharine Maria Sedgwick, *Means and Ends; or, Self-Training* (Boston: Marsh, Capen, Lyon, & Webb, 1839). See the chapter "What to Read, and How to Read," especially 241, 244, 248–49.

12. See Lawrence C. Stedman and Carl F. Kaestle, "Part Two: Americans' Reading Abilities," in *Literacy in the United States: Readers and Reading since 1880*, ed. Carl F. Kaestle et al. (New Haven: Yale University Press, 1991), 114–15, 118, 119–23.

13. Theodore R. Sizer proposes this term to designate "a set of widely accepted symbols and ideas that give meaning to being American" (10) and situates it in "shared experience," especially through popular culture (11). See "Public Literacy: Puzzlements of a High School Watcher," in *The Right to Literacy*, ed. Andrea A. Lunsford, Helene Moglen, and James Slevin, 9–12 (New York: MLA, 1990).

14. Catharine Maria Sedgwick, *The Boy of Mount Rhigi* (Boston: Charles H. Peirce, 1848), 5–6.

15. Charles Schuster, "The Ideology of Literacy: A Bakhtinian Perspective," in Lunsford, Moglen, and Slevin, *The Right to Literacy*, 227, 225–31.

16. Brian V. Street's description of "the 'New Literacy Studies'" is relevant: he applauds "the rejection by many writers of the dominant view of literacy as a 'neutral,' technical skill, and the conceptualization of literacy instead as an ideological practice, implicated in power relations and embedded in specific cultural meanings and practices" (1). See *Social Literacies: Critical Approaches to Literacy in Development, Ethnography, and Education* (New York: Longman, 1995).

17. Shirley Brice Heath, *Ways with Words: Language, Life, and Work in Communities and Classrooms* (New York: Cambridge University Press, 1983), 386 n. 2.

18. Noel, "Social Lyceum," *Ladies' Magazine* 4 (Apr. 1831): 160, 160–61, 164.

19. See, as a prime example of this influential scholarship, *American Literature*'s award-winning "No More Separate Spheres!" issue. As Cathy N. Davidson observes there, "the binaric version of nineteenth-century American history is ultimately unsatisfactory because it is simply too crude an instrument—too rigid and totalizing—for understanding the different, complicated ways that nineteenth-century American society or literary production functioned" (444). See "Preface: No More Separate Spheres!" *American Literature* 70 (Sept. 1998): 443–64.

20. Amy Kaplan, "Manifest Domesticity," *American Literature* 70 (Sept. 1998): 599.

21. Noel, "Social Lyceum," 164; Sarah Josepha Hale, "Remarks," *Ladies' Magazine* 4 (Apr. 1831): 165, 166–67.

22. See Sandra Harding, "Rethinking Standpoint Epistemology: 'What Is Strong Objectivity?'" in *Feminist Epistemologies*, ed. Linda Alcoff and Elizabeth Potter (New York: Routledge, 1993), 54.

23. Glenda Riley depicts the ideal of the moral mother as arising in the context of the new nation's trying to ensure its future and therefore assigning the responsibility for protecting its virtue/morality to women, who were charged with educating future citizens. See *Inventing the American Woman: A Perspective on Women's History* (Arlington Heights: Harlan Davidson, 1987), 46.

24. Marilyn Jacoby Boxer, *When Women Ask the Questions* (Baltimore: Johns Hopkins University Press, 1998), 142–43.

25. Scholars participating in *American Literature*'s "No More Separate Spheres!" issue might fault Nina Baym for organizing her argument around a model of separation between the work of "men increasingly invested in work outside of the home site" and that of "women [who] made an argument for the utility of a system allotting their own sex intellectual and belletristic labor that could [be] done at home" (30). Nonetheless, Baym's recent emphasis on nineteenth-century women's role as history writers (e.g., Child in *Hobomok*), as well as her characterization of the mother figures in dialogue books as quite different from the "true woman" of "passive submissiveness," shows that the underlying conception of domesticity in her 1990s analysis is more public-oriented than in her 1970s and 1980s interpretations (44). See especially "Maternal Historians, Didactic Mothers" in Baym's *American Women Writers and the Work of History, 1790–1860,* 29–45 (New Brunswick: Rutgers University Press, 1995).

26. See, for instance, Patricia Okker, *Our Sister Editors: Sarah J. Hale and the Tradition of Nineteenth-Century American Women Editors* (Athens: University of Georgia Press, 1995); Gillian Brown, *Domestic Individualism: Imagining Self in Nineteenth-Century America* (Berkeley: University of California Press, 1990).

27. Lydia Sigourney, *The Boy's Book* (New York: Turner, Hughes, & Hayden, 1845), iv.

28. Zitkala-Ša's 1900 *Atlantic* series of essays ("Impressions of an Indian Childhood," "The School Days of an Indian Girl," and "An Indian Teacher Among Indians") are reprinted in *American Indian Stories,* ed. Dexter Fisher (Lincoln: University of Nebraska Press, 1979).

29. See my "Gendering the History of the Antislavery Narrative: Juxtaposing *Uncle Tom's Cabin* and *Benito Cereno, Beloved* and *Middle Passage,*" *American Quarterly* 49 (Sept. 1997): 531–73.

30. "Literary Notices," *Ladies' Magazine* 6 (May 1833): 237–39.

31. Sarah Josepha Hale, "Introduction," *Ladies' Magazine* 1 (Jan. 1828): 2–3.

32. Sarah Josepha Hale, "Our Title," *American Ladies' Magazine* 7 (Jan. 1834): 48.

33. See, for example, Benedict Anderson's "Census, Map, Museum" chapter in *Imagined Communities: Reflections on the Origin and Spread of Nationalism,* rev. ed. (New York: Verso, 1991), 43.

34. For an example, see Lucy Larcom's memoir. Larcom sets her accounts of reading "English reprints" by authors like Miss Edgeworth next to praise for narratives like those in "Mrs. Lydia Maria Child's . . . the 'Girl's Own Book,'—which it was the joy of my heart to read." See Lucy Larcom, *A New England Girlhood Outlined from Memory* (1889; repr., Boston: Northeastern University Press, 1986), 99, 101.

35. Lydia Sigourney, ed. *The Works of Hannah More, with a Sketch of Her Life, in Two Volumes* (Philadelphia: J. J. Woodward, 1832), 6.

36. Sarah Josepha Hale, "Miss Harriet Martineau," *American Ladies' Magazine* 7 (Apr. 1834): 13–17. The actual physical movement back and forth across the Atlantic of both individual women writers and print texts was, of course, a

central force in the development of the domestic literacy genre, even up through Jane Addams's day.

37. Catharine Maria Sedgwick, introduction to *Women and Work: With an Introduction by Catherine M. Sedgwick,* by Barbara Leigh Smith Bodichon (New York: C. S. Francis, 1859), n.p.

38. One section of an 1832 *Ladies' Magazine* book review of Lydia Maria Child's biographies of Madame de Staël and Madame Roland exemplifies how adapting European models could involve invoking both national and class identity. The reviewer praises de Staël's "lustre of genius" but also notes that her experience showed how an un-American cultural milieu limited the learning opportunities available to the French woman: "She was gifted, highly so, but she was fashioned for the part she acted, by her education," an education "for display"—focused more on performative oral conversation in the salon than on the fuller intellectual development available to 1830s American women readers. See "Literary Notices," *Ladies' Magazine* 5 (July 1832): 330–31.

39. The close connections between improvements in women's education in the United States and cultural arbiters' emphasis on idealizing its benefits to the nation exemplify one of Frederic Jameson's points in *The Political Unconscious*—that some aspects of nationalism can be salutary, even utopian in their vision (298). Jameson insists that "all nationalism is both healthy and morbid," including "progress" as well as "regress" (298).

40. Qtd. in Riley, *Inventing the American Woman,* 51. Rush's statement is, of course, but one of many examples of the way this ideology could be manipulated to both empower and restrain women. Assigned full control over "manners and character" for the nation, women were still denied their own vote—a fact that Rush obscures rhetorically by casting women as in a position to "administer" laws. This inside/outside position left women with a complicated choice—whether to demand more sociopolitical power or to concentrate on exploiting the power they already had.

41. For instance, in the introduction of the inaugural *Ladies' Magazine* referenced earlier, Hale explains that improved education would allow "each individual [to] lend her aid to perfect the moral and intellectual character of those within her sphere. It is that mothers may be competent to the task of instructing their children, training them from infancy to the contemplation and love of all that is great and good, and the practice of piety and virtue" (1–2).

42. John A. Bolles, "The Influence of Women on Society," *Ladies' Magazine* 4 (June 1831): 256.

43. See Rhonda F. Levine, introduction to *Social Class and Stratification: Classic Statements and Theoretical Debates,* ed. Rhonda F. Levine (Lanham: Rowman and Littlefield, 1998), 3.

44. See Erik Olin Wright, "Class Analysis," in Levine, *Social Class and Stratification,* 148. See also the introduction to *Bourdieu: Critical Perspectives,* ed. Craig Calhoun, Edward LiPuma, and Moishe Postone (Chicago: University of Chicago Press, 1993), where the editors describe Bourdieu's interpretation of the organization and reproduction of culture as "intended to elucidate the workings of social power and offer a critical, not just a neutral, understanding of social life" (10). Significantly for this study of a class-sustaining narrative genre, they also point to ways that Bourdieu emphasized how "language use" works "as social action" (8) and "illuminate[s] the social and cultural reproduction of inequality," including "how the habitus of dominated groups can veil the conditions of their subordination" (6).

45. This group might be positioned, economically and often in social practice, as including both the "lower-upper class" and the "upper-middle class." However, following the historians whose work is discussed below, I see the nineteenth-century middle class(es) as constantly in flux both individually and as a group.

46. Louise L. Stevenson, *The Victorian Homefront: American Thought and Culture, 1860–1880* (New York: Twayne, 1991); Stow Persons, *The Decline of American Gentility* (New York: Columbia University Press, 1973).

47. Persons, like Stevenson, describes the privileged middle class as suffering, especially at midcentury, from a fear of the newly moneyed, whom they perceived as ranging from being obsessed with fashion to genuinely dangerous (*Decline of American Gentility,* 26). Along those lines, in his discussion of the 1820–80 "American Exception" era, Robert H. Wiebe notes that many Europeans were appalled at the American elevation of the "sovereign mob" over "men of talent" and, presumably, refinement (62). (In this respect, the alliance of the privileged American classes with European counterparts is significant.) See *Self-Rule: A Cultural History of American Democracy* (Chicago: University of Chicago Press, 1995).

48. Addams's preface to the latter text articulates just the kind of class-connected social concerns Stevenson ascribes to her fellow Victorian intellectuals. Clearly her proclaimed wish to "serve the need of a rapidly growing public" is bound up with her class-based sense of social responsibility, which, in turn, is closely related to her ability to access, generate, and interpret print text for the good of the larger community. (She alludes, for instance, to her position as "head of the Publication Committee," and her text implicitly acknowledges the heightened access to print culture available to someone who can "assemble" and "set down" information for others to read.) Further, she implies that this enlightened perspective has given her the ability to understand the issue of white slavery both emotionally and rationally and thus, in Stevenson's words, "to educate the public morally and intellectually" (*Victorian Homefront,* 180). Like so many of the educational texts of her culture-controlling class, Addams's preface speaks in a purportedly self-effacing maternal voice that is actually working hard at managing the public setting. See Jane Addams, *A New Conscience and an Ancient Evil* (New York: Macmillan, 1914), ix–xi.

49. Steven Mintz argues that authors like Sedgwick and Stowe came from families having "a strong sense of their own gentility" and an associated commitment to "communal responsibility" that could be fulfilled through "the role of writer" (195). In fact, he suggests that one factor lying behind the moral focus of nineteenth-century American literature was the "quasi-religious" role literature played in the lives of this social class. Emphasizing this stance's connection with Scottish moral philosophy, with which members of this class tended to affiliate strongly, Mintz points to their related belief in the ability to use language to shape society (8, 29, 195). See *A Prison of Expectations: The Family in Victorian Culture* (New York: New York University Press, 1983).

50. Dana D. Nelson, *National Manhood: Capitalist Citizenship and the Imagined Fraternity of White Men* (Durham: Duke University Press, 1998).

51. Studies of the professionalization of women's writing and the feminization of the literary marketplace include chapters in Cathy N. Davidson's *Revolution and the Word: The Rise of the Novel in America* (New York: Oxford University Press, 1986) and a collection of essays she edited: *Reading in America: Literature and Social History* (Baltimore: Johns Hopkins University Press, 1989). Other texts that treat authorial professionalization, though with less focus on women's writing, are Lawrence Buell's *New England Literary Culture from Revolution*

through Renaissance (Cambridge: Cambridge University Press, 1989) and Christopher P. Wilson's *The Labor of Words: Literary Professionalism in the Progressive Era* (Athens: University of Georgia Press, 1985).

52. Susan Margaret Coultrap-McQuin, *Doing Literary Business: American Women Writers in the Nineteenth Century* (Chapel Hill: University of North Carolina Press, 1990), 2–4, 5–6.

53. Mary Kelley, *Private Woman, Public Stage: Literary Domesticity in Nineteenth-Century America* (New York: Oxford University Press, 1984), 138.

54. See Nina Baym's discussions of literary value, morality, and healthy texts in *Novels, Readers, and Reviewers: Responses to Fiction in Antebellum America* (Ithaca: Cornell University Press, 1984).

55. Generalizing this difference is only a first step. To recover the place of the domestic literacy genre in literary history, we must build a more nuanced and developmental view of various groups' participation in the contested process defining the place of literature in American culture, creating literary value measures over the course of the nineteenth century, and seeking ways of imposing those systems on the larger society. In developing this theme, I will, of course, build on earlier work like Cathy N. Davidson's and Jane Tompkins's, which has shown that didactic goals and sentimental modes for literature were viewed more positively in the early Republic through the antebellum era. See, for instance, Davidson's *Revolution and the Word* and Tompkins's *Sensational Designs: The Cultural Work of American Fiction, 1790–1860* (New York: Oxford University Press, 1985). In contrast, focusing on a later period (1850–1910) and its regularizing set of criteria, more recent scholarship by Nancy Glazner elucidates the increasing tendency for cultural arbiters to separate "high tastes and low appetites" in considerations of the literary and to link the high-culture literary (with its predilection for refined realism) with the "belletristic publishing" values of such venues as the *Atlantic* group (and its assertive imposition of formalist literary criteria). See *Reading for Realism: The History of a U.S. Literary Institution, 1850–1910* (Durham: Duke University Press, 1997), 20, 24. Taken together, such studies help us see how changing uses of literature in the United States have been closely connected to efforts by powerful subclasses (whether ministers, publishers, or the professorate) to impose their criteria for defining "good" American literature.

56. Bolles, "Influence," 265.

57. "Madame Roland," in "Literary Notices," *Ladies' Magazine* 5 (July 1832): 333.

58. In this context, see Hazel V. Carby, *Reconstructing Womanhood: The Emergence of the Afro-American Woman Novelist* (New York: Oxford University Press, 1987), especially her reading of Frances Harper's *Iola Leroy.*

59. See my "Gendering the History."

60. See analysis of the important role literary groups played in the lives of antebellum white and African American women in Mary Kelley, "'A More Glorious Revolution': Women's Antebellum Reading Circles and the Pursuit of Public Influence," *New England Quarterly* 76 (June 2003): 163–96. For a parallel study of the publicly significant literacy practices among clubwomen from a later era, see Anne Ruggles Gere, *Intimate Practices: Literacy and Cultural Work in U.S. Women's Clubs, 1880–1920* (Urbana: University of Illinois Press, 1997).

61. One manifestation of this stance is the negative reaction I repeatedly elicited when trying out the first version of my name for the domestic literacy movement: "domestic didactics" was sometimes critiqued as being uninformative, other times misinterpreted as referring only to "children's literature."

62. See Glazner, *Reading for Realism,* where she outlines how overt didacticism became one of the traits to be denigrated as part of an effort to tout realism's difficulty (106).

63. Robert Walsh, *Didactics: Social, Literary, and Political,* 2 vols. (Philadelphia: Carey, Lea, and Blanchard, 1836), 1: vii, ix. While not a familiar name today, Walsh (1784–1859) was an influential figure in nineteenth-century culture making, especially through writing and editing for periodicals. First editor of the monthly *Museum,* the leading American eclectic for twenty years, Walsh also edited the *American Quarterly Review* (1827–37) and the *American Register,* a review of history, politics, and literature.

64. Mariolina Salvatori, ed., *Pedagogy: Disturbing History, 1819–1929* (Pittsburgh: University of Pittsburgh Press, 1996), 7, 11. Salvatori notes that recent attempts to rehabilitate "pedagogy" have often been associated with radical or at least student-centered teaching agendas like Paulo Freire's, and she comments on the fact that compositionists (versus literature scholars) have been viewed as appropriate researchers and theorists of pedagogy—perhaps in line with their role as providers of service-oriented writing courses. In the first case, Salvatori notes "such phrases as liberatory pedagogy, critical pedagogy, and radical pedagogy" and proposes that "the fact that pedagogy's positive valence is pegged on the adjective—critical, liberatory, radical—seems to underscore its perceived conceptual inadequacy" (1). William A. Mowry's educational memoir describes a particular instructional strategy as "good pedagogical teaching"—suggesting that mere "teaching" was then void of the reflective analysis he praises in his example (21). See *Recollections of a New England Educator, 1838–1908: Reminiscences—Biographical, Pedagogical, Historical* (New York: Silver, Burdett, and Company, 1908).

65. See Richard H. Brodhead, "Sparing the Rod: Discipline and Fiction in Antebellum America," *Representations* 21 (Winter 1988): 67–96; Laura Wexler, "Tender Violence: Literary Eavesdropping, Domestic Fiction, and Educational Reform," in *The Culture of Sentiment: Race, Gender, and Sentimentality in Nineteenth-Century America,* ed. Shirley Samuels, 9–38 (New York: Oxford University Press, 1992).

Chapter 2

1. Lydia Sigourney, *The Book for Girls, Consisting of Original Articles in Prose and Poetry* (New York: Turner & Hayden, 1844).

2. This goal of gendering instructional literature is consistent with a pattern Patricia Crain documents in *The Story of A: The Alphabetization of America from* The New England Primer *to* The Scarlet Letter (Stanford: Stanford University Press, 2000). Crain points out that, in the years between the founding of the Republic and the Civil War, "women played an increasingly central role in the nation's literacy, as readers, writers, students, and teachers" (105).

3. Historicizing literature (as an analytical category) is a key component of the process, of course, as Larzer Ziff forcefully shows. In *Writing in the New Nation,* Ziff explains that "most who thought about the matter" during the early republican era "defined literature as all of written knowledge, which is to say that belles lettres constituted a very small part of what they regarded as literature" (ix). This expansive view of literature made for fluid genres and contributed to the productive interaction between politics and literature making.

4. Circulation figures for the *Lady's Book* (the eventual name of Hale's periodical) are quite telling in this regard. Patricia Okker points to the ongoing upswing in subscriptions throughout the antebellum era, setting the rate at 40,000

by 1849 and 150,000 by 1860; she also reminds us that the "numbers of readers, not simply subscribers, were even higher" (*Our Sister Editors,* 56).

5. Magazines where Stowe published in the 1830s and 1840s included *Christian Keepsake, Temperance Offering, Ladies' Magazine,* and regional publications in the Cincinnati area during her family's time there.

6. Rowson's writerly identity has most often been linked to *Charlotte Temple,* a best-selling seduction romance, so we have sometimes lost sight of her contemporaries' view of her as a didactic author. Yet one review of *Charlotte's Daughter* (a sequel) emphasizes the latter view: "Mrs. Rowson has lived to enjoy considerable celebrity as an instructress, and a writer. Her works, composed, as they professedly were, with strict reference to the moral improvement of the young of her own sex," were, this male reviewer said, dedicated mainly to teaching the reader. See "Critical Notices," review of *Charlotte's Daughter,* by Susanna Rowson, *Ladies' Magazine* 1 (Apr. 1828): 190.

7. Barbauld's primer was printed under a variety of names in both England and America. J. Johnson of London, who published other major juvenile authors as well, issued the first edition as *Lessons for Children* and included subtitles designating the various age levels for each volume (e.g., *from Two to Three Years Old*). American titles often incorporated the author's name, as in *Mrs. Barbauld's Lessons for Children.* Some focused on the child character, as in *Little Charles, embellished with coloured engravings.* For detailed discussion of the Americanization of Barbauld's *Lessons,* and of Barbauld herself as a maternal teaching model, see my "Re-making Barbauld's Primers: A Case Study of the 'Americanization' of British Literary Pedagogy," *Children's Literature Association Quarterly* 21 (Winter 1996–97): 158–69.

8. The plethora of surviving editions of Barbauld's *Lessons* at the American Antiquarian Society, the Library of Congress, the Library Company of Philadelphia, and the Boston Public Library attest to her popularity. Multiple copies of many editions are extant, with publication dates ranging from the early 1800s through the 1870s. (Judging by their inscriptions, many of these had been family copies for several generations before being donated to the libraries.) For a discussion of the implications that various textual appropriations of Barbauld had for the development of female authorship in America, see my "Distributed Authorship: A Feminist Case-Study Framework for Studying Intellectual Property," *College English* 66 (Nov. 2003): 31–47.

9. Mary Hughs, ed. *Selections from the Works of Mrs. Barbauld with Extracts from Miss Aikin's Memoir of That Lady* (Philadelphia: R. H. Small, 1828); Grace Ellis, *A Memoir of Mrs. Anna Laetitia Barbauld with Many of Her Letters,* 2 vols. (Boston: James R. Osgood and Co., 1874).

10. Sarah Josepha Hale, ed., *Things by Their Right names* (Boston: Marsh, Capen, Lyon, & Webb, 1840), frontmatter.

11. Gillian Avery, *Behold the Child: American Children and Their Books, 1621–1922* (Baltimore: Johns Hopkins University Press, 1994), 50.

12. Warren Burton includes a passage from Barbauld's *Lessons* in the introduction to *The District School as It Was* (1850; repr., New York: Arno Press, 1969), but he does not seem to realize that Barbauld was the author.

13. See my "*Lessons for Children* and Teaching Mothers: Mrs. Barbauld's Primer for the Textual Construction of Middle-Class Pedagogy," *Lion and the Unicorn* 17 (Dec. 1993): 135–51.

14. Page numbers here refer to an 1807 Charleston imprint, an American reprint very consistent with Barbauld's first English edition. See Anna Laetitia Barbauld, *Lessons for Children,* 3 vols. (Charleston: J Hoff, 1807), 3: 3–4. Subse-

quent references to this edition will be designated "C." Later in this chapter, I will cite several other American editions. I will distinguish among particular editions within the body of the essay by citing publisher, city, and date of issue.

15. A central feature of Vicki Tolar Collins's construction of material rhetoric as a feminist methodology of discourse analysis is her position that "who is speaking and who controls the materiality of the messages matters very much," especially when the speaker's authority position is tenuous and therefore relatively easy to undermine (545). She argues that women writers' authority as speakers has often been appropriated and reshaped by way of various editorial emendations and interventions, so that others' "desires" are layered onto a text, with the "speaker" thereby being "respoken" (547). See "The Speaker Respoken: Material Rhetoric as Feminist Methodology," *College English* 61 (May 1999): 545–73.

16. Some of these language changes were relatively straightforward, aligning vocabulary with (an already) Americanized English but not altering tone, emphasis, or meaning. For example, part 2 of the 1821 Philadelphia edition of *Lessons* begins with Barbauld's own phrase, "Good morrow, little boy!", while the 1861 Boston edition uses "Good morning, little boy!"

17. I found three copies of *Little Marrian*, put out by two different publishers, at the American Antiquarian Society. Intriguingly, given the gender switch of the title, one of them is inscribed as follows: "a present from Aunt Hunting to Ezra Herrick Sovill, Millbury, January 1st, 1847" (Boston: Phillips & Sampson, 1845). Later in this "Marrian" version of *Lessons*, "Charles" suddenly reappears for one episode—the adventure where he runs away from school. Perhaps such behavior was unimaginable for a young American girl.

18. Anna Laetitia Barbauld, *Mrs. Barbauld's Lessons for Children* (Boston: Munroe and Francis, 1850), 188–92.

19. Stowe eventually had a personal connection to Barbauld's legacy through Harriet Martineau, who met the Beecher family during her American travels. Martineau's father had been one of Barbauld's prized students at Palgrave Academy, and Martineau treasured memories of Barbauld's visits to her family.

20. Lydia Maria Child, *The Mother's Book*, 2d ed. (Boston: Carter and Hendee, 1831; repr., Bedford: Applewood Books, 1992), 99. Gillian Avery, who observes that Mrs. Barbauld's juvenile literature was "very popular in America" (*Behold the Child*, 45), also discusses the profound influence Barbauld had on Lydia Maria Child's writing for children. In Avery's view, Child was, in fact, "too much dominated by her model," even though Avery does acknowledge that, in the *Evenings in New England* (1824) inspired by Barbauld's and her brother John Aikin's *Evenings at Home*, Child gave her anthology distinctively "American scenes and American characters" so as to create a "delightful locality" for her tales (*Behold the Child*, 47).

21. "Literary Notices," *Ladies' Magazine* 5 (Mar. 1832): 138–39.

22. Sarah Josepha Hale, *Woman's Record; or, Sketches of all Distinguished Women from the Creation to A.D. 1854*, 2d ed., rev. (New York: Harper, 1855), 196–97.

23. Sarah Josepha Hale, "The Four Portraits," *Ladies' Magazine* 3 (Mar. 1830): 96–110. Hale marveled at Barbauld's renowned teaching abilities, joined with "intellectual eminence and Christian humility" (98).

24. Child, *Looking Toward Sunset*, 68.

25. Lydia Sigourney, *Memoir of Mary Anne Hooker* (Philadelphia: American Sunday School Union, 1840), 115.

26. Elizabeth Sedgwick later used as a headnote for her *Lessons Without*

Books a quotation from the English author: "Do you ask, then, what will educate your son? Your example will educate him; your conversation; the business he sees you transact; the likings and dislikings you express; these will educate him; the society you live in, will educate him." The quotation comes from Barbauld's "On Education" essay, which was regularly reprinted in its entirety in nineteenth-century American didactic publications. See Elizabeth Sedgwick, *Lessons Without Books. By the Author of "The Beatitudes"* (Boston: L. C. Bowles, 1830). The letter to which Catharine Sedgwick refers may be found in Mary E. Dewey, ed., *Life and Letters of Catharine M. Sedgwick* (New York: Harper & Brothers, 1871), 170–71. Sedgwick's excitement over receiving praise from Barbauld accords with her extolling her English mentor in a journal entry several years later. In particular, Sedgwick, who is speculating about the career of Harriet Martineau as the main topic of this entry, rates Barbauld's "genius" as "superior" to Martineau's (*Life and Letters,* 241). As Mary Kelley points out, Sedgwick eventually grew to admire Martineau very much, partly based on having met her during the trip the English writer made to the United States—the same journey when Martineau met Harriet Beecher Stowe in Cincinnati. See Mary Kelley, "Negotiating a Self: The Autobiography and Journals of Catharine Maria Sedgwick," *New England Quarterly* 66 (Sept. 1993): 395.

27. The Americanized editions of Barbauld's *Lessons* and other texts that I list in the bibliography represent only a very small sample of her reach into the U.S. literary marketplace. For a fuller sense of her impact, see my "Distributed Authorship" and "Re-making Barbauld's Primers."

28. Mary P. Ryan credits much of their early success to the supportive network provided by "friends, family, and community leaders." See *The Empire of the Mother: American Writing about Domesticity 1830–1860* (New York: Haworth Press, 1982), 116.

29. Nina Baym, "Reinventing Lydia Sigourney," in *The (Other) American Traditions: Nineteenth-Century Women Writers,* ed. Joyce W. Warren (New Brunswick: Rutgers University Press, 1993), 55.

30. A recent, important correction to this view has been provided by Karcher's biography, *The First Woman.*

31. For examples of the range of readings of *Hope Leslie,* see Judith Fetterley, "'My Sister! My Sister!': The Rhetoric of Catharine Sedgwick's *Hope Leslie,*" *American Literature* 70 (Sept. 1998): 491–549; and Margaret R. Higonnet, "Comparative Reading: Catharine M. Sedgwick's *Hope Leslie,*" *Legacy* 15 (1998): 17–22.

32. "Clarence; or, A Tale Of Our Own Time," review of *Clarence; or, A Tale of Our Own Time,* by Catharine Maria Sedgwick, *Ladies' Magazine* 3 (July 1830): 320–25.

33. "Clarence," 320, 325. Sedgwick's and the reviewer's emphasis on the role paternal teaching played in proper feminine education is a good reminder that, despite their arguments for maternal literacy management, male mentorship was also valued in many antebellum texts.

34. "Sketches, by Mrs. Sigourney. Philadelphia; Key and Biddle," review of *Sketches,* by Lydia Sigourney, *Ladies' Magazine* 7 (June 1834): 284–85. See also "Letters to Young Ladies. By a Lady. Hartford: printed by P. Canfield," review of *Letters to Young Ladies,* by Lydia Sigourney, *Ladies' Magazine* 6 (Aug. 1833): 373–74.

35. "Literary Notices," *Ladies' Magazine* 6 (May 1833): 237–39. The review includes positive comments about *Hobomok, The Coronal, The Frugal Housewife, The Girls' Own Book,* and *The Mother's Book,* as well as Child's editing of the *Juvenile Miscellany* (237).

36. See Linda K. Kerber's influential *Women of the Republic: Intellect and Ideology in Revolutionary America* (Chapel Hill: University of North Carolina Press, 1980). Kerber emphasizes the ideology's links to Judith Sargent Murray and Mary Wollstonecraft, as well as to post-Revolutionary American women, arguing that "they could be better wives and mothers for the next generation of virtuous republican citizens" if they developed intellectually themselves (92).

37. See Nancy Cott's preface to her twentieth-anniversary edition of *The Bonds of Womanhood: "Woman's Sphere" in New England, 1780–1835* (New Haven: Yale University Press, 1997), where she notes "that notions of gender are continually mutable—historical products always in the making and remaking—in every time and place being forged, disseminated, contested, reworked, and in some guise reaffirmed" (xxviii).

38. Mary Beth Norton, "The Evolution of White Women's Experience in Early America," *American Historical Review* 89 (1984): 616–18. For another discussion highlighting the continuity amid shifts in gender roles in American politics prior to the nineteenth century, see Mary Beth Norton, *Founding Mothers and Fathers: Gendered Power and the Forming of American Society* (New York: Vintage Books, 1997).

39. Norton, "Evolution," 609, 616. Interestingly, although Norton's seminal essay characterizes the evolution of white women's experience as complex and incremental, some configurations of republican motherhood have oversimplified the role, erasing overlaps between the home and the polis that were actually a part of the ideology from its inception. In a more expansive vein, Nancy Theriot analyzes how women's educational work in their families, even in the early Republic, garnered them a kind of imperial agency: rather than constraining self-development, she asserts, "the mother role was a vehicle for female self-expression and female power." See *Mothers and Daughters in Nineteenth-Century America: The Biosocial Construction of Femininity* (Louisville: University Press of Kentucky, 1995), 25.

40. Baym astutely describes the home as part of public culture in Habermas's sense of the public sphere as distinct from "the official sphere" of the state yet still a site of influential social interaction, particularly in the formation of public opinion (*American Women Writers,* 6). Dana Nelson's reading of the Federalist Papers offers a useful male-focused counterpoint to discussions of middle-class women's home-based yet outward-reaching social roles. Nelson suggests that the Federalist Publius aims at a republican-oriented "relocating [of] manhood, moving its emotional investment beyond the family. A man's managerial role within the family will prepare him for civic fraternity, where his best energies more properly will reside" (*National Manhood,* 45).

41. See Nina Baym, *Feminism and American Literary History: Essays* (New Brunswick: Rutgers University Press, 1992), 167–68. Baym sees Hale's politics as evolving and sometimes "oscillating . . . between a residual republican rationalism" and a more Victorian emphasis on gendered spirituality (173). See also sections on Willard and Peabody (121–35, 136–50).

42. "Woman," *Ladies' Magazine* 3 (Sept. 1830): 441.

43. "The Influence of Manners," *Ladies' Magazine* 7 (July 1834): 217.

44. Michael Schudson, *The Good Citizen: A History of American Civic Life* (Cambridge: Harvard University Press, 1998), 91. Whereas Schudson pays particular attention to links between this sociopolitical transformation and the development of the common school curriculum, my analysis focuses on education in the home. Overlaps between the ideology of maternal teaching at home and new ped-

agogies for the schools became more prevalent as the century progressed and more women worked as schoolteachers.

45. Wiebe, *Self-Rule,* 62–63. See also Carl F. Kaestle, *Pillars of the Republic: Common Schools and American Society 1780–1860* (New York: Hill and Wang, 1983), 5.

46. Lora Romero, *Home Fronts: Domesticity and Its Critics in the Antebellum United States* (Durham: Duke University Press, 1997). Romero cites both Judith Sargent Murray and Benjamin Rush as early proponents of the view that "in their capacity as mothers women exercised a determining power over the fate of the Republic in the values they taught boys who would grow up to lead the nation" (14).

47. Bruce Burgett, *Sentimental Bodies: Sex, Gender, and Citizenship in the Early Republic* (Princeton: Princeton University Press, 1998), 87. Burgett draws on Habermas to note how the women of Abigail Adams's day "were factually and legally excluded from the political public sphere" yet able to take an "active part in the literary public sphere" (86). Burgett's analysis of connections between the eighteenth-century salon and the involvement of American women in the domestication of politics is especially salient (101, 111).

48. According to the *Encyclopedia of Southern Culture,* by the early 1800s, it was likely that a book "published in the North would receive a national distribution, but southern-issued books were rarely even read in neighboring states" (865). By the time the Civil War was looming on the horizon, Southerners had grown particularly resentful of Northerners' domination of school textbook production and of the way that abolitionists could call upon the more extensive circulation powers of their publishing houses, which were becoming national in their reach. See "Literature," in *Encyclopedia of Southern Culture,* ed. Charles Reagan Wilson and William M. Ferris, 865 (Chapel Hill: University of North Carolina Press, 1989).

49. Jennifer E. Monaghan, "Literacy Instruction and Gender in Colonial New England," in Davidson, *Reading in America,* 53–80.

50. An echo of this self-effacing voice can sometimes be identified even in works by the highly successful authors of the antebellum era. For instance, in the preface to her anthology of biographical pieces, *Good Wives,* Child apologizes: "I shall be asked, with a smile, what *I* hope to do to alter the current of public feeling, and change the hue of national character? Truly, I expect to do but little." See *Good Wives* (Boston: Carter, Hendee, and Co., 1833), xi. See also Warner, *Letters of the Republic,* 15–16.

51. Lydia Maria Child herself complained in "Old Bachelors" that "until within the last half-century, books have been written almost entirely by men" (*Looking Toward Sunset,* 225).

52. Along those lines, in *Our Sister Editors,* Okker makes a distinction between the acceptance of female editors whose work focused clearly on a female audience and the fact that "those women who spoke to (or were perceived to speak to) audiences other than women and children at times" generated "harsh rebukes" (16).

53. "Critical Notices," 191.

54. An apt example of the kind of careful positioning these writers often sought is Sigourney's introduction to *Noble Deeds of American Women.* She simultaneously praises her countrywomen's contributions to the nation and cautions that they should avoid attempting to redirect their energies into nondomestic, unfeminine channels. Insisting that "her patriotism is, to labor in the sanctuary of

home, and in every allotted department of education, to form and train a race that shall bless their country, and serve their God" (xx–xxi), Sigourney avers that the "Creator has assigned different spheres of action to the sexes" (xxii) and that the "true nobility of Woman is to keep her own sphere" (xxiii). See *Noble Deeds of American Women; with Biographical Sketches of Some of the More Prominent* (Auburn and Buffalo: Miller, Orton, & Mulligan, 1854).

55. John Guillory, *Cultural Capital: The Problem of Literary Canon Formation* (Chicago: University of Chicago Press, 1993), ix.

56. Like Guillory, I think that literary texts need to be positioned as "the vector of ideological notions which do not inhere in the works themselves but in the context of their institutional presentation, or more simply, in the way they are taught" (*Cultural Capital*, ix). The school, however, has not always been the primary teaching site for distributing literary cultural capital. By neglecting the nineteenth-century home as a location of literary pedagogy, we have obscured the social position, in American literature, of didactic writing in general and of the domestic literacy narrative in particular.

57. Derek Robbins, *The Work of Pierre Bourdieu: Recognizing Society* (Boulder: Westview Press, 1991), 58.

58. Bourdieu, "Concluding Remarks," 268.

59. Heath expands upon her own definition in ways that further link her theories of "social interactional" literacy with the key scenes in domestic literacy narratives. Heath explains that, for some, literacy events have been viewed as falling into two types—one a reading event wherein an audience tries to understand an encoded graphic message, the other a writing event with a would-be author attempting to produce such a text. Heath emphasizes an oral literacy that is "rule-governed"—so that participants who are familiar with a group's cultural practices know how to participate effectively in a particular event's production of or interaction with a written text (e.g., in a school discussion or, in the context of this essay, in parlor talk about a book). See *Ways with Words*, 386 n. 2.

60. Catharine Maria Sedgwick, *The Poor Rich Man, and the Rich Poor Man* (New York: Harper & Brothers, 1836), 40.

61. An important difference between early nineteenth- and late twentieth-century print-reading practices should be noted here. Our tendency to dichotomize "oral" literacy practices and the consumption of print text is closely related to current practices of reading silently and privately. As Joan D. Hedrick notes, white middle-class reading in antebellum America was very often a social act, as family members gathered in parlors to "hear" books together. See "Parlor Literature: 1833–1834," in Hedrick's *Harriet Beecher Stowe: A Life,* 76–88 (New York: Oxford University Press, 1994), 76–77.

62. Catharine Maria Sedgwick, *Facts and Fancies for School-Day Reading, a Sequel to "Morals and Manners"* (New York: G. P. Putnam's Sons, 1873); *Stories for Young Persons* (New York: Wiley & Putnam, 1848; repr., New York: Harper & Brothers, 1841).

63. Deborah Fitts, "Una and the Lion: The Feminization of District School-Teaching and Its Effects on the Roles of Students and Teachers in Middle-Class Massachusetts," in *Regulated Children/Liberated Children: Education in Psychohistorical Perspective,* ed. Barbara Finkelstein, 140–57 (New York: Psychohistory Press, 1979).

64. My view of the dialogic dimension of instruction in the antebellum era has been enriched through discussions with Charlene Avallone, who is at work on a manuscript about conversational learning in the nineteenth century.

65. In distinguishing between individual literacy events and recurring literacy

practices, I draw on Heath (*Ways with Words*) and Street (*Social Literacies*). The power of any single literacy event derives in part from its being recognized by participants as representative of a recurring literacy practice in accord with their beliefs about language and its use for social purposes.

66. Elizabeth Sedgwick, *Lessons Without Books*, 80–83.

67. Of course, Frank's analysis also suggests that he is still reading the narrative more literally than figuratively, as when he declares that "no boy will ever beat [Lord Nelson] in climbing." In line with the antebellum era's ideas about children's underdeveloped analytical abilities, in other words, Frank can get at part of the text's social implications by way of his mother's guidance, but he has not fully grasped the significance of the story. In any event, the middle-class mothers reading Elizabeth Sedgwick's book could attain a more sophisticated level of interpretation, dedicated to honing their sons' competitive career abilities.

68. On links connecting Fuller's study of Richard Whately's rhetoric, her teaching at Greene Street School in Providence, her later management of the Boston conversations, and her writing for the *Dial* and elsewhere, see Annette Kolodny, "Inventing a Feminist Discourse: Rhetoric and Resistance in Margaret Fuller's *Woman in the Nineteenth Century*," in *Reclaiming Rhetorica: Women and the Rhetorical Tradition*, ed. Andrea A. Lunsford (Pittsburgh: University of Pittsburgh Press, 1995), 137–66. For a useful discussion of Fuller's *conversaziones* in the larger context of women's literary groups, see Kelley, "A More Glorious Revolution," 163–96. Elizabeth McHenry's groundbreaking work on nineteenth-century African American literary societies provides an important reminder that such middle-class organizations were not limited to whites. See *Forgotten Readers: Recovering the Lost History of African American Literary Societies* (Durham: Duke University Press, 2002).

69. Lydia Sigourney, *Letters to Mothers* (Hartford: Hudson and Skinner, 1838; 2d ed., New York: Harper & Brothers, 1839), 185. Sigourney's "The Rainy Day" in *The Child's Book* exemplifies this approach. Opening with a daughter's complaint about the weather, this narrative redirects her attitude with an oral Bible story and other literacy activities with her mother, such as singing "a sweet hymn or two." See *The Child's Book* (New York: Turner and Hayden, 1844), n.p.

70. Lydia Maria Child, *The Mother's Book* (Boston: Carter and Hendee, 1831; repr., Old Sturbridge, Mass.: Applewood Books, 1992), 88.

71. Sigourney, *Letters to Mothers*, 92. Child's *Emily Parker* (1827) offers an appealing portrait of at-home maternal teaching in its early scenes, then underscores the dangers of unguided literacy. Before dying, Mrs. Parker tells her daughter: "There are many things in my heart, which you are not old enough to understand now; but go to the Good Book; that will guide you, whatever may be your trials." Emily's failure to heed that advice is, of course, one reason for her undoing. See *Emily Parker; or, Impulse Not Principle. Intended for Young Persons* (Boston: Isaac R. Butts & Co., 1827), 9.

72. See Lydia Sigourney's "Educational Remembrances" chapter in *Letters of Life* (New York: Appleton, 1866). After explaining how much she values her own journal as a guide, she outlines her efforts to develop similar literacy practices among her students: "I made a number of blank books . . . and each pupil encouraged to write therein, at the close of each week, a brief synopsis of whatever had occurred around her, or within herself, that she deemed worthy of preservation. . . . I appointed a time every Saturday to have them read aloud" (219–20).

73. Catharine Maria Sedgwick, *Stories for Young Persons*, 96.

74. Michael Warner, *Letters of the Republic,* xiii.

75. Lydia Sigourney, *Letters to Young Ladies,* 3d ed. (New York: Harper & Brothers, 1837).

76. For instance, Sigourney's "Mrs. Martha Laurens Ramsay" added such elements as "Astronomy, Chronology, Philosophy, and an extensive course of voyages" to her children's home literacy training. See *Examples from the Eighteenth and Nineteenth Centuries* (New York: Charles Scribner, 1857), 204–5. Notable for its focus on a *Southern* matron, this story exemplifies the rare choice of a New England author's looking outside her own region for a national model. Sigourney explains that this worthy matron "studied the Greek and Latin classics until she was qualified to be a profitable instructor in these languages" and that "she prosecuted Botany" so as "to be useful to her children" in their study of science (205). She also "prepared questions for them in . . . history" (204); memorized Psalms and prayer books to be able to quote key passages; and maintained a course of reading, diary keeping, and letter writing that informed her teaching (206–7).

77. For a related trend in public discourse on housework, see Jeanne Boydston, *Home and Work: Housework, Wages, and the Ideology of Labor in the Early Republic* (New York: Oxford University Press, 1991).

78. The need for effective maternal teachers was not the only rationale used to promote enhanced education for females. Religious and self-development benefits to individual women were invoked as well. Educated women were also depicted as being better wives, able to guide their husbands' manners and intellectual growth. As the century progressed, middle-class women's work focused more on child rearing than on being a supportive mate, and preparing mother-teachers came to the forefront in arguments about women's education.

79. Here are examples from Hale's campaign: "How Ought Women to be Educated," *Ladies' Magazine* 5 (Nov. 1832): 508–15; "Female Seminaries I," *Ladies' Magazine* 6 (Mar. 1833): 139–42; "Female Seminaries II," *Ladies' Magazine* 6 (Apr. 1833): 176–79; "Troy Female Seminary," *Ladies' Magazine* 6 (Sept. 1833): 402–5.

80. See Eldred and Mortensen, "Monitoring Columbia's Daughters," 51; and Averil Evans McClelland, *The Education of Women in the United States: A Guide to Theory, Teaching, and Research* (New York: Garland Publishing, 1992), 56–57.

81. "Miss Fiske's School for Young Ladies," *Ladies' Magazine* 6 (Dec. 1833): 552–56. See also "Convents Are Increasing," *Ladies' Magazine* 7 (Dec. 1834): 560–64. Complaining that "Catholics have endowed private seminaries, or convents, and they are reaping the reward of their efforts in their increasing influence," an anonymous author (Hale? Catharine Beecher?) worries over the tendency of some "fashionable" Protestant families to send their daughters to Catholic convents, a trend with dangerous implications for the republic (560–61).

82. In contrast, a rural/urban difference may not have been as pronounced— at least within New England. William J. Gilmore points to the "mass culture of the printed word" as a reason why rural regions were active in the movement creating new institutions—e.g., Windsor Female Academy—and enhancing female learning at home. See *Reading Becomes a Necessity of Life: Material and Cultural Life in Rural New England, 1780–1835* (Knoxville: University of Tennessee Press, 1989), 44–45.

83. Qtd. in Riley, *Inventing the American Woman,* 51.

84. Susanna Rowson. *A Present for Young Ladies: Containing Poems, Dialogues, Addresses, &c. as Recited by the Pupils of Mrs. Rowson's Academy at the Annual Exhibitions* (Boston: John West, 1811).

85. McClelland notes that, around this same period, girls' common school at-

tendance in New England gradually began changing from a marginal status (allowing them entry only during the summer when boys were doing farmwork and either before or after boys' attendance hours during the rest of the year). By the end of the 1830s–40s, coeducational common schools had emerged as the norm (*Education of Women*, 56).

86. "Female Education," *Ladies' Magazine* 1 (Jan. 1828): 21–30.

87. Emma Willard and Sarah Josepha Hale, "Mrs. Willard on Female Education," *Ladies' Magazine* 7 (Apr. 1834): 162.

88. See, for instance, "Perseverance" and "Easy Studies" in Lydia Sigourney, *The Girl's Reading-Book; in Prose and Poetry. For Schools* (New York: J. Orville Taylor and "American Common School Union," 1838; 15th ed., Newburgh, [N.Y.]: Proudfoot and Banks, 1847), in which female studies, imagined as including difficult subjects like Latin even at an early age, were still being cast as preparation for proper domesticity. McClelland implicitly relates this lingering trend to the continued reluctance to argue for scholarly achievement for its own sake: "It is important to remember that the ability to go to school was not ever perceived as a prelude to higher learning. Indeed, the 'learned woman' was in as much disrepute as ever for higher learning was thought to ruin a woman for useful life. Rather, what was needed was a stronger, more literate, knowledgeable and moral mother" (*Education of Women*, 57).

89. Elizabeth Alden Green, *Mary Lyon and Mount Holyoke: Opening the Gates* (Hanover: University Press of New England, 1979).

90. See S. F. W., "Female Education." *Ladies' Magazine* 7 (Nov. 1834): 500.

91. Lydia Sigourney, *The Pictorial Reader* (New York: Turner & Hayden, 1844), 8–9.

92. This same pattern is also evident in Sigourney's "Reverend John Wesley," in *Examples from the Eighteenth and Nineteenth Centuries*, where the main character's mother's letters are described as "a great assistance in strengthening and confirming his religious earnestness" during his study at Oxford (7–8). See also (in *Examples from the Eighteenth*) "Mrs. May Lovell Ware," in which Mrs. Ware "found time for a kind of journalizing epistles" to her stepson, so that he later declares, "Surely God never gave a boy such a mother, nor a man such a friend" (341).

93. Sigourney, *The Boy's Book*, 89. Here Sigourney implies that spending time away from home at a local day school can be a complement to domestic teaching, while leaving for extended study at a boarding facility might be more dangerous. On other occasions she was unenthusiastic even about day schools, at least for the very young. In "Reverend John Wesley," in the *Examples from the Eighteenth and Nineteenth Centuries* anthology, for instance, Sigourney said of Wesley's mother: "She exerted herself to be the sole instructress of her children, and did not permit them to attend school, in their tender years, fearing they might be subjected to unskilled training, or to the influence of bad example" (7–8). The question of when it would be desirable (or even safe) for middle-class mothers to send their children to school challenged writers working in this tradition for decades. Barbara Beatty describes the 1820s and 1830s as periods of particularly intense competition between "infant schools" (adapted from the charity schools to serve middle-class clientele) and what she calls "family school" models (20, 29–32). She suggests that back-and-forth tension between home schooling and feminized instruction in schools as ideals for young (up to age six) children can be traced in enrollment patterns as well as advice literature. See *Preschool Education in America: The Culture of Young Children from the Colonial Era to the Present* (New Haven: Yale University Press, 1995).

94. When reading such assertions of the superiority of feminine domestic education over masculine boarding schools, we must remember that lines dividing home and educational institutions were far less distinct in the antebellum era than later in the century, when expanded academies, seminaries, and colleges spread across the country. For example, Harriet Beecher Stowe's mother and Harriet herself both educated young neighborhood children as day students in their homes, as did many other middle-class women in colonial New England. Jane C. Nylander reports on one such domestic teaching enterprise that was actually shared by Ruth Bascom and her husband, Ezekial, who had nearly a dozen boarding students in 1813. See *Our Own Snug Fireside: Images of the New England Home 1760–1860* (New York: Yale University Press, 1994), 24–25. Furthermore, many students attending antebellum academies and seminaries boarded with families rather than living in dormitories, joining the mixed-gender environment of parlor culture in the evenings after attending classes during the day. So the moves in some domestic literacy narratives to dichotomize masculine boarding and feminine home education may be more argumentative than descriptive.

95. Consistent with this hesitancy to make overt claims of political power is Lydia Maria Child's observation in her *History of the Condition of Women, in Various Ages and Nations* (Boston: John Allen & Co., 1835) that the "women of the United States have no direct influence in politics," followed almost immediately by her statement that "perhaps there is no country in the world, where women, as wives, sisters, and daughters, have more influence" (265).

96. Catharine Maria Sedgwick, *A Love Token for Children: Designed for Sunday-School Libraries* (New York: Harper & Brothers, 1838), 137.

97. Sigourney, *Examples from the Eighteenth*, 231–32. This narrative portrays a Congressman "indebted to his maternal guide, for the hallowed precepts which were early incorporated with his character," through her having "induced him in childhood to read religious books" (232). The power of her influence could be measured in part, Sigourney suggests, by her son's treasuring a book from which she taught him, which "he continued to use till his dying day" (232).

98. Sigourney's "Child at the Mother's Grave" narrative poem depicts just such a literacy bond, outlasting death. See *The Girl's Reading Book,* 192.

99. Sedgwick, *Love Token for Children,* 20–25. Sigourney's "A Father to his Motherless Children" offers a telling parallel examination of the difficulties encountered by a father struggling to nurture his "little smitten flock" after the death of their "blessed" mother, whose home teaching practices he tries to imitate as they "say the prayer she taught," sing her songs, and retell favorite stories. See *Illustrated Poems* (New York: Allen Brothers, 1869), 373–74.

100. The "Topics" list in the first issue of the *Mother's Magazine* is telling in this regard. For example, by setting as one goal for the periodical "to make public any successful experiments parents may have made, in the education and management of their families," the list stresses the overlap between domestic teaching and the public good. And, in planning to write about "maternal associations," the magazine celebrates their "salutary influence" on public culture. See *Mother's Magazine* 1 (Jan. 1833): 4–5.

101. Sigourney, *Letters to Mothers,* 10. Sigourney's quoting of Queen Elizabeth's lament is striking: "My cousin Mary of Scotland, hath a fair son born unto her, and I am but a dead tree" (9). Sigourney implies here that a mother with no overt political power may, in the end, have more influence than a childless queen.

102. Nina Baym points out that "in the early 1840s, as the cult of Washington's mother took hold," Sarah Hale praised the first president's mother by declaring that, under her "maternal guidance, and in the common school," he

gained the "physical, intellectual, and moral elements which formed his greatness." For Baym, Hale's linking of home and school learning here is significant, in line with the era's (and especially Emma Willard's) view of "the schoolroom" as "producing teacher-mothers" (*Feminism and American Literary History*, 131). Other popular models drew from colonial New England history (e.g., Ann Eliot and Mrs. Winthrop). See Lydia Sigourney, *Examples of Life and Death* (New York: Charles Scribner, 1851).

103. Sigourney, *The Boy's Book*, 66. Similarly, the *Ladies' Magazine* marked the dedication of a monument to Mary Washington by printing a speech President Andrew Jackson had delivered for the occasion and introducing it with a reaffirmation of "the Mother of Washington" as a model for women's shaping society through the education of sons. See "Mary, the Mother of Washington," *Ladies' Magazine* 6 (June 1833): 266–69. See also "Woman's Way to Eminence," *Ladies' Magazine* 7 (July 1834): 385–87.

104. Albert Bushnell, *My Mother: With Poetry and a Preface by Mrs. Lydia H. Sigourney* (Oberlin, [Ohio]: Fitch, 1848). In her preface's portrait of this missionary-making mother, Sigourney echoes Bushnell: "How far his own self-devotedness to the work of missions, may have been the result of her own instructions to his infant mind, can never be fully known, till that day, when the secrets of all hearts shall be made manifest" (vi).

105. Examples of texts specifically identifying the Bible as appropriate or even essential reading include Sedgwick's *The Poor Rich Man* and her "Ella" and "Saturday Night" narratives in *Stories for Young Persons;* and Sigourney's "Mrs. Martha Laurens Ramsey" biography in *Examples from the Eighteenth and Nineteenth Centuries* and her "Child at the Mother's Grave" in *The Girl's Reading Book.*

106. Ann Douglas, *The Feminization of American Culture* (New York: Doubleday, 1977). Much work remains to be done to understand links between the ongoing changes in Protestant religious thought, especially among Congregationalists and Evangelicals, and theories and practices of maternal domestic teaching. Steven Mintz, for instance, charts a close relationship between increased emphasis on the maternal role in childrearing and "the rise of more liberal religious doctrines that reject the notion of original sin and regard salvation as a gradual process in which the natural and supernatural join together," as well as "individualistic sentiments, evident in religious doctrines stressing human will and ability" (*Prison of Expectations*, 190–91).

107. See, for instance, "Mrs. Mary Lovell Ware" in Sigourney's *Examples from the Eighteenth and Nineteenth Centuries,* where the "revered" Dr. Channing "conversed with [Mrs. Ware] to *learn,* as well as to *teach,*" and "requested her to make visits of instruction to a disconsolate person whom he could not awaken to religious hope, trusting that her gentle sympathy and clear views might shed a ray of light that would point to the day" (346).

Chapter 3

1. Child, *The Mother's Book*, title page.

2. In literacy studies, cross-class relationships' influence on literacy development has been a major concern, but most analyses have focused on late twentieth-century experiences rather than earlier periods. See, for example, Brandt's "Sponsors of Literacy," 165–85.

3. Important work on the study of class is available in Jean Pfaelzer and Sharon M. Harris, eds., "Discourses of Women and Class," special issue, *Legacy* 16 (1999).

4. Amy Kaplan's "Manifest Domesticity" highlights the racist and imperialist stance of women working in this tradition, such as Sarah Josepha Hale (592–99) and Catharine Beecher (587–91).

5. Catharine Maria Sedgwick's preface to *Live and Let Live* declares that, among members of her own class, she hopes to awaken "sleeping consciences" so women "feel their duties" to others (vi). Her dedication page identifies this same group as her target audience. See *Live and Let Live; or, Domestic Service Illustrated* (New York: Harpers, 1837).

6. For a review of scholarship on social class, from Marx through recent feminist reexaminations setting class in a network with other social categories, see Levine, *Social Class and Stratification,* especially Levine's "Conclusion" (249–60) and Patricia Hill Collins's "Toward a New Vision: Race, Class, and Gender as Categories of Analysis and Connection" (231–47).

7. I quote the phrase "inferiors in position" from the preface to *Live and Let Live* (vi). Sedgwick's placing the phrase in quotation marks underscores the ongoing unease middle-class women writers felt about using such terminology to delineate social rank in a democracy.

8. Mintz, *Prison of Expectations,* 206.

9. See Stevenson, *Victorian Homefront,* and Persons, *Decline of American Gentility.* In "Toward an Historical Archaeology of Materialistic Domestic Reform," Suzanne Spencer-Wood situates nineteenth-century reformists' work in and outside the home within a context of concern over "industrialization, urbanization, and massive immigration" (238). See *The Archaeology of Inequality,* ed. Randall H. McGuire and Robert Paynter, 231–86 (Oxford: Blackwell, 1991). See too Mintz, *Prison of Expectations,* 154.

10. These terms—*enlightened* and *benevolent*—were often presented as interactive. Women's study of society, through their own domestic literacy, rendered them enlightened, so that they sought opportunities for benevolence. Being benevolent, in turn, enlightened women (made them holy and more knowledgeable about themselves, society, and moral good). Both "Infant Schools," *Ladies' Magazine* 5 (Apr. 1832): 179–82, and Lydia Sigourney, "Mrs. Jerusha Lathrop," in *The Girl's Reading Book* (1838), 147–48, use these terms.

11. This was a troubling reality that writers of domestic literacy narratives usually did not emphasize to their middle-class readership. For one exception, see the introduction Catharine Maria Sedgwick wrote for an American edition of a British author's tract urging that young ladies be educated for paid professions. Sedgwick points to parents' responsibility to prepare their daughters for "the exigencies of life. They expect their daughters to marry and thus be provided for. . . . But . . . marriage may come, and a life of pecuniary adversity, or a widowhood of penury may follow" (qtd. in Bodichon, *Women and Work,* 5).

12. Susan Warner, *The Wide, Wide World by Elizabeth Wetherell* [pseud.] (New York: George P. Putnam, 1851, 1892; repr., New York: Feminist Press, 1987), 24, 30–36. See also Nina Baym's discussion of Alice Humphreys's instructing Ellen later in the novel. See *Woman's Fiction: A Guide to Novels by and about Women in America 1820–70,* 2d ed. (Urbana: University of Illinois Press, 1993), 147.

13. See Catharine Maria Sedgwick's portrayal of the citified young girls in her "Ella" tale from *Stories for Young Persons,* 95–112; and her portrayal of the heroine's unpleasant relatives in *A New-England Tale; or, Sketches of New-England Character and Manners,* ed. Victoria Clements (New York: Oxford University Press, 1995).

14. Forten's Civil War–era diaries, composed during her teaching in the South, as well as her essays for the *Atlantic Monthly*, are usually read in the context of African American literary history, but the interclass relations evident in Forten's views of her teaching are also worth explicating. See Charlotte Forten Grimké, *The Journals of Charlotte Forten Grimké*, ed. Brenda Stevenson (New York: Oxford University Press, 1988); "Life on the Sea Islands, Part I," *Atlantic Monthly* 13 (May 1864): 587–96; and "Life on the Sea Islands, Part II," *Atlantic Monthly* 13 (June 1864): 666–76. For a class-oriented analysis of Forten's writing, see Lisa A. Long, "Charlotte Forten's Civil War Journals and the Quest for 'Genius, Beauty, and Deathless Fame,'" *Legacy* 16 (1999): 37–48. See also Jane Addams, *Twenty Years at Hull-House with Autobiographical Notes*, ed. James Hurt (1910; repr., Urbana: University of Illinois Press, 1990); and Addams, *New Conscience*.

15. Sigourney, "Mrs. Jerusha Lathrop," in *The Girl's Reading Book*, 147–48.

16. "Infant Schools," 181, 179. Amy Dru Stanley points out that, besides recognizing the social benefits benevolent workers accrued through tasks like managing infant schools, we need to realize that some of these "charitable" middle-class women were being paid salaries. These "altruistic ladies who administered the vast benevolent empire of the antebellum era," Stanley shows, were not always motivated by pure altruism. See "Home Life and Morality of the Market," in *The Market Revolution in America: Social, Political, and Religious Expressions, 1800–1880*, ed. Melvyn Stokes and Stephen Conway (Charlottesville: University Press of Virginia, 1996), 79.

17. This essay, in fact, goes further than most pieces of its kind to acknowledge the challenges that prevented working-class mothers from fulfilling the middle-class ideal of teaching at home: "The poor mother is obliged to go out to her day's work, that she may earn food for her children. . . . To these poor anxious mothers the Infant School is a blessed asylum" (180–81).

18. See Nelson, *National Manhood*, especially the introduction.

19. *Mother's Magazine* 1 (Jan. 1833): 4. I thank the Nineteenth-Century Women Writers' Study Group, whose discussions have greatly assisted my analysis of this text and many others.

20. Since the "Topics" list is unsigned, I attribute it to Mrs. Whittelsey. The description of the magazine's contents printed above it is signed "L. H. S.," perhaps denoting Lydia Howard Sigourney, then active in magazine writing and editing.

21. Harriet Beecher Stowe, "Trials of a Housekeeper," in *Household Papers and Stories*, 487–93 (Cambridge: Riverside Press, 1896). For samples of the class-distinguishing advertising cards that circulated throughout the century, visit the "Managing the Help" series within the "Domesticity" section of the "Women's Work in the Long Nineteenth Century" Web site that Ann Pullen and I have designed: <http://www.kennesaw.edu/hss/wwork/>.

22. Throughout the nineteenth century and into the twentieth, *ladies* was a code word used to underscore differences based on social class. See Sedgwick's *Live and Let Live*, where, once the snobby Mrs. Ardley discovers that the person she is interviewing about a domestic servant position may have once been of higher social status, she changes her attitude dramatically: "Mrs. Ardley felt a sympathy for a fallen *possible* lady, that she never would have dreamed of for a *mere poor woman*" (31).

23. Cf. "Infant Schools," 179–82. The article explains that the need for this supervision should not reflect negatively on the mothers of such children, who

may be "very poor even though they be worthy and industrious" (180). The clientele of the school is described as the children of the "poor mother" who is "obliged to go out to her day's work, that she may earn food for her children," mothers who can still (in theory at least) maintain a middle-class-like teaching relationship with their children after "5 o'clock in the afternoon" (180).

24. The education of orphans was clearly safe to take on, in this regard. Thus, in Whittelsey's *Mother's Magazine,* the "orphans of . . . deceased friends" are described as a "flock" to be saved (4). Earlier, the educative needs of the children of deceased missionaries are singled out as concerns of the periodical. While the editorial statements assume complete control over orphans, how much the class of mothers being constructed in these texts should be involved in "the wants of the children of ignorance and penury" is not specified (4).

25. Michael Argyle, *The Psychology of Social Class* (New York: Routledge, 1994), 1.

26. "Infant Schools" contains similar distance/power assertions, insisting on a class hierarchy even while touting purported mobility. Only "the children of the poor" need to have their weekday teaching closely monitored; for them (versus for middle-class children), Sunday school alone cannot "redeem the moral degradation" of their weekdays; weeklong middle-class intervention is required (181–82).

27. While the *Lowell Offering* has often been interpreted as embodying the desire of factory girls to take on middle-class literacy practices and social values, the relatively brief life and character of that publication need to be remembered. Only 2 percent of Lowell workers subscribed to the *Offering,* yet it was hailed as the voice of the mill girls, especially by mill owners, who recognized its propaganda value. During the same period when the *Offering* was portraying happy, healthy industrialism, a substantial number of workers signed an 1845 petition to the Massachusetts legislature detailing fourteen-hour days, speedups in the machines, lack of exercise, and poor nutrition among the workers. I thank historian Ann Pullen for this information. Many of the insights on interclass relations in this chapter come from regularly team-teaching a course on women's work with Professor Pullen.

28. Bruce C. Daniels, *The Fragmentation of New England: Comparative Perspectives on Economic, Political, and Social Divisions in the Eighteenth Century* (New York: Greenwood Press, 1988). For Daniels, this "clash between equality of opportunity and equality of condition" was "rooted in the pre-Revolutionary eighteenth century," when colonial regions even as purportedly homogeneous as New England became increasingly heterogeneous, paving the way for a national culture based partly on cross-regional alliances among similar social classes, as they recognized differences (such as religion, race, or class) within local cultures (183).

29. See Noel Ignatiev, *How the Irish Became White* (New York: Routledge, 1995). Ignatiev convincingly demonstrates that nativist opposition to Irish assimilation encompassed "several origins and manifestations," including "snobbery," "partisan" politics, "doctrinal" differences (Protestant versus Catholic), associations of the Irish with intemperance, and questions about the Irish's apparent support for slavery (148–49). To Ignatiev's list, I would add issues about domestic teaching and related concerns about language and literacy practices.

30. Hasia R. Diner, *Erin's Daughters in America: Irish Immigrant Women in the Nineteenth Century* (Baltimore: Johns Hopkins University Press, 1983), 86. Diner describes fears about the possibility of Irish domestic workers being "disguised agents of the Pope bent on converting the Protestant children in their charge" (85).

31. Sigourney, *Letters to Mothers*, 42–43.

32. Sedgwick, *Means and Ends*, 238–39.

33. Catharine Maria Sedgwick, *Tales and Sketches. Second Series* (New York: Harper & Brothers, 1844), 191. Judging by Sedgwick's "Notice," this story was reprinted, along with others in the anthology, from an earlier magazine version (7).

34. Diner reports that complaints circulating about "Irish girls" included their inability to cook well, their uncleanliness, and their unreliability (*Erin's Daughters in America*, 85).

35. Patricia Collins's class stratification model for interpreting the "interlocking nature of race, class, and gender" provides a helpful gloss for this story ("Toward a New Vision," 235). Collins follows Sandra Harding in suggesting that three main dimensions of oppression require close scrutiny: the institutional, the symbolic, and the individual. In this tale, Sedgwick uses the symbolic representations of language (Mrs. Ray's stereotype-resisting characterizations of Margaret) to suggest that, within the institutional setting of domesticity, Margaret could be Americanized consistent with the national ideology for middle-class motherhood. However, the individual prejudice of old Mr. Maxwell, who can see Margaret only in terms of her static racial/ethnic identity and not her potentially mobile class identity, ends up destroying her efforts to be Americanized via an idealized gendered role ("Toward a New Vision," 235–40).

36. This same change in direction also marks Sedgwick's lack of understanding about the usual life choices of actual—as opposed to fictional—Irish female domestic workers. As Diner convincingly shows, these women were more likely to *choose* to remain single than to marry—so much so that Irish American leaders worried over the low marriage rate (*Erin's Daughters in America*, 91–92). Although Margaret does not appear, in Sedgwick's children's story, to have literally "lost her virtue," traits of the seduction-and-fall plotline are obvious in "The Irish Girl."

37. For fuller treatments of both novels as benevolent domestic literacy narratives, see my "Periodizing Authorship, Characterizing Genre: Reading Catharine Maria Sedgwick's Benevolent Literacy Narratives," *American Literature* 76 (Mar. 2004): 1–29.

38. Rose's text has been highly influential. See Mike Rose, *Lives on the Boundary* (New York: Penguin, 1990). Both Villanueva and Rodriguez address social class issues while also highlighting language differences connected to race and ethnicity. See Victor Villanueva, *Bootstraps: From an American Academic of Color* (Urbana: NCTE, 1993); Richard Rodriguez, *Hunger of Memory* (New York: Bantam, 1983).

39. My reference to this "double bind" calls to mind one often invoked by scholars pointing to challenges faced by African American women, restricted by both race and gender. I of course do not mean to suggest that the lived experiences of free working-class white women were basically similar to those of nineteenth-century African American women, whether slave or free. Narratives like Harriet Jacobs's underscore the heightened constraints placed upon enslaved African American women, including restrictions on their literacy development and use. Still, as Elizabeth McHenry has recently argued, it is important that we not overgeneralize nineteenth-century American blacks' experiences and that, more specifically, we acknowledge the rich and self-directed interactions with literacy going on among middle-class blacks. See especially McHenry's introduction to *Forgotten Readers*, 14–15. Bringing class, gender, and race together as analytical tools for understanding domestic literacy narratives' various subgenres in-

volves making the kinds of subtle distinctions within "white" culture—for example, the differences between Irish domestics or Appalachian mill workers and
white, well-to-do Protestants—that McHenry has outlined for studying nineteenth-
and early twentieth-century black culture.

40. Elizabeth Stuart Phelps, *The Silent Partner* (Boston: J. R. Osgood, 1871;
repr., New York: Feminist Press, 1983), 234–35. Citations are to the Feminist
Press edition.

41. I thank Marjorie Pryse for alerting me to the recent republication of
Cooke's novel. See Grace MacGowan Cooke, *The Power and the Glory* (New York:
Doubleday, Page & Co., 1910; repr., Boston: Northeastern University Press,
2003), 104.

42. See, for instance, *Hull-House Bulletin 7* (Chicago: Hull-House, 1905–6);
Hull-House Year Book; September 1, 1906–September 1, 1907 (Chicago: Hull-
House, 1907).

43. Even when the story was finally published in the late 1980s, by an aca-
demic press, a cover description stressed the author's "lifelong connection with
Jane Addams" rather than Polacheck's own experiences of Hull-House's educa-
tional programs. See Hilda Satt Polacheck, *I Came a Stranger: The Story of a
Hull-House Girl*, ed. Dena J. Polacheck Epstein (Urbana: University of Illinois
Press, 1989).

44. Delia Caparoso Konzett, "Administered Identities and Linguistic Assimilation: The Politics of English in Anzia Yezierska's *Hungry Hearts*," *American Literature* 69 (Sept. 1997): 611.

45. Anzia Yezierska, *Salome of the Tenements* (1923; repr., Urbana: University
of Illinois Press, 1995), 135.

46. Cara-Lynn Ungar, "Discourses of Class and the New Jewish Working
Woman in Anzia Yezierska's *Arrogant Beggar*," *Legacy* 16 (1999): 85; Anzia
Yezierska, *Arrogant Beggar*, ed. Katherine Stubbs (1927; repr., Durham: Duke
University Press, 1996).

47. See Joanna Levin, "'Neither Strictly Native Nor Wholly Foreign': Bohemian New York at the Turn-of-the-Century" (paper presented at the annual
meeting of the Modern Language Association, New York, Dec. 2002).

48. Sheryl Greenwood Gowen, *The Politics of Workplace Literacy: A Case
Study* (New York: Teachers College Press, 1992); Hanna Arlene Fingeret and Cassandra Drennon, *Literacy for Life: Adult Learners, New Practices* (New York:
Teachers College Press, 1997); Glenda Hull, "Hearing Other Voices: A Critical Assessment of Popular Views on Literacy and Work," in *Changing Work, Changing
Workers: Critical Perspectives on Language, Literacy, and Skills*, ed. Glenda Hull,
3–31 (Albany: State University of New York Press, 1997).

49. "In 1870, women made up 61 percent of the teaching force, and 71 percent in 1900" (Stevenson, *Victorian Homefront*, 124). Barbara Sicherman emphasizes that the feminization process applied only to the classroom, not to administration, and not at the collegiate level. Her figures for percentages of women in
the classroom, though, are compatible with others: 1870—59 percent, 1920—86
percent. See "College and Careers: Historical Perspectives on the Lives and Work
Patterns of Women College Graduates," in *Women and Higher Education in
American History*, ed. John Mack Faragher and Florence Howe (New York: Norton, 1988), 147.

50. Geraldine Joncich Clifford, "Women's Liberation and Women's Professions: Reconsidering the Past, Present and Future," in Faragher and Howe,
Women and Higher Education, 171. See also Jo Anne Preston, "Domestic Ideology, School Reformers, and Female Teachers: Schoolteaching Becomes Women's

Work in Nineteenth-Century New England," *New England Quarterly* 66 (Dec. 1993): 531–51.

51. Mintz stresses the intensity of the bond Sedgwick had with her siblings, especially her brothers. Mintz speculates that her occasionally anxious writings about having a useful role in the lives of her siblings and their children may have been typical of "the needs and insecurities of a particular class of people—isolated spinsters who [otherwise] felt themselves barred from productive lives" (*Prison of Expectations*, 164–65). See too Catharine Maria Sedgwick, *Married or Single?* (New York: Harper, 1857).

52. Sigourney offered a variation on this argument. She suggested that teaching one's children at home rather than sending them to school was easier if a mother had "in the family a sister, friend, or well-trained dependent, capable of acting as assistant or substitute" (*Letters to Mothers*, 120). As in Sedgwick's Bond family, a mother's focus on domestic literacy management is supported rather than replaced by others.

53. Larcom, *New England Girlhood*, 66–67.

54. Jean E. Friedman, *Ways of Wisdom: Moral Education in the Early National Period, Including the Diary of Rachel Mordecai Lazarus* (Athens: University of Georgia Press, 2001), 10–11.

55. See also Lydia Sigourney, *Whisper to the Bride*, 2d ed. (Hartford: William Hamersley, 1850).

56. Child, *Looking Toward Sunset*, 138.

57. Child's own position as a childless woman writing for mothers and children is noteworthy here. Barbara Beatty outlines a similar stance for Peabody. The kindergarten pioneer wrote about her work as maternal, even though she was childless. Beatty says Peabody characterized "motherliness" as "a quality of the soul, not the body," so that physically being a mother was different from motherliness, which was "not confined to mothers of the body," who were sometimes "really lacking" those ideal qualities. See *Preschool Education in America*, 62.

58. Lydia Sigourney, *Great and Good Women: Biographies for Girls* (Edinburgh: William P. Nimmo, 1872).

59. Catharine Maria Sedgwick, "Old Maids," in *Tales and Sketches by Miss Sedgwick* (Philadelphia: Carey, Lea, and Blanchard, 1835), 116.

60. See Walter Herbert Small, "The Dame School and the School Dame," in *Early New England Schools*, 162–86 (Boston: Ginn and Company, 1914; repr., New York: Arno Press, 1969). Citations are to the Arno edition.

61. Larcom, *A New England Girlhood*, 39, 44. The memoir depicts Aunt Hannah's teaching as a complex yet appealing blend of masculine and feminine teaching strategies: "Aunt Hannah was very kind and motherly, but she kept us in fear of her ferule" (42). For a fictional example of a female-run school being established as a preparatory experience for very young children, see Catharine Maria Sedgwick's *A New-England Tale*, where the heroine, Jane, describes her very early teaching (103).

62. Even though the actual experience in such schools could be more coercive than gently domestic for students, middle-class women *represented* their work there as a form of enlightened motherhood. Ryan points out that some poor children were classified as delinquents, then "sentenced to reform schools and houses of refuge" against their will (*Empire of the Mother*, 101–2).

63. As Preston points out, New England reformers like Horace Mann used women's willingness to work for less as a way of making proposed reforms more palatable to a cost-conscious public ("Domestic Ideology," 538).

64. Catharine Beecher, *Educational Reminiscences and Suggestions* (New York: J. B. Ford, 1874), 98. Elizabeth Alden Green describes similar arguments by Mary Lyon in a plea for funds for Mount Holyoke. Lyon presented donations to her program as a bargain, since the women teachers trained there would later cost communities little to hire. "She made it clear," Green explains, "that she was only asking to prepare them for jobs that young men would not accept and that she considered it 'Providence' that had shut off women from business careers" (*Mary Lyon and Mount Holyoke*, 119).

65. Joel Perlmann and Robert A. Margo have assembled detailed statistics showing not only the differences between male and female pay levels for teaching but also ways in which those differences varied widely by region and locality, depending upon the degree to which women were needed in other types of work. See *Women's Work? American Schoolteachers 1650–1920* (Chicago: University of Chicago Press, 2001), 9.

66. McClelland, *Education of Women,* 75.

67. McClelland, *Education of Women,* 76.

68. Riley, *Inventing the American Woman,* 48.

69. Qtd. in Fitts, "Una and the Lion," 143.

70. A Father, "The Question." *Ladies' Magazine* 7 (Oct. 1834): 477.

71. Kaestle says that "harsh and frequent punishments seem to have been characteristic of early nineteenth-century schools" until the campaign favoring moral suasion, which he describes as linked to the increasing tendency to hire women teachers. According to Kaestle, "although not all women teachers abstained from corporal punishment, they were less likely to beat their students than men, partly because of gentler feminine stereotypes and partly because the older boys were often stronger than they were" (*Pillars of the Republic,* 19). Mowry's educational memoir affirms Kaestle's points, noting that hiring women in the summer was made more likely by the absence of the older, potentially more troublesome boys, who would be working in the field. Mowry also affirms Kaestle's description of the typical schoolmaster as using "a rod of iron" for "severe punishments" that made the teacher "a savage tyrant" (*Recollections of a New England Educator,* 43–44).

72. For Horace Mann's rhetoric favoring moral suasion over corporal punishment, see Brodhead, "Sparing the Rod," 75–76.

73. Qtd. in Polly Welts Kaufman, *Women Teachers on the Frontier* (New Haven: Yale University Press, 1984), 28, 30.

74. For a comparative portrait of female education in England in 1830, see Mrs. S. C. Hall, *Chronicles of a School Room* (Boston: Cottons and Barnard, 1830), an American edition of the British text. Hall's book recounts the memories of a refined educator who taught a small group of young ladies in her home. The program that Hall's main character (Mrs. Ashburton) provides for her young students is a virtual replicate of Foster's decades earlier, showing no signs of the reforms carried out by leading American educators like Mary Lyon, Zilpah Grant, Catharine Beecher, and Emma Willard. The main goal for Hall, in fact, is to prepare her charges for the marriage market. The glowing review *Chronicles of a School Room* received in the *Ladies' Magazine* shows that we need to be cautious about assuming that the beliefs and practices of would-be leaders like Beecher and Lyon were universally accepted during their own lifetimes. See "Chronicles of a School Room; Published by Cottons and Barnard," review of *Chronicles of a Schoolroom,* by Mrs. S. C. Hall, *Ladies' Magazine* 3 (Aug. 1830): 375–79.

75. Hannah Foster, *The Boarding School; or, Lessons of a Preceptress to Her Pupils* (Boston: I. Thomas and E. T. Andrews, 1798), 26.

76. Emma Willard, "From Emma Hart Willard, A Plan for Improving Female Education (1819)," in *Pedagogy: Disturbing History, 1819–1929*, ed. Mariolina Rizzi Salvatori (Pittsburgh: University of Pittsburgh Press, 1996), 74.

77. *Catalogue of the Officers, Teachers, and Pupils, of the Hartford Female Seminary for the Summer Term of 1828*, Hartford Female Seminary Catalogue, folder 320, Beecher-Stowe Family Papers, Schlesinger Library, Radcliffe Institute, Harvard University. Whereas Foster's program was fictional, and Willard's a proposal, the catalog for Beecher's seminary describes a curriculum actually in use.

78. Almira Hart Lincoln Phelps, sister of Emma Willard, distinguished between some things that should be taught at home and the more specialized learning best provided in a seminary. Phelps described the "awkward, ignorant" daughter of an acquaintance whose mother kept her in homeschooling until she was past sixteen. According to Phelps, the mother wrongly thought she could teach her daughter more than "letters," more than "reading, spelling, writing, geography, grammar, arithmetic"—that is, that she was also capable of teaching "the higher branches of education" (97). Phelps complained about the "indulgences" of excessive at-home teaching, which could "render [a girl's] intellect dull and torpid" (98). See "Lectures to Young Ladies: Comprising Outlines and Applications of the Different Branches of Female Education for the Use of Female Schools, and Private Libraries (1833)," in Salvatori, *Pedagogy*, 95–102.

79. According to William J. Gilmore, the Hartford seminary was typical in this regard. Researching female learning patterns in the Upper Connecticut Valley, Gilmore found that, as elsewhere in the United States, academies added "grammar, rhetoric, and composition," as well as accounting, geometry, nursing, belles-lettres, philosophy, religion, geography and history. See *Reading Becomes a Necessity of Life: Material and Cultural Life in Rural New England, 1780–1835* (Knoxville: University of Tennessee Press, 1989), 47.

80. Catharine Beecher, *Suggestions Respecting Improvements in Education, Presented to the Trustees of the Hartford Female Seminary, and published at their request* (Hartford: Packard & Butler, 1829). To note differences between Beecher's positions and those of male contemporaries in parallel leadership positions, see "Female Education: Notice of an Address on Female Education . . . ," *Ladies' Magazine* 1 (Jan. 1828): 21–27; "A Lecture on the Education of Females . . . ," *Ladies' Magazine* 5 (Mar. 1832): 140–44; and "Female Seminaries—No. III. Scottsboro Institute," *Ladies' Magazine* 6 (May 1833): 228–31.

81. Evidently, this emphasis survived the departure of the Beecher sisters for Cincinnati. In a report on the Hartford school as it was being administered by John Brace several years later, a *Ladies' Magazine* piece included the "*personal influence of teachers*" as a strong point of the program. Brace, who had been Harriet Beecher's favorite instructor at Litchfield Academy, was a caring teacher with a regionwide reputation. Still, as if anticipating questions about having a male assume Beecher's position when many were advocating female teachers for females, this qualifier was appended: "*ladies* fill all the subordinate branches of instruction," with one exception ("Female Seminaries II," 178, 176).

82. Kaestle reports that, between 1800 and 1830, versions of the Lancaster method were adopted all over the country with great enthusiasm. Although some brave leaders objected to its "rigid lock-step procedures" and mechanistic tone, the cheapness of the program, which sometimes required but a single instructor to monitor as many as five hundred children with the help of submonitors, was popular with administrators and community leaders (*Pillars of the Republic*, 41–43).

83. For an example of this ongoing balancing act as it was played out at one

Midwestern institution, see my "Rereading the History of Nineteenth-Century Women's Higher Education: A Reexamination of Jane Addams' Rockford Education as Preparation for her *Twenty Years at Hull-House* Teaching," *Journal of the Midwest History of Education Society* 21 (1994): 27–46.

84. Rosemary Hennessy, "Subjects, Knowledges, . . . and All the Rest: Speaking for What?" in *Who Can Speak? Authority and Critical Identity,* ed. Judith Roof and Robyn Wiegman (Urbana: University of Illinois Press, 1995), 146–47.

85. I affirm Hennessy's view that "feminism's criterion for evaluating any knowledge" is "the interests and effects of truth claims on the social reality they construct" ("Subjects, Knowledges," 142), so that we need to consider the hoped-for results and the actual impact women writers' participation in these promotions of domesticated teaching actually had, instead of focusing only on the limits of their thinking as seen through our own current lens.

86. The idea that nineteenth-century women's writing provided models for life choices is not, of course, new. See Nina Baym's discussion of how women's novels operated "by engaging and channeling the emotions of readers" so that they could "accept the author's solution to [the heroine's] difficulties as pertinent to their own lives" (*Woman's Fiction,* 17).

87. Preston, "Domestic Ideology," 542.

88. Lydia Maria Child, "Louisa Preston," in *A Lydia Maria Child Reader,* ed. Carolyn L. Karcher, 101–11 (Durham: Duke University Press, 1997), 111; originally published in *Juvenile Miscellany* 4 (Mar. 1828): 56–81.

89. Lydia Sigourney, *Scenes in My Native Land* (Boston: James Munroe, 1845), 193.

90. Larcom, *New England Girlhood,* 256–60.

91. Lydia Sigourney, *Letters to My Pupils: With Narrative and Biographical Sketches,* 2d ed. (New York: Robert Carter & Brothers, 1856), 155.

92. Sigourney describes prized former pupils as follows: "It was . . . no surprise to hear, in future years, that . . . they were prompt to teach others, either in the Sunday-school, the household, or the licensed places of public instruction" (*Letters to My Pupils,* 189). Despite this characterization, the letters also contain clear signs of her former students' continued joy in scholarship, such as the missionary's wife who revels in her study of Siamese (190) or the minister's wife living in the West who casts her teaching as a "duty" but also an avenue for study (193–94).

93. Grimké, *Journals;* Ida B. Wells-Barnett, *Crusade for Justice: The Autobiography of Ida B. Wells,* ed. Alfreda M. Duster (Chicago: University of Chicago Press, 1970), 31; Shirley Marchalonis, "Legacy Profile: Lucy Larcom (1824–1893)," *Legacy* 5 (1988): 46–47; Larcom, *New England Girlhood,* 264–69.

94. Sedgwick, "Ella," in *Stories for Young Persons,* 98.

95. Sedgwick, "Self Education," in *Facts and Fancies,* 118.

96. For examples, see primary documents such as "From: James Gordon Carter, *Essays Upon Popular Education with an Outline of an Institution for the Education of Teachers*" (81–84) and "From: Albert Bushnell Hart, 'The Teacher as a Professional Expert' (1833)" (257–60), both in Salvatori, *Pedagogy.*

97. Augusta Jane Evans, *Beulah,* ed. Elizabeth Fox-Genovese (1859, 1900; repr., Baton Rouge: Louisiana State University Press, 1992); Anzia Yezierska, *Bread Givers* (1925; repr., New York: Persea Books/Doubleday, 1975). The lead character in each story successfully acquires more genteel status by taking on the role of schoolteacher.

98. Sedgwick, *Women and Work,* 4.

99. Elizabeth Sedgwick, *A Talk With My Pupils* (New York: John Hopper, 1863), 90.

Chapter 4

1. Eric J. Sundquist reports fifty thousand copies of the novel sold within eight weeks, one million in England and America by 1853. See his introduction to *New Essays on* Uncle Tom's Cabin, ed. Eric J. Sundquist (Cambridge: Cambridge University Press, 1986), 18. Thomas F. Gossett contends that the book may well have had ten readers for every copy purchased. See Uncle Tom's Cabin *and American Culture* (Dallas: Southern Methodist University Press, 1985), 165–70. Also, many readers encountered the narrative first in serial form in the *National Era* before it was published as a book.

2. *Uncle Tom's Cabin* was first advertised in the *Era*'s May 8, 1851, issue as an upcoming feature. In the winter of 1852, episodes were still appearing in the periodical, alongside a range of texts—for example, political analyses, sentimental stories, poetry—suited to its middle-class parlor audience. For the match between venue and content that publication in the *Era* represented, see my "Gendering the History," 540–42.

3. Harriet Beecher Stowe to Sarah Josepha Hale, November 10, 1851, HM24166, The Huntington Library, San Marino, Calif. Reproduced with permission.

4. Harriet Beecher Stowe, *A Key to Uncle Tom's Cabin: Presenting the Original Facts and Documents upon Which the Story is Founded* (1853; facs. ed., Bedford, [Mass.]: Applewood Books, 1998), 5. (Some sources set the first edition's publishing date as 1852.)

5. The translations I cite for Roland Barthes's and Michel Foucault's essays appear in *Modern Criticism and Theory: A Reader,* ed. David Lodge, 166–71, 197–210 (London: Longman, 1988).

6. Stowe's novel elicited an outpouring of response texts supporting slavery as a benevolent institution. See, for example, Mrs. Mary H. Eastman, *Aunt Phillis' Cabin; or, Southern Life as It Is* (Philadelphia: Lippincott, 1852). In contrast, a number of twentieth-century African American writers critiqued Stowe's racism and reimagined African American life after slavery. See, for example, Richard Wright, *Uncle Tom's Children* (1938; repr., New York: Harper, 1993).

7. The Beechers' links to Harriet Martineau were facilitated through correspondence and Martineau's travel to the United States. As noted earlier, Harriet Martineau was the daughter of one of Barbauld's favorite students. Martineau's memories of her own early contacts with Barbauld were sentimental and vivid. Stowe's contemporaries recognized shared value systems and community-building approaches as binding their social group with Dissenting-tradition counterparts across the Atlantic; we see those self-conscious links in a letter from one of Stowe's New England relatives who, after meeting Martineau while the English author was in Connecticut, predicted that Harriet Beecher would achieve prominence like the English "Harriet." See Anne Jean Lyman to Abby Lyman Greene, Nov. 3, n.d., MSS/1 G812 r/RM, item 74, box 3, Greene-Roelker papers, Research Library, The Cincinnati Historical Society. Later in her American journey, Martineau traveled to Cincinnati, where she met young Harriet Beecher, with whom she reconnected during Stowe's triumphant tour of England after publication of *Uncle Tom's Cabin.* Intellectually and socially, the role that the Beecher family played in the United States had an earlier parallel in the work of Barbauld's father, John Aikin, a minister who helped found the well-regarded Warrington Dis-

senting Academy, and her brother, John, a prominent physician and author—not to mention Barbauld herself.

8. Mintz argues that a self-conscious "gentility" among these families was closely bound up with their sense of civic duty (*Prison of Expectations,* 195). He stresses that this trans-Atlantic social class's strong belief in their own ability to lead society was intimately related to their sense of personal identity (8, 29, 31). See too Persons, *Decline of American Gentility;* Stevenson, *Victorian Homefront.* See also my discussions of social class in chapters 1 and 3.

9. Joan D. Hedrick's monumental biography of Stowe looks backward at the author's life as preparing for and then carrying out a career in literature writing. Hedrick provides invaluable analysis of Stowe's increasingly confident view of herself as a writer. See, for example, Hedrick's chapters "Parlor Literature" and "A Literary Woman," as well as "The *Atlantic* and the Ship of State" and "Professional Writer," in *Harriet Beecher Stowe: A Life.* Earlier biography, less nuanced than Hedrick's, casts Stowe as a crusader using literature for political aims but undervalues the didactic dimension of her work. See, for example, Forrest Wilson, *Crusader in Crinoline: The Life of Harriet Beecher Stowe* (New York: Lippincott, 1941).

10. See my "Gendering Gilded Age Periodical Professionalism: Reading Stowe's *Hearth and Home* Prescriptions for Women's Writing," in *The Only Efficient Instrument: American Women Writers and the Periodical, 1837–1916,* ed. Aleta Feinsod Cane and Susan Alves, 45–65 (Iowa City: University of Iowa Press, 2001). See also Christopher P. Wilson, *Labor of Words.*

11. See my "Gendering the Antislavery Narrative," 540.

12. For a review of Stowe's treatment by literary criticism, see Sundquist's introduction to *New Essays,* where he contrasts Stowe's decline with Melville's ascent among academic readers seeking "complex philosophical intent and dense literary allusiveness" (2). For an example of readings that purportedly credit her artistry but, in the end, demean or damn with faint praise, see James M. Cox, "Harriet Beecher Stowe: From Sectionalism to Regionalism," *Nineteenth Century* 38 (1984): 444–66. Cox acknowledges her historical importance but rejects Stowe via comparison with Hawthorne and suggests that "she tended to stay serenely, if not complacently, within sentimental and didactic models" (452).

13. See, for instance, Lora Romero, "Bio-Political Resistance in Domestic Ideology and *Uncle Tom's Cabin,*" *American Literary History* 1 (1989): 715–34; Joan D. Hedrick, "'Peaceable Fruits': The Ministry of Harriet Beecher Stowe," *American Quarterly* 40 (June 1988): 307–32; Stephen Railton, "Mothers, Husbands, and Uncle Tom," *Georgia Review* 38 (1984): 129–44.

14. Jeanne Boydston, Mary Kelley, and Anne Margolis helpfully describe the complexity of the sisters' relationship. They note that Catharine took advantage of Harriet's teaching abilities at both the Hartford Seminary and the Western Female Institute. Further, they point out that Catharine "grew proprietary about her sister's [authorial] work," assertively trying to take command of negotiations over royalty payments (226). See *The Limits of Sisterhood: The Beecher Sisters on Women's Rights and the Woman's Sphere* (Chapel Hill: University of North Carolina Press, 1988). Laurie Crumpacker's discussion identifies some of the links in the educational thought and work of Harriet and Catharine (78). See "Four Novels of Harriet Beecher Stowe: A Study in Nineteenth-Century Androgyny," in *American Novelists Revisited: Essays in Feminist Criticism,* ed. Fritz Fleischmann, 78–106 (Boston: Hall, 1982).

15. The sisters' contrasting attitudes toward teaching in 1830s Cincinnati are relevant. Catharine describes herself in *Educational Reminiscences* as spending

these years "employ[ing] my pen" to write *Domestic Economy* texts and giving over management of the school to "my former teachers" from Hartford, including Harriet (86). But Harriet devoted an enormous amount of energy to the classroom itself, even as she also published an elementary textbook in 1833. For a description of Stowe's schoolwork on a typical day at the seminary, see Charles Edward Stowe and Lyman Beecher Stowe, *Harriet Beecher Stowe: The Story of Her Life* (New York: Houghton, 1911), 76–77.

16. For a lively portrait of Harriet's charismatic brother Henry Ward Beecher, as viewed by a contemporary, see the reissuing of Lyman Abbott's biography *Henry Ward Beecher,* ed. William G. McLoughlin (New York: Houghton Mifflin, 1903; repr., New York: Chelsea House, 1980).

17. For a discussion of Harriet Beecher's participation in the Semicolon Club, see my "Gendering the Antislavery Narrative," 541.

18. Douglas, *Feminization of American Culture,* 3–13.

19. Tompkins, *Sensational Designs,* especially xvi–xix, 122–46.

20. Gossett dates Lyman's oath in 1819 (Uncle Tom's Cabin *and American Culture,* 15).

21. This biography (*Harriet Beecher Stowe*) includes a slightly different declaration from Lyman, expressed during shared chore time at the Beechers': "I wish Harriet were a boy! She would do more than any of them!" (9). The 1911 edition of the biography that I used lists two authors, "her son Charles Edward Stowe and her grandson Lyman Beecher Stowe" (title page). The 1911 edition frequently differs in details and wording from an 1889 version listing Charles as sole author. Still, to avoid confusing the younger Lyman with Harriet's father, and to simplify sentence structure throughout, I will reference only Charles as author of the 1911 text throughout chapter 4.

22. Like Anna Laetitia Barbauld, Maria Edgeworth exercised considerable influence on American domestic pedagogy in the early nineteenth century—as well as on the domestic literacy narrative. For another example of the trans-Atlantic reach of Edgeworth's educational texts, see Jean E. Friedman's account of Rachel Mordecai's attempt to apply the Edgeworthian model to teaching her half-sister Eliza. Rachel studied Edgeworth's texts and also corresponded with the Edgeworth family (*Ways of Wisdom,* especially 132–33). Barbauld's and Edgeworth's pedagogical theories—as well as their didactic literature—promoted compatible models, in part because both authors were so closely connected to the innovative thinkers in the Lunar Society, in which Joseph Priestley (Barbauld's own favorite teacher) and Maria Edgeworth's father, Richard Edgeworth, were leading members. Initial publication of Barbauld's *Lessons* (see chapter 2) actually predated the 1781 founding of the Lunar Society and influenced texts about teaching children that emerged from society members, including the Edgeworths' *Early Lessons,* the Frank stories Stowe references, and Thomas Day's popular *Sanford and Merton* book series. For a history of the Lunar Society, see Brian Simon, *Studies in the History of Education: 1780–1870* (London: Lawrence & Wishart, 1960).

23. She was also, evidently, learning to use the earmarks of the domestic literacy narrative to characterize her own literacy acquisition—for example, the didactic book, the collaborative evening reading activity, the linkage between such reading and moral education.

24. For instance, Charles reports on her discovery of Shakespeare via a reading of *The Tempest.* The episode, according to Charles, would reappear in *The Pearl of Orr's Island,* when Mara finds a partial copy of the play and deems it a "treasure" (*Harriet Beecher Stowe,* 15).

25. See Elizabeth Ammons's insightful essay "Stowe's Dream of the Mother-Savior: *Uncle Tom's Cabin* and American Women Writers before the 1920s," in Sundquist, *New Essays on* Uncle Tom's Cabin, 155–95. See also Dorothy Berkson, "'So We All Became Mothers': Harriet Beecher Stowe, Charlotte Perkins Gilman, and the New World of Woman's Culture," in *Feminism, Utopia, and Narrative,* ed. Sarah Webster Goodwin and Libby F. Jones (Knoxville: University of Tennessee Press, 1990), 109.

26. Harriet Beecher Stowe, *Uncle Tom's Cabin; or, Life Among the Lowly,* ed. Ann Douglas (1852; repr., New York: Penguin, 1986), 68.

27. I take his actions and George's corrections to be more a sign of Stowe's portraying Tom, at this stage, as a novice reader, exhibiting traits that would be considered developmentally appropriate by a teacher working, as Stowe often did, with beginning-level students. In other words, I interpret Tom's letter reversal as an indication that Stowe is characterizing him as a childlike learner—not a deficient one. Marvin Cohn and George Stricker show that "letter recognition errors may be the result of children going through normal stages of development" (33). See "Inadequate Perception vs. Reversals," *Reading Teacher* 30 (1976): 33–36. Also see Hortense Spillers, "Changing the Letter: The Yokes, the Jokes of Discourse, or, Mrs. Stowe, Mr. Reed," in *Slavery and the Literary Imagination,* ed. Deborah E. McDowell, 25–61 (Baltimore: Johns Hopkins University Press, 1989).

28. That slave states' outlawing such teaching was a concern to Northern educational leaders is seen in Horace Mann's *Go Forth and Teach: An Oration Delivered Before the Authorities of the City of Boston, July 4, 1842 by Horace Mann, also Other Materials Relating to His Life,* ed. Hugh Taylor Birch (Washington: Committee on the Horace Mann Centennial, National Education Association, 1937). Mann observed: "What is most painful and humiliating to reflect upon, in all the principal slave states . . . [is that] the highest homage which is paid to the beneficent power of education is the terrible homage of making it a severely punishable offense to educate a slave!" (77).

29. Barbara Finkelstein, "Reading, Writing and the Acquisition of Identity in the United States, 1790–1860," in Finkelstein, *Regulated Children/Liberated Children,* 128. A phenomenon related to the tendency to perceive black literacy as dangerous was the tendency to doubt the very possibility of African American literacy, even when confronted with its most evident products. Thus, for example, arguments raged for years about the degree of editorial versus authorial role exercised by Lydia Maria Child over Harriet Jacobs's *Incidents in the Life of a Slave Girl: Written By Herself.* See Jean Fagan Yellin's description of Jacobs's text as being "transformed," by "discovery of a cache of her letters," from "a questionable slave narrative into a well-documented pseudonymous autobiography." See "Written By Herself: Harriet Jacobs' Slave Narrative," *American Literature* 53 (Sept. 1981): 479.

30. In this regard, Stowe offers commentary in the *Key* to parallel Douglass's experiences with those of her character George Harris (16).

31. Qtd. in Finkelstein, "Reading," 128. The Harriet Beecher Stowe House in Cincinnati provided me with a biographical sketch of Henson that describes one strategy in his literacy acquisition as frequently hiding just "outside the 'white' church, which he was never allowed to enter, to listen to the preaching" ("Josiah Henson," 1). Finkelstein's treatment of class, gender, and racial differences in literacy practices of the nineteenth century connects her work with studies of white, female literacy by Cathy N. Davidson and Janice Radway. Taken together, these studies show how, for both slave and white women readers, literacy prac-

tices have often been cast as secret, private pleasures that could lead to major changes in self-image, while also promoting an enhanced sense of community through the sharing of those very practices. See Davidson, *Revolution and the Word*, 98; Janice Radway, *Reading the Romance: Women, Patriarchy, and Popular Literature* (Chapel Hill, University of North Carolina Press, 1991), 12, 17.

32. Whereas Spillers (in "Changing the Letter") classifies Tom as "semiliterate" (45) and Michie describes him as "quasi-literate" (203), I want to emphasize how Stowe portrays Tom as gradually acquiring and sharing a very complex range of literacy practices. Although some of these practices are not highly valued within the context of the "literate" behaviors of current academic culture, they would have been appreciated by Stowe and her contemporaries—especially those viewing literacy as social and multifaceted, traits central to domestic literacy narratives. See Helena Michie, "Dying between Two Laws: Girl Heroines, Their Gods, and Their Fathers in *Uncle Tom's Cabin* and the *Elsie Dinsmore* Series," in *Refiguring the Father: New Feminist Readings of Patriarchy*, ed. Patricia Yaeger and Beth Kowaleski-Wallace, 188–206 (Carbondale: Southern University Press, 1989).

33. Here, as elsewhere in the novel, Stowe's depiction of slave literacy practices coincides with historical research. For example, Finkelstein argues that, even when "learning to read and write required slaves to remove themselves from the centers of community activity" by hiding out to steal literacy initially, "their isolation was neither total, nor . . . necessarily alienating. Rather, . . . they used their literary skills to expand, enhance, dignify, and deepen the sacred world. . . . Rather than diluting the predominance of the oral tradition, . . . literacy actually became an instrument of community enrichment prior to emancipation" ("Reading," 129).

34. For a classic example of an African American male reader resisting Uncle Tom's characterization, see James Baldwin's well-known essay "Everybody's Protest Novel," in *Critical Essays on Harriet Beecher Stowe*, ed. Elizabeth Ammons, 92–97 (Boston: G. K. Hall, 1980); originally published in *Partisan Review* 16 (1949): 578–85. For an apt review of various black male readers' responses to the narrative during the antebellum era, see Marva Banks, "*Uncle Tom's Cabin* and Antebellum Black Response," in *Readers in History: American Literature and the Contexts of Response*, ed. James L. Machor (Baltimore: Johns Hopkins University Press, 1993), 209–27. Banks recounts enthusiastic readings by William Still and Henry Bibb but also points to Martin Delany's and William Allen's complaints about the novel (e.g., Allen's view that Tom has "too much piety" [223]; Delany's critique of Stowe's colonialist stance).

35. Although I teach only excerpts from *Uncle Tom's Cabin* in my undergraduate American literature classes, I have regularly included it as an option for individualized reading assignments. Over the past decade, I've noticed two striking patterns: more women than men select the novel for the independent reading assignment, and the women who select it often report highly positive, emotional responses. In particular, at a university where a significant number of students are married white women attending part-time while also working or raising a family, I've repeatedly had such readers describe themselves, unprompted, as staying up late at night or even "hiding" in rooms away from their spouses or other family members to read it for hours, "crying" over close identification with Uncle Tom and "learning lessons" of great moral importance to their lives.

36. Jacqueline Jones, *Soldiers of Light and Love: Northern Teachers and Georgia Blacks, 1865–1873* (Chapel Hill: University of North Carolina Press, 1980),

153–54. Jones notes that the Northern teachers also made use of characters from Stowe's novel (e.g., Topsy) to describe their students to readers back home (250 n. 36).

37. Richard H. Brodhead's reading of Ophelia and her pedagogy is set in context with other literary movements by appearing as a chapter in his *Cultures of Letters: Scenes of Reading and Writing in Nineteenth-Century America*, 13–47 (Chicago: University of Chicago Press, 1994). See also Susan Ryan's discussion "Pedagogies of Emancipation" in *The Grammar of Good Intentions: Race and the Antebellum Culture of Benevolence*, 109–42 (Ithaca: Cornell University Press, 2003). For a more overtly political reading of the Ophelia episode, see David Grant, "*Uncle Tom's Cabin* and the Triumph of Republican Rhetoric," *New England Quarterly* 71 (Sept. 1998): 429–48.

38. That the school was considered by the family to be Catharine's enterprise was never in any doubt. The *Catalogue of the Officers, Teachers, and Pupils of the Hartford Female Seminary* for 1828 specifically states that "the institution is under the care of Miss C. E. Beecher, assisted by *eight* other teachers [of whom Harriet was one] and by *two* assistant pupils" (7). See the Hartford Female Seminary Catalogue, folder 320, Beecher-Stowe Family Papers, Schlesinger Library, Radcliffe Institute, Harvard University.

39. See the 1828 Hartford *Catalogue*'s description of the school curriculum, which emphasizes such hallmarks of control as having one "teacher . . . constantly . . . enforcing order, . . . and sending the classes to recite" (7). Lists of the actual courses of study later in the catalog abound with male authors. Major subheadings later in the brochure include "Things Forbidden" and "Things Required" (11–12). See the Hartford Female Seminary Catalogue, folder 320, Beecher-Stowe Family Papers, Schlesinger Library, Radcliffe Institute, Harvard University.

40. Beecher, *Educational Reminiscences*, 73–74.

41. Beecher family members frequently reprinted pieces of each other's texts when writing about themselves. I do see a difference, though, between their typical use of this technique (as exemplified by Charles Stowe, when he folds corroborating letters in with analysis) and Catharine's, when she presents in *Educational Reminiscences* a series of letters from Harriet but ignores contradictions between their view of events and her own.

42. When Harriet married Calvin Stowe in 1836, she was already twenty-five: though perhaps not an "old-maid schoolteacher," neither was she a young bride. Harriet's letters to New England friends in the years before her marriage depict teaching as fully engaging her interest and energy.

43. Mentioning that Harriet's geography book was wrongly credited to Catharine, Coultrap-McQuin observes: "Harriet did not complain about the book's misattribution; the self-confidence of her later career had not yet emerged" (*Doing Literary Business*, 82). I suspect another cause of silence was that she still prioritized classroom teaching over publication. Charles Stowe reports on a conversation Harriet had with an admirer of the book: "Bishop Purcell visited our school to-day, and expressed himself as greatly pleased that we had opened such an one here. He spoke of my poor little geography and thanked me for the unprejudiced manner in which I had handled the Catholic question in it. I was of course flattered that he should have known anything about the book" (*Harriet Beecher Stowe*, 75).

44. A letter to Calvin in May–June 1844 tells stories about their daughter Hatty's insightful versions of stories from the Bible and contains Stowe's assertion that all her children "do seem at times to be influenced by the religious

truths that are constantly & daily inculcated upon them." Stowe expresses "trust" that "Christ has accepted the dedication" she was giving to her in-home school (folder 68, Beecher-Stowe Family Papers, Schlesinger Library, Radcliffe Institute, Harvard University).

45. Harriet Beecher Stowe to Calvin Stowe, 1844, folder 69, Beecher-Stowe Family Papers, Schlesinger Library, Radcliffe Institute, Harvard University.

46. See Warren Burton's accounts of Mary Smith (7ff.) and Mehitbel Holt (24ff.) in *The District School as It Was*.

47. Stowe's opening explication of Ophelia in the *Key* mirrors, in capsule form, the tonal shift around Ophelia in the novel, as it progresses from lightly ironic critique to more straightforward censure on moral grounds: "Miss Ophelia," the author explains, "stands as the representative of a numerous class of the very best of Northern people; to whom, perhaps, if our Lord should again address his churches a letter, as he did those of old time, he would use the same words as then: 'I know thy works, and thy labor, and thy patience, and how thou canst not bear them which are evil; and thou hast . . . labored and hast not fainted. Nevertheless, I have somewhat against thee, because thou hast left thy first love'" (30).

48. I base my supposition in part on a series of letters Catharine sent to one of her Hartford seminary students, Sarah Terry. Although this young lady was clearly one of Catharine's favorites, Miss Beecher repeatedly wrote out exhortations for improving one's character and pleas to examine one's conscience, rather than engaging in the kind of friendly epistolary conversation that could have downplayed Catharine's position of authority over her student. In tone and content, Catharine's written efforts to reform this young student represent a serious version of the comic exchanges Stowe presents in Ophelia's initial efforts to train Topsy in upright Christianity. See Catharine Beecher, letter to Sarah Terry, 1829, Katharine S. Day Collection, Stowe-Day Library.

49. Compare, for instance, the description of the Hartford seminary curriculum under Catharine's leadership with Ophelia's first training program for Topsy, which the New Englander administers with rules-based rigor.

50. Stowe elaborates on this point in her *Key* section on Ophelia by noting that "it is very easy to see that although slavery has been abolished in the New England States, it has left behind it the most baneful feature of the system—that which makes American worse than Roman slavery—the prejudice of caste and color. In the New England States the negro has been treated as belonging to an inferior race of beings; forced to sit apart by himself in the place of worship; his children excluded from the schools; himself excluded from the railroad-car and the omnibus, and the peculiarities of his race made the subject of bitter contempt and ridicule" (31).

51. Brace took over the principalship at Hartford seminary after Catharine and Harriet moved to Cincinnati. The quotations from Isabella Hooker's speech about Brace represent her quoting of Stowe, and page numbers refer to the printed program for the 1892 Hartford Female Seminary Reunion, held by the American Antiquarian Society.

52. Harriet Beecher Stowe to Calvin Stowe, 1844, folder 68, Beecher-Stowe Family Papers, Schlesinger Library, Radcliffe Institute, Harvard University.

53. Harriet Beecher Stowe to Calvin Stowe, 1844, folder 68, Beecher-Stowe Family Papers, Schlesinger Library, Radcliffe Institute, Harvard University; Lydia Sigourney, "The Rainy Day," in *The Child's Book,* n.p.

54. Annie Fields, ed., *The Life and Letters of Harriet Beecher Stowe* (Boston: Houghton, 1897), 155. Fields's position of influence in the literary society of

Stowe's day gives her interpretation added weight. See Susan K. Harris, *The Cultural Work of the Late Nineteenth-Century Hostess: Annie Adams Fields and Mary Gladstone Drew* (New York: Palgrave/Macmillan, 2002). Harris's emphasis on Annie Fields's reading circle as "engag[ing] most passionately with works that spoke to their social concerns" (9), on the group's "demand" that art be used for moral or "ideological ends" (102), as well as on "the empathetic limitations" in Fields's and her circle's benevolent reform work (139), provides important context for my reading of *Uncle Tom's Cabin*.

55. Fitts, "Una and the Lion," 143.

56. George's letter is full of "various refreshing items of home intelligence" that could only have been gathered through multiple conversations, when, we assume, Tom's own "letter homeward" would have been socially read as well (378–79). Eva and Tom's many readings of George's letter attest to Stowe's assumption that her readers would be familiar with the domestic literacy narrative convention of American middle-class males maintaining ties with loved ones by writing often when away. In this case, both Tom and George carry out that enterprise, though in different contexts.

57. Stowe's treatment of Eva's literacy-linked influence from beyond the grave recalls Lydia Sigourney's "Child at the Mother's Grave" poem in *The Girl's Reading Book* (192). Sigourney constructs a similar nexus connecting social literacy, a motherly teacher (like Eva), and a child-learner (like Topsy)—all joined in a bond outlasting death. Topsy's use of literacy-inflected memories to remain tied to Eva also foreshadows Augustine St. Clare's attempts to reconnect with literacy-related memories of his mother.

58. In the early stages of this conversation, St. Clare exclaims, "O that I could believe what my mother taught me, and pray as I did when I was a boy!" (437).

59. An echo of this scene affirming Eva's continuing ability to teach, even from beyond the grave, occurs in the episode when St. Clare discovers that Topsy has been saving a book Eva gave her. Observing that Topsy's "real sorrow" is clear from her treasuring of the book, with Eva's curl, St. Clare agrees that Ophelia can set Topsy free (444ff.).

60. See Paolo Freire, *Pedagogy of the Oppressed*, thirtieth anniversary ed., trans. Myra Bergman Ramos (New York: Continuum, 2000); *Education for a Critical Consciousness*, trans. Myra Bergman Ramos (New York: Continuum, 1974); and *Pedagogy of Hope: Reliving Pedagogy of the Oppressed*, trans. Robert R. Barr (New York: Continuum, 1995). Freire argues for an activist literacy based on development of a critical consciousness (versus a Christian moral sense) that can lead to political power and change.

61. Stowe did change her position on colonization later, but her endorsement of it in *Uncle Tom's Cabin* has been troubling to many readers. For details on Stowe's renunciation of colonization, see Susan Ryan, "Charity Begins at Home: Stowe's Antislavery Novels and the Forms of Benevolent Citizenship," *American Literature* 72 (Dec. 2000): 779 n. 33.

Chapter 5

1. P. Gabrielle Foreman and Carla L. Peterson both comment on *Iola Leroy*'s efforts to reach a mixed audience of white and black readers. Foreman describes the complex generic implications of the novel's simultaneously appealing to different "subsets" of readers, including "white reformers" and "the politicized segment of Black press readers." See "'Reading Aright': White Slavery, Black Referents, and the Strategy of Histotextuality in *Iola Leroy*," *Yale Journal of Criticism:*

Interpretation in the Humanities 10 (Fall 1997): 329, 332. Certainly Harper's poetry, throughout her career, was read by both races, and many of her lectures in the Northeast before the Civil War drew white abolitionists as well as blacks. See Frances Foster's discussion of Harper's Reconstruction poetry, especially the long narrative *Moses: A Story of the Nile,* as being directed to "a variety of readers ranging from the newly literate to the more experienced and well educated" and potentially including such diverse groups as white women's rights leaders and recently freed black Southerners. See "Doers of the Word: The Reconstruction Poetry of Frances Ellen Watkins Harper," in *Written by Herself: Literary Production by African American Women, 1746–1892,* (Bloomington: Indiana University Press, 1993), 140. As Carla Peterson observes elsewhere, however, Harper's work in the *Christian Recorder* addresses "a primarily black audience." See "'Further Liftings of the Veil': Gender, Class, and Labor in Frances E. W. Harper's *Iola Leroy,*" in *Listening to Silences: New Essays in Feminist Criticism,* ed. Elaine Hedges and Shelley Fisher Fishkin (New York: Oxford University Press, 1994), 99. Special thanks to Peterson for her generous contributions to my work on this chapter and other projects.

2. See Melba Joyce Boyd, *Discarded Legacy: Politics and Poetics in the Life of Frances E. W. Harper, 1825–1911* (Detroit: Wayne State University Press, 1994). I am building upon Boyd's view of Harper as an educator not only of the freedmen but of the American nation as a whole (208).

3. "'Uncle Tom' and Grandchild," *Harper's Weekly* (Nov. 3, 1866): 689–90. The note just below the illustration on page 689 both identifies its title and directs the reader to "See Page 690."

4. See Homi K. Bhabha, *The Location of Culture* (London: Routledge, 1994). Bhabha characterizes "colonial mimicry" as "the desire for a reformed, recognizable Other, *as a subject of a difference that is almost the same, but not quite.* Which is to say, that the discourse of mimicry is constructed around an ambivalence. . . . Mimicry is, thus[,] the sign of a double articulation; a complex strategy of reform, regulation and discipline, which 'appropriates' the Other as it visualizes power" (86). I would maintain that the *Harper's* illustration represents an apt example of Bhabha's point, especially through its simultaneous construction of similarity and difference in evoking but reforming the familiar image of teaching from domestic literacy narratives.

5. Toni Morrison, *Playing in the Dark: Whiteness and the Literary Imagination* (New York: Vintage Books, 1992), 44. Morrison explains that "the image of reined-in, bound, suppressed, and repressed darkness became objectified in American literature as an Africanist persona," and she stresses how "the duties of that persona. . . helped to form the distinguishing characteristics of a proto-American literature" (38–39), an "ego-reinforcing" resource for whites (45).

6. Escaped slaves' personal literacy acquisition stories offer one forceful rejection of these demeaning stereotypes. Frederick Douglass's description of learning to read and write gains added power when reexamined within the context of the domestic literacy narrative's stock scene of the white mother teaching her male child. Douglass positions himself within that tradition when describing his mistress's initial efforts to teach him, but he also asserts a race-based experience of having to acquire literacy without maternal aid when, at the urging of her husband, this "kind and tender-hearted woman" shifted from humanely empowering him through teaching to denying him further support for literacy development. See "Narrative of the Life of Frederick Douglass" (1845), in *The Classic Slave Narratives,* ed. Henry Louis Gates Jr., 276–77 (New York: Mentor/Penguin, 1987).

7. A Northern teacher of "contrabands" during the final stages of the Civil

278 / Notes to Pages 163-65

War and of freed people afterward, Elizabeth Hyde Botume underscored the urgency behind Southern outlawing of literacy instruction for slaves. Bitterly attacking a Southerner's position that slaves *"can't* learn," Botume demanded, "Then . . . will you be so kind as to tell me why they made stringent laws at the South against doing what *could not be done?"* (4). See *First Days Amongst the Contrabands* (1893; repr., New York: Arno Press, 1968).

8. Although I am not detailing examples here of links between these nineteenth-century representations of African American learners and recurring counterparts today, current journalism about the "crisis" in African American schooling and home life, popular film portrayals of African American male students, and legislation purporting to "reform" public education testify to the lingering ideological power of these discursive identity formations.

9. Situating his critique of Tuskegee and of Booker T. Washington as "a master executioner" (97) within the larger context of ongoing constraint of the (male) African American body (politic), Houston A. Baker Jr. notes how the "carceral network that has continuously held the black-South body in a state of 'suspended rights'" can be theorized through reference to Foucault's "brilliant genealogy of penality" (93). Connecting the ideology behind Tuskegee *plantation* with the white state's wish to control the black body, Baker contrasts the "zones of discipline and confinement" associated with Tuskegee with the "black modernism in historical progress" seen in Montgomery civil rights actions many years later. See *Turning South Again: Re-thinking Modernism/Re-reading Booker T.* (Durham: Duke University Press, 2001).

10. Michel Foucault, *Discipline and Punish: The Birth of the Prison* (New York: Vintage Books, 1979), 308.

11. Rosemary Hennessy, *Materialist Feminism and the Politics of Discourse* (New York: Routledge, 1993), 43.

12. In *Minnie's Sacrifice,* Harper critiques Northern whites' views of blacks after the war and the impact this attitude had on her race's position in American society. The hero, Louis, declares to Minnie, "What saddens me most is to see so many people of the North clasping hands with these rebels and traitors, and to hear it repeated that [the freed] people are too ignorant to vote" (76-77). See *Minnie's Sacrifice, Sowing and Reaping, Trial and Triumph: Three Rediscovered Novels by Frances E. W. Harper,* ed. Frances Smith Foster (Boston: Beacon Press, 1994).

13. A key element in that scholarship is Frances Smith Foster's recovery of a trio of texts Harper originally published in serialized form in periodicals. See note 12 above. Foster's inspiring scholarship and her generous personal support have guided my work on this chapter and other projects. Generative evaluations of Harper's *Iola Leroy* have been provided by scholars such as Claudia Tate, who examines that text as an example of "literary interventionism" participating in a tradition of domestic fiction, and Hazel Carby, who emphasizes Harper's political activism for a range of causes. See Tate, *Domestic Allegories of Political Desire: The Black Heroine's Text at the Turn of the Century* (New York: Oxford University Press, 1992), 95, 134-35; Carby, *Reconstructing Womanhood.* Emphasizing Harper's influence as a lecturer and her skill as a poet, along with her fiction writing, Carla L. Peterson highlights the author's persistent work for a range of causes including temperance and women's rights as well as abolitionism. See *"Doers of the Word": African-American Women Speakers and Writers in the North (1830-1880)* (New York: Oxford University Press, 1995), 120-35, 155-56, 171-73. John Ernest credits Harper with responding through her novel *Iola Leroy* to white racist literature and thought in the last decades of the nineteenth century

(497). See "From Mysteries to Histories: Cultural Pedagogy in Frances E. W. Harper's *Iola Leroy*," *American Literature* 64 (Sept. 1992): 497–518.

14. Jacqueline Jones Royster, *Traces of a Stream: Literacy and Social Change among African American Women* (Pittsburgh: University of Pittsburgh Press, 2000), 4.

15. Lauren Berlant relates Harper's interventions in political culture to equally distinctive efforts by Harriet Jacobs and Anita Hill in different time periods. Berlant argues that Harper's final novel "seizes the scene of citizenship from white America and rebuilds it, in the classic sense, imagining a liberal public sphere located within the black community" (561). See "The Queen of America Goes to Washington City: Harriet Jacobs, Frances Harper, Anita Hill," *American Literature* 65 (Sept, 1993): 549–74. See also Jean Fagan Yellin's introduction to her groundbreaking edition of Harriet Jacobs's *Incidents in the Life of a Slave Girl, Written By Herself* (1861; repr., Cambridge: Harvard University Press, 1987). Yellin outlines Jacobs's adept appropriation of several gendered genres to promote white women readers' affiliation with her experiences as a slave.

16. Elizabeth Keckley, *Behind the Scenes: Thirty Years a Slave and Four Years in the White House* (New York: G. W. Carleton, 1868).

17. Dorothy Sterling, *Black Foremothers: Three Lives* (New York: Feminist Press, 1988), 57–58.

18. Josephine Ruffin, a leader of the African American clubwomen's movement and editor of the *Women's Era,* issued a call for active response to the letter composed by Jacks, whose position as president of the Missouri Press Association made his published attack on African American women especially aggravating. Characterizing them as "wholly devoid of morality" and all classifiable as "prostitutes, thieves and liars," Jacks actually inspired African American women from around the country to make their club movement more strategic so as to prove his claims false. Victoria Earle Matthews's speech at an 1895 Boston clubwomen's gathering was just one of a number of presentations countering Jacks's statements. Matthews singled out Harper twice in the speech as one of the makers of race literature resisting the negative depictions of blacks in much white American literature. See "The Value of Race Literature: An Address Delivered at the First Congress of Colored Women of the United States (1895)," in *With Pen and Voice: A Critical Anthology of Nineteenth-Century African-American Women,* ed. Shirley Wilson Logan, 126–48 (Carbondale: Southern Illinois University Press, 1995). See too Anne Ruggles Gere and Sarah R. Robbins, "Gendered Literacy in Black and White: Turn-of-the-Century African-American and European-American Club Women's Printed Texts," *Signs* 21 (Spring 1996): 643–78.

19. In contrast, writing a letter to Ednah Cheney about a visit back to Edenton, North Carolina, after the war, Jacobs focuses not on the constraints that kept her from mothering her children while still enslaved but instead on the "community of [black] people whose love and devotion" "made the few sunny spots in that dark life sacred to me" (qtd. in Peterson, *"Doers of the Word,"* 202).

20. Peterson, *"Doers of the Word,"* 192. Peterson quotes key lines from one of Forten's poems from this period: "May those, whose holy task it is / To guide impulsive youth, / Fail not to cherish in their souls / A reverence for truth" (*"Doers of the Word,"* 181). Peterson also references Forten's allusions to aiding "the poor and oppressed" (*"Doers of the Word,"* 181).

21. Forten was certainly not the only African American woman whose writing about teaching admitted to facing frustration. See, for example, Ida B. Wells-Barnett's description of her choice to leave a segregated California school—"a makeshift one-room building" that made an "odious" contrast with the "commodi-

ous building up on the hill" for "the white, Indian, and half-breed Mexican and Indian children" (*Crusade for Justice,* 26–27).

22. Frances Smith Foster, ed., *A Brighter Coming Day: A Frances Ellen Watkins Harper Reader* (New York: Feminist Press, 1990), 274. Having searched in vain for any *Atlantic* piece written by a "Miss Foster" during this period, I do think Harper is referring to Forten. Subsequent references to primary and interpretive material from this anthology will be designated as coming from *Brighter Coming Day.*

23. See Forten Grimké, "Life on the Sea Islands, Part II," 675.

24. Susan Paul, *Memoir of James Jackson: The Attentive and Obedient Scholar, Who died in Boston, October 31, 1833, Aged Six Years and Eleven Months. By His Teacher,* ed. Lois Brown (1835; repr., Cambridge: Harvard University Press, 2000).

25. Lois Brown reports that, although several schools for African American youth had opened in Boston by this time, many black children were not attending (Paul, *Memoir of James Jackson,* 22).

26. Not all white benevolent literacy narratives adopted a holier-than-thou stance. Exceptions include texts by Lydia Maria Child, as well as some narratives by white women involved in the education of "contrabands" during the Civil War and freed slaves afterward. See, for instance, Wayne E. Reilly, ed., *Sarah Jane Foster, Teacher of the Freedmen: A Diary and Letters* (Charlottesville: University Press of Virginia, 1990).

27. As Lois Brown notes, "The name Paul was synonymous with African American education and uplift in the early 1800s" (Paul, *Memoir of James Jackson,* 9), and Paul herself gained renown through such projects as her direction of a youth choir.

28. See Lois Brown's introduction to Paul, *Memoir of James Jackson,* 29. Brown's point about the shift in content for Sabbath school education after the Nat Turner rebellion is significant in this context. Based on their heightened fear of slave literacy, she explains, whites running schools for enslaved blacks generally enacted "a shift away from reading and writing instruction to oral training and rote memorization," skills considered less dangerous.

29. See Frances Smith Foster's discussion in *Brighter Coming Day,* 38–39.

30. See my "Gendering the Debate over African Americans' Education in the 1880s: Frances Harper's Reconfiguration of Atticus Haygood's Philanthropic Model," *Legacy* 19 (2002): 81–89.

31. To say that white writers had dominated the genre does not, of course, lessen the role that African Americans played in the construction of its ideology. See, in this context, Morrison, *Playing in the Dark.*

32. Another serial Harper published in the *Christian Recorder, Sowing and Reaping,* addresses temperance issues. Its content is quite consistent with Harper's education program, especially her affirmation of moral suasion–based reform.

33. See, for example, Berlant, "Queen of America,"; Ernest, "From Mysteries to Histories"; Foreman, "'Reading Aright'"; and Peterson, *"Doers of the Word"* and "'Further Liftings of the Veil.'" See also Elizabeth Young, "Warring Fictions: *Iola Leroy* and the Color of Gender," *American Literature* 64 (June 1992): 273–97. For a related perspective on Harper's writing as creatively in dialogue with post-Reconstruction's white stereotypes of black women, see Claudia Tate's *Domestic Allegories,* chapter 4, especially her discussion of the "true black woman" as "domestic nurturer, spiritual counselor, moral advocate, social activist, and academic teacher" in Harper's writing (97).

34. On Harper's reworking of slavery narrative conventions in *Minnie's Sacrifice* and for an analysis of how recovery of this text promotes reevaluation of such race novels as *Iola Leroy*, see M. Giulia Fahi, "Reconstructing Literary Genealogies: Frances E. W. Harper's and William Dean Howells's Race Novels," in *Soft Canons: American Women Writers and Masculine Tradition*, ed. Karen L. Kilcup, 48–66 (Iowa City: University of Iowa Press, 1999). Peterson's "'Further Liftings of the Veil'" provides insightful analysis of both *Minnie's Sacrifice* and *Trial and Triumph* in the context of Harper's rich career.

35. Eric Foner, *A Short History of Reconstruction, 1863–77* (New York: Harper and Row, 1990), 43.

36. Harper had stepchildren from her marriage to Ohio widower Fenton Harper, with whom she lived on a farm from 1860 until his death in 1864. She and Fenton had one child of their own—Mary—who moved with her mother to New England after Fenton Harper's death (*Brighter Coming Day*, 18).

37. We do have some impressive reviews of Harper's lectures. Shirley Wilson Logan cites Grace Greenwood's enthusiastic description of Harper as a "bronze muse" speaking "without notes, with gestures few and fitting," and in a "manner marked by dignity and composure," "never assuming, never theatrical." Logan also says that African American abolitionist Mary Ann Shadd Cary dubbed Harper "the greatest female speaker" ever to come to Detroit. See *With Pen and Voice: A Critical Anthology of Nineteenth-Century African-American Women* (Carbondale: Southern Illinois University Press, 1995), 31. Melba Joyce Boyd presents a white South Carolinian newspaper report on one of Harper's Southern speeches, including the comment that Harper "left the impression on our mind that she was not only intelligent and educated, but—the great end of education—she was enlightened. She comprehends perfectly the situations of her people, to whose interests she seems ardently devoted" (*Discarded Legacy*, 121).

38. Interestingly, this comment recalls Augustine St. Clare's observations to Ophelia in *Uncle Tom's Cabin:* "You send thousands of dollars to foreign missions; but could you endure to have the heathen sent into your towns and villages, and give your time, and thoughts, and money, to raise them to the Christian standard?" (452).

39. On the work of Yankee schoolmarms and Freedmen's Bureau officials, see Robert C. Morris, *Reading, 'Riting, and Reconstruction: The Education of Freedmen in the South, 1861–1870* (Chicago: University of Chicago Press, 1981).

40. Calling for increased governmental protection and support, she exclaimed: "How have our people been murdered in the South, and their bones scattered at the grave's mouth! Oh, when will we have a government strong enough to make human life safe?" (*Brighter Coming Day*, 132). Harper would have been well aware that a local black woman's successfully claiming the schoolteacher role would be unusual in the early days of Reconstruction—and thus all the more impressive. For a case study illustrating these difficulties, see Whittington B. Johnson, "A Black Teacher and Her School in Reconstruction Darien: The Correspondence of Hettie Sabattie and J. Murray Hoag, 1868–1869," *Georgia Historical Quarterly* 85 (Spring 1991): 90–105.

41. Foner links the content of Reconstruction-era education programs for blacks, and specifically their emphasis on "social control," with the fact that "few Northerners involved in black education could rise above the conviction that slavery had produced a 'degraded' people in dire need of instruction in frugality, temperance, honesty, and the dignity of labor. In classrooms, alphabet drills and multiplication tables alternated with exhortations to piety, cleanliness, and punctuality" (*Short History of Reconstruction*, 66).

42. Individual sections of the report, submitted by superintendents working in the various Southern states, sometimes counter this trend. For instance, the account from Virginia includes this observation on the "capability" of African Americans in the schools: "I believe the finest intellectual achievements are possible to these colored children; no one who listened to the prompt answers, or perceived the 'snap' of the pupils during the late exercises, can doubt it. What I was most gratified with was the enthusiasm for, and pride in, knowledge, which is a motive power that, if given play, will carry them up to noble attainments." See J. W. Alvord, *Fourth Semi-Annual Report on Schools for Freedmen, July 1, 1867* (Washington: Government Printing Office, 1867–68), 15.

43. Harper echoes Alvord's insistence that a debt is owed to America's former slaves, but by praising their accomplishments in the context of strengths derived from the suffering of slavery, she grants them a nobility not evident in his Bureau report. For instance, having traveled to Georgia in 1870, Harper observes "that the interest of the grown-up people in getting education [had] somewhat subsided." However, she also states: "I don't think that I have visited scarcely a place since last August where there was no desire for a teacher," and she references an official who "thought some time since that there were more colored than white who were learning or had learned to read" (*Brighter Coming Day*, 126). James D. Anderson contends that Alvord's attitudes changed over time. Anderson credits Alvord's "growing awareness of a distinctly black perspective on educational and social matters" (6). See *The Education of Blacks in the South, 1860–1935* (Chapel Hill: University of North Carolina Press, 1988).

44. John W. DeForest, "The Man and Brother, II," *Atlantic Monthly* 22 (Oct. 1868): 416 (hereafter cited by part and page number). DeForest was, according to Ellery Sedgwick, one of editor James Fields's protégés during this period, having numerous pieces published in the magazine—a fact giving the opinions in his Freedmen's Bureau essays added weight. See *The Atlantic Monthly, 1857–1909: Yankee Humanism at High Tide and Ebb* (Amherst: University of Massachusetts Press, 1994), 98.

45. In "Three Months among the Reconstructionists" an anonymous author conflates the negative traits of Southern freedmen with those of poor rural whites to argue that Northern whites needed to uplift the whole Southern region. Despite its disdain for the uneducated lower classes of whites and its biting condemnation of slavery, the essay insists that the "negro is no model of virtue or manliness," since he "loves idleness," "has little conception of right and wrong, and . . . is improvident to the last degree of childishness." The author maintains that former slaves are "anxious to learn" and fortunately quite "tractable," but requiring "almost infinite patience" because they can come only "very slowly to moral comprehensions." See "Three Months among the Reconstructionists," *Atlantic Monthly* 17 (Feb. 1866): 243.

46. Depictions of African Americans in the *Atlantic* were far from uniformly negative. Numerous essays supported radical Republicanism, emphasizing the need for the South to accept the Thirteenth, Fourteenth, and Fifteenth Amendments to the U.S. Constitution. Contributors included Frederick Douglass and William Parker, highly positive models of black civic responsibility. See William Parker's two-part personal narrative, "The Freedmen's Story," *Atlantic Monthly* 17 (Feb. 1866): 152–66; (Mar. 1866): 276–95. White advocates like T. W. Higginson, meanwhile, argued for fair treatment of the freedmen and cast them as deserving full political equality. Having surveyed the periodical's treatment of Reconstruction, I would describe the range of perspectives there as mixed, with the

Atlantic's fluctuating stance far less enlightened than we might expect, given its links to idealists like Thoreau and Emerson.

47. John W. DeForest, "The Man and Brother, I," *Atlantic Monthly* 22 (Sept. 1868): 343 (hereafter cited by part and page number). DeForest declares, "That the freedmen should be ignorant and unintelligent does not appear strange when it is considered that they were brought to us, not so very long ago, in the condition of savages, and that since they have been among us they have been kept down as bondsmen or cast out as pariahs" (337–38). Later, he damns with faint praise by explaining, "In the matter of honesty the freedmen are doing as well as could be expected, considering their untoward education, first as savages and then as slaves" (344).

48. DeForest even implies that Emancipation might turn out *not* to be beneficial to the Negro. Commenting on the stresses facing "the blacks" as they cope with "emancipation," DeForest pities their having lost the control provided by their masters, who he declares could be counted on to encourage such moral behaviors as marriage and child support, as well as to regulate work habits. DeForest predicts, "This new, varied, costly life of freedom, this struggle to be at once like a race which has passed through a two thousand years' growth in civilization, will unquestionably diminish the productiveness of the negro, and will terribly test his vitality." Thus, he opines that "abrupt emancipation," while "a mighty experiment," should be seen as "fraught with as much menace as hope" (II, 425).

49. In direct contrast to DeForest's implication that Southern blacks expected corporal punishment to be a part of their children's education, see Charles Chesnutt's journals about his South Carolina teaching experiences in the 1870s: "No one need tell me, that a school cannot be governed without the administration of corporal punishment, unless it is a very bad school indeed." Chesnutt notes that he had "taught five weeks without it, and can very probably teach five more" (80). See Richard H. Brodhead, ed., *The Journals of Charles W. Chesnutt* (Durham: Duke University Press, 1993).

50. J. W. Alvord, *Sixth Semi-Annual Report on Schools for Freedmen, July 1, 1868* (Washington: Government Printing Office, 1868). I am not claiming that Harper studied annual reports of the Freedmen's Bureau. What I do believe is that she would have been well aware of the prejudices embedded in the reports, since, as public government documents, they would have been reflective of values and language circulating among social arbiters during this era.

51. Harper herself, like other antislavery speakers and writers, often emphasized the horror of slavery's impact on motherhood. See her poems "The Slave Mother" and "To Mrs. Harriet Beecher Stowe" (*Brighter Coming Day*, 58–59, 57). What I want to emphasize here, though, is that Harper adapted her rhetoric to the new situation of Reconstruction, moving from arguing that slavery undermined black motherhood to imagining the possibility of a new version of American motherhood enhanced by the knowledge gained through and after slavery.

52. Peterson, *"Doers of the Word,"* 264.

53. For a telling contrast between Harper's choice of the *Christian Recorder* and Charlotte Forten's positioning of her work "mainly in white newspapers and magazines such as the *National Anti-Slavery Standard,* the *Liberator,* and the *Atlantic Monthly,*" and only occasionally in the *Christian Recorder,* see Peterson, *"Doers of the Word,"* 179, 209, 214, and 216. Elizabeth McHenry places the *Christian Recorder* within a cluster of important black periodicals—including the *Weekly Anglo-African* and the *Colored American,* as well as *Frederick Douglass' Paper*—helping promote "an ideal of community that affirmed reading and other literary

activities as acts of public good on which the intellectual life and civic character of its members could be grounded" (*Forgotten Readers,* 87).

54. Frances Smith Foster, "African Americans, Literature, and the Nineteenth-Century Afro-Protestant Press," in *Reciprocal Influences: Literary Production, Distribution, and Consumption in America,* ed. Steven Fink and Susan S. Williams (Columbus: Ohio State University Press, 1999), 29. Foster argues that, unless we recover a sense of the "intricate connection between religion and literature and science and art and Afro-Protestantism's commitment to a gospel of social reform," we will obscure important traits of African American culture and its influence on the larger American society (34).

55. See Street's *Social Literacies* for a critique of "great divide" theories of literacy that privilege written discourse over oral literacy practices and his call instead for understandings of literacy practices grounded in the study of particular social contexts. Underpinning my argument about Harper's Reconstruction-era reformation of the domestic literacy narrative is a sense that, through her observations of postbellum Southern rural black culture, she inductively arrived at many of the same views now espoused by Street and other ethnographic researchers of folk literacy in various cultural contexts.

56. Illiteracy rates among the freed people of the South have been estimated at as high as 96 percent in the first years after the war. See J. M. Stephen Peeps, "Northern Philanthropy and the Emergence of Black Higher Education—Do-Gooders, Compromisers, or Co-Conspirators?" *Journal of Negro Education* 50 (1981): 253. Therefore, arguing that oral literacy practices could play a role in the kind of teaching New England white mothers centered in print texts would have opened up this social role to a large number of women otherwise excluded from it. James D. Anderson's detailed portrait of African American education after the Civil War suggests Harper's portrayal of Minnie and Louis's work in their community was realistic as well as idealistic. Anderson argues that, although blacks accepted assistance from white Northern missionaries, their own effort—"informed by an ethic of mutuality—was the primary force that brought schools to the children of freed men and women" (*Education of Blacks,* 5). For an example of effective black/white collaboration later in the century, see Sarah Robbins, Deborah Mitchell, and Ed Hullender, "Uplifting a 'New' South," available at <http:// www.kennesaw.edu/english/kmwp/AmerCommunities/thematic_content/ educating_for_citizenship/eduhome.html>.

57. Here Harper may be calling, by implication, for an extension of the productive model for learning that had been serving middle-class African Americans through learning societies tied to print literacy, as outlined in Elizabeth McHenry's pioneering study, *Forgotten Readers.* In discussing two Northeastern literary societies active between 1880 and the early twentieth century, McHenry points to the way in which—like various black antebellum groups preceding them—these two organizations emphasized "literary study" as an avenue to "becoming, as a race, better prepared for the demands of citizenship" by acquiring a "learned identity far removed from the intellectual poverty associated with slavery" (141). Harper's implied program for literary study affiliates with the tradition of print-oriented uplift in such Northern literacy societies but also values texts retrieved from the oral folk culture tradition maintained by Southern slaves.

58. See Kimberly A. C. Wilson, "The Function of the 'Fair' Mulatto: Complexion, Audience, and Mediation in Frances Harper's *Iola Leroy,*" *Cimarron Review* 106 (Jan. 1994): 104–13. Wilson relates Harper's focus on mulatto characters to her mixed audience of white and black Sunday school readers. Wilson says the

latter group could have felt marginalized by that choice: "it seems impossible that her Sunday-school readers would have found empowerment in or been uplifted by the marginalization of those characters whom they most closely resembled" (109). Contrast Carby's reading in *Reconstructing Womanhood*. Carby argues that the "figure of the mulatto should be understood and analyzed as a narrative device of mediation" and points out that Iola's mulatto status "enabled Harper to express the relationship between white privilege and black lack of privilege" (89).

59. N. S. Shaler, "An Ex-Southerner in South Carolina," *Atlantic Monthly* 26 (July 1870): 57. Shaler's racist commentary is especially distressing, given that he fought for the Union, so his rantings can't be dismissed as posturing by a Southerner still dedicated to the Rebel cause.

60. Harper says of Minnie: "While some of the authors of the present day have been weaving their stories about white men marrying beautiful quadroon girls, who, in so doing were lost to us socially, I conceived of one of that same class to whom I gave a higher, holier destiny; a life of lofty self-sacrifice and beautiful self-consecration, finished at the post of duty, and rounded off with the fiery crown of martyrdom" (*Minnie's Sacrifice*, 91).

61. Fabi makes a similar argument about the heroine's mulatto status in *Iola Leroy*: "By portraying Iola's acceptance of her black ancestry and her subsequent experiences as a member of the African American community, Harper succeeds in moving beyond the tragic mulatta trope, not by erasing the representation of blackness, but by reconstructing black cultural distinctiveness on different grounds." According to Fabi, Iola's mulatto status helps shift "blackness from a visible, ostensibly unambiguous signifier of inferiority and oppression" to "a force of cultural change, a grand social mission to construct a new, more egalitarian civilization" ("Reconstructing Literary Genealogies," 57).

62. The range of topics Minnie and Louis discuss in their home underscores the idea that, especially in this particular time, "protecting" black women from politics was inappropriate (and perhaps impossible). For instance, when a visitor (Mr. Jackson) arrives soon afterward to describe being tempted by a proposed bribe for his vote, Minnie is included in discussion (75–77).

63. Foner stresses that "a wave of violence . . . raged almost unchecked in large parts of the postwar South" and that the "pervasiveness of violence reflected whites' determination" to limit freedom by "resist[ing] black efforts to establish their autonomy, whether in matters of family, labor, or personal demeanor" (*Short History of Reconstruction*, 52–53).

64. Although lynchings certainly victimized men more than women, Harper is historically accurate in portraying the grave dangers women involved in Reconstruction often faced. See, for example, Bertram Wyatt-Brown, who points out that, partly because they tended to board with local African American families, black Northern women teaching in the South were more likely than their white counterparts to become embroiled in local controversies. See "Black Schooling during Reconstruction," in *The Web of Southern Social Relations: Women, Family, and Education*, ed. Walter L. Fraser Jr., R. Frank Saunders Jr., and Jon L. Wakelyn, 146–65 (Athens: University of Georgia Press, 1985). For an example of how white women teachers working in the South were also directly endangered, see Reilly, *Sarah Jane Foster*, 75. See also Morris, *Reading*, 31.

65. Contrast this relatively brief exchange with the more fully conceived domestic teaching scene in Harper's *Trial and Triumph*, where Mrs. Lasette interprets a similar school experience of Annette's as an opportunity for her to learn to accept God's valuing of all different races. Complaining that her Irish class-

mate Mary Joseph "had no business calling me a nigger" (217), Annette admits
to having traded race-related insults with the girl, suggesting that "her mother
. . . [ate] with the pigs in the old country" and labeling her "a poor white mick"
(216). By the time Mrs. Lasette has directed her conversation with Annette to the
same question Anna uses less effectively with Minnie ("Does God ever make any
mistakes?"[219]), Harper's re-vision of a domestic lesson on inclusive race pride
shows how underdeveloped Anna's teaching had been in the 1860s narrative.

66. See Camilla's efforts to use Uncle Isaac's story to reform her father's
views (*Minnie's Sacrifice*, 13).

67. "Social equality" became an especially controversial issue during Reconstruction, as some Northern teachers and government administrators who journeyed south to support the freedmen established friendly relations with them.
Even Southerners who saw potential benefit to their region from the education
of former slaves tended to be strongly opposed to social interaction between the
races. See Morris, *Reading*, 230.

68. Boyd stresses the role Chloe could have played in "literacy programs"
serving Southern freed peoples, who Boyd feels could have easily identified with
Chloe (*Discarded Legacy*, 150). For Boyd, *Sketches* shows Harper as "a teacher"
who "viewed her literature as 'Songs for the People,'" whereby "the application of
her poetry for teaching was a practical function of her literacy campaign and of
her political aesthetics" (150).

69. Chloe's reversal of position with her mistress over the course of the poem
sequence is striking in this regard, especially in the context of the white middle-
class model for women influencing politics through the sons they guide. When
the kindhearted, beloved son "Mister Thomas" leaves his mother to fight for the
Confederacy, Chloe observes to Uncle Jacob, "Now old Mistus feels the sting, /
For this parting with your children / Is a mighty dreadful thing" (*Brighter Coming Day*, 200). On equal terms as they both pray for the return of lost children,
Chloe can see the irony in her mistress's suffering as slaves had when their children were "sold away" (*Brighter Coming Day*, 196). Significantly, it is Chloe who
is reunited with her son, as her mistress mourns the death of Mister Thomas
(*Brighter Coming Day*, 208).

70. See Frances Smith Foster's insightful analysis of Harper's audience
awareness in poetry writing: "Harper played her audience, used her poetry to
strike chords of sentiment, to improvise upon familiar themes, and, thereby, to
create songs more in harmony with what she knew as the dictates of Christianity
and democracy" (*Brighter Coming Day*, 30). Like Foster's view of Harper as using
straightforward poetic techniques (e.g., simple rhyme and regular rhythm), my
sense of Harper's use of Chloe would emphasize the character's likely appeal for
middle-class Northern whites. For the black audience being exclusively addressed
in *Minnie's Sacrifice* and the rhetorical purpose of providing Reconstruction-era
models for teaching and learning by members of her race, Harper chose a more
complicated interplay between Miriam and other former slave mothers, as well as
between Miriam and the white motherly figure of Camilla.

71. Aunt Susan's conflation of her daughter's folk wisdom and Minnie's
school-educated knowledge recalls Carby's observation that in *Iola Leroy* Harper
would "illustrate the potential basis of alliance between intellectuals and the folk,
between the literate and the illiterate" (*Reconstructing*, 82).

72. Harper's anecdote was more radical in its day than it may now appear.
She both appropriated and resisted a recurring icon associated with education of
the freedmen in publicity depicting the American Missionary Association's
(AMA's) white Northern teachers' work. Jacqueline Jones reports on a circular

sent to the AMA's white women teachers in Atlanta in October 1867, urging that they have photographs taken of themselves reading to black families at home, with the whole group cast as childlike recipients of the Yankee teachers' motherly instruction. Harper reframes that image to show black learners as having a depth of understanding—and an ability to communicate it proactively—well beyond anything depicted in such AMA publicity. See *Soldiers of Light and Love,* 149.

73. Harper was probably referring to Fanny Jackson Coppin. See Linda M. Perkins's allusions to Coppin's study at Oberlin and her later teaching in "The Education of Black Women in the Nineteenth Century," in Faragher and Howe, *Women and Higher Education in American History,* 71, 73.

74. Perkins argues that, around the 1880s, "blacks were attempting to 'uplift' themselves to the standards of the majority culture," including "Victorian gender roles [that] may have been desired by some black males" even though "in reality" a separate spheres ideology was neither practical nor consistent with the "reality" of African American life, since "married black women had to work, and a disproportionate number of black women in the North were single" ("Education of Black Women," 76-77).

Chapter 6

1. Mrs. Shaw, "China—Tung-Chow," *Woman's Work for Woman* 6 (Feb. 1877): 400. I will use *WWW* to refer to this publication in future citations.

2. Mary Louise Pratt, *Imperial Eyes: Travel Writing and Transculturation* (New York: Routledge, 1992). Pratt developed the concept of the "contact zone" "to invoke the spatial and temporal copresence of subjects previously separated by geographic and historical disjunctures, and whose trajectories now intersect" (7). While Pratt focuses on the "European male subject . . . whose imperial eyes passively look out and possess" (7), her framework illuminates how missionary women interacted with natives. See, for example, Miss H. M. Eddy, "Syria—Sidon," *WWW* 7 (Feb. 1877): 410-11; Mrs. Capp, "China—Tungchow," *WWW* 7 (July 1877): 145-47.

3. Jameson, *Political Unconscious,* 106.

4. Frances Smith Foster's rediscovery of the novels Frances Harper first published in the *Christian Recorder* has highlighted ways that the church promoted African American women's literacy and literature after the Civil War. (See chapter 5.) As an example, for the role religion played as an organizing principle in Southern white women's lives after the Civil War, see Mary E. Frederickson, "Shaping a New Society," in *Women in New Worlds: Historical Perspectives on the Wesleyan Tradition,* ed. Hilah F. Thomas and Rosemary Skinner Keller, 1: 345-61 (Nashville: Abingdon, 1981).

5. Devitt, "Integrating Rhetorical and Literary Theories," 696-718.

6. I will focus on missionary publishing between about 1870 and about 1915. Setting a precise post-Civil War start date for the emergence of the subgenre would be deceptive, since forerunner texts during the antebellum era helped shape the form. Similarly, no clear-cut end date can be set. One turning point might be 1910-11, as discussed later in chapter 6, when a world congress of women missionaries and American Jubilee year celebrations were presented in numerous women's narratives as climactic moments in the movement's history.

7. See Anne Firor Scott's analysis of how "women learned," through organizational participation, "to conduct business, carry on meetings, speak in public, manage money." These skills were all important to the shared literacy practices

of the foreign mission movement's literature making. Additionally, Scott's interpretation of how "values and attitudes were developed" through "collective experience" leads to ideas about how reading and writing mission literature shaped the social selves of women in this community. See *Natural Allies: Women's Associations in American History* (Urbana: University of Illinois Press, 1991), 2.

8. Anne Ruggles Gere's study of turn-of-the-century clubwomen's collaborative literacy shows that the "intimate practices" of their literacy did significant public work for themselves and American society (*Intimate Practices*, 5).

9. Patricia R. Hill, *The World Their Household: The American Woman's Foreign Mission Movement and Cultural Transformation, 1870–1920* (Ann Arbor: University of Michigan Press, 1985), 3.

10. I do not mean to imply that the movement was flush with excess funds or that individual foreign missionaries lived in luxury. In fact, women leaders in the United States and overseas often painted a picture of embattled budgets endangering the enterprise. Sometimes such portraits were accurate; sometimes they were heightened for effect. In either case, well into the twentieth century, the organizations' balance sheets climbed continually upward.

11. Helen Barrett Montgomery, *Western Women in Eastern Lands: An Outline Study of Fifty Years of Women's Work in Foreign Missions* (New York: Macmillan, 1910–11).

12. Dana L. Robert, *American Women in Mission: A Social History of Their Thought and Practice* (Macon: Mercer University Press, 1996), 256.

13. "One Hundred Thousand Dollars: What It Means," *WWW* 9 (Sept. 1879): 300–302. The previous edition of the periodical identifies the sixteen states sending representatives; brags that "the ladies" came "from the North, South, East and West"; and extols the "inspiration" provided by the "occasion" itself, especially its "grand aims and lofty purposes." See "The Meeting at Saratoga," *WWW* 9 (Aug. 1879): 259.

14. "Miss Fannie Heck Enters Into Rest," *Raleigh News and Observer,* August 26, 1915. The clipping is from the Fannie E. S. Heck Papers, Wake Forest University Archives and Special Collections, Z. Smith Reynolds Library, Wake Forest University.

15. Hill, *World Their Household*, 3.

16. For a discussion of this relationship penned by one of the movement's own activists, see Laura A. Haygood, "Relation of Female Education to Home Mission Work," reprinted in the biography created largely from her letters (89–95). See Oswald Eugene Brown and Anna Muse Brown, *Life and Letters of Laura Askew Haygood* (Nashville: Smith and Lamar, Publishing House of the M. E. Church, South, 1904).

17. Robert cites as one example Mary Hawes, a mission wife who attended Catharine Beecher's Hartford Seminary. Signaling one of many instances of the Beecher family's far-reaching influence on American culture, Robert also notes that Harriet Lathrop Winslow (missionary wife to Ceylon) and Eliza Hart Spalding (missionary wife to the Nez Perce Indians) had theological training with Lyman Beecher (*American Women in Mission,* 8).

18. Marjorie King points out that late nineteenth-century mission-movement leaders in China, eager to convince the locals that girls needed schooling, reworked arguments that had been used in the antebellum United States to gain educational opportunity for women. See "Exhorting Femininity, Not Feminism: Nineteenth-Century U.S. Missionary Women's Efforts to Emancipate Chinese Women," in *Women's Work for Women: Missionaries and Social Change in Asia,* ed. Leslie A. Flemming (Boulder: Westview Press, 1989), 121.

19. Amanda Porterfield, *Mary Lyon and the Mount Holyoke Missionaries* (New York: Oxford University Press, 1997), 6.

20. Maria T. True, "Tokio Japan," *WWW* 12 (Jan. 1882): 15–16. Mrs. True repeated the association in a letter to the journal: "I have in my mind a Japanese Mt. Holyoke as the possible outgrowth of this Bancho school!" She used the comparison to convince her readers to send money. See "Japan," *WWW* 12 (Apr, 1882): 122.

21. "The Huguenot Seminary of South Africa," *WWW* 12 (July 1882): 217–20.

22. One reason British and American missionaries tended to have comfortable social relations was that, from the beginning, there had been extensive cross-fertilization between the two enterprises. For instance, as Dana L. Robert indicates, William Carey, one of the early organizers of British foreign missionary initiatives, had been inspired by reading accounts of David Brainerd's preaching to North American Indians. Later, Americans found printed stories of Carey's adventures as a foreign missionary so uplifting that they founded fundraising drives for such work (*American Women in Mission*, 5).

23. Conditions in the interior tended to be very different from those in port cities and to vary from country to country. The more isolated the mission post, the less involved mission families would be in European-style social concerns.

24. Although Jane Hunter cites multiple examples of American missionaries seeking support from U.S. government legations in disputes with natives before the turn of the century, she points out that, until President William Henry Harrison ordered gunboat diplomacy in 1893, the Boxer Rebellion occurred in 1900, and the Philippines were acquired, American missionaries generally perceived their government as anti-imperial. See *The Gospel of Gentility: American Women Missionaries in Turn-of-the-Century China* (New Haven: Yale University Press, 1984), 6–7.

25. Hunter, *Gospel of Gentility*, 152. Hunter points to Theodore Roosevelt, Grover Cleveland, William Howard Taft, and Woodrow Wilson as leaders who favored territorial expansion at one time but who came to prefer a more Progressive agenda of uplift. Clearly, from today's perspective, such efforts to replace "the repression of life" with "the cultivation and direction of life" (quoting Roosevelt) were still imperialistic, but Hunter maintains the shift in U.S. attitudes did bring the missionary movement and the government to a compatible perspective toward native Others—one allowing leaders like Roosevelt to promote contributions to the foreign mission enterprise (*Gospel of Gentility*, 7–9).

26. The missionary women whose biographies will be discussed in detail later in this chapter—Laura Haygood and Harriet Shuck—both expressed a humble dedication to learning Chinese for teaching purposes. Although Haygood predicted, after months of study, that she would need "two years before [she would] be able to teach Bible classes" in the local language, she persevered (Brown and Brown, *Life and Letters*, 126). Later, hoping that "knowledge of the language" would "open many doors" into "the work that may be done for women and girls," Haygood felt that she had made progress (143–44) but kept striving to achieve "a better knowledge of the language" since she still felt "restricted by [her] ignorance" from doing all she could for God and the Chinese (222). However misguided Haygood's conviction that Christianity was crucial to uplifting the Chinese might seem to us, we should note her commitment to reaching her local neighbors through the medium of their own language. Henrietta Shuck's experience was similar. See J. B. Jeter, *A Memoir of Mrs. Henrietta Shuck, The First American Female Missionary to China* (Boston: Gould, Kendall and Lincoln, 1846), 98–107.

27. For discussion of British colonial women learning the local language being encouraged to see that effort as a vehicle toward imperial power, see Rosemary Marangoly George, "Homes in the Empire, Empires in the Home," *Cultural Critique* 26 (Winter 1993-94): 95-127.

28. Irwin T. Hyatt Jr., *Our Ordered Lives Confess: Three Nineteenth-Century American Missionaries in East Shantung* (Cambridge: Harvard University Press, 1976), 69.

29. Hyatt, *Our Ordered Lives Confess,* 16. The role language use and learning played in shaping American mission women's work needs more detailed analysis than can be provided here.

30. To say that these writers deemphasized the political aspects of their work does not mean they ignored its connections to nationalism. Indeed, they consistently portrayed their teaching as an "American" enterprise, but one focused more on America as a site of religious commitment than on imperial aspirations. See, for example, "At Home: Semi-Annual Meeting," *WWW* 7 (Nov. 1877): 286-88.

31. For a helpful analysis in the British context, see Vron Ware's tracing of Annette Ackroyd's career in India. Ackroyd was a British liberal educator who, Ware argues, became an advocate of imperialist politics. Ware's reading of Ackroyd's letters highlights how this Victorian woman's sense of solidarity with her Indian "sisters" before she traveled to the colony to teach was undermined by her internalization of imperial values once she had worked on the scene. See *Beyond the Pale: White Women, Racism and History* (London: Verso, 1992), 122.

32. "At Home: Child-Marriage" describes both benefits and drawbacks of arranged marriages for very young girls in India. See *WWW* 7 (Feb. 1877): 412-15.

33. "Abroad: The Chinese in America," *WWW* 9 (Nov. 1879): 361-67. This piece criticizes the undemocratic treatment of California's Chinese immigrants, who were cast in a pivotal *Woman's Work* report as hard workers unfairly victimized—but also as childlike figures in need of Christian mission schooling to be civilized.

34. "Gleanings," *WWW* 9 (Nov. 1879): 392-93.

35. *Woman's Work for Woman,* published by and for Presbyterian women, concentrated on readers in the Northeast and Midwest. For an example of a comparable Southern periodical, see *Royal Service.* For a case study of *Woman's Work* as emblematic of the foreign mission movement's engagement with print culture, see my *"Woman's Work for Woman:* Collaborative Print Culture in Gendered Mission Narratives," in *Women in Print,* ed. James Danky and Wayne Wiegand (Madison: University of Wisconsin Press), forthcoming.

36. Mrs. Murray Mitchell, "A Day in India." *WWW* 13 (Apr. 1883): 115.

37. For stories on the influence of local auxiliaries making good use of mission literacy practices, see "Notes from Room 48," *WWW* 9 (Feb. 1879): 68-70; "Cheering Words from Auxiliaries," *WWW* 9 (Jan. 1879): 20-21; and "Conducting a Prayer Meeting," *WWW* 9 (May 1879): 158-59.

38. "At Home: Semi-Annual Meeting," 286-87.

39. "India," *WWW* 13 (Jan. 1883): 10. See also "Abroad—India," *WWW* 7 (Sept. 1877): 226-27.

40. Helen S. C. Nevius, *Our Life in China* (New York: Robert Carter & Brothers, 1869), 127.

41. Jeter, *Memoir of Mrs. Henrietta Shuck,* 42.

42. Brown and Brown, *Life and Letters,* 50.

43. Brown and Brown, *Life and Letters,* 125.

44. Warner observes: "It becomes possible to imagine oneself, in the act of reading, becoming part of an arena of the national people that cannot be realized except through such mediating imaginings" (*Letters of the Republic,* xiii).

45. Bushnell, *My Mother,* 75. Sigourney declares: "How far his own self-devotedness to the work of missions, may have been the result of her own instructions . . . , can never be fully known, till that day, when the secrets of all hearts shall be made manifest" (Bushnell, *My Mother,* vi). The influence of Bushnell's mother was not unique. Howard Crumley, a young neighbor of Laura Haygood before she became a missionary, enjoyed over fourteen years of correspondence with her, which encouraged him to become a minister (Brown and Brown, *Life and Letters,* 34, 40–49).

46. In Sigourney's *Lucy Howard's Journal* (New York: Harper & Brothers, 1858), the potentially incompatible categories of appealing child and dangerous heathen were merged in the female figure of the Indian girl, whose own point of view is obscured by the author's focus on the white maternal heroine. For the Ophelia-Topsy, New England–Africa missionary circuit, see chapter 4. Ironically, outside of Liberia, it could be difficult for African American women to secure sponsorship for African missionary teaching, as in the case of Mary McCloud (Bethune), whose application to the Presbyterian foreign mission program in Africa was denied, even though she had trained at Dwight Moody's famed Institute for Home and Foreign Missions in Chicago. See "Bethune, Mary McLeod," in *Black Women in America: An Historical Encyclopedia,* ed. Darlene Clark Hine, Elsa Barkley Brown, and Rosalyn Terborg-Penn, 1: 114 (Bloomington: Indiana University Press, 1933).

47. Hyatt notes that Martha Foster's early dreams of missionary work were discouraged by her local pastor and others, until she was safely wed to T. P. Crawford and sent to China to work alongside him, although often, Hyatt implies, in his shadow (*Our Ordered Lives Confess,* 6). During the antebellum era, while a number of male missionaries went overseas alone, most took wives with them, providing a two-for-one bargain for their sponsoring organizations—for example, Mr. and Mrs. Nevius, Mr. and Mrs. Judson, and Mr. and Mrs. Beighton.

48. Hill, *World Their Household,* 13–14.

49. Even private narratives (journals, diaries, letters) reflect the tendency to exalt the male minister and his work over his wife and her teaching. Thus, Martha Crawford felt such intense anxiety when her efforts to learn Chinese surpassed her husband's that she wrote in her diary about praying that he might soon be "outstripping me," and she agonized when he viewed her skill with a "bitter" sense of inferiority (Hyatt, *Our Ordered Lives Confess,* 8). Later, after the success of her first small school for girls apparently irritated her husband, she redirected her energies for a time to more overtly domestic (though nonetheless successful) pursuits, including writing a popular 1866 cookbook designed "to help other foreign wives" "communicate better" with members of their "domestic staff" (Hyatt, *Our Ordered Lives Confess,* 16). When her request to open a boys' boarding school in their home initially prompted Mr. Crawford's response that "straight preaching" and not teaching was the true mission agenda, she won his support by convincing him that the students could help him gain access to outlying villages, with his own preaching still being predominant (16).

50. Besides writing for American readers of *Woman's Work for Woman,* Mrs. Nevius composed didactic narratives in Chinese, especially "The Life of Rose Mills" (published in Shanghai in 1875) and "The Swiss boy, or the story of Sahpe" (published in Shanghai in 1883). Hyatt says Mrs. Nevius's "Chinese-language Christian literature for women . . . constitutes probably the most note-

worthy body of such material done by one individual" (*Our Ordered Lives Confess*, 68).

51. Rev. S. Newell, *Memoirs of Mrs. Harriet Newell, Wife of the Rev. S. Newell, American Missionary to India* (London: James Nisbet, 1823). This book's title itself presents an early missionary woman in a typically subordinate position vis-à-vis her husband. Downplaying his own contribution as a "compiler" of Harriet's writing, her husband nonetheless emphasizes the "unambitious, delicate" aspects of her nature and declares that the memoir itself "would have been kept within the circle of her particular friends, had not the closing scenes of her life, and the Missionary zeal, which has recently been kindled in this country, excited in the public mind a lively interest in her character, and given the Christian community a kind of property in the productions of her pen" (advertisement). This concept of women's originally personal missionary writing—and subsequent publications of it—as "community . . . property" would pervade the movement's use of the domestic literacy narrative in later decades too. See also Rev. Daniel C. Eddy, *The Three Mrs. Judsons, and Other Daughters of the Cross* (Boston: Thayer and Eldridge, 1855, 1860), which depicts all its subjects as loyal, supportive missionary wives.

52. See Jeter, *Memoir of Mrs. Henrietta Shuck*. Scott E. Casper describes the "constructive, cultural purposes" of American biographies. Casper argues that, in the nineteenth century, "the predominant message of American-written biographies was didactic and nationalistic" (4). See *Constructing American Lives: Biography and Culture in Nineteenth-Century America* (Chapel Hill: University of North Carolina Press, 1999).

53. Jeter's editorial control is evident, nonetheless. For instance, when recording Henrietta's conversion, Jeter stresses that "her deliverance" was part of a campaign by "many pious parents" to lead "their children" "before the throne of God" (*Memoir of Mrs. Henrietta Shuck*, 18). Thus, even as he credits her piety, he frames his presentation to depict her as matching social expectations for middle-class American Protestant girls.

54. One way Jeter furthers his agenda of presenting Mrs. Shuck as a replicable role model is by inviting other women "of high reputation" who had crossed her path to comment on what others might learn from her example. Henrietta's former teacher Mrs. Little, for example, describes the young Miss Hall as having been a worthy "member of my school and family" and hopes that the biography will be "a valuable gift to the public" (*Memoir of Mrs. Henrietta Shuck*, 15).

55. One of Henrietta's letters to her former teacher Mrs. Little asks for guidance: "When you write, tell me what books you think it would be advisable for me to read. I . . . will take care to peruse with great attention all you mention" (Jeter, *Memoir of Mrs. Henrietta Shuck*, 24). That Mrs. Shuck and her mission-movement contemporaries maintained a strong connection between their work and their national identities is suggested by such anecdotes as Henrietta's writing home about the possibility, if she left China, of transferring her students to another missionary couple who, though Presbyterians and not Baptists like herself, she deemed to be able Christian leaders by virtue of their being "from America" (Jeter, *Memoir of Mrs. Henrietta Shuck*, 141).

56. Sigourney recommends that middle-class women adopt "a child of the poor" to teach, with this curriculum including household tasks but also writing and "the simpler operations of arithmetick," as well as "strict moral principle" (Lydia Sigourney, *Letters to Mothers*, 199–200). Sigourney's description of this instruction and the "benevolent pleasure" it earns for the mother underscores the

close connections between the rhetoric of foreign missionary motherhood and the original models for benevolent literacy management.

57. Brown and Brown, *Life and Letters*, 430.

58. For a description of Mrs. Lambuth's efforts to Christianize young Chinese women with teaching and prayer meetings, see "Woman's Work," *WWW* 9 (Feb. 1879): 40–41. Lambuth's writing for *Woman's Work for Woman*, like Helen Nevius's, marks her as a transitional figure between Henrietta Shuck and Laura Haygood. Nevius and Lambuth both initially saw themselves as support for their spouses, but their connections with the women's foreign mission movement's literacy network fostered increasing pride in their own gendered contributions to the mission enterprise.

59. Brown and Brown, *Life and Letters*, 385.

60. Like the Shuck biography in its era, the Haygood narrative was not unique. Two biographies published in the decades after Haygood's attest to the continuing professionalization trend. Sara Estelle Haskin's 1920 collection of sketches on the careers of Methodist women emphasizes the administrative ability and broadly secular influence of single missionaries like Lochie Rankin, Mary White, Virginia Atkinson, and Haygood. See *Women and Missions in the Methodist Episcopal Church, South* (Nashville: M. E. Church, Smith and Lamar, 1920). In an autobiography several decades later, Jennie Manget Logan stresses professionalization and secularization for women's involvement in foreign fields. Logan spent over forty years in China as, first, a colleague of her physician husband and, later, a medical-care provider in her own right. See *Little Stories of China* (N.p., n.d.).

61. For today's readers, the length of this section could be a surprise, as China's more exotic setting is thus postponed. Such episodes would have been seen as vital in Haygood's day, however. For instance, a reader schooled in the imagery of the domestic literacy narrative would recognize the moral suasion ideal in a detail declaring that Mrs. Haygood "poured out the fullness of her Christian faith and love into the heart and mind of her daughter Laura" (Brown and Brown, *Life and Letters*, 13).

62. Haygood's grandmother, according to the Browns, rendered Laura's vocation for religious maternal teaching virtually inevitable: "It was at her grandmother's feet that she heard over and over again those stories of Bible heroes, until she could not miss the lesson that every man's true life is planned of God" (*Life and Letters*, 10).

63. A thorough analysis of the ways in which their gender differences shaped their two careers in community service would be worthwhile indeed. For more on Atticus Haygood as a New South leader with a keen interest in education and religion, see my "Gendering the Debate over African Americans' Education."

64. Examples of her followers' moves to present Haygood's influence as maternal abound. For instance, Miss Atkinson, one of her protégées at the Shanghai station, wrote after Haygood's death that her mentor had been "a mother as well as friend and advisor" (Brown and Brown, *Life and Letters*, 496).

65. Several years earlier, when justifying her choice not to write Mollie much about mission conferences held in China, Haygood had noted: "There will be some reports of them in the papers now, I suppose, and full minutes by and by" (Brown and Brown, *Life and Letters*, 221). So, too, while describing her pleasure at meeting the renowned Lottie Moon in 1888, Haygood wrote to Abbie Callaway: "You must know something of her work through your Church papers" (219). The tendency of lady missionary authors to frame their periodical articles as letters

to friends is notable in this context. Rather than representing a staged move, using this form was consistent with their knowledge that personal friends would be reading their submissions.

66. "Conducting a Ladies' Prayer Meeting," *WWW* 9 (Feb. 1879): 54. Language in pieces like this one clearly anticipates the rhetoric of today's on-line listservs. Though the conversation is asynchronous, participants' diction has an intimate quality, based on trust that others will respond. These linguistic parallels suggest that the frequent touting of on-line discussion's unique capabilities for escaping the boundaries of "old" technologies may be off the mark. Networks like women's mission-movement publications served similar purposes in very similar ways.

67. J. H. J., "A Suggestive Incident," *WWW* 13 (Feb. 1883): 66.

68. "From Home Letters," *WWW* 9 (May 1879): 161.

69. "The Prayer Meeting Again," *WWW* 9 (July 1879): 235.

70. Mrs. W. A. Niles, "What Are the Best Methods for Enlisting Christian Women in Persistent Efforts for the Conversion of the Heathen?" *WWW* 9 (Aug. 1879): 272.

71. One of the tributes after her death noted that Heck was "present when the Union was organized in Richmond, Virginia, in 1888" and helped push its growth "from ten states to eighteen, from 1500 to over 13000 organizations." See "Editorial: The Day, Thy Day," *Royal Service* 10 (Oct. 1915): 5.

72. Fannie E. S. Heck, "A Great Event" (N.p., n.d.), Fannie E. S. Heck Papers, Wake Forest University Archives and Special Collections, Z. Smith Reynolds Library, Wake Forest University.

73. Fannie E. S. Heck, "The Things That . . . Remain" (Richmond: Foreign Mission Board, S.B.C., n.d.), Fannie E. S. Heck Papers., Wake Forest University Archives and Special Collections, Z. Smith Reynolds Library, Wake Forest University.

74. "Miss Fannie Heck Enters Into Rest." Fannie E. S. Heck Papers, Wake Forest University Archives and Special Collections, Z. Smith Reynolds Library, Wake Forest University.

75. "Editorial: Fannie Exile Scudder Heck," *Biblical Recorder,* Sept. 1, 1915.

76. See "Editorial: The Day, Thy Day," where Heck's editorship is credited with raising the subscriptions for *Our Mission Fields/Royal Service* from "its first free list of 6000" to a "paid-up subscription of over 21000" (5). (The name of the periodical was changed from *Our Mission Fields* to *Royal Service* to capitalize on audiences' familiarity with Heck's book and its themes.)

77. Susie M. Heck Smith, "A Portrait: Fannie E. S. Heck," Fannie E. S. Heck Papers, Wake Forest University Archives and Special Collections, Z. Smith Reynolds Library, Wake Forest University.

Conclusion

1. One trend evident in print publications for the clubwomen's movement—in both European American and African American clubs—involved efforts to make study groups more formal and professional. See Gere and Robbins, "Gendered Literacy in Black and White," 643–78.

2. On the history of conceptions of literacy driving school instructional programs, see Sarah Robbins, Mary Miesiezek, and Beth Andrews, "Promoting a Relevant Classroom Literacy," in *The Relevance of English: Teaching That Matters in Students' Lives,* ed. Robert P. Yagelski and Scott A. Leonard (Urbana: NCTE, 2002), 157–82. See also Myers, *Changing Our Minds.*

3. The genre had always been able to operate in hybrid ways—whether by interacting with forms like antislavery writing (as in Stowe) or with biographies, travel writing, and so on. However, narratives written around the time of Haygood's and Addams's texts tend to exhibit a different degree of "blending," with more textual elements coming from masculine, professional traditions.

4. See my "Rereading the History," 27–46. For Addams's use of literacy management techniques while writing for student publications, see her editorials for the *Rockford Seminary Magazine* (Dec. 1880): 280–82; (Feb. 1881): 54; (Mar. 1881): 85–88.

5. It is instructive to juxtapose the coverage of Hull-House in periodical pieces around the time of its founding with Addams's treatment of the settlement in her *Twenty Years* narrative. See the Hull-House Scrapbook, vol. 1, Hull-House Association Records, Jane Addams Memorial Collection, Special Collections, The University Library, University of Illinois at Chicago. Articles about Hull-House include many quotes from Addams describing the enterprise in terms of domestic benevolence.

6. Jane Addams, *Twenty Years at Hull-House*, 61.

7. See, for example, Mary Jo Deegan, *Jane Addams and the Men of the Chicago School, 1892–1918* (New Brunswick: Transition Books, 1990).

8. Shannon Jackson, *Performance, Historiography, Hull-House Domesticity* (Ann Arbor: University of Michigan Press, 2000). Jackson observes: "With thinkers such as Mead and Dewey constantly visiting the settlement—whether to teach a college extension class or to share an evening meal[–]Chicago pragmatism and Hull-House domesticity continually fed off of each other" (14–15).

9. Addams's being among the first generation of college women helped make her networking with university professionals possible, since she could confidently capitalize on her prior knowledge of academic fields formerly closed to even the most well-to-do of her sex.

10. James Hurt comments that "Addams's essentialist beliefs in women's natural intuitive powers and instincts toward benevolence and nurturance" continued to dominate her work, limiting her interest in suffrage and leading her to maintain a focus on "traditional roles" for women as "sacrificial caretakers of others." See Hurt's introduction to *Twenty Years at Hull-House*, xvii–xviii. Other commentators see her politics in more radical terms. Certainly, Addams did not hesitate to take an active part in controversial campaigns like workers' pursuit of legislation against sweatshops, and such interventions led to Hull-House losing some donors.

11. I have found no evidence that Addams was directly familiar with Frances E. W. Harper's models for community teaching, such as the portraits of androgynous activism in *Minnie's Sacrifice*. But Addams was aware of the work of African American women leaders in community reform, so she may have encountered Harper's writing through that connection. Ida B. Wells-Barnett's autobiography recounts contacts between Wells-Barnett and Addams, including one call to Hull-House by Wells-Barnett that resulted in the women collaborating to prevent Chicago's schools from being segregated. See Wells-Barnett, *Crusade for Justice*, 276–77.

12. Nancie Atwell, *In the Middle: New Understandings about Writing, Reading and Learning* (Portsmouth: Heinemann, 1998); Lucy McCormick Calkins, *Lessons from a Child* (Portsmouth: Heinemann, 1983); and Katie Wood Ray, *Wondrous Words: Writers and Writing in the Elementary Classroom* (Urbana: NCTE, 1999).

13. Constance Weaver, *Understanding Whole Language: From Principles to Practice* (Portsmouth: Heinemann, 1990), 3–4.

14. R. Mark Hall argues that, based upon its "enormous influence" on reading choices, Oprah's Book Club deserves increased "attention from the academic community," in particular from "literacy specialists," who need, among other things, to explore the ways Winfrey has advanced "the notion that reading makes life better." See "The 'Oprahfication' of Literacy: Reading 'Oprah's Book Club,'" *College English* 65 (July 2003): 647, 665. In referencing the "original" book club, I refer to the period between 1996 and 2002, before Winfrey suspended her regular recommendations for reading. After a hiatus during which several other television personalities started up similar enterprises but failed to have the same impact, Oprah began a new version of the club, making only occasional recommendations. The first choice under this new guise was John Steinbeck's *East of Eden* in mid-2003. In 2004, Oprah selected Gabriel García Márquez's *One Hundred Years of Solitude*.

15. As Laura Miller observes, from the outset, Franzen's reaction and Oprah's clearly miffed response were cast in gendered and class-based terms connected to popular-culture/high-culture biases. See Jonathan Franzen, *The Corrections* (New York: Farrar, Straus and Giroux, 2001); "Book Lovers' Quarrel," available at <http://www.salon.com/books/feature/2001/10/26/franzen_winfrey/index. html>.

16. Some faulted Oprah for choosing so many female-as-victim books like Ann-Marie MacDonald's *Fall on Your Knees* (with its incest-related plot), Janet Fitch's *White Oleander* (chronicling multiple types of abuse directed against a foster child), and Joyce Carol Oates's *We Were the Mulvaneys* (charting the devastating impact of a young girl's rape on her whole family). In fact, Franzen's initially negative comments about the book club seemed grounded in the negative perceptions that had grown up around such selections, giving little notice to choices like Isabel Allende's *Daughter of Fortune,* which centers on a strong female character taking control of historically significant challenges, or Ernest Gaines's *A Lesson Before Dying,* which focuses on an evolving teacher/learner relationship between two black men.

17. In this context, it is striking that Oprah's second version of the club was pegged to "classic" literary texts and that her first selection was by a canonical white male author.

18. As Elizabeth McHenry reminds us, Oprah's guidance of literacy also needs to be viewed within the context of African Americans' middle-class literary organizations in the nineteenth and early twentieth centuries. See McHenry, *Forgotten Readers,* 307–15.

19. Of course, many of these dual-career families may be consciously choosing to share child nurturance responsibilities, so as to allow both partners to work outside the home.

20. See "The Personal Responsibility and Work Opportunity Reconciliation Act of 1996," available at <http://www.acf.dhhs.gov/programs/opa/ facts/prwora96.htm>.

21. See Ron Kind, "Welfare Reform Must Continue to Promote Responsibility, While Empowering Individuals," available at <http://www.house.gov/kind/press/columns/108welfarebill.htm>.

22. See "Other Side of Welfare: Real Stories from a Single Mother," available at <http://www.drlaura.com/reading/?mode+view&id+172>.

23. Radway, *Reading the Romance,* 57–59, 86–118, 213.

24. Unidentified member of Oprah's Book Club, *The Oprah Winfrey Show,* July 6, 2001.

25. Amy Kaplan, "Manifest Domesticity," 584, 599, 602.

26. Along related lines, as I was revising this book in the summer of 2003, Office Depot repeatedly broadcast a television commercial of a mother taking her son shopping for school supplies. Though tongue in cheek, the advertisement seemed a marker of current attitudes about domestic literacy management. The commercial depicts the mother as imagining that arranging a quick purchase of the right items for the classroom is all she needs to do to ensure that her child will one day discover a galaxy, name it after his mother, and win the Nobel Prize. In today's consumer culture, it seems, the fantasy of buying easy school success has, at least for some of us, replaced the hard work of parental literacy management at home. Home schooling, in this context, has comlex social, political, and economic significance.

27. This quotation is as accurate as I could make it in notes I took just after audience members had left. Uncertain as I have felt about offering what might seem a too-perfect stereotype (e.g., through the soccer-mom reference), this mother's seemingly sincere stance led me to include her comments here.

Selected Bibliography

A Note on Conventions

In the nineteenth century, especially during the antebellum era, the idea of authorship as appropriate women's work had not yet been clearly established. Publishers often left works by women writers unsigned. In addition, books written by married women were as likely to use "Mrs." and the last name of the author as to identify her given name. Thus, the title pages for books by the writer we generally call "Lydia Sigourney" today might, in the nineteenth century, have named the author as "Mrs. L. H. Sigourney" or simply "Mrs. Sigourney," and sometimes her works were left unsigned. In this bibliography and in the endnotes, I have used the authors' first and last names, as we refer to them today. So, for instance, there are alphabetized listings for Elizabeth Sedgwick, Anna Laetitia Barbauld, and Lydia Sigourney, rather than mixed listings of "Mrs." names and given names that would reflect the inconsistent patterns on actual title pages for books I have used.

Abbott, Lyman. *Henry Ward Beecher.* New York: Houghton Mifflin, 1903. Edited by William G. McLoughlin. Reprint, New York: Chelsea House, 1980.

"Abroad—India." *Woman's Work for Woman* 7 (September 1877): 226–27.

"Abroad: The Chinese in America." *Woman's Work for Woman* 9 (November 1879): 361–67.

Addams, Jane. *Democracy and Social Ethics.* New York: Macmillan, 1902.

———. "Editorial." *Rockford Seminary Magazine* (December 1880): 280–82.

———. "Editorial." *Rockford Seminary Magazine* (February 1881): 54.

———. "Editorial." *Rockford Seminary Magazine* (March 1881): 85–88.

———. *Hull-House, A Social Settlement: An Outline Sketch, February, 1894.* Chicago: Hull-House, [1894].

———. *A New Conscience and an Ancient Evil.* New York: Macmillan, 1914.

———. *Twenty Years at Hull-House, with Autobiographical Notes.* 1910. Edited and with an introduction by James Hurt. Reprint, Urbana: University of Illinois Press, 1990.

Aikin, Dr. John, and Anna Laetitia Barbauld. *Evenings At Home by Mrs. Barbauld and Dr. Aikin. No. 3.* Philadelphia: Thomas Ash, 1828.

Allende, Isabel. *Daughter of Fortune.* New York: HarperCollins, 1999.

Alvord, J. W. *Fourth Semi-Annual Report on Schools for the Freedmen, July 1, 1867.* Washington: Government Printing Office, 1867–68.

———. *Sixth Semi-Annual Report on Schools for the Freedmen, July 1, 1868.* Washington: Government Printing Office, 1868.

American Popular Lessons, Chiefly Selected from the Writings of Mrs. Barbauld, Miss Edgeworth and other Approved Authors. Designed particularly for the younger classes of children in schools. New York: Heustis, 1820.

Ammons, Elizabeth. "Stowe's Dream of the Mother-Savior: *Uncle Tom's Cabin* and American Women Writers before the 1920s." In Sundquist, *New Essays on* Uncle Tom's Cabin, 155–95.

Anderson, Benedict. *Imagined Communities: Reflections on the Origin and Spread of Nationalism.* Rev. ed. London: Verso, 1991.

Anderson, James D. *The Education of Blacks in the South, 1860–1935.* Chapel Hill: University of North Carolina Press, 1988.

Argyle, Michael. *The Psychology of Social Class.* New York: Routledge, 1994.

"At Home: Child Marriage." *Woman's Work for Woman* 7 (February 1877): 412–15.

"At Home: Semi-annual Meeting." *Woman's Work for Woman* 7 (November 1877): 286–88.

Atwell, Nancie. *In the Middle: New Understandings about Writing, Reading and Learning.* Portsmouth: Heinemann, 1998.

Avery, Gillian. *Behold the Child: American Children and Their Books, 1621–1922.* Baltimore: Johns Hopkins University Press, 1994.

Baker, Houston A., Jr. *Turning South Again: Re-thinking Modernism/Re-reading Booker T.* Durham: Duke University Press, 2001.

Bakhtin, M. M. *The Dialogic Imagination: Four Essays.* Edited by Michael Holquist. Translated by Caryl Emerson and Michael Holquist. Austin: University of Texas Press, 1981.

Baldwin, James. "Everybody's Protest Novel." In *Critical Essays on Harriet Beecher Stowe,* edited by Elizabeth Ammons, 92–97. Boston: G. K. Hall, 1980. Originally published in *Partisan Review* 16 (1949): 578–85.

Banks, Marva. "*Uncle Tom's Cabin* and Antebellum Black Response." In *Readers in History: American Literature and the Contexts of Response,* edited by James L. Machor, 209–27. Baltimore: Johns Hopkins University Press, 1993.

Barbauld, Anna Laetitia. *Hymns in Prose, for the Use of Children.* Revised by the Community of the Publication of the American Sunday School Union. Philadelphia: American Sunday School Union, 1827.

——. *Lessons for Children.* Charleston: J. Hoff, 1807.

——. *Lessons for Children.* Boston: William Carter and Brother, 1861.

——. *Lessons for Children, by Mrs. Barbauld. With Engravings.* Greenfield, [N.H.]: A. Phelps, 1843.

——. *Lessons for Children in Four Parts.* Philadelphia: Benjamin Warner, 1818.

——. *Lessons for Children in Four Parts.* New York: W. B. Gilley, 1825.

——. *Lessons for Children in Four Parts with Engravings.* Philadelphia: Anthony Finley, 1821.

——. *Little Charles, embellished with coloured engravings.* Boston: Lilly, Wait, and Co., 1833–34.

——. *Little Marrian.* Edited by Mrs. Colman. Boston: Phillips & Sampson, 1845.

——. *Little Marrian.* Boston: William Carter and Brother, 1861.

——. *Mrs. Barbauld's Lessons, admirably adapted to the capacities of children.* New York: D. Bliss, 1806.

——. *Mrs. Barbauld's Lessons for Children.* Boston: Munroe and Francis, 1850.

Barbauld, Anna Laetitia, and Lucy Aikin. *The Works of Anna Laetitia Barbauld, with a Memoir by Lucy Aikin.* Edited by Lucy Aikin. 2 vols. London: Longman, 1825.

Barbauld, Anna Laetitia, and Maria Edgeworth. *Lessons for Children with Eight Coloured Engravings.* New York: S. King, 1823.

Barker, Paula. "The Domestication of Politics: Women and American Political Society, 1780–1920." *American Historical Review* 89 (June 1984): 593–619.

Barthes, Roland. "The Death of the Author." In Lodge, *Modern Criticism and Theory: A Reader,* 166–71.

Bates, Clara Doty. "Our Lady of the House." 1892. Partial clipping. Scrapbooks, vol. 1. Hull-House Association Records. Jane Addams Memorial Collection. Special Collections, The University Library, University of Illinois at Chicago.

Baym, Nina. *American Women Writers and the Work of History, 1790–1860*. New Brunswick: Rutgers University Press, 1995.

———. *Feminism and American Literary History: Essays*. New Brunswick: Rutgers University Press, 1992.

———. *Novels, Readers, and Reviewers: Responses to Fiction in Antebellum America*. Ithaca: Cornell University Press, 1984.

———. "Reinventing Lydia Sigourney." In *The (Other) American Traditions: Nineteenth-Century Women Writers*, edited by Joyce W. Warren, 54–72. New Brunswick: Rutgers University Press, 1993.

———. *Woman's Fiction: A Guide to Novels by and about Women in America, 1820–70*. 2d ed. Urbana: University of Illinois Press, 1993.

Beatty, Barbara. *Preschool Education in America: The Culture of Young Children from the Colonial Era to the Present*. New Haven: Yale University Press, 1995.

Beecher, Catharine. *Educational Reminiscences and Suggestions*. New York: J. B. Ford, 1874.

———. Letter to Sarah Terry. 1829. Katharine S. Day Collection. Stowe-Day Library.

———. *Suggestions Respecting Improvements in Education, Presented to the Trustees of the Hartford Female Seminary, and published at their request*. Hartford: Packard & Butler, 1829.

Beecher-Stowe Family Papers. Schlesinger Library, Radcliffe Institute, Harvard University.

Berkson, Dorothy. "'So We All Became Mothers': Harriet Beecher Stowe, Charlotte Perkins Gilman, and the New World of Woman's Culture." In *Feminism, Utopia, and Narrative*, edited by Sarah Webster Goodwin and Libby F. Jones, 100–115. Tennessee Studies in Literature 32. Knoxville: University of Tennessee Press, 1990.

Berlant, Lauren. "The Female Complaint." *Social Text* 19 (Fall 1988): 237–59.

———. "The Queen of America Goes to Washington City: Harriet Jacobs, Frances Harper, and Anita Hill." *American Literature* 65 (September 1993): 549–74.

"Bethune, Mary McLeod." In *Black Women in America: An Historical Encyclopedia*, edited by Darlene Clark Hine, Elsa Barkley Brown, and Rosalyn Terborg-Penn, 1: 113–26. Bloomington: Indiana University Press, 1993.

Bhabha, Homi K. *The Location of Culture*. London: Routledge, 1994.

Bodichon, Barbara Leigh Smith. *Women and Work. With an Introduction by Catherine M. Sedgwick*. New York: C. M. Francis, 1859.

Bolles, John A. "The Influence of Women in Society." *Ladies' Magazine* 4 (June 1831): 265.

"Books and Authors." *American Ladies' Magazine* 7 (January 1834): 43.

Botume, Elizabeth Hyde. *First Days Amongst the Contrabands*. 1893. Reprint, New York: Arno Press, 1968.

Bourdieu, Pierre. "Concluding Remarks." In Calhoun, LiPuma, and Postone, *Bourdieu: Critical Perspectives*, 263–75.

Boxer, Marilyn Jacoby. *When Women Ask the Questions: Creating Women's Studies in America*. Baltimore: Johns Hopkins University Press, 1998.

Boyd, Melba Joyce. *Discarded Legacy: Politics and Poetics in the Life of Frances E. W. Harper, 1825–1911*. Detroit: Wayne State University Press, 1994.

Boydston, Jeanne. *Home and Work: Housework, Wages, and the Ideology of Labor in the Early Republic*. New York: Oxford University Press, 1991.

Boydston, Jeanne, Mary Kelley, and Anne Margolis. *The Limits of Sisterhood: The*

Beecher Sisters on Women's Rights and the Woman's Sphere. Chapel Hill: University of North Carolina Press, 1988.

Brandt, Deborah. "Sponsors of Literacy." *CCC: College Composition and Communication* 49 (May 1998): 165–85.

Brodhead, Richard H. *Cultures of Letters: Scenes of Reading and Writing in Nineteenth-Century America.* Chicago: University of Chicago Press, 1994.

———. "Sparing the Rod: Discipline and Fiction in Antebellum America." *Representations* 21 (Winter 1988): 67–96.

———, ed. *The Journals of Charles W. Chesnutt.* Durham: Duke University Press, 1993.

Brown, Gillian. *Domestic Individualism: Imagining Self in Nineteenth-Century America.* Berkeley: University of California Press, 1990.

Brown, Oswald Eugene, and Anna Muse Brown. *Life and Letters of Laura Askew Haygood.* Nashville: Smith and Lamar, Publishing House of the M. E. Church, South, 1904.

Buell, Lawrence. *New England Literary Culture from Revolution through Renaissance.* Cambridge: Cambridge University Press, 1989.

Burgett, Bruce. *Sentimental Bodies: Sex, Gender, and Citizenship in the Early Republic.* Princeton: Princeton University Press, 1998.

Burton, Warren. *The District School as It Was.* 1850. Reprint, New York: Arno Press, 1969.

Bushnell, Albert. *My Mother: With Poetry and a Preface by Mrs. Lydia H. Sigourney.* Oberlin, [Ohio]: Fitch, 1848.

Calhoun, Craig, Edward LiPuma, and Moishe Postone, eds. *Bourdieu: Critical Perspectives.* Chicago: University of Chicago Press, 1993.

Calkins, Lucy McCormick. *Lessons from a Child.* Portsmouth: Heinemann, 1983.

Capp, Mrs. "China–Tungchow." *Woman's Work for Woman* 7 (July 1877): 145–47.

Carby, Hazel V. *Reconstructing Womanhood: The Emergence of the Afro-American Woman Novelist.* New York: Oxford University Press, 1987.

Casper, Scott E. *Constructing American Lives: Biography and Culture in Nineteenth-Century America.* Chapel Hill: University of North Carolina Press, 1999.

Catalogue of the Officers, Teachers, and Pupils of the Hartford Female Seminary for the Summer Term of 1828. Hartford Female Seminary Catalogue. Folder 320, Beecher-Stowe Family Papers. Schlesinger Library, Radcliffe Institute, Harvard University.

"Cheering Words from Auxiliaries." *Woman's Work for Woman* 9 (January 1879): 20–21.

Chesnutt, Charles W. *The House Behind the Cedars.* Boston: Houghton Mifflin, 1900.

Child, Lydia Maria. *Emily Parker; or, Impulse, Not Principle. Intended for Young Persons.* Boston: Isaac R. Butts & Co., 1827.

———. *Flowers for Children.* New York: C. S. Francis and Co., 1854; Boston: J. H. Francis, 1854.

———. *Good Wives.* Boston: Carter, Hendee, and Co., 1833.

———. *The History of the Condition of Women, In Various Ages and Nations.* 2 vols. Boston: John Allen & Co., 1835.

———. *Hobomok and Other Writings on Indians.* Edited by Carolyn L. Karcher. New Brunswick: Rutgers University Press, 1991.

———. "Louisa Preston." In *A Lydia Maria Child Reader,* edited by Carolyn L. Karcher, 101–11. Durham: Duke University Press, 1997. Originally published in *Juvenile Miscellany* 4 (March 1828): 56–81.

———. *The Mother's Book.* 2d ed. Boston: Carter and Hendee, 1831. Reprint, Old Sturbridge, [Mass.]: Applewood Books, 1992.

———. ed. *Looking Toward Sunset.* Boston: Ticknor and Fields, 1865.

"Chronicles of a School Room; Published by Cottons and Carnard." Review of *Chronicles of a Schoolroom*, by Mrs. S. C. Hall. *Ladies' Magazine* 3 (August 1830): 375–79.

"Clarence; or, A Tale of Our Own Time." Review of *Clarence; or, A Tale of Our Own Time*, by Catharine Maria Sedgwick. *Ladies' Magazine* 3 (July 1830): 320–25.

Clifford, Geraldine Joncich. "Women's Liberation and Women's Professions: Reconsidering the Past, Present and Future." In Faragher and Howe, *Women and Higher Education in American History*, 165–82.

Cohn, Marvin, and George Stricker. "Inadequate Perception vs. Reversals." *Reading Teacher* 30 (1976): 33–36.

Collins, Patricia Hill. "Toward a New Vision: Race, Class, and Gender as Categories of Analysis and Connection." In Levine, *Social Class and Stratification: Classic Statements and Theoretical Debates*, 231–47.

Collins, Vicki Tolar. "The Speaker Respoken: Material Rhetoric as Feminist Methodology." *College English* 61 (May 1999): 545–73.

"Conducting a Ladies' Prayer Meeting." *Woman's Work for Woman* 9 (February 1879): 54.

"Conducting a Prayer Meeting." *Woman's Work for Woman* 9 (May 1879): 158–59.

"Convents Are Increasing." *Ladies' Magazine* 7 (December 1834): 560–64.

Cooke, Grace MacGowan. *The Power and the Glory.* New York: Doubleday, Page & Co., 1910. Reprint, Boston: Northeastern University Press, 2003.

Cott, Nancy. *The Bonds of Womanhood: "Woman's Sphere" in New England, 1780–1835.* New Haven: Yale University Press, 1997.

Coultrap-McQuin, Susan Margaret. *Doing Literary Business: American Women Writers in the Nineteenth Century.* Chapel Hill: University of North Carolina Press, 1990.

Cox, James M. "Harriet Beecher Stowe: From Sectionalism to Regionalism." *Nineteenth Century* 38 (1984): 444–66.

Crain, Patricia. *The Story of A: The Alphabetization of America from* The New England Primer *to* The Scarlet Letter. Stanford: Stanford University Press, 2000.

"Critical Notices." Review of *Charlotte's Daughter*, by Susanna Rowson. *Ladies' Magazine* 1 (April 1828): 190–95.

Crumpacker, Laurie. "Four Novels of Harriet Beecher Stowe: A Study in Nineteenth-Century Androgyny." In *American Novelists Revisited: Essays in Feminist Criticism*, edited by Fritz Fleischmann, 78–106. Boston: Hall, 1982.

Daniels, Bruce C. *The Fragmentation of New England: Comparative Perspectives on Economic, Political, and Social Divisions in the Eighteenth Century.* New York: Greenwood Press, 1988.

Davidson, Cathy N. "Preface: No More Separate Spheres!" *American Literature* 70 (September 1998): 443–64.

——. *Revolution and the Word: The Rise of the Novel in America.* New York: Oxford University Press, 1986.

——, ed. *Reading in America: Literature and Social History.* Baltimore: Johns Hopkins University Press, 1989.

Deegan, Mary Jo. *Jane Addams and the Men of the Chicago School, 1892–1918.* New Brunswick: Transition Books, 1990.

DeForest, John W. "The Man and Brother, I." *Atlantic Monthly* 22 (September 1868): 337–48.

——. "The Man and Brother, II." *Atlantic Monthly* 22 (October 1868): 414–25.

Devitt, Amy J. "Integrating Rhetorical and Literary Theories of Genre." *College English* 62 (July 2000): 696–718.

Dewey, Mary E., ed. *Life and Letters of Catharine M. Sedgwick.* New York: Harper & Brothers, 1871.

Diner, Hasia R. *Erin's Daughters: Irish Immigrant Women in the Nineteenth Century.* Baltimore: Johns Hopkins University Press, 1983.

Douglas, Ann. *The Feminization of American Culture.* New York: Doubleday, 1977.

Douglass, Frederick. "Narrative of the Life of Frederick Douglass." 1845. In *The Classic Slave Narratives,* edited by Henry Louis Gates Jr., 243–332. New York: Mentor/Penguin, 1987.

Eastman, Mrs. Mary H. *Aunt Phillis' Cabin; or, Southern Life as It Is.* Philadelphia: Lippincott, 1852.

Eddy, Rev. Daniel C. *The Three Mrs. Judsons, and Other Daughters of the Cross.* Boston: Thayer and Eldridge, 1855, 1860.

Eddy, Miss H. M. "Syria—Sidon." *Woman's Work for Woman* 7 (February 1877): 410–11.

"Editorial: Fannie Exile Scudder Heck." *Biblical Recorder,* September 1, 1915.

"Editorial: The Day, Thy Day." *Royal Service* 10 (October 1915): 5.

Eldred, Janet Carey, and Peter Mortensen. "Monitoring Columbia's Daughters: Writing as Gendered Conduct." *Rhetoric Society Quarterly* 23 (Summer–Fall 1993): 46–69.

——. "'Persuasion Dwelt on Her Tongue': Female Civic Rhetoric in Early America." *College English* 60 (February 1998): 173–88.

Ellis, Grace. *A Memoir of Mrs. Anna Laetitia Barbauld with Many of Her Letters.* 2 vols. Boston: James R. Osgood and Co., 1874.

Ernest, John. "From Mysteries to Histories: Cultural Pedagogy in Frances E. W. Harper's *Iola Leroy.*" *American Literature* 64 (September 1992): 497–518.

Evans, Augusta Jane. *Beulah.* 1859, 1900. Edited by Elizabeth Fox-Genovese. Reprint, Baton Rouge: Louisiana State University Press, 1992.

Fabi, M. Giulia. "Reconstructing Literary Genealogies: Frances E. W. Harper's and William Dean Howells's Race Novels." In *Soft Canons: American Women Writers and Masculine Tradition,* edited by Karen L. Kilcup, 48–66. Iowa City: University of Iowa Press, 1999.

Fannie E. S. Heck Papers. Wake Forest University Archives and Special Collections, Z. Smith Reynolds Library, Wake Forest University.

Faragher, John Mack, and Florence Howe, eds. *Women and Higher Education in American History.* New York: Norton, 1988.

A Father. "The Question." *Ladies' Magazine* 7 (October 1834): 476–78.

"Female Education." *Ladies' Magazine* 7 (November 1834): 499–502.

"Female Education: Notice of an Address on Female Education, delivered in Portsmouth, N. H., October 26, 1827. By the Rev. Charles Burroughs." *Ladies' Magazine* 1 (January 1828): 21–27.

"Female Seminaries I." *Ladies' Magazine* 6 (March 1833): 139–42.

"Female Seminaries II." *Ladies' Magazine* 6 (April 1833): 176–79.

"Female Seminaries—No. III. Scottsboro Institute." *Ladies' Magazine* 6 (May 1833): 228–31.

Fetterley, Judith. "'My Sister! My Sister!': The Rhetoric of Catharine Sedgwick's *Hope Leslie.*" *American Literature* 70 (September 1998): 491–549.

Fields, Annie, ed. *The Life and Letters of Harriet Beecher Stowe.* Boston: Houghton, 1897.

Fingeret, Hanna Arlene, and Cassandra Drennon. *Literacy for Life: Adult Learners, New Practices.* New York: Teachers College Press, 1997.

Finkelstein, Barbara. "Reading, Writing and the Acquisition of Identity in the United States, 1790–1860." In Finkelstein, *Regulated Children/Liberated Children,* 114–39.

———, ed. *Regulated Children/Liberated Children: Education in Psychohistorical Perspective.* New York: Psychohistory Press, 1979.

Fitch, Janet. *White Oleander.* New York: Little, Brown, 1999.

Fitts, Deborah. "Una and the Lion: The Feminization of District School-Teaching and Its Effects on the Roles of Students and Teachers in Middle-Class Massachusetts," In Finkelstein, *Regulated Children/Liberated Children,* 140–57.

Foner, Eric. *A Short History of Reconstruction, 1863–77.* New York: Harper and Row, 1990.

Foreman, P. Gabrielle. "'Reading Aright': White Slavery, Black Referents, and the Strategy of Histotextuality in *Iola Leroy.*" *Yale Journal of Criticism: Interpretation in the Humanities* 10 (Fall 1997): 327–54.

Foster, Frances Smith. "African Americans, Literature, and the Nineteenth-Century Afro-Protestant Press." In *Reciprocal Influences: Literary Production, Distribution, and Consumption in America,* edited by Steven Fink and Susan S. Williams, 24–35. Columbus: Ohio State University Press, 1999.

———. *Written By Herself: Literary Production by African American Women, 1746–1892.* Bloomington: Indiana University Press, 1993.

———, ed. *A Brighter Coming Day: A Frances Ellen Watkins Harper Reader.* New York: Feminist Press, 1990.

Foster, Hannah. *The Boarding School; or, Lessons of a Preceptress to Her Pupils.* Boston: I. Thomas and E. T. Andrews, 1798.

Foucault, Michel. *Discipline and Punish: The Birth of the Prison.* New York: Vintage Books, 1979.

———. "What Is an Author?" In Lodge, *Modern Criticism and Theory: A Reader,* 197–210.

———. "What Is an Author?" In *Textual Strategies: Perspectives in Post-Structuralist Criticism,* edited by Josué V. Harari, 141–60. Ithaca: Cornell University Press, 1979.

Franzen, Jonathan. *The Corrections.* New York: Farrar, Straus and Giroux, 2001.

Frederickson, Mary E. "Shaping a New Society." In *Women in New Worlds: Historical Perspectives on the Wesleyan Tradition,* edited by Hilah F. Thomas and Rosemary Skinner Keller, 1: 345–61. Nashville: Abingdon, 1981.

Freire, Paulo. *Education for a Critical Consciousness.* Translated by Myra B. Ramos. New York: Continuum, 1974.

———. *Pedagogy of Hope: Reliving Pedagogy of the Oppressed.* Translated by Robert R. Barr. New York: Continuum, 1995.

———. *Pedagogy of the Oppressed.* Thirtieth anniversary ed. Translated by Myra Bergman Ramos. New York: Continuum, 2000.

Friedman, Jean E. *Ways of Wisdom: Moral Education in the Early National Period, Including the Diary of Rachel Mordecai Lazarus.* Athens: University of Georgia Press, 2001.

"From Home Letters." *Woman's Work for Woman* 9 (May 1879): 161.

Gaines, Ernest. *A Lesson before Dying.* New York: Knopf, 1993.

George, Rosemary Marangoly. "Homes in the Empire, Empires in the Home." *Cultural Critique* 26 (Winter 1993–94): 95–127.

Gere, Anne Ruggles. *Intimate Practices: Literacy and Cultural Work in U.S. Women's Clubs, 1880–1920.* Urbana: University of Illinois Press, 1997.

Gere, Anne Ruggles, and Sarah R. Robbins. "Gendered Literacy in Black and White: Turn-of-the-Century African-American and European-American Club Women's Printed Texts." *Signs* 21 (Spring 1996): 643–78.

Gilmore, William J. *Reading Becomes a Necessity of Life: Material and Cultural Life in Rural New England, 1780–1835.* Knoxville: University of Tennessee Press, 1989.

Ginzberg, Lori D. *Women and the Work of Benevolence: Morality, Politics, and Class in the Nineteenth-Century United States.* New Haven: Yale University Press, 1990.

Glazner, Nancy. *Reading for Realism: The History of a U.S. Literary Institution, 1850–1910.* Durham: Duke University Press, 1997.

"Gleanings." *Woman's Work for Woman* 9 (November 1879): 392–93.

Gossett, Thomas F. Uncle Tom's Cabin *and American Culture.* Dallas: Southern Methodist University Press, 1985.

Gowen, Sheryl Greenwood. *The Politics of Workplace Literacy: A Case Study.* New York: Teachers College Press, 1992.

Grant, David. "*Uncle Tom's Cabin* and the Triumph of Republican Rhetoric." *New England Quarterly* 71 (September 1998): 429–48.

Green, Elizabeth Alden. *Mary Lyon and Mount Holyoke: Opening the Gates.* Hanover: University Press of New England, 1979.

Greenblatt, Stephen. "Culture." In *Critical Terms for Literary Study,* edited by Frank Lentricchia and Thomas McLaughlin, 2d ed., 225–32. Chicago: University of Chicago Press, 1995.

Greene-Roelker Papers. MSS/q G812 r/RM. Research Library, The Cincinnati Historical Society.

Grimké, Charlotte Forten. *The Journals of Charlotte Forten Grimké.* Edited by Brenda Stevenson. New York: Oxford University Press, 1988.

——. "Life on the Sea Islands, Part I." *Atlantic Monthly* 13 (May 1864): 587–96.

——. "Life on the Sea Islands, Part II." *Atlantic Monthly* 13 (June 1864): 666–76.

Guillory, John. *Cultural Capital: The Problem of Literary Canon Formation.* Chicago: University of Chicago Press, 1993.

Hale, Sarah Josepha. "The Four Portraits." *Ladies' Magazine* 3 (March 1830): 96–110.

——. "Introduction." *Ladies' Magazine* 1 (January 1828): 1–4.

——. "Miss Harriet Martineau." *American Ladies' Magazine* 7 (April 1834): 13–17.

——. "Our Title." *American Ladies' Magazine* 7 (January 1834): 48.

——. "Remarks." *Ladies' Magazine* 4 (April 1831): 165–69.

——, ed. *Things by Their Right names, and Other Stories, Fables, and Moral Pieces, in Prose and Verse, Selected and Arranged From the Writings of Mrs. Barbauld, with a Sketch of Her Life, by Mrs. S. J. Hale.* Boston: Marsh, Capen, Lyon, & Webb, 1840.

——, ed. *Woman's Record; or, Sketches of All Distinguished Women from the Creation to A.D. 1854. Arranged in four eras, with selections from female writers of every age.* 2d ed., rev. New York: Harper, 1855.

Hall, David D. *Cultures of Print: Essays in the History of the Book.* Amherst: University of Massachusetts Press, 1996.

Hall, R. Mark. "The 'Oprahfication' of Literacy: Reading 'Oprah's Book Club.'" *College English* 65 (July 2003): 646–68.

Hall, Mrs. S. C. *Chronicles of a School Room.* Boston: Cottons and Barnard, 1830.

Harding, Sandra. "Rethinking Standpoint Epistemology: 'What Is Strong Objectivity?'" In *Feminist Epistemologies,* edited by Linda Alcoff and Elizabeth Potter, 49–82. New York: Routledge, 1993.

Harper, Frances E. W. *Iola Leroy; or, Shadows Uplifted.* 1892. Edited by Frances Smith Foster. Reprint, New York: Oxford University Press, 1988.

——. *Minnie's Sacrifice, Sowing and Reaping, Trial and Triumph: Three Rediscovered Novels.* Edited by Frances Smith Foster. Boston: Beacon Press, 1994.

Harris, Susan K. *The Cultural Work of the Late Nineteenth-Century Hostess: Annie Adams Fields and Mary Gladstone Drew.* New York: Palgrave/Macmillan, 2002.

Haskin, Sara Estelle. *Women and Missions in the Methodist Episcopal Church, South.* Nashville: M. E. Church, Smith and Lamar, 1920.

Haygood, Laura A. "Relation of Female Education to Home Mission Work." In *Life and Letters of Laura Askew Haygood*, edited by Oswald Eugene Brown and Anna Muse Brown, 89–95. Nashville: Smith and Lamar, Publishing House of the M. E. Church, South, 1904.

Heath, Shirley Brice. *Ways with Words: Language, Life, and Work in Communities and Classrooms*. New York: Cambridge University Press, 1983.

Heck, Fannie E. S. "A Great Event." N.p., n.d. Fannie E. S. Heck Papers. Wake Forest University Archives and Special Collections, Z. Smith Reynolds Library, Wake Forest University.

——. "The Things That . . . Remain." Richmond: Foreign Mission Board, S. B. C., n.d. Fannie E. S. Heck Papers. Wake Forest University Archives and Special Collections, Z. Smith Reynolds Library, Wake Forest University.

Hedrick, Joan D. *Harriet Beecher Stowe: A Life*. New York: Oxford University Press, 1994.

——. "'Peaceable Fruits': The Ministry of Harriet Beecher Stowe." *American Quarterly* 40 (June 1988): 307–32.

Hennessy, Rosemary. *Materialist Feminism and the Politics of Discourse*. New York: Routledge, 1993.

——. "Subjects, Knowledges, . . . and All the Rest: Speaking for What?" In *Who Can Speak? Authority and Critical Identity*, edited by Judith Roof and Robyn Wiegman, 137–50. Urbana: University of Illinois Press, 1995.

Higonnet, Margaret R. "Comparative Reading: Catharine M. Sedgwick's *Hope Leslie*." *Legacy* 15 (1998): 17–22.

Hill, Patricia R. *The World Their Household: The American Woman's Foreign Mission Movement and Cultural Transformation, 1870–1920*. Ann Arbor: University of Michigan Press, 1985.

Hooker, Isabella. Speech for the 1892 Hartford Female Seminary Reunion. Reprinted in the Program for the Reunion. American Antiquarian Society.

Howard, June. "What is Sentimentalism?" *American Literary History* 11 (Spring 1999): 63–81.

"How Ought Women to be Educated." *Ladies' Magazine* 5 (November 1832): 508–15.

Hughs, Mary, ed. *Selections from the Works of Mrs. Barbauld with Extracts from Miss Aikin's Memoir of That Lady*. Philadelphia: R. H. Small, 1828.

"The Huguenot Seminary of South Africa." *Woman's Work for Woman* 12 (July 1882): 217–20.

Hull, Glenda. "Hearing Other Voices: A Critical Assessment of Popular Views on Literacy and Work." In *Changing Work, Changing Workers: Critical Perspectives on Language, Literacy, and Skills*, edited by Glenda Hull, 3–31. Albany: State University of New York Press, 1997.

Hull-House Bulletin 1.1. Hull-House Association Records. Jane Addams Memorial Collection. Special Collections, The University Library, University of Illinois at Chicago.

Hull-House Bulletin 7. Chicago: Hull-House, 1905–6.

Hull-House Scrapbook. Vol. 1. Hull-House Association Records. Jane Addams Memorial Collection. Special Collections, The University Library, University of Illinois at Chicago.

Hull-House Year Book; September 1, 1906–September 1, 1907. Chicago: Hull-House, 1907.

Hunter, Jane. *The Gospel of Gentility: American Women Missionaries in Turn-of-the-Century China*. New Haven: Yale University Press, 1984.

Hunter, Tera W. *To 'Joy My Freedom: Southern Black Women's Lives and Labors after the Civil War*. Cambridge: Harvard University Press, 1997.

Hurt, James. Introduction to *Twenty Years at Hull House, with Autobiographical Notes*, by Jane Addams. Edited by James Hurt. Urbana: University of Illinois Press, 1990.

Hyatt, Irwin T., Jr. *Our Ordered Lives Confess: Three Nineteenth-Century American Missionaries in East Shantung*. Cambridge: Harvard University Press, 1976.

Ignatiev, Noel. *How the Irish Became White*. New York: Routledge, 1995.

"India." *Woman's Work for Woman* 13 (January 1883): 10.

"Infant Schools." *Ladies' Magazine* 5 (April 1832): 179–82.

"The Influence of Manners." *Ladies' Magazine* 7 (1834): 216–17.

"The Influence of Women on Society." *Ladies' Magazine* 4 (June 1831): 256–69.

Jackson, Shannon. *Performance, Historiography, Hull-House Domesticity*. Ann Arbor: University of Michigan Press, 2000.

Jacobs, Harriet. *Incidents in the Life of a Slave Girl*. 1861. Edited by Jean Fagan Yellin. Reprint, Cambridge: Harvard University Press, 1987.

Jameson, Fredric. *The Political Unconscious: Narrative as a Socially Symbolic Act*. Ithaca: Cornell University Press, 1981.

Jane Addams Memorial Collection. Special Collections, The University Library, University of Illinois at Chicago.

Jeter, J. B. *A Memoir of Mrs. Henrietta Shuck, The First American Female Missionary to China*. Boston: Gould, Kendall, and Lincoln, 1846.

J. H. J. "A Suggestive Incident." *Woman's Work for Woman* 13 (February 1883): 66.

Johnson, Whittington B. "A Black Teacher and Her School in Reconstruction Darien: The Correspondence of Hettie Sabattie and J. Murray Hoag, 1868–1869." *Georgia Historical Quarterly* 85 (Spring 1991): 90–105.

Jones, Jacqueline. *Soldiers of Light and Love: Northern Teachers and Georgia Blacks, 1865–1873*. Chapel Hill: University of North Carolina Press, 1980.

"Josiah Henson." Pamphlet. Cincinnati: The Harriet Beecher Stowe House, 1991.

Kaestle, Carl F. *Pillars of the Republic: Common Schools and American Society 1780–1860*. New York: Hill and Wang, 1983.

Kaestle, Carl F., et al., eds. *Literacy in the United States: Readers and Reading since 1880*. New Haven: Yale University Press, 1991.

Kaplan, Amy. "Manifest Domesticity." *American Literature* 70 (September 1998): 581–606.

Karcher, Carolyn. *The First Woman in the Republic: A Cultural Biography of Lydia Maria Child*. Durham: Duke University Press, 1994.

——, ed. *A Lydia Maria Child Reader*. Durham: Duke University Press, 1997.

Kaufman, Polly Welts. *Women Teachers on the Frontier*. New Haven: Yale University Press, 1984.

Keckley, Elizabeth. *Behind the Scenes: Thirty Years a Slave and Four Years in the White House*. New York: G. W. Carleton, 1868.

Kelley, Mary. "'A More Glorious Revolution': Women's Antebellum Reading Circles and the Pursuit of Public Influence." *New England Quarterly* 76 (June 2003): 163–96.

——. "Negotiating a Self: The Autobiography and Journals of Catharine Maria Sedgwick." *New England Quarterly* 66 (September 1993): 366–98.

——. *Private Woman, Public Stage: Literary Domesticity in Nineteenth-Century America*. New York: Oxford University Press, 1984.

——, ed. *The Power of Her Sympathy: The Autobiography and Journals of Catharine Maria Sedgwick*. Boston: Massachusetts Historical Society, 1993.

Kerber, Linda K. "Separate Spheres, Female Worlds, Woman's Place: The Rhetoric of Woman's History." *Journal of American History* 75 (1988): 9–39.

———. *Women of the Republic: Intellect and Ideology in Revolutionary America.* Chapel Hill: University of North Carolina Press, 1980.

Kind, Ron. Congressman, Third Congressional District of Wisconsin. "Welfare Reform Must Continue to Promote Responsibility, While Empowering Individuals." Available at <http://www.house.gov/kind/press/columns/108welfarebill.htm>.

King, Marjorie. "Exhorting Femininity, Not Feminism: Nineteenth-Century U.S. Missionary Women's Efforts to Emancipate Chinese Women." In *Women's Work for Women: Missionaries and Social Change in Asia,* edited by Leslie A. Flemming, 117–36. Boulder: Westview Press, 1989.

Kolodny, Annette. "Inventing a Feminist Discourse: Rhetoric and Resistance in Margaret Fuller's Woman in the Nineteenth Century." In *Reclaiming Rhetorica: Women in the Rhetorical Tradition,* edited by Andrea A. Lunsford, 137–66. Pittsburgh: University of Pittsburgh Press, 1995.

Konzett, Delia Caparose. "Administered Identities and Linguistic Assimilation: The Politics of Immigrant English in Anzia Yezierska's *Hungry Hearts.*" *American Literature* 69 (September 1997): 595–620.

Landry, Donna. "Figures of the Feminine: An Amazonian Revolution in Feminist Literary History?" In *The Uses of Literary History,* edited by Marshall Brown, 107–28. Durham: Duke University Press, 1995.

Larcom, Lucy. *A New England Girlhood: Outlined from Memory.* 1889. Reprint, Boston: Northeastern University Press, 1986.

"A Lecture on the Education of Females. Delivered before the American Institute of Instruction, August 1831. By George B. Emerson. Boston: Hilliard, Gray, Little & Willkins." *Ladies' Magazine* 5 (March 1832): 140–44.

"Letters to Young Ladies. By a Lady. Hartford: printed by P. Canfield." Review of *Letters to Young Ladies,* by Lydia Sigourney. *Ladies' Magazine* 6 (August 1833): 377–74.

Levin, Joanna. "'Neither Strictly Native Nor Wholly Foreign': Bohemian New York at the Turn-of-the-Century." Paper presented at the annual meeting of the Modern Language Association, New York, December 2002.

Levine, Rhonda F. "Conclusion." In Levine, *Social Class and Stratification: Classic Statements and Theoretical Debates,* 249–60.

———, ed. *Social Class and Stratification: Classic Statements and Theoretical Debates.* Lanham: Rowman and Littlefield, 1998.

L. H. S. "Comparative Intellect of the Sexes." *Ladies' Magazine* (June 1834): 242–43.

LiPuma, Edward. "Culture and the Concept of Culture in a Theory of Practice." In Calhoun, LiPuma, and Postone, *Bourdieu: Critical Perspectives,* 14–34.

"Literary Notices." *Ladies' Magazine* 5 (March 1832): 138–40.

"Literary Notices." *Ladies' Magazine* 5 (July 1832): 329–32.

"Literary Notices." *Ladies' Magazine* 6 (May 1833): 237–39.

"Literature." In *Encyclopedia of Southern Culture,* edited by Charles Reagan Wilson and William M. Ferris, 865. Chapel Hill: University of North Carolina Press, 1989.

Lodge, David, ed. *Modern Criticism and Theory: A Reader.* London: Longman, 1988.

Logan, Jennie Manget. *Little Stories of China.* N.p., n.d.

Logan, Shirley Wilson, ed. *With Pen and Voice: A Critical Anthology of Nineteenth-Century African-American Women.* Carbondale: Southern Illinois University Press, 1995.

Long, Lisa A. "Charlotte Forten's Civil War Journals and the Quest for 'Genius, Beauty, and Deathless Fame.'" *Legacy* 16 (1999): 37–48.

Lunsford, Andrea A., Helene Moglen, and James Slevin, eds. *The Right to Literacy.* New York: MLA, 1990.

Lyman, Anne Jean. Letter to Abby Lyman Greene. November 3, [n.d.]. MSS/q G812 r/RM, Greene-Roelker Papers. Research Library, The Cincinnati Historical Society.

——. Letter to Abby Lyman Greene. April 17, 1838. MSS/q G812r/RM, Greene-Roelker Papers. Research Library, The Cincinnati Historical Society.

MacDonald, Ann-Marie. *Fall on Your Knees*. New York: Simon and Schuster, 1996.

"Madame Roland: Literary Notices." Review of *Madame Roland*, by Lydia Maria Child. *Ladies' Magazine* 5 (July 1832): 332–34.

Mann, Horace. *Go Forth and Teach: An Oration Delivered Before the Authorities of the City of Boston, July 4, 1842 by Horace Mann, also Other Materials Relating to His Life*. Edited by Hugh Taylor Birch. Washington: Committee on the Horace Mann Centennial, National Education Association, 1937.

——. *Lectures on Education*. Boston: W. B. Fowle and N. Capen, 1845.

Marchalonis, Shirley. "Legacy Profile: Lucy Larcom (1824–1893)." *Legacy* 5 (1988): 46–47.

Márquez, Gabriel García. One Hundred Years of Solitude. Translated by Gregory Rabassa. New York: Harper and Row, 1970.

"Mary, the Mother of Washington." *Ladies' Magazine* 6 (June 1833): 266–69.

Matthews, Victoria Earle. "The Value of Race Literature: An Address Delivered at the First Congress of Colored Women of the United States (1895)." In *With Pen and Voice: A Critical Anthology of Nineteenth-Century African-American Women*, edited by Shirley Wilson Logan, 126–48. Carbondale: Southern Illinois University Press, 1995.

McClelland, Averil Evans. *The Education of Women in the United States: A Guide to Theory, Teaching, and Research*. New York: Garland Publishing, 1992.

McGuire, Randall H. and Robert Paynter, eds. *The Archeology of Inequity*. Oxford: Blackwell, 1991.

McHenry, Elizabeth. *Forgotten Readers: Recovering the Lost History of African American Literary Societies*. Durham: Duke University Press, 2002.

"The Meeting at Saratoga." *Woman's Work for Woman* 9 (August 1879): 259.

Michie, Helena. "Dying between Two Laws: Girl Heroines, Their Gods, and Their Fathers in *Uncle Tom's Cabin* and the *Elsie Dinsmore* Series." In *Refiguring the Father: New Feminist Readings of Patriarchy*, edited by Patricia Yaeger and Beth Kowaleski-Wallace, 188–206. Carbondale: Southern Illinois University Press, 1989.

Miller, Alice. Untitled article on Hull House's founding. *The Charities Review*. 1892. Hull-House Association Records. Scrapbooks, vol. 1. Jane Addams Memorial Collection. Special Collections, The University Library, University of Illinois at Chicago.

Miller, Laura. "Book Lovers' Quarrel." Available at <http://www.salon.com/books/feature/2001/10/26/franzen_winfrey/index.html>.

Mintz, Steven. *A Prison of Expectations: The Family in Victorian Culture*. New York: New York University Press, 1983.

"Miss Fannie Heck Enters Into Rest." *Raleigh News and Observer*, August 26, 1915. Fannie E. S. Heck Papers. Wake Forest University Archives and Special Collections, Z. Smith Reynolds Library, Wake Forest University.

"Miss Fiske's School for Young Ladies." *Ladies' Magazine* 6 (December 1833): 552–56.

"Miss Harriet Martineau." *American Ladies' Magazine* 7 (April 1834): 13–17.

Mitchell, Mrs. Murray. "A Day in India." *Woman's Work for Woman* 13 (April 1883): 115.

Moi, Toril. "Feminist, Females, Feminine." In *The Feminist Reader: Essays in Gender and the Politics of Literary Criticism*, edited by Catherine Belsey and Jane Moore, 117–32. Cambridge: Blackwell, 1989.

Monaghan, E. Jennifer. "Literacy Instruction and Gender in Colonial New England." In Davidson, *Reading in America: Literature and Social History*, 53–80.

Montgomery, Helen Barrett. *Western Women in Eastern Lands: A Outline Study of Fifty Years of Woman's Work in Foreign Missions*. New York: Macmillan, 1910–11.

Morris, Robert C. *Reading, 'Riting, and Reconstruction: The Education of Freedmen in the South, 1861–1870*. Chicago: University of Chicago Press, 1981.

Morrison, Toni. *Playing in the Dark: Whiteness and the Literary Imagination*. New York: Vintage Books, 1992.

Mossell, Mrs. N. F. *The Work of the Afro-American Woman*. 1894. Reprint, New York: Oxford University Press, 1988.

Mowry, William A. *Recollections of a New England Educator, 1838–1908: Reminiscences–Biographical, Pedagogical, Historical*. New York: Silver, Burdett, and Company, 1908.

Murray, Judith Sargent. "Story of Margaretta." 1798. In *Selected Writings of Judith Sargent Murray*, edited by Sharon M. Harris, 153–272. New York: Oxford University Press, 1995.

Myers, Miles. *Changing Our Minds: Negotiating English and Literacy*. Urbana: NCTE, 1996.

Nash, Margaret A. "Rethinking Republican Motherhood: Benjamin Rush and the Young Ladies' Academy of Philadelphia." *Journal of the Early Republic* 17 (Summer 1997): 171–91.

Nelson, Dana D. *National Manhood: Capitalist Citizenship and the Imagined Fraternity of White Men*. Durham: Duke University Press, 1998.

Nevius, Helen S. C. *Our Life in China*. New York: Robert Carter & Brothers, 1869.

Newell, Rev. S. *Memoirs of Mrs. Harriet Newell, Wife of the Rev. S. Newell, American Missionary to India*. London: James Nisbet, 1823.

Nieman, Donald G., ed. *African Americans and Education in the South, 1865–1900*. New York: Garland Publishing, 1994.

Niles, Mrs. W. A. "What Are the Best Methods for Enlisting Christian Women in Persistent Efforts for the Conversion of the Heathen?" *Woman's Work for Woman* 9 (August 1879): 272.

Noel. "Social Lyceum." *Ladies' Magazine* 4 (April 1831): 160–65.

Norton, Mary Beth. "The Evolution of White Women's Experience in Early America." *American Historical Review* 89 (June 1984): 593–619.

———. *Founding Mothers and Fathers: Gendered Power and the Forming of American Society*. New York: Vintage Books, 1997.

"Notes from Room 48." *Woman's Work for Woman* 9 (February 1879): 68–70.

Nylander, Jane C. *Our Own Snug Fireside: Images of the New England Home 1760–1860*. New York: Yale University Press, 1994.

Oates, Joyce Carol. *We Were the Mulvaneys*. New York: Plume, 1997.

Okker, Patricia. *Our Sister Editors: Sarah J. Hale and the Tradition of Nineteenth-Century American Women Editors*. Athens: University of Georgia Press, 1995.

"One Hundred Thousand Dollars: What It Means." *Woman's Work for Woman* 9 (September 1879): 300–302.

"Other Side of Welfare: Real Stories from a Single Mother." Available at <http://www.drlaura.com/reading/?mode_view&id=172>.

Parker, William. "The Freedmen's Story." *Atlantic Monthly* 17 (February 1866): 152–66.

———. "The Freedmen's Story, II." *Atlantic Monthly* 17 (March 1866): 276–95.

Paton, Fiona. "Beyond Bakhtin: Towards a Cultural Stylistics." *College English* 63 (November 2000): 166–93.

Paul, Susan. *Memoir of James Jackson: The Attentive and Obedient Scholar, Who Died in Boston, October 31, 1833, Aged Six Years and Eleven Months. By His Teacher.* 1835. Edited and with an introduction by Lois Brown. Reprint, Cambridge: Harvard University Press, 2000.

Paynter, Robert, and Randall H. McGuire. "The Archeology of Inequality: Material Culture, Domination, and Resistance." In McGuire and Paynter, *The Archeology of Inequality,* 1–27.

Peabody, Elizabeth. *Record of a School: Exemplifying the General Principles of Spiritual Culture.* Boston: James Munroe, 1835.

Peeps, J. M. Stephen. "Northern Philanthropy and the Emergence of Black Higher Education—Do-Gooders, Compromisers, or Co-Conspirators?" *Journal of Negro Education* 50 (1981): 251–69.

Perkins, Linda M. "The Education of Black Women in the Nineteenth Century." In Faragher and Howe, *Women and Higher Education in American History,* 64–86.

Perlmann, Joel, and Robert A. Margo. *Women's Work? American Schoolteachers 1650–1920.* Chicago: University of Chicago Press, 2001.

"The Personal Responsibility and Work Opportunity Reconciliation Act of 1996." Available at <http://www.acf.dhhs.gov/programs/opa/facts/prwora96.htm>.

Persons, Stow. *The Decline of American Gentility.* New York: Columbia University Press, 1973.

Peterson, Carla L. *"Doers of the Word": African-American Women Speakers and Writers in the North (1830–1880).* New York: Oxford University Press, 1995.

——. "'Further Liftings of the Veil': Gender, Class, and Labor in Frances E. W. Harper's *Iola Leroy.*" In *Listening to Silences: New Essays in Feminist Criticism,* edited by Elaine Hedges and Shelley Fisher Fishkin, 97–112. New York: Oxford University Press, 1994.

Pfaelzer, Jean, and Sharon M. Harris, eds. "Discourses of Women and Class." Special issue, *Legacy* 16 (1999).

Phelps, Almira Hart Lincoln. "Lectures to Young Ladies: Comprising Outlines and Applications of the Different Branches of Female Education for the Use of Female Schools, and Private Libraries (1833)." In Salvatori, *Pedagogy: Disturbing History, 1819–1929,* 95–102.

Phelps, Elizabeth Stuart. *The Silent Partner.* Boston: J. R. Osgood, 1871. With an afterword by Mari Jo Buhle and Florence Howe. Reprint, New York: Feminist Press, 1983.

Polacheck, Hilda Satt. *I Came a Stranger: The Story of a Hull-House Girl.* Edited by Dena J. Polacheck Epstein. Urbana: University of Illinois Press, 1989.

Porterfield, Amanda. *Mary Lyon and the Mount Holyoke Missionaries.* New York: Oxford University Press, 1997.

Pratt, Mary Louise. *Imperial Eyes: Travel Writing and Transculturation.* New York: Routledge, 1992.

"The Prayer Meeting Again." *Woman's Work for Woman* 9 (July 1879): 235.

Preston, Jo Anne. "Domestic Ideology, School Reformers, and Female Teachers: Schoolteaching Becomes Women's Work in Nineteenth-Century New England." *New England Quarterly* 66 (December 1993): 531–51.

Radway, Janice. *Reading the Romance: Women, Patriarchy, and Popular Literature.* Chapel Hill: University of North Carolina Press, 1991.

Railton, Stephen. "Mothers, Husbands, and Uncle Tom." *Georgia Review* 38 (1984): 129–44.

Ray, Katie Wood. *Wondrous Words: Writers and Writing in the Elementary Classroom.* Urbana: NCTE, 1999.

Reilly, Wayne E., ed. *Sarah Jane Foster, Teacher of the Freedmen: A Diary and Letters.* Charlottesville: University Press of Virginia, 1990.

Reunion: Hartford Female Seminary, June 9, 1892. Hartford: Case, Lockwood, and Brainard, 1892.

Riley, Glenda. *Inventing the American Woman: A Perspective on Women's History.* Arlington Heights: Harlan Davidson, 1987.

Robbins, Derek. *The Work of Pierre Bourdieu: Recognizing Society.* Boulder: Westview Press, 1991.

Robbins, Sarah. "Distributed Authorship: A Feminist Case-Study Framework for Studying Intellectual Property." *College English* 66 (November 2003): 31–47.

———. "'The Future Good and Great of Our Land': Republican Mothers, Female Authors, and Domesticated Literacy in Antebellum New England." *New England Quarterly* 75 (December 2002): 562–91.

———. "Gendering Gilded Age Periodical Professionalism: Reading Stowe's *Hearth and Home* Prescriptions for Women's Writing." In *The Only Efficient Instrument: American Women Writers and the Periodical, 1837–1916,* edited by Aleta Feinsod Cane and Susan Alves, 45–65. Iowa City: University of Iowa Press, 2001.

———. "Gendering the Debate over African Americans' Education in the 1880s: Frances Harper's Reconfiguration of Atticus Haygood's Philanthropic Model." *Legacy* 19 (2002): 81–89.

———. "Gendering the History of the Antislavery Narrative: Juxtaposing *Uncle Tom's Cabin* and *Benito Cereno, Beloved* and *Middle Passage.*" *American Quarterly* 49 (September 1997): 531–73.

———. "*Lessons for Children* and Teaching Mothers: Mrs. Barbauld's Primer for the Textual Construction of Middle-Class Pedagogy." *Lion and the Unicorn* 17 (December 1993): 135–51.

———. "Periodizing Authorship, Characterizing Genre: Reading Catharine Maria Sedgwick's Benevolent Literacy Narratives." *American Literature* 76 (March 2004): 1–29.

———. "Re-making Barbauld's Primers: A Case Study of the 'Americanization' of British Literary Pedagogy." *Children's Literature Association Quarterly* 21 (Winter 1996–97): 158–69.

———. "Rereading the History of Nineteenth-Century Women's Higher Education: A Reexamination of Jane Addams' Rockford Education as Preparation for her *Twenty Years at Hull-House* Teaching." *Journal of the Midwest History of Education Society* 21 (1994): 27–46.

———. "*Woman's Work for Woman:* Collaborative Print Culture in Gendered Mission Narratives." In *Women in Print,* edited by James Danky and Wayne Wiegand. Madison: University of Wisconsin Press, forthcoming.

Robbins, Sarah, Mary Miesiezek, and Beth Andrews. "Promoting a Relevant Classroom Literacy." In *The Relevance of English: Teaching That Matters in Students' Lives,* edited by Robert P. Yagelski and Scott A. Leonard, 157–82. Urbana: NCTE, 2002.

Robbins, Sarah, Deborah Mitchell, and Ed Hullender. "Uplifting a 'New' South." Available at <http://www.kennesaw.edu/english/kmwp/AmerCommunities/thematic_content/educating_for_citizenship/eduhome.html>.

Robert, Dana L. *American Women in Mission: A Social History of Their Thought and Practice.* Macon: Mercer University Press, 1996.

Rockford Seminary Catalogue: Annual Catalogue of the Officers and Students of Rockford Seminary, Rockford, Illinois. Rockford: N.p., 1878.

Rodriguez, Richard. *Hunger of Memory: The Education of Richard Rodriguez.* New York: Bantam, 1983.

Romero, Lora. "Bio-Political Resistance in Domestic Ideology and *Uncle Tom's Cabin.*" *American Literary History* 1 (1989): 715–34.

———. *Home Fronts: Domesticity and Its Critics in the Antebellum United States.* Durham: Duke University Press, 1997.

Rose, Mike. *Lives on the Boundary.* New York: Penguin, 1990.

Rowson, Susanna. *Biblical Dialogues Between a Father and His Family.* Boston: Richardson and Lord, 1822.

———. *A Present for Young Ladies; Containing Poems, Dialogues, Addresses, &c. as Recited by the Pupils of Mrs. Rowson's Academy at the Annual Exhibitions.* Boston: John West, 1811.

———. *Reuben and Rachel; or, Tales of Old Times.* Boston: Manning & Loring, 1798.

———. *Sarah; or, The Exemplary Wife.* Boston: C. Williams, 1813.

Royster, Jacqueline Jones. *Traces of a Stream: Literacy and Social Change among African American Women.* Pittsburgh: University of Pittsburgh Press, 2000.

Rudnick, Lois. "A Feminist American Success Myth: Jane Addams' *Twenty Years at Hull-House.*" In *Tradition and the Talents of Women,* edited by Florence Howe, 145–67. Urbana: University of Illinois Press, 1991.

Ryan, Mary P. *The Empire of the Mother: American Writing about Domesticity 1830–1860.* New York: Haworth Press, 1982.

Ryan, Susan. "Charity Begins at Home: Stowe's Antislavery Novels and the Forms of Benevolent Citizenship." *American Literature* 72 (December 2000): 751–82.

———. *The Grammar of Good Intentions: Race and the Antebellum Culture of Benevolence.* Ithaca: Cornell University Press, 2003.

Salvatori, Mariolina Rizzi, ed. *Pedagogy: Disturbing History, 1819–1929.* Pittsburgh: University of Pittsburgh Press, 1996.

Schudson, Michael. *The Good Citizen: A History of American Civic Life.* Cambridge: Harvard University Press, 1998.

Schuster, Charles. "The Ideology of Literacy: A Bakhtinian Perspective." In Lunsford, Moglen, and Slevin, *The Right to Literacy,* 225–34.

Scott, Anne Firor. *Natural Allies: Women's Associations in American History.* Urbana: University of Illinois Press, 1991.

Sedgwick, Catharine Maria. *The Boy of Mount Rhigi.* Boston: Charles Peirce, 1848.

———. "Ella." In *Stories for Young Persons,* 95–114.

———. *Facts and Fancies for School-Day Reading, a Sequel to "Morals and Manners."* New York: Wiley & Putnam, 1848. Reprint, New York: G. P. Putnam's Sons, 1873.

———. "The Irish Girl." In *Tales and Sketches. Second Series,* 191–214.

———. *Live and Let Live; or, Domestic Service Illustrated.* New York: Harper & Brothers, 1837.

———. *A Love Token for Children: Designed for Sunday-School Libraries.* New York: Harper & Brothers, 1838.

———. *Married or Single?* New York: Harper, 1857.

———. *Means and Ends; or, Self-Training.* Boston: Marsh, Capen, Lyon, & Webb, 1839.

———. "Mill-Hill." In *A Love Token for Children,* 78–136.

———. *A New-England Tale; or, Sketches of New-England Character and Manners.* 1822. Edited by Victoria Clements. reprint. New York: Oxford University Press, 1995.

———. "Old Maids." In *Tales and Sketches by Miss Sedgwick,* 97–116.

———. *The Poor Rich Man, and the Rich Poor Man.* New York: Harper & Brothers, 1836.

———. "Self Education." In *Facts and Fancies for School-Day Reading,* 116–35.

———. *Stories for Young Persons.* New York: Harper & Brothers, 1841.

———. *Tales and Sketches by Miss Sedgwick.* Philadelphia: Carey, Lea, and Blanchard, 1835.

———. *Tales and Sketches. Second Series.* New York: Harper & Brothers, 1844.

———. Introduction to *Women and Work. With an Introduction by Catherine M. Sedgwick,* by Barbara Leigh Smith Bodichon. New York: C. M. Francis, 1859.

Sedgwick, Elizabeth. *Lessons Without Books. By the Author of "The Beatitudes."* Boston: L. C. Bowles, 1830.

———. *A Talk With My Pupils.* New York: John Hopper, 1863.

Sedgwick, Ellery. *The* Atlantic Monthly, *1857–1909: Yankee Humanism at High Tide and Ebb.* Amherst: University of Massachusetts Press, 1994.

Semicolon Club Papers. MSS S 471. Research Library, The Cincinnati Historical Society.

S. F. W. "Female Education." *Ladies' Magazine* 7 (November 1834): 500.

Shaler, N. S. "An Ex-Southerner in South Carolina." *Atlantic Monthly* 26 (July 1870): 53–61.

Shaw, Mrs. "China—Tung-Chow." *Woman's Work for Woman* 6 (February 1877): 400.

Sicherman, Barbara. "College and Careers: Historical Perspectives on the Lives and Work Patterns of Women College Graduates." In Faragher and Howe, *Women and Higher Education in American History,* 130–64.

———. "Sense and Sensibility: A Case Study of Women's Reading in Late-Victorian America." In Davidson, *Reading in America,* 201–25.

Sigourney, Lydia. *The Book for Girls, Consisting of Original Articles in Prose and Poetry.* New York: Turner & Hayden, 1844.

———. *The Boy's Book; Consisting of Original Articles in Prose and Poetry.* New York: Turner, Hughes, & Hayden, 1845.

———. *The Child's Book: Consisting of Original Articles in Prose and Poetry.* New York: Turner & Hayden, 1844.

———. *Examples from the Eighteenth and Nineteenth Centuries.* New York: Charles Scribner, 1857.

———. *Examples of Life and Death.* New York: Charles Scribner, 1851.

———. *The Faded Hope.* New York: Robert Carter & Brothers, 1853.

———. *The Girl's Reading-Book; in Prose and Poetry. For Schools.* New York: J. Orville Taylor, at the "American Common School Union," 1838. 15th ed., Newburgh, [N.Y.]: Proudfit and Banks, 1847.

———. *Great and Good Women: Biographies for Girls.* Edinburgh: William P. Nimmo, 1872.

———. *Illustrated Poems.* New York: Allen Brothers, 1869.

———. *Letters of Life.* New York: Appleton, 1866.

———. *Letters to Mothers.* Hartford: Hudson and Skinner, 1838. 2d ed., New York: Harper & Brothers, 1839.

———. *Letters to My Pupils: With Narrative and Biographical Sketches.* 2d ed. New York: Robert Carter & Brothers, 1856.

———. *Letters to Young Ladies.* 3d ed. New York: Harper & Brothers, 1837.

———. *Lucy Howard's Journal.* New York: Harper & Brothers, 1858.

———. *Memoir of Mary Anne Hooker, Author of "The Life of David," etc. Written for the American Sunday-School Union and revised by the Committee of Publication.* Philadelphia: American Sunday School Union, 1840.

———. "Miss Ann Maria Hyde." In *Examples from the Eighteenth and Nineteenth Centuries,* 244–63.

———. "Mrs. Jerusha Lathrop." In *The Girl's Reading Book,* 143–51. Reprinted in *Examples from the Eighteenth and Nineteenth Centuries,* 63–72.

——. *Noble Deeds of American Women; with Biographical Sketches of Some of the More Prominent.* Auburn and Buffalo: Miller, Orton, & Mulligan, 1854.

——. *The Pictorial Reader, Consisting of Original Articles for the Instruction of Young Children; Being an Introduction to "The Boy's Reading Book," and "The Girls' Reading Book," by the Same Author.* New York: Turner & Hayden, 1844.

——. *Scenes in My Native Land.* Boston: James Munroe, 1845.

[——]. *Songs for the Little Ones at Home.* New York: American Tract Society, 1852.

——. *Whisper to the Bride.* 2d ed. Hartford: William Hamersley, 1850.

——, ed. *The Works of Hannah More, with a Sketch of Her life, in Two Volumes.* Philadelphia: J. J. Woodward, 1832.

Simon, Brian. *Studies in the History of Education: 1780–1870.* London: Lawrence & Wishart, 1960.

Sizer, Theodore R. "Public Literacy: Puzzlements of a High School Watcher." In Lunsford, Moglen, and Slevin, *The Right to Literacy,* 9–12.

"Sketches, by Mrs. Sigourney. Philadelphia; Key and Biddle." Review of *Sketches,* by Lydia Sigourney. *Ladies' Magazine* 7 (June 1834): 284–85.

Small, Walter Herbert. "The Dame School and the School Dame." In *Early New England Schools,* 162–86. Boston: Ginn and Company, 1914. Reprint, New York: Arno Press, 1969.

Smith, Susie M. Heck. "A Portrait: Fannie E. S. Heck." Fannie E. S. Heck Papers. Wake Forest University Archives and Special Collections, Z. Smith Reynolds Library, Wake Forest University.

Spencer-Wood, Suzanne. "Toward an Historical Archeology of Materialistic Domestic Reform." In McGuire and Paynter, *The Archeology of Inequality,* 231–86.

Spillers, Hortense. "Changing the Letter: The Yokes, the Jokes of Discourse, or, Mrs. Stowe, Mr. Reed." In *Slavery and the Literary Imagination,* edited by Deborah E. McDowell, 25–61. Baltimore: Johns Hopkins University Press, 1989.

Stanley, Amy Dru. "Home Life and the Morality of the Market." In *The Market Revolution in America: Social, Political, and Religious Expressions, 1800–1880,* edited by Melvyn Stokes and Stephen Conway, 74–96. Charlottesville: University Press of Virginia, 1996.

Stedman, Lawrence C., and Carl F. Kaestle. "Part Two: Americans' Reading Abilities." In *Literacy in the United States: Readers and Reading since 1880,* edited by Carl F. Kaestle et al., 114–23. New Haven: Yale University Press, 1991.

Steinbeck, John. *East of Eden.* New York: Viking Press, 1952.

Sterling, Dorothy. *Black Foremothers: Three Lives.* New York: Feminist Press, 1988.

Stevenson, Louise L. *The Victorian Homefront: American Thought and Culture, 1860–1880.* New York: Twayne, 1991.

Stowe, Charles Edward, and Lyman Beecher Stowe. *Harriet Beecher Stowe: The Story of Her Life.* New York: Houghton, 1911.

Stowe, Harriet Beecher. *A Key to Uncle Tom's Cabin: Presenting the Original Facts and Documents upon Which the Story is Founded.* 1853. Facs. ed., Bedford, [Mass.]: Applewood Books, 1998.

——. Letter to Calvin Stowe. May 25, [1844]. Folder 68, Beecher-Stowe Family Papers. Schlesinger Library, Radcliffe Institute, Harvard University.

——. Letter to Calvin Stowe. May–June 1844. Folder 68, Beecher-Stowe Family Papers. Schlesinger Library, Radcliffe Institute, Harvard University.

——. Letter to Calvin Stowe. July 1844. Folder 69, Beecher-Stowe Family Papers. Schlesinger Library, Radcliffe Institute, Harvard University.

——. Letter to Calvin Stowe. August 1844. Folder 70, Beecher-Stowe Family Papers. Schlesinger Library, Radcliffe Institute, Harvard University.

——. Letter to Sarah Josepha Hale. HM 24166, The Huntington Library, San Marino, Calif.

——. *The May Flower and Miscellaneous Writings.* Boston: Phillips, Sampson, & Co., 1855.

——. "Trials of a Housekeeper." In *Household Papers and Stories,* 487–93. Cambridge: Riverside Press, 1896.

——. *Uncle Tom's Cabin; or, Life Among the Lowly.* 1852. Edited by Ann Douglas. Reprint, New York: Penguin, 1986.

Street, Brian V. *Social Literacies: Critical Approaches to Literacy in Development, Ethnography, and Education.* London: Longman, 1995.

Sundquist, Eric J. Introduction to Sundquist, *New Essays on* Uncle Tom's Cabin, 1–44.

——, ed. *New Essays on* Uncle Tom's Cabin. Cambridge: Cambridge University Press, 1986.

Tate, Claudia. *Domestic Allegories of Political Desire: The Black Heroine's Text at the Turn of the Century.* New York: Oxford University Press, 1992.

Theriot, Nancy. *Mothers and Daughters in Nineteenth-Century America: The Biosocial Construction of Femininity.* Louisville: University Press of Kentucky, 1995.

"Three Months among the Reconstructionists." *Atlantic Monthly* 17 (February 1866): 237–45.

Tompkins, Jane. *Sensational Designs: The Cultural Work of American Fiction, 1790–1860.* New York: Oxford University Press, 1985.

"Troy Female Seminary." *Ladies' Magazine* 6 (September 1833): 402–5.

True, Maria T. "Japan." *Woman's Work for Woman* 12 (April 1882): 122.

——. "Tokio Japan." *Woman's Work for Woman* 12 (January 1882): 15–16.

"'Uncle Tom' and Grandchild." *Harper's Weekly* (November 3, 1866): 689–90.

Ungar, Cara-Lynn. "Discourses of Class and the New Jewish Working Woman in Anzia Yezierska's *Arrogant Beggar.*" *Legacy* 16 (1999): 82–92.

Villanueva, Victor. *Bootstraps: From an American Academic of Color.* Urbana: NCTE, 1993.

Walsh, Robert. *Didactics: Social, Literary, and Political.* 2 vols. Philadelphia: Carey, Lea, and Blanchard, 1836.

Ware, Vron. *Beyond the Pale: White Women, Racism and History.* London: Verso, 1992.

Warner, Michael. *The Letters of the Republic: Publication and the Public Sphere in Eighteenth-Century America.* Cambridge: Harvard University Press, 1990.

Warner, Susan. *The Wide, Wide World by Elizabeth Wetherell* [pseud.]. New York: George P. Putnam, 1851, 1892. Reprint of the 1892 edition, New York: Feminist Press, 1987.

Weaver, Constance. *Understanding Whole Language: From Principles to Practice.* Portsmouth: Heinemann, 1990.

Wells-Barnett, Ida B. *Crusade for Justice: The Autobiography of Ida B. Wells.* Edited by Alfreda M. Duster. Chicago: University of Chicago Press, 1970.

Wexler, Laura. "Tender Violence: Literary Eavesdropping, Domestic Fiction, and Educational Reform." In *The Culture of Sentiment: Race, Gender, and Sentimentality in Nineteenth-Century America,* edited by Shirley Samuels, 9–38. New York: Oxford University Press, 1992.

Whittelsey, Mrs. A. G., ed. *Mother's Magazine* 1 (January 1833).

Wiebe, Robert H. *Self-Rule: A Cultural History of American Democracy.* Chicago: University of Chicago Press, 1995.

Willard, Emma. *Advancement of Female Education: or, A Series of Addresses, in favor of establishing At Athens, In Greece, a Female Seminary, especially designed to instruct female teachers.* Troy: Norman Tuttle, 1833.

———. "From Emma Hart Willard, A Plan for Improving Female Education (1819)." In Salvatori, *Pedagogy: Disturbing History, 1819–1929,* 74–78.

Willard, Emma, and Sarah Josepha Hale. "Mrs. Willard on Female Education." *Ladies' Magazine* 7 (April 1834): 163–73.

Wilson, Christopher P. *The Labor of Words: Literary Professionalism in the Progressive Era.* Athens: University of Georgia Press, 1985.

Wilson, Forrest. *Crusader in Crinoline: The Life of Harriet Beecher Stowe.* New York: Lippincott, 1941.

Wilson, Kimberly A. C. "The Function of the 'Fair' Mulatto: Complexion, Audience, and Mediation in Frances Harper's *Iola Leroy.*" *Cimarron Review* 106 (January 1994): 104–13.

Wollstonecraft, Mary. *A Vindication of the Rights of Woman.* 1792. Edited by Miriam Brody. Reprint, New York: Penguin, 1986.

"Woman." *Ladies' Magazine* 3 (September 1830): 441–47.

"Woman's Way to Eminence." *Ladies' Magazine* 7 (July 1834): 385–87.

"Woman's Work." *Woman's Work for Woman* 9 (February 1879): 40–41.

"The Women of America." *Ladies' Magazine* 3 (March 1830): 105.

"Women's Work in the Long Nineteenth Century." Available at <http://www.kennesaw.edu/hss/wwork>.

Wright, Erik Olin. "Class Analysis." In Levine, *Social Class and Stratification: Classic Statements and Theoretical Debates,* 141–65.

Wright, Richard. *Uncle Tom's Children.* 1938. Reprint, New York: Harper, 1993.

Wyatt-Brown, Bertram. "Black Schooling during Reconstruction." In *The Web of Southern Social Relations: Women, Family, and Education,* edited by Walter L. Fraser Jr., R. Frank Saunders Jr., and Jon L. Wakelyn, 146–65. Athens: University of Georgia Press, 1985.

Yellin, Jean Fagan. "Doing It Herself: *Uncle Tom's Cabin* and Woman's Role in the Slavery Crisis." In Sundquist, *New Essays on* Uncle Tom's Cabin, 85–105.

———. "Written By Herself: Harriet Jacobs' Slave Narrative." *American Literature* 53 (September 1981): 479–86.

Yezierska, Anzia. *Arrogant Beggar.* 1927. Edited by Katherine Stubbs. Reprint, Durham: Duke University Press, 1996.

———. *Bread Givers.* 1925. Reprint, New York: Persea/Doubleday, 1970.

———. *Salome of the Tenements.* 1923. Reprint, Urbana: University of Illinois Press, 1995.

———. *Hungry Hearts.* Boston: Houghton Mifflin, 1920.

Young, Elizabeth. "Warring Fictions: *Iola Leroy* and the Color of Gender." *American Literature* 64 (June 1992): 273–97.

Zagarell, Sandra A. "Narrative of Community: The Identification of a Genre." *Signs* 13 (1988): 498–527.

Ziff, Larzer. *Writing in the New Nation: Prose, Print, and Politics in the Early United States.* New Haven: Yale University Press, 1991.

Zitkala-Ša. *American Indian Stories.* Edited by Dexter Fisher. Lincoln: University of Nebraska Press, 1979.

Index

Spillers, Hortense, 130
standpoint theory, 20, 109–10
Sterling, Dorothy, 165
Stevenson, Louise L., 29, 122–23
Stewart, Maria W., 165
Still, William, 172
Stories for Young Persons (C. Sedgwick), 57, 61
Story of Margaretta, The (Murray), 14
Stowe, Calvin, 47, 141–42, 148, 150
Stowe, Charles, 126–28, 140–41
Stowe, Harriet Beecher, 13, 15, 47, 258n94;
biography by son, 126–28, 140–41;
brother Henry Ward, 125, 141–42; as
child able to teach adult, 147–48; construction as author, 121–24; contribution
to domestic literacy narrative, 40; as eager to learn from child, 148–49; on enfranchisement for African Americans,
154; on family move to Cincinnati,
140–41; father of, 125–28, 140, 146–48,
271n21; gender restriction on, 127–28;
on housekeeping, 81; husband of, 141–42,
148; literary acquisition/education of,
126–27, 146–48; literary club and, 33;
mother of, 127; personal identity pre–
Uncle Tom's Cabin, 117–18, 123–24; race
restriction on, 128; as rhetor, 123; sense
of teaching retained by, 141–42, 274n42;
sisters of, 274n38, 274n41; social background of, 29, 246n49; as teacher at
Hartford Female Seminary, 138–39. *See
also* Beecher, Catherine; Hooker, Isabella
Beecher; *Uncle Tom's Cabin*
Street, Brian V., 17, 243n16, 284n55
Stricker, George, 272n27
suffrage, 14, 245n40
*Suggestions Respecting Improvements in
Education* (C. Beecher), 107–8
symbolic capital, 55–57, 58; and symbolic-
knowledge capital, 59

Tales and Sketches (C. Sedgwick), 86, 98
Tate, Claudia, 278n13
teacher, mother as, 20–25; education of,
62–66; gender and, 23–25; honoring,
66–68; male reader/writer and, 23–24;
motherhood ideal and, 20–21; political
significance of, 21–22; social class and,
23, 245n44, 246nn48–49
teacher, single woman as, 93–98, feminization of teaching and, 94, 125, 264n49;
formal training for, 102; and natural ability to guide children, 99–100, 101–2; popular image of, 102–3; salary for, 100,
261n16, 266n65; shifting view of childhood and, 101; social class of teacher
and, 112–14; as stepping-stone to mother-

hood, 100–101; support for, as paid
teacher, 93–98; text used in formal training for, 104–9; instructional method,
114–15, 266n71, 267n82; motivation for
teaching of, 110–12; proper qualifica-
tions/training of, 112–14; relationship
with student, 115
teaching, by well-taught child, 146–49
teaching, by woman as "natural instructor of
youth," 98–103
teaching from beyond the grave, 70–71,
276nn57, 59
textbooks, 40–41, 274n43
Tompkins, Jane, 31, 125
Trial and Triumph (Harper), 158, 170–71,
285n65–286n65
Trueheart, Mrs. S. C., 206, 221, 222
Twenty Years at Hull House (Addams), 13,
78, 234

"'Uncle Tom' and His Grandchild," 158–62
Uncle Tom's Cabin (H. B. Stowe), 13, 15; attack on corporal punishment in, 143–45;
Bible reading/study in, 125, 128, 132–33,
134, 144, 149, 150, 151; characterization
of Uncle Tom in, 128–33, 273n32; child-
teaches-adult motif in, 129, 130–31, 149,
152–53, 272n27; collaborative literacy
management in, 133, 150, 151; community-building literacy practices in,
133–34; denial of free blacks' control
over own education/life in, 153–56; depiction of Mrs. Shelby in, 136–38; domestic literacy management in, 129, 130,
134, 146; as domestic literacy narrative,
125–26, 129, 130, 136–37, 142; ideal female educator in, 138, 141–42, 144–45,
156; influence of, 269n6; intended audience for, 134, 136; *Key* as interpretive
framework for, 119, 131–33, 136–37, 152,
275nn47–50; learning-through-feminine-
sensibility paradigm in, 150–52; maternal voice in, 21–22; middle-class value
system in, 29; popularity of, 269n1; radi-
calism in, 131; satire in, 142–43, 144,
275nn48–49; teaching-to-Christianize-the-
heathen sequence in, 208; twentieth-century resistance to Tom, 134,
273nn34–35; woman of fashion in, 138
Ungar, Cara-Lynn, 92–93
"Unmarried Women" (Child), 96–97
uplift literacy narrative, 89–90, 170, 172–73,
184, 191–93

Villanueva, Victor, 75, 89, 263n38

Walsh, Robert, 34, 36, 248n63
Warner, Michael, 61–62, 205, 241n4